# BASIC
# ENGLISH
# GRAMMAR
## Second Edition

# Betty Schrampfer Azar

PRENTICE HALL REGENTS
A VIACOM COMPANY

PRENTICE HALL REGENTS
Upper Saddle River, New Jersey 07458

**Library of Congress Cataloging-in-Publication Data**

Azar, Betty Scrampfer, 1941-
  Basic English grammar / Betty Schrampfer Azar. -- 2nd ed.
    p.    cm.
  Includes indexes.
  ISBN 0-13-368317-6
  ISBN 0-13-368424-5 (v. 1). -- ISBN 0-13-368358-3 (v. 2)
  1. English language--Textbooks for foreign speakers.  2. English
language--Grammar--Problems, exercises, etc.    I. Title.
PE1128.A96    1995
428.2'4--dc20                                        92-25711
                                                       CIP

Publisher: *Tina B. Carver*
Director of Production and Manufacturing: *Aliza Greenblatt*
Editorial Production/Design Manager: *Dominick Mosco*
Editorial/Production Supervision: *Janet Johnston*
Editorial Assistant: *Shelley Hartle*
Production Coordinator: *Ray Keating*
Cover Coordinator: *Merle Krumper*
Cover Production: *Molly Pike Riccardi*
Cover Design: *Joel Mitnick Design*
Interior Design: *Ros Herion Freese*
Illustrations: *Don Martinetti*

Published by PRENTICE HALL REGENTS
Prentice-Hall, Inc.
A Simon & Schuster Company
Upper Saddle River, New Jersey 07458

Printed in the United States of America.

10 9 8 7 6 5 4 3

ISBN 0-13-368317-6
ISBN 0-13-368424-5 (Vol. A)
ISBN 0-13-368358-3 (Vol. B)

Prentice-Hall International (UK) Limited, *London*
Prentice-Hall of Australia Pty., Limited, *Sydney*
Prentice-Hall Canada Inc., *Toronto*
Prentice-Hall Hispanoamericana, S.A., *Mexico*
Prentice-Hall of India Private Limited, *New Delhi*
Prentice-Hall of Japan, Inc., *Tokyo*
Simon & Schuster Asia Pte. Ltd., *Singapore*
Editora Prentice-Hall do Brasil, Ltda., *Rio de Janeiro*

# Contents

## Chapter 3  EXPRESSING PRESENT TIME (PART 2)

## Chapter 4  NOUNS AND PRONOUNS

## Chapter 5   EXPRESSING PAST TIME

## Chapter 6   EXPRESSING FUTURE TIME

## Chapter 7 EXPRESSING ABILITY

## Chapter 8 NOUNS, PRONOUNS, AND ADJECTIVES

## Chapter 9  MAKING COMPARISONS

## Chapter 10  EXPRESSING IDEAS WITH VERBS

# Preface to the Second Edition

*Basic English Grammar* remains a developmental skills text for students of English as a second or foreign language. Serving as both a reference and a workbook, it introduces students to the form, meaning, and usage of basic structures in English. It provides ample opportunities for practice through extensive and varied exercises leading to communicative activities. Although it focuses on grammar, it promotes the development of all language skills.

This second edition has a greatly expanded range of contents to provide a solid core of basic English grammar for lower-level or beginning students. It includes numerous new exercises with, at the end of each chapter, cumulative review exercises that include additional communicative and interactive student-centered tasks.

Also available are an *Answer Key*, with answers only, and a *Teacher's Guide*, with teaching suggestions as well as the answers to the exercises.

#  Acknowledgments

Writing English grammar texts is a pleasure for me. In this pursuit, I am helped by many wonderful people: dedicated teachers who give presentations at conferences and write articles for regional newsletters or international journals; researchers who explore the hows and whys of second language acquisition; grammarians who present their observations clearly and convincingly; past and present authors of other ESL/EFL grammar materials who show creative and sound approaches to helping students gain understanding and usage ability of English; colleagues who give me valuable feedback and share their pedagogical insights; and publishing professionals who know how to mold and market educational materials. We all rely on one another.

Above all, I am indebted to my students, who have taught me a great deal about the language acquisition process by openly sharing with me their learning experiences and practical needs.

In sum, I am indebted to the ESL/EFL community of teachers, researchers, authors, publishers, and students.

In particular, I thank Tina Carver, Janet Johnston, and Shelley Hartle for their invaluable professionalism as well as friendship. I also wish to thank Barbara Matthies, Irene Juzkiw, Stacy Hagen, Nancy Price, Lawrence Cisar, Don Martinetti, Lizette Reyes, Stella Reilly, Marita Froimson, Joy Edwards, R.T. Steltz, Sue Van Etten, Ken Kortlever, Generessa Arielle, and Chelsea Azar. My gratitude goes also to the many wonderful teachers and publishers I met in Korea, Japan, and Taiwan on my trip to Asia in 1994.

# CHAPTER 1
# Using *Be* and *Have*

■ **EXERCISE 1:**  Learn the names of your classmates and teacher.  Write their names in the spaces below.

_____    _____

_____    _____

_____    _____

_____    _____

_____    _____

_____    _____

_____    _____

_____    _____

_____    _____

_____    _____

## 1-1 NOUN + IS + NOUN: SINGULAR

| | |
|---|---|
| NOUN + IS + NOUN<br>(a) **Canada** **is** a **country.** | "Singular" means "one, not two or more."<br>In (a): *Canada* = a singular noun<br> *is* = a singular verb<br> *country* = a singular noun |
| (b) Mexico is **a c**ountry. | **A** frequently comes in front of singular nouns.<br>In (b): **a** comes in front of the singular noun *country*. **A** is called "an article." |
| (c) **A** cat is **an** animal. | **A** and **an** have the same meaning. They are both articles.<br>**A** is used in front of words that begin with consonants: *b, c, d, f, g, h, j, k, etc.* Examples: *a bed, a cat, a dog, a friend, a girl*<br>**An** is used in front of words that begin with *a, e, i,* and *o.*★<br>Examples: *an animal, an ear, an island, an office* |

★**An** is also sometimes used in front of words that begin with *u.* See Chart 4-7.
The letters *a, e, i, o,* and *u* are called "vowels."
All of the other letters in the alphabet are called "consonants."

■ **EXERCISE 2:** Complete the sentences. Use an ARTICLE, **a** or **an**.

1. ___A___ horse is ___an___ animal.

2. English is _____ language.

3. Chicago is _____ city.

4. Korea is _____ country.

5. Europe is _____ continent.

6. _____ dictionary is _____ book.

7. _____ hotel is _____ building.

8. _____ bear is _____ animal.

9. _____ bee is _____ insect.

10. _____ ant is _____ insect.

■ **EXERCISE 3:** Complete the sentences. Use an ARTICLE (***a*** or ***an***) and the words in the list.

| | | |
|---|---|---|
| animal | continent | insect |
| city | country | language |

1. Arabic is ____*a language*____ .

2. Rome is ____*a city*____ .

3. A cat is ____*an animal*____ .

4. Asia is _____ .

5. Tokyo is _____ .

6. Spanish is _____ .

7. Mexico is _____ .

8. London is _____ .

9. A bee is _____ .

10. South America is _____ .

11. A dog is _____ .

12. China is _____ .

13. Russian is _____ .

14. A cow is _____ .

15. A fly is _____ .

■ **EXERCISE 4—ORAL:** Complete the sentences with your own words. Think of more than one possible completion.

1. . . . is a language.
   → *English is a language.*
   → *Spanish is a language.*
   → *Arabic is a language.*
   → *Etc.*

2. . . . is a country.

3. . . . is a city.

4. . . . is a continent.

5. . . . is an animal.

6. . . . is an insect.

| | |
|---|---|
| NOUN  +  *ARE*  +  NOUN<br>(a)  **Cats        are        animals.** | "Plural" means "two, three, or more."<br>*Cats* = a plural noun<br>*are* = a plural verb<br>*animals* = a plural noun |
| (b)  SINGULAR:  a cat, an animal.<br>     PLURAL:     cat**s**, animal**s** | Plural nouns end in **-s**.<br>**A** and **an** are used only with singular nouns. |
| (c)  SINGULAR:  a cit**y**, a countr**y**.<br>     PLURAL:     cit**ies**, countr**ies** | Some singular nouns that end in **-y** have a special plural form: They omit the **-y** and add **-ies**.* |
| NOUN    *and*    NOUN  +  *ARE*  +  NOUN<br>(d)  **Canada and China      are      countries.**<br>(e)  **Dogs        and    cats        are      animals.** | Two nouns connected by **and** are followed by **are**.<br>In (d): *Canada* is a singular noun.  *China* is a singular noun.  They are connected by **and**.  Together they are plural, i.e., "more than one." |

*See Chart 2-6 for more information about adding **-s/-es** to words that end in **-y**.

■ **EXERCISE 5:**  Change the singular sentences to plural sentences.

SINGULAR                                                                 PLURAL

1. An ant is an insect.        →        _____Ants are insects._____

2. A computer is a machine.    →        _____

3. A dictionary is a book.     →        _____

4. A chicken is a bird.        →        _____

5. A rose is a flower.         →        _____

6. A carrot is a vegetable.    →        _____

7. A rabbit is an animal.      →        _____

■ **EXERCISE 6:** Complete the sentences with *is* or *are* and one of the nouns in the list. Use the correct singular form of the noun (using *a* or *an*) or the correct plural form.

| | | |
|---|---|---|
| animal | country | language |
| city | insect | machine |
| continent | | |

1. A dog _____ *is an animal* _____.

2. Dogs _____ *are animals* _____.

3. Spanish _____.

4. Spanish and Chinese _____.

5. Asia _____.

6. Asia and Africa _____.

7. Thailand and Viet Nam _____.

8. Thailand _____.

9. Butterflies _____.

10. A butterfly _____.

11. An automobile _____.

12. Automobiles _____.

13. London _____.

14. London and Baghdad _____.

■ **EXERCISE 7—ORAL:** Complete the sentences with your own words.

*Example:* ... a country.
*Response:* (Brazil is) a country.

1. ... a country.
2. ... countries.
3. ... languages.
4. ... a language.
5. ... a city.
6. ... cities.
7. ... animals.
8. ... an insect.
9. ... a peninsula.
10. ... streets in this city.
11. ... countries in Asia.
12. ... a city in Europe.
13. ... a plant.
14. ... a vegetable.
15. ... a season.

■ **EXERCISE 8—ORAL (BOOKS CLOSED):** What are the following things?

*Example:* Cows
*Response:* Cows are animals.

1. English
2. England
3. Butterflies
4. Chickens
5. Europe
6. Roses
7. A carrot

8. Russian and Arabic
9. Spring
10. Japan and Venezuela
11. A computer
12. A bear
13. Bees
14. An ant

15. Winter and summer
16. September and October
17. A dictionary
18. Typewriters
19. A Honda
20. (*names of cars, cities, countries, continents, animals, insects*)

## 1-3 PRONOUN + *BE* + NOUN

| SINGULAR | | | PLURAL | | | | |
|---|---|---|---|---|---|---|---|
| PRONOUN | + BE + | NOUN | PRONOUN | + BE | + NOUN | | |
| (a) **I** | am | a student. | (f) **We** | are | students. | I<br>you<br>she<br>he<br>it<br>we<br>they | = pronouns |
| (b) **You** | are | a student | (g) **You** | are | students. | | |
| (c) **She** | is | a student | (h) **They** | are | students. | | |
| (d) **He** | is | a student | | | | am<br>is<br>are | = forms of *be* |
| (e) **It** | is | a country. | | | | | |

| | |
|---|---|
| (i) *Rita* is in my class. **She** is a student.<br>(j) *Tom* is in my class. **He** is a student.<br>(k) *Rita* and *Tom* are in my class. **They** are students. | Pronouns refer to nouns.<br>In (i): *she* (feminine) = Rita<br>In (j): *he* (masculine) = Tom<br>In (k): *they* = Rita and Tom |

■ **EXERCISE 9:** Complete the sentences. Use a VERB: *am*, *is*, or *are*. Use a NOUN: *a student* or *students*.

1. We _____*are students*_____.

2. I _____.

3. Rita goes to school. She _____.

4. Rita and Tom go to school. They _____.

5. You (*one person*) _____.

6. You (*two persons*) _____.

■ **EXERCISE 10—ORAL (BOOKS CLOSED):** Complete the sentences with *a form of* **be** *+ a*
*student/students.* Indicate the subject or subjects with your hand.

*Example:* ( . . . ) *(The teacher supplies the name of a student.)*
*Response:* (Yoko) is a student. *(The responding student indicates Yoko.)*

1. ( . . . )                    6. ( . . . )
2. ( . . . ) and ( . . . )      7. ( . . . ) and ( . . . )
3. I                            8. They
4. ( . . . ) and I              9. You
5. We                          10. ( . . . ) and ( . . . ) and ( . . . )

Now identify the given people as students and, in addition, tell what country or
continent they are from.

11. ( . . . )
   → *(Yoko) is a student. She is from Japan.*
12. ( . . . ) and ( . . . )
   → *(Luis) and (Pablo) are students. They are from South America.*
13. ( . . . )
14. ( . . . ) and ( . . . )
15. Etc.

---

| 1-4 | CONTRACTIONS WITH *BE* |
|---|---|

| | | | | | | | When people speak, they often push two words together. *A contraction* = two words that are pushed together. |
|---|---|---|---|---|---|---|---|---|
| **AM** | PRONOUN | + | *BE* | → | CONTRACTION | | | |
| | I | + | am | → | ***I'm*** | (a) | ***I'm*** a student. | |
| **IS** | she | + | is | → | ***she's*** | (b) | ***She's*** a student. | Contractions of a *subject pronoun* + ***be*** are used in both speaking and writing. |
| | he | + | is | → | ***he's*** | (c) | ***He***'s a student. | |
| | it | + | is | → | ***it's*** | (d) | ***It's*** a city. | |
| **ARE** | you | + | are | → | ***you're*** | (e) | ***You're*** a student. | |
| | | | | | | | ***You're*** students. | PUNCTUATION: The mark in the middle of a contraction is called an "apostrophe" ('). |
| | we | + | are | → | ***we're*** | (f) | ***We're*** students. | |
| | they | + | are | → | ***they're*** | (g) | ***They're*** students. | |

NOTE: Write an apostrophe above the line. Do not write an apostrophe on the line.

CORRECT:     *I'm a student.*

INCORRECT:     *I,m a student.*

■ **EXERCISE 11:** Complete the sentences. Use CONTRACTIONS (*pronoun + be*).

1. *Sara* is a student. _____*She's*_____ in my class.

2. *Jim* is a student. _____ in my class.

3. I have *one brother*. _____ twenty years old.

4. I have *two sisters*. _____ students.

5. I have *a dictionary*. _____ on my desk.

6. I like *my classmates*. _____ friendly.

7. I have *three books*. _____ on my desk.

8. *My brother* is twenty-six years old. _____ married.

9. *My sister* is twenty-one years old. _____ single.

10. *Yoko and Ali* are students. _____ in my class.

11. I like *my books*. _____ interesting.

12. I like *grammar*. _____ easy.

13. *Kate and I* live in an apartment. _____ roommates.

14. *We* live in *an apartment*. _____ on Pine Street.

15. *I* go to school. _____ a student.

16. I know *you*. _____ in my English class.

## 1-5  NEGATIVE WITH *BE*

| | |
|---|---|
| (a) Tom $\begin{bmatrix} \textbf{\textit{is not}} \\ \textbf{\textit{isn't}} \end{bmatrix}$ a teacher.  He is a student. | ***Not*** makes a sentence negative.<br><br>***Not*** can be contracted with ***is*** and ***are***:<br>CONTRACTION:  ***is*** + ***not*** = ***isn't***<br>CONTRACTION:  ***are*** + ***not*** = ***aren't*** |
| (b) Tom and Ann $\begin{bmatrix} \textbf{\textit{are not}} \\ \textbf{\textit{aren't}} \end{bmatrix}$ teachers. | |
| (c) I ***am not*** a teacher. | ***Am*** and ***not*** are not contracted. |

■ **EXERCISE 12:** Complete the sentences with the correct information.

1. Korea _____*isn't*_____ a city. It *'s a country* _____.

2. Horses _____ insects. They _____.

3. Asia _____ a country. It _____.

4. Bees and ants _____ animals. They _____.

5. Arabic _____ a country. It _____.

6. I _____ a professional photographer. I _____.

Ms. Black

Jim

Mr. Rice

Mike

Ann

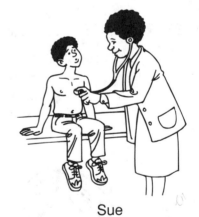

Sue

7. Ann _____ a gardener. She _____.

8. Mike _____ a gardener. He _____ an artist.

9. Jim _____ a bus driver. He _____.

10. Sue _____ a photographer. She _____.

11. Mr. Rice _____ a police officer. He isn't _____.

12. Ms. Black isn't _____. She _____.

| | NOUN | + | BE | + | ADJECTIVE |
|---|---|---|---|---|---|
| (a) | A ball | | is | | **round**. |
| (b) | Balls | | are | | **round.** |
| (c) | Mary | | is | | **intelligent**. |
| (d) | Mary and Tom | | are | | **intelligent.** |

| | PRONOUN | + | BE | + | ADJECTIVE |
|---|---|---|---|---|---|
| (e) | I | | am | | **hungry**. |
| (f) | She | | is | | **young**. |
| (g) | They | | are | | **happy**. |

round
intelligent
hungry          } = adjectives
young
happy

Adjectives often follow a form of **be** (*am*, *is*, *are*).  Adjectives describe or give information about a noun or pronoun that comes at the beginning of a sentence.*

*The noun or pronoun that comes at the beginning of a sentence is called a "subject." See Chart 4-1.

■ **EXERCISE 13:**   Complete the drawings.

> STUDENT A:   Make the faces **happy**, **sad**, and **angry**.   Show your drawings to Student B.
>
> STUDENT B:   Identify the emotions that Student A showed in the drawings.  For example: *She is angry.  He is sad.  They are happy.*

■ **EXERCISE 14:** Find the ADJECTIVE in the first sentence. Then complete the second sentence with **be** + an adjective that has an opposite meaning. Use the adjectives in the list. Use each adjective only one time.

| | | |
|---|---|---|
| beautiful | expensive | open |
| clean | fast | poor |
| cold | ✔ happy | short |
| dangerous | noisy | sour |
| easy | old | tall |

1. I'm not sad.  I *'m happy* _____.

2. Ice isn't hot.  It _____.

3. Mr. Thomas isn't rich.  He _____.

4. My hair isn't long.  It _____.

5. My clothes aren't dirty. They _____.

6. Flowers aren't ugly.  They _____.

7. Cars aren't cheap. They _____.

8. Airplanes aren't slow.  They _____.

9. Grammar isn't difficult.  It _____.

10. My sister isn't short.  She _____.

11. My grandparents aren't young.  They _____.

12. The dormitory isn't quiet.  It _____.

13. The door isn't closed.  It _____.

14. Guns aren't safe.  They _____.

15. Lemons aren't sweet.  They _____.

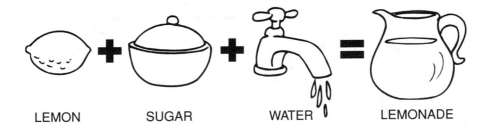

LEMON        SUGAR        WATER        LEMONADE

■ **EXERCISE 15—ORAL (BOOKS CLOSED):** Use ADJECTIVES to describe things in the classroom. Suggestions are given in parentheses.

*Example:* round, square, flat

To STUDENT A: *(The teacher writes the words on the board:* round, square, flat, *and then touches or points to something round, for example, a ring or a circle drawn on the board.)*
Tell me about this ring that I'm holding. Use one of the words on the board.

STUDENT A: It's round.

To STUDENT B: Tell me about this coin.

STUDENT B: It's round. It's flat.

1. round (a ring, a coin, a circle drawn on the board)
2. square (a box, a desk, a figure drawn on the board)
3. flat (a coin, a desktop)
4. full (a pocket, a hand)
5. empty (a pocket, a hand)
6. wet (a street on a rainy day, a licked finger)
7. dry (indoors on a rainy day, an unlicked finger)
8. dirty (a hand or a piece of paper rubbed on the floor)
9. clean (a hand or a piece of paper not rubbed on the floor)
10. long (a string, a strip of paper, someone's hair)
11. short (a string, a strip of paper, someone's hair)
12. heavy (a desk, a pile of books)
13. light (a piece of paper, a pen)
14. loud (a knock on a door or desk top, one's speaking voice)
15. soft (a knock on a door or desk top, one's speaking voice)
16. quiet (no sound at all in the classroom)

■ **EXERCISE 16:** Make sentences by using *is* or *are* and an ADJECTIVE from the following list. Use each adjective only one time.

| | | |
|---|---|---|
| · beautiful | ✔ hot | · sour |
| · cold | important | · square |
| · dry | · large/big | · sweet |
| flat | · round | · wet |
| · funny | · small/little | |

1. Fire _____*is hot*_____.

2. Ice and snow _____.

3. A box _____.

4. Balls and oranges _____.

5. Sugar _____.

6. An elephant _____,

   but a mouse _____.

7. A rain forest _____,

   but a desert _____.

8. A lemon _____.

9. A joke _____.

10. Good health _____.

11. Flowers _____.

12. A coin _____ small, round, and _____.

■ **EXERCISE 17:** Complete the sentences. Use *is, isn't, are,* or *aren't*.

1. A ball _____*isn't*_____ square.

2. Balls _____*are*_____ round.

3. A mouse _____ big.

4. Lemons _____ yellow.

   Ripe bananas _____ yellow too.

5. A lemon _____ sweet. It _____ sour.

6. A diamond _____ cheap.

7. Diamonds _____ expensive.

8. Apples _____ expensive.

9. The earth _____ flat. It _____ round.

10. My pen _____ heavy. It _____ light.

11. This room _____ dark. It _____ light.

12. English grammar _____ hard. It _____ easy.

13. This exercise _____ difficult. It _____ easy.

14. My classmates _____ friendly.

15. A turtle _____ slow.

16. Airplanes _____ slow.

    They _____ fast.

17. The floor in the classroom _____ clean.

    It _____ dirty.

18. The weather _____ cold today.

19. The sun _____ bright today.

20. Ice cream and candy _____ sour. They _____ sweet.

21. My shoes _____ comfortable.

22. My desk _____ comfortable.

23. Flowers _____ ugly. They _____ beautiful.

24. Traffic at rush hour _____ noisy. It _____ quiet.

■ **EXERCISE 18—ORAL:** Do any of these words describe you?

*Example:* Hungry?
*Response:* I'm hungry. OR: I'm not hungry.

1. hungry?
2. thirsty?
3. sleepy?
4. tired?
5. old?
6. young?
7. happy?
8. homesick?
9. married?
10. single?
11. angry?
12. nervous?
13. friendly?
14. lazy?
15. hardworking?
16. famous?
17. sick?
18. healthy?
19. friendly?
20. shy?

■ **EXERCISE 19—ORAL:**   Do any of these words describe this city?

1. big?
2. small?
3. old?
4. modern?
5. clean?

6. dirty?
7. friendly?
8. unfriendly?
9. safe?
10. dangerous?

■ **EXERCISE 20—ORAL (BOOKS CLOSED):**   Make sentences.  Use *is/isn't* or *are/aren't*.

*Example:* A ball \ round
*Response:* A ball is round.
*Example:* Balls \ square
*Response:* Balls aren't square.

1. A box \ square
2. A box \ round
3. The earth \ flat
4. The earth \ round
5. Bananas \ red
6. Bananas \ yellow
7. Diamonds \ expensive
8. Diamonds \ cheap
9. Apples \ expensive
10. Air \ free
11. Cars \ free
12. A pen \ heavy
13. A pen \ light
14. Flowers \ ugly
15. A rose \ beautiful
16. A turtle \ fast

17. A turtle \ slow
18. Airplanes \ slow
19. Airplanes \ fast
20. English grammar \ difficult
21. English grammar \ easy
22. This exercise \ hard
23. The weather \ hot today
24. The weather \ cold today
25. Lemons \ sweet
26. Ice cream and candy \ sour
27. Traffic \ noisy
28. City streets \ quiet
29. Education \ important
30. Good food \ important
31. Good food and exercise \ important
32. The students in this class \ very intelligent

■ **EXERCISE 21—ORAL (BOOKS CLOSED):**   Name things that the given ADJECTIVES can describe.

*Example:*   round
TEACHER:  Name something that is round.
STUDENT:  (A ball, an orange, the world, my head, etc.) is round.

1. hot
2. square
3. sweet
4. sour
5. large

6. flat
7. little
8. important
9. cold
10. funny

11. beautiful
12. expensive
13. cheap
14. free
15. delicious

## 1-7 *BE* + A LOCATION

| | |
|---|---|
| (a) Maria is **here**.<br>(b) Bob was **at the library**. | In (a): *here* = a location.<br>In (b): *at the library* = a location.<br>**Be** is often followed by *a location*. |
| (c) Maria is $\begin{cases} \textbf{\textit{here}}. \\ \textbf{\textit{there}}. \\ \textbf{\textit{downstairs}}. \\ \textbf{\textit{upstairs}}. \\ \textbf{\textit{inside}}. \\ \textbf{\textit{outside}}. \\ \textbf{\textit{downtown}}. \end{cases}$ | A location may be one word, as in the examples in (c). |
| (d) Bob was $\begin{array}{ll} \text{PREPOSITION} + \text{NOUN} \\ \begin{cases} \textbf{\textit{at}} & \textbf{\textit{the library}}. \\ \textbf{\textit{on}} & \textbf{\textit{the bus}}. \\ \textbf{\textit{in}} & \textbf{\textit{his room}}. \\ \textbf{\textit{at}} & \textbf{\textit{work}}. \\ \textbf{\textit{next to}} & \textbf{\textit{Maria}}. \end{cases} \end{array}$ | A location may be a prepositional phrase, as in (d).<br>*A preposition + a noun* is called a "prepositional phrase."<br>*At the library* = a prepositional phrase. |
| SOME COMMON PREPOSITIONS<br><br>*above*      *between*      *next to*<br>*at*      *from*      *on*<br>*behind*      *in*      *under* | |

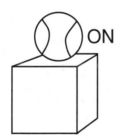 ON

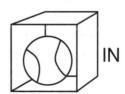 IN

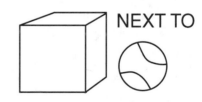 NEXT TO

ABOVE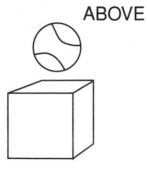

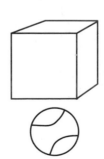

UNDER

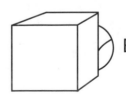 BEHIND

■ **EXERCISE 22:** Complete the sentences with PREPOSITIONS that describe the pictures. Use each preposition one time.

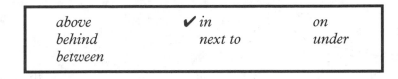

| above | ✔ in | on |
| behind | next to | under |
| between | | |

1.

The cat is _____*in*_____ the desk.

2.

The cat is _____ the desk.

3.

The cat is _____ the desk.

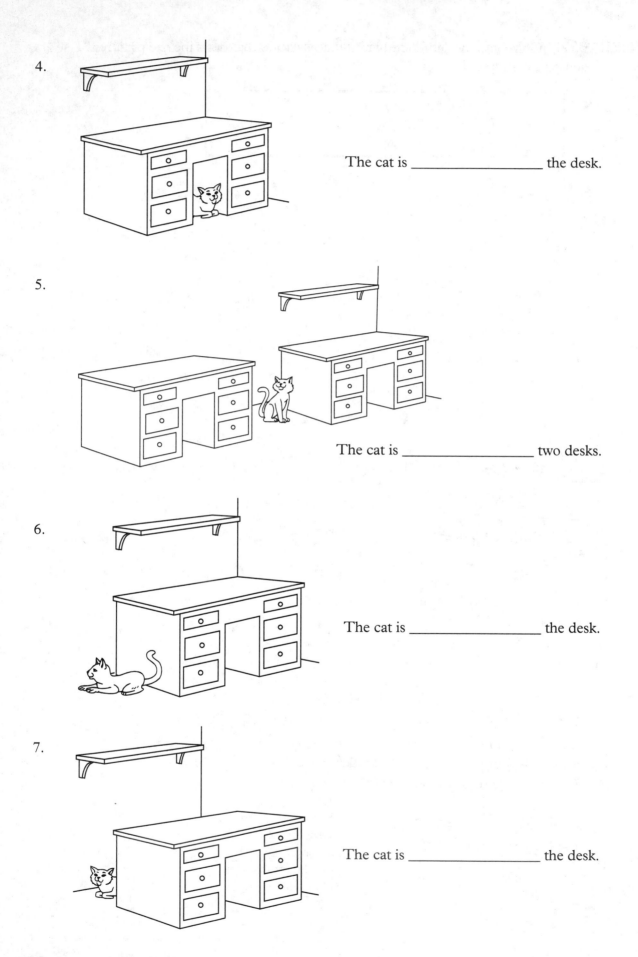

4. The cat is _____ the desk.

5. The cat is _____ two desks.

6. The cat is _____ the desk.

7. The cat is _____ the desk.

■ **EXERCISE 23:** Find the PREPOSITIONS and the PREPOSITIONAL PHRASES in the following sentences.

1. Mike is in his apartment.
   → *in = a preposition*
   → *in his apartment = a prepositional phrase*

2. Mr. Lee is at the airport.

3. Ali is from Egypt.

4. My book is on my desk.

5. Bob's pen is in his pocket.

6. The post office is on First Street.

7. The post office is next to the bank.

8. My feet are under my desktop.

9. My nose is between my cheeks.

10. My apartment is on the third floor. It is above Mr. Kwan's apartment.

■ **EXERCISE 24—ORAL (BOOKS CLOSED):** Practice using PREPOSITIONS of location.

| | | |
|---|---|---|
| *Example:* | under | |
| TEACHER | Put your hand under your chair. Where is your hand? | |
| STUDENT: | My hand is under my chair. / It's under my chair. | |

1. *on* — Put your pen on your book. Where is your pen?
2. *in* — Put your pen in your book. Where's your pen?
3. *under* — Put your pen under your book. Where's your pen?
4. *next to* — Put your pen next to your book. Where's your pen?
5. *on* — Put your hand on your ear. Where's your hand?
6. *next to* — Put your hand next to your ear. Where's your hand?
7. *above* — Put your hand above your head. Where's your hand?
8. *next to* — Stand next to ( . . . ). Where are you?
9. *between* — Stand between ( . . . ) and ( . . . ). Where are you?
10. *between* — Put your pen between two books. Where's your pen?
11. *behind* — Put your hand behind your head. Where's your hand?
12. Follow these directions: Put your pen  in your hand.
    . . . on your arm.
    . . . behind your neck.
    . . . between your hands.
    . . . under your book.
    . . . next to your book.
    . . . above your book.

## 1-8 SUMMARY: SENTENCE PATTERNS WITH BE

| | |
|---|---|
| (a) SUBJECT + BE + NOUN<br> I     am     *a student.*<br><br>(b) SUBJECT + BE + ADJECTIVE<br> He    is     *intelligent.*<br><br>(c) SUBJECT + BE + A LOCATION<br> We    are    *in class.* | The noun or pronoun that comes at the beginning of a sentence is called the "subject."<br><br>**Be** is a "verb." Almost all English sentences have a subject and a verb. |
| | Notice in the examples: There are three basic completions for sentences that begin with a *subject + the verb* **be**:<br> • *a noun*, as in (a)<br> • *an adjective*, as in (b)<br> • *an expression of location*, as in (c) |

■ **EXERCISE 25:** Write the form of **be** (**am**, **is**, or **are**) that is used in each sentence. Then write the grammar structure that follows **be**.

|  | BE | + | COMPLETION |
|---|---|---|---|
| 1. We're students. → | are | + | N *(a noun)* |
| 2. Anna is in Rome. → | is | + | LOC *(a location)* |
| 3. I'm hungry. → | am | + | ADJ *(an adjective)* |
| 4. Dogs are animals. → | _____ | + | _____ |
| 5. Jack is at home. → | _____ | + | _____ |
| 6. He's sick. → | _____ | + | _____ |
| 7. They're artists. → | _____ | + | _____ |
| 8. I'm in class. → | _____ | + | _____ |
| 9. Gina is upstairs. → | _____ | + | _____ |
| 10. My pockets are empty. → | _____ | + | _____ |

■ **EXERCISE 26—ORAL:** *Is* and *are* are often contracted with nouns in spoken English. Listen to your teacher say the contractions in the following sentences and practice saying them yourself.

1. Grammar is easy.
   ("Grammar's easy.")

2. Rita is a student.

3. My book is on the table.

4. My books are on the table.

5. The weather is cold today.

6. My brother is twenty-one years old.

7. The window is open.

8. The windows are open.

9. My money is in my wallet.

10. Mr. Smith is a teacher.

11. Tom is at home now.

12. The sun is bright today.

13. My roommate is from Chicago.

14. My roommates are from Chicago.

15. My sister is a student in high school.

## 1-9  YES/NO QUESTIONS WITH *BE*

| QUESTION | STATEMENT | In a question, *be* comes in front of the subject. |
|---|---|---|
| *BE* + SUBJECT | SUBJECT + *BE* | *Punctuation:* A question ends with a question mark (?). |
| (a) *Is* *she* a student? | *She* *is* a student. | A statement ends with a period (.). |
| (b) *Are* *they* at home? | *They* *are* at home. | |

When people answer a question, they usually give only a "short answer" (but sometimes they give a "long answer" too). Notice in the short answers below:
After yes, *be* is not contracted with a pronoun.★
After *no*, two contractions of *be* are possible with no differences in meaning.

| QUESTION | SHORT ANSWER + (LONG ANSWER) | |
|---|---|---|
| (c) *Is she* a student? → | Yes, *she is.*★ | *(She's a student.)* |
| → | No, *she's not.* | *(She's not a student.)* OR: |
| → | No, *she isn't.* | *(She isn't a student.)* |
| (d) *Are they* at home? → | Yes, *they are.*★ | *(They're at home.)* |
| → | No, *they're not.* | *(They're not at home.)* OR: |
| → | No, *they aren't.* | *(They aren't at home.)* |

★ INCORRECT: *Yes, she's.*
  INCORRECT: *Yes, they're.*

■ **EXERCISE 27:**   Make questions and give short answers.

1. A: _____*Are you tired?*_____

   B: _____*No, I'm not.*_____ (I'm not tired.)

2. A: _____*Is Anna in your class?*_____

   B: _____*Yes, she is.*_____ (Anna is in my class.)

3. A: _____

   B: _____ (I'm not homesick.)

4. A: _____

   B: _____ (Bob is homesick.)

5. A: _____

   B: _____ (Sue isn't here today.)

6. A: _____

   B: _____ (The students in this class are intelligent.)

7. A: _____

   B: _____ (The chairs in this room aren't comfortable.)

8. A: _____

   B: _____ (I'm not married.)

9. A: _____

   B: _____ (Tom and I are roommates.)

10. A: _____

   B: _____ (A butterfly is not a bird.)

■ **EXERCISE 28—ORAL (BOOKS CLOSED):**  Ask and answer questions.

STUDENT A:  Your book is open.  Ask a classmate a question.  Use "*Are you . . . ?*"
STUDENT B:  Your book is closed.  Answer Student A's question.
*Example:*  hungry
STUDENT A:  (Yoko), are you hungry?
STUDENT B:  Yes, I am.  OR:  No, I'm not.

1. hungry
2. sleepy
3. thirsty
4. married
5. single
6. tired
7. homesick
8. lazy
9. cold
10. comfortable
11. a student
12. a teacher
13. a famous actor
14. in the middle of the room

*Switch roles.*

15. in the back of the room
16. in the front of the room
17. in class
18. in bed
19. at the library
20. at home
21. in (*name of this city*)
22. in (*name of another city*)
23. in Canada
24. in the United States
25. from the United States
26. from (*name of country*)
27. a student at (*name of school*)

■ **EXERCISE 29—ORAL (BOOKS CLOSED):**  Ask a classmate a question.

STUDENT A:  Your book is open.  Ask a classmate a question.  Use "*Are you . . . ?*"
STUDENT B:  Your book is closed.  Answer Student A's question.
*Example:*  a ball \ round
STUDENT A:  ( . . . ), is a ball round?
STUDENT B:  Yes, it is.
*Example:*  a ball \ square
STUDENT A:  ( . . . ), is a ball square?
STUDENT B:  No, it isn't.  OR:  No, it's not.

*Switch roles.*

1. a mouse \ big
2. sugar \ sweet
3. lemons \ sweet
4. ice cream and candy \ sour
5. the world \ flat
6. the world \ round
7. your desk \ comfortable
8. your shoes \ comfortable
9. your eyes \ brown
10. the sun \ bright today
11. the weather \ cold today
12. your pen \ heavy
13. apples \ expensive
14. diamonds \ cheap
15. English grammar \ easy
16. the floor in this room \ clean
17. butterflies \ beautiful
18. turtles \ intelligent
19. your dictionary \ under your desk
20. your books \ on your desk
21. your desk \ in the middle of the room
22. your pen \ in your pocket

## 1-10 QUESTIONS WITH *BE*: USING *WHERE*

**Where** asks about location. **Where** comes at the beginning of the question, in front of **be**.

|  | QUESTION | SHORT ANSWER + (LONG ANSWER) |
|---|---|---|
|  | *BE* + SUBJECT |  |
| (a) | **Is** **the book** on the table? → | Yes, **it is.** *(The book is on the table.)* |
| (b) | **Are** **the books** on the table? → | Yes, **they are.** *(The books are on the table.)* |
|  | *WHERE* + *BE* + SUBJECT |  |
| (c) **Where** | **is** **the book?** | → **On the table.** *(The book is on the table.)* |
| (d) **Where** | **are** **the books?** | → **On the table.** *(The books are on the table.)* |

■ **EXERCISE 30:** Make questions.

1.  A: _____*Is Kate at home?*_____
    B: Yes, she is.  (Kate is at home.)

2.  A: _____*Where is Kate?*_____
    B: At home.  (Kate is at home.)

3.  A: _____
    B: Yes, it is.  (Cairo is in Egypt.)

4.  A: _____
    B: In Egypt.  (Cairo is in Egypt.)

5.  A: _____
    B: Yes, they are.  (The students are in class today.)

6.  A: _____
    B: In class.  (The students are in class today.)

7.  A: _____
    B: On Main Street.  (The post office is on Main Street.)

8.  A: _____
    B: Yes, it is.  (The train station is on Grand Avenue.)

9.  A: _____
    B: Over there.  (The bus stop is over there.)

10. A: _____
    B: At the zoo.  (Sue and Ken are at the zoo today.)

■ **EXERCISE 31—ORAL (BOOKS CLOSED):** Ask a classmate a question. Use *where.*

*Example:* your pen
STUDENT A: Where is your pen?
STUDENT B: *(free response)*

1. your grammar book
2. your dictionary
3. your money
4. your books
5. ( . . . )

6. ( . . . ) and ( . . . )
7. your sunglasses
8. your pen
9. your apartment

10. your parents
11. the post office
12. *(the names of places in this city: a store, landmark, restaurant, etc.)*

■ **EXERCISE 32—ORAL:** Ask and answer questions using *where* and the map of North America.

*Example:* Washington, D.C.
STUDENT A: Where's Washington, D.C.?
STUDENT B: *(Pointing at the map)* It's here.

*Suggestions:*
1. New York City
2. Los Angeles
3. Montreal
4. Miami
5. Toronto
6. Washington, D. C.
7. the Great Lakes
8. the Rocky Mountains
9. the Mississippi River
10. Mexico City

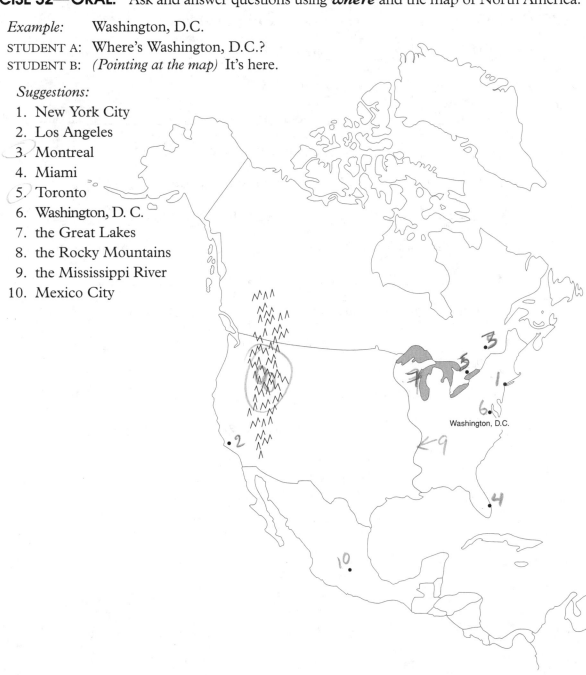

Washington, D.C.

## 1-11 USING *HAVE* AND *HAS*

|  | SINGULAR | | PLURAL | | | |
|---|---|---|---|---|---|---|
| | | | | | *I* | |
| (a) | *I* **have** a pen. | (f) | *We* **have** pens. | | *you* | + **have** |
| (b) | *You* **have** a pen. | (g) | *You* **has** pens. | | *we* | |
| (c) | *She* **has** a pen. | (h) | *They* **have** pens. | | *they* | |
| (d) | *He* **has** a pen. | | | | *she* | |
| (e) | *It* **has** blue ink. | | | | *he* | + **has** |
| | | | | | *it* | |

■ **EXERCISE 33:** Complete the sentences. Use **have** and **has.**

1. We _____*have*_____ grammar books.

2. I _____ a dictionary.

3. Kate _____ a blue pen. She _____ a blue notebook too.

4. You _____ a pen in your pocket.

5. Bob _____ a notebook on his desk.

6. Anna and Bob _____ notebooks. They _____ pens too.

7. Samir is a student in our class. He _____ a red grammar book.

8. I _____ a grammar book. It _____ a red cover.

9. You and I are students. We _____ books on our desks.

10. Mike _____ a wallet in his pocket. Sara _____ a wallet in her purse.

11. Nadia isn't in class today because she _____ the flu.

12. Mr. and Mrs. Johnson _____ two daughters.

## 1-12 USING MY, YOUR, HIS, HER, OUR, THEIR

|  | SINGULAR | PLURAL |
|---|---|---|
| (a) | **I** have a book. *My* book is red. | (e) **We** have books. *Our* books are red. |
| (b) | **You** have a book. *Your* book is red. | (f) **You** have books. *Your* books are red. |
| (c) | **She** has a book. *Her* book is red. | (g) **They** have books. *Their* books are red. |
| (d) | **He** has a book. *His* book is red. | |

| SUBJECT FORM | | POSSESSIVE FORM |
|---|---|---|
| *I* | → | *my* |
| *you* | → | *your* |
| *she* | → | *her* |
| *he* | → | *his* |
| *we* | → | *our* |
| *they* | → | *their* |

I *possess* a book. = I *have* a book. = It is *my* book.

*My, our, her, his, our,* and *their* are called "possessive adjectives." They come in front of nouns.

■ **EXERCISE 34:**     Complete the sentences.  Use *my*, *your*, *his*, *her*, *our*, or *their*.

1. I have a pen. _____My_____ pen is blue.

2. You have a pen. _____ pen is black.

3. Kate has a pen. _____ pen is green.

4. Jim has a pen. _____ pen is yellow.

5. Sara and I have pens. _____ pens are gray.

6. Sara and you have pens. _____ pens are red.

7. Sam and Kate have pens. _____ pens are orange.

8. I have a sister. _____ sister is twenty-one years old.

9. Ann has a car. _____ car is a Ford.

10. You have a pen. _____ pen is a ballpoint.

11. Jim and you have mustaches. _____ mustaches are dark.

12. Ann and Alex have a baby. _____ baby is eight months old.

13. Alice and I have notebooks. _____ notebooks are green.

14. Ann has a brother. _____ brother is in high school.

15. Ken has a coat. _____ coat is brown.

16. We have a dog. _____ dog is gray and white.

■ **EXERCISE 35:** Complete the sentences. Use **have** or **has**. Use **my**, **your**, **her**, **his**, **our**, or **their**.

1. I _____have_____ a book. _____My_____ book is interesting.

2. Bob _____ a bookbag. _____ bookbag is green.

3. You _____ a raincoat. _____ raincoat is brown.

4. Kate _____ a raincoat. _____ raincoat is red.

5. Ann and Jim are married. They _____ a baby. _____ baby is six months old.

6. Ken and Sue _____ a daughter. _____ daughter is ten years old.

7. John and I _____ a son. _____ son is seven years old.

8. I _____ a brother. _____ brother is sixteen.

9. We _____ grammar books. _____ grammar books are red.

10. Tom and you _____ bookbags. _____ bookbags are green.

11. Ann _____ a dictionary. _____ dictionary is red.

12. Mike _____ a car. _____ car is blue.

■ **EXERCISE 36:** Complete the sentences with **my**, **your**, **her**, **his**, **our**, or **their**.

1. Rita is wearing a blouse. _____ blouse is light blue.

2. Tom is wearing a shirt. _____ shirt is yellow and brown.

3. I am wearing jeans. _____ jeans are blue.

4. Bob and Tom are wearing boots. _____ boots are brown.

5. Sue and you are wearing dresses. _____ dresses are red.

6. Ann and I are wearing sweaters. _____ sweaters are green.

7. You are wearing shoes. _____ shoes are dark brown.

8. Sue is wearing a skirt. _____ skirt is black.

9. John is wearing a belt. _____ belt is white.

10. Sue and Ann are wearing slacks. _____ slacks are dark gray.

11. Tom is wearing slacks. _____ slacks are dark blue.

12. I am wearing earrings. _____ earrings are gold.

---

## VOCABULARY CHECKLIST

| COLORS | CLOTHES | JEWELRY |
|---|---|---|
| black | belt | bracelet |
| blue, dark blue, light blue | blouse | earrings |
| blue green | boots | necklace |
| brown, dark brown, light brown | coat | ring |
| gray, dark gray, light gray | dress | watch/wristwatch |
| green, dark green, light green | gloves | |
| orange | hat | |
| pink | jacket | |
| purple | jeans | |
| red | pants | |
| tan, beige | sandals | |
| white | shirt | |
| yellow | shoes | |
| gold | skirt | |
| silver | slacks | |
| | suit | |
| | sweater | |
| | tie, necktie | |
| | T-shirt | |

---

■ **EXERCISE 37—ORAL (BOOKS CLOSED):** Name some of the colors and then some of the articles of clothing and jewelry in the room. Then describe an article of clothing/jewelry and its color, using this pattern:

*possessive adjective + noun + **is/are** + color*

*Examples:*
TEACHER: Look at Ali. Tell me about his shirt. What color is his shirt?
STUDENT: His shirt is blue.

TEACHER: Look at Rosa. What is this?
STUDENT: A sweater.
TEACHER: Tell me about her sweater. What color is it?
STUDENT: Her sweater is red.

TEACHER: Look at me. What am I touching?
STUDENT: Your shoes.
TEACHER: Tell me about the color.
STUDENT: Your shoes are brown.

| | |
|---|---|
| (a)  I have a book in my hand. **This book** is red. | *this* book = the book is near me. |
| (b)  I see a book on your desk. **That book** is blue. | *that* book = the book is not near me. |
| (c)  **This** is my book. | |
| (d)  **That** is your book. | |
| (e)  **That's** her book. | CONTRACTION:  *that is = that's* |

THIS
BOOK

THAT BOOK

■ **EXERCISE 38—ORAL (BOOKS CLOSED):**  Use *this* and *that*.  Touch and point to things in the classroom.

*Example:* book
*Response:* This is my book.  That is your book.

| | | |
|---|---|---|
| 1. book | 5. dictionary | 9. pencil |
| 2. pen | 6. bookbag | 10. pencil sharpener |
| 3. notebook | 7. coat | 11. watch |
| 4. purse | 8. hat | 12. nose |

■ **EXERCISE 39—ORAL (BOOKS CLOSED):**  Use *this* and *that*.  Touch and point to things in the classroom.

*Example:* red \ yellow
*Response:* This (book) is red.  That (shirt) is yellow.

| | |
|---|---|
| 1. red \ blue | 7. red \ pink |
| 2. red \ green | 8. dark blue \ light blue |
| 3. red \ yellow | 9. black \ gray |
| 4. blue \ black | 10. gold \ silver |
| 5. white \ black | 11. dark brown \ tan |
| 6. orange \ green | 12. purple \ red |

## 1-14 USING *THESE* AND *THOSE*

| | SINGULAR | | PLURAL |
|---|---|---|---|
| (a) My books are on my desk. **These** are my books. | *this* | → | *these* |
| (b) Your books are on your desk. **Those** are your books. | *that* | → | *those* |

■ **EXERCISE 40:** Complete the sentences. Use the words in parentheses.

1. (This, These) _____ *These* _____ books belong to me. (That, Those)

   _____ *That* _____ book belongs to Kate.

2. (This, These) _____ coat is black. (That, Those) _____

   coats are tan.

3. (This, These) _____ earrings are gold. (That, Those) _____

   earrings are silver.

4. (This, These) _____ pencil belongs to Alex. (That, Those)

   _____ pencil belongs to Alice.

5. (This, These) _____ sunglasses belong to me. (That, Those)

   _____ sunglasses belong to you.

6. (This, These) _____ exercise is easy. (That, Those) _____

   exercises are hard.

7. Students are sitting at (this, these) _____ desks, but (that, those)

   _____ desks are empty.

8. (This, These) _____ book is on my desk. (That, Those)

   _____ books are on your desk.

■ **EXERCISE 41—ORAL (BOOKS CLOSED):** Use *these* and *those*. Touch and point to things in the classroom.

*Example:* books
*Response:* These are my books. Those are your books.

1. books
2. pens
3. shoes
4. earrings
5. jeans
6. things
7. glasses/sunglasses
8. notebooks

■ **EXERCISE 42—ORAL (BOOKS CLOSED):** Use *this*, *that*, *these*, or *those*. Touch and point to things in the classroom.

*Example:* book
*Response:* This is my book. That is your book.
*Example:* books
*Response:* These are my books. Those are your books.

| | |
|---|---|
| 1. book | 6. coats |
| 2. books | 7. shoes |
| 3. dictionary | 8. wallet |
| 4. pens | 9. purse |
| 5. pen | 10. glasses |

---

### 1-15 ASKING QUESTIONS WITH *WHAT* AND *WHO* + *BE*

| | |
|---|---|
| (a) **What is** this (thing)? → It's a pen. <br> (b) **Who is** that (man)? → That's Mr. Lee. <br><br> (c) **What are** those (things)? → They're pens. <br> (d) **Who are** they? → They're Mr. and Mrs. Lee. | **What** asks about things. <br> **Who** asks about people. <br> NOTE: In questions with **what** and **who**, <br> • *is* is followed by a singular word. <br> • *are* is followed by a plural word. |
| (e) **What's** this? <br> (f) **Who's** that man? | CONTRACTIONS <br> *who is = who's* <br> *what is = what's* |

---

■ **EXERCISE 43:** Complete the questions with *what* or *who* and *is* or *are*.

1. A: _____*Who is*_____ that woman?
   B: She's my sister. Her name is Sonya.

2. A: _____ those things?
   B: They're ballpoint pens.

3. A: _____ that?
   B: That's Ms. Walenski.

4. A: _____ this?
   B: That's my new notebook.

5. A: Look at those people over there. _____ they?
   B: I'm not sure, but I think they're new students from Thailand.

6. A: _____ your name?
   B: Anita.

7. A: _____ your grammar teacher?
   B: Mr. Cook.

8. A: _____ your favorite teachers?
   B: Mr. Cook and Ms. Rosenberg.

9. A: _____ a rabbit?
   B: It's a small furry animal with big ears.

10. A: _____ bats?
    B: They're animals that can fly. They're not birds.

■ **EXERCISE 45—ORAL:** Talk about things and people in the classroom. Ask your classmates the given questions.

*Example*:      What's this?
STUDENT A:   What's this? *(pointing at his/her grammar book)*
STUDENT B:   It's your grammar book.
*Example*:      Who's that?
STUDENT A:   Who's that? *(indicating a classmate)*
STUDENT B:   That's Ivan.

1. What's this?
2. What's that?
3. Who's this?
4. Who's that?
5. What are those?
6. What are these?

■ **EXERCISE 46:**  Study the names of the parts of the body in Picture A. Then cover Picture A and write in the names of the body parts in Picture B.

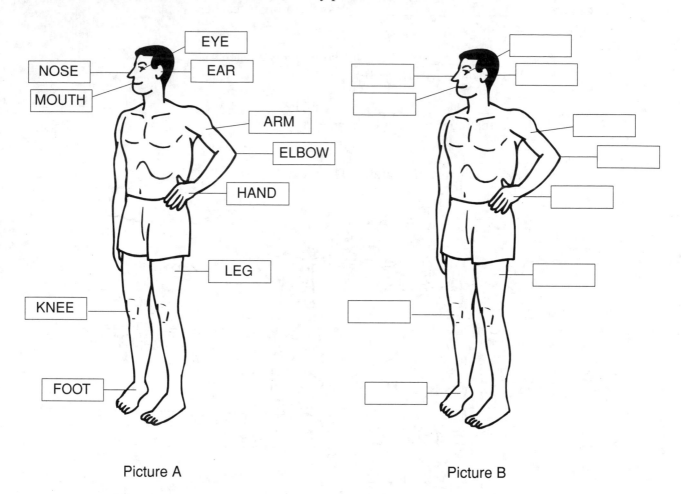

Picture A                                Picture B

■ **EXERCISE 47—ORAL (BOOKS CLOSED):**  Use ***this***, ***that***, ***these***, and ***those***.

*Example:*  hand
TEACHER:  What is this? *(The teacher indicates her or his hand.)*
STUDENT:  That is your hand.

OR

TEACHER:  What is that? *(The teacher indicates a student's hand.)*
STUDENT:  This is my hand.

1. nose                6. knee
2. eyes                7. foot
3. arm                 8. shoulder
4. elbow               9. fingers
5. legs               10. ears

■ **EXERCISE 48—ORAL:** Ask a classmate questions about the picture. Use **What's this?**
**What's that? What are these? What are those?** and any other questions you want
to ask.

*Example:*
STUDENT A: What's this? *(pointing at the tree)*
STUDENT B: That's a tree.
STUDENT A: What are those? *(pointing at the horses)*
STUDENT B: Those are horses.
Etc.

■ **EXERCISE 49:** Draw a picture and then answer a classmate's question about it. Use ***What's this? What's that? What are these? What are those?*** and any other questions you want to ask.

*Suggestions for the picture you draw:*
1. this classroom
2. some of the people in this classroom
3. your family
4. your room / apartment / house
5. a scene at a zoo
6. an outdoor scene

■ **EXERCISE 50—REVIEW:** Underline the NOUNS, ADJECTIVES, PRONOUNS, POSSESSIVE ADJECTIVES, and PREPOSITIONAL PHRASES.

*PART I:* Find the NOUNS and ADJECTIVES.

     *noun*     *adj.*
1. Balls are round.

2. Flowers are beautiful.

3. Birds have wings.

4. Bats aren't birds.

5. Bats aren't blind.

*PART II:* Find the PRONOUNS and POSSESSIVE ADJECTIVES.

               *pronoun*               *poss. adj.*
6. Bats have wings, but they aren't birds. Bats use their wings to fly.

7. I have a grammar book. It's red. My dictionary is red too.

8. My book is red, and your book is red too.

9. An egg isn't square. It's oval.

10. Tina has three sons. She is at home today. They are at school. Her sons are good

students.

*PART III:* Find the PREPOSITIONAL PHRASES.

11. Libya is in Africa.

*prep. phr.*

12. Po is from Beijing.

13. My books are on my desk.

14. I'm at school.

15. My middle finger is between my index finger and my ring finger.

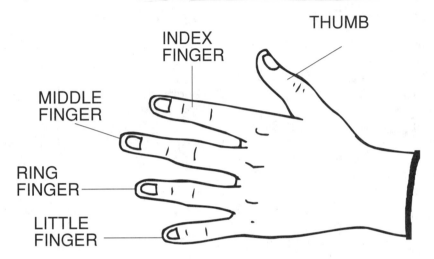

■ **EXERCISE 51—REVIEW:**  Correct the mistakes in the sentences.

1. We is students.

   *are*

2. I no hungry.

3. I am student.  He is teacher.

4. Yoko not here.  She at school.

5. I'm from Mexico.  Where you are from?

6. Roberto he is a student in your class?

7. Those pictures are beautifuls.

8. This is you dictionary.  It not my dictionary.

9. Mr. Lee have a brown coat.

10. They are n't here today.

11. This books are expensive.

12. Cuba is a island.

13. Florida and Korea is peninsula.


■ **EXERCISE 52—REVIEW:** Choose the correct completion.

*Example*:

Those _____ *B* _____ expensive.
    A. book is        B. books are        C. books is

1. Ann _____ a grammar book.
    A. have        B. is        C. has

2. This floor _____.
    A. dirty is        B. dirty        C. is dirty

3. _____ yellow.
    A. A banana are        B. A banana is        C. Bananas is

4. *Bob:* _____ is your apartment?
   *Ann:* It's on Forest Street.
    A. What        B. Where        C. Who

5. Mike is _____ engineer.
    A. a        B. an        C. on

6. Give this to Ann. It is _____ dictionary.
    A. she        B. an        C. her

7. *Yoko:* _____ these?
   *Gina:* My art books. I'm taking an art history course this semester.
    A. What is        B. Who are        C. What are

8. *Tom:* Are you hungry?

   *Sue:* Yes, _____.
    A. I'm        B. I'm not        C. I am

9. _____ books are really expensive.
    A. Those        B. They        C. This

10. *Tina:* _____ that?
    *Jim:*  That's Paul Carter.
         A.  Who's          B.  What's          C.  Where's

11. That is _____.
         A.  a mistakes     B.  mistakes        C.  a mistake

12. *Paul:* _____ in your class?
    *Eric:* No.
         A.  Mr. Kim        B.  Is Mr. Kim      C.  Mr. Kim is he

■ **EXERCISE 53—REVIEW:**  Complete the sentences with *am, is,* or *are*.  Use *not* if necessary.

1. Lemons _____ vegetables.

2. A lemon _____ a kind of fruit.

3. I _____ from the United States.

4. We _____ human beings.

5. Eggs _____ oval.

6. Chickens _____ birds, but bats _____ birds.

7. Salt _____ sweet.  Sugar _____ sweet.

8. Soccer _____ a sport.

9. Soccer and basketball _____ sports.

10. Africa _____ a country.  It _____ a continent.

■ **EXERCISE 54—REVIEW:**  Complete the sentences.

1. A: _____*Are*_____ you a student at this school?

   B: Yes, _____.

   A: Where _____ you from?

   B: I _____ Korea.


2. A: Where _____ your book?

   B: Yoko _____ it.

   A: Where _____ your notebooks?

   B: Ali and Roberto _____ my notebooks.

3. A: _____ this?

   B: It _____ picture of my family.

   A: _____ this?

   B: That's _____ father.

   A: _____ they?
   B: My brother and sister.

4. A: Are you a _____?

   B: No, _____ not.  I'm a _____.

5. A: Are _____ expensive?

   B: Yes, _____.

   A: Is _____ expensive?

   B: No, _____.

6. A: What's _____?
   B: I don't know.  Ask someone else.

   A: What's _____?

   B: It's _____.

7. A: _____ an animal?
   B: Yes.

   A: _____ animals?
   B: Yes.

   A: _____ an insect?
   B: No, it's not.  It's an animal too.

8. A: _____ countries in Asia?
   B: Yes, they are.

   A: _____ a country in South America?
   B: Yes, it is.

   A: _____ a country in Africa?

   B: No, it's not.  It's a country in _____.

9. A: Where _____?

   B: He's _____.

   A: Where _____?

   B: They're _____.


10. A: _____ a turtle?
    B: Just a minute. Let me look in my dictionary. Okay. A turtle is a reptile.

    A: _____ a reptile?

    B: _____ an animal that has cold blood.

    A: _____ snakes reptiles too?

    B: Yes. _____ reptiles too.


■ **EXERCISE 55—REVIEW:** Work in pairs.

   STUDENT A: Give directions. Your book is open.
   STUDENT B: Draw what Student A tells you to draw. Your book is closed.

   1. Draw a ball on a box.
   2. Draw a ball above a box.
   3. Draw a ball next to a box.
   4. Draw a ball under a box.
   5. Draw a ball in a box.
   6. Draw a banana between two apples.
   7. Draw a square above a circle.
   8. Draw a flower. Draw a tree next to the flower. Draw a bird above the tree. Draw a turtle under the flower.

   *Switch roles.*
   9. Draw a circle next to a triangle.
   10. Draw a circle in a triangle.
   11. Draw a circle above a triangle.
   12. Draw a triangle between two circles.
   13. Draw a circle under a triangle.
   14. Draw an apple on a banana. Draw an apple above a banana.
   15. Draw a tree. Draw a person next to the tree. Draw the sun above the tree.
   16. Draw a cloud. Draw a bird under the cloud. Draw a bird above the cloud. Draw a bird in the cloud.

■ **EXERCISE 56—REVIEW:** Work in pairs.

STUDENT A: Give directions. Use the given prepositions.
STUDENT B: Perform the action.

*Example:*    in
STUDENT A: Put your pen in your pocket.
STUDENT B: *(Student B puts her/his pen in her/his pocket.)*

*Switch roles.*

1. in
2. on
3. above
4. under
5. between
6. next to
7. behind

8. in
9. between
10. behind
11. above
12. on
13. next to
14. under

■ **EXERCISE 57—REVIEW:** Complete the sentences in this composition by Carlos.

(1)    My name _____*is*_____ Carlos. ____*I am* OR *I'm*____ from Mexico.

(2)    _____ a student. _____ twenty years old.

(3)    My family lives in Mexico City. _____ father _____ a

(4)    businessman. _____ fifty-one years old. _____ mother

(5)    _____ a housewife. _____ forty-nine years old.

(6)    I _____ two sisters and one brother. The names of my sisters

(7)    _____ Rosa and Patricia. Rosa _____ a teacher.

(8)    _____ twenty-eight years old. Patricia _____ a student.

(9)    _____ eighteen years old. The name of _____ brother

(10)   _____ Pedro. _____ an engineer. He is married. He

(11)   _____ two children.

(12)   I live in a dormitory. _____ a tall building. _____ on

(13)   Pine Street. My address _____ 3225 Pine St. I live with my roommate.

(14)   _____ name is Bob. _____ from Chicago.

(15)   _____ nineteen years old.

(16)   I like my classes. _____ interesting. I like _____

(17)   classmates. _____ friendly.

■ **EXERCISE 58—REVIEW:** Write a composition by completing the sentences. (Use your own paper.) NOTE: A sentence begins with a capital letter (a big letter) and a sentence ends with a period ( . )*

My name _____. I _____ from _____. _____ a student. _____ years old.

My family lives in _____. _____ father _____ years old. _____ mother _____ years old.

I have _____ sister(s) and _____ brother(s). The name(s) of my sister(s) _____. _____ is a/an _____. _____ years old. *(Write about each sister.)* The name(s) of my brother(s) _____. _____ is a _____. _____ years old. *(Write about each brother.)*

I live in *(a dormitory, a house, an apartment)* _____. My address _____. I live with _____. _____ name(s) _____.

I like _____ classes. _____ are _____ and _____. I like _____ classmates. They _____.

———————————
*In British English, a period is called a "full stop."

# CHAPTER *2*
# Expressing Present Time (Part 1)

## 2-1 FORM AND BASIC MEANING OF THE SIMPLE PRESENT TENSE

|  | SINGULAR | PLURAL |
|---|---|---|
| 1st PERSON | I *talk* | we *talk* |
| 2nd PERSON | you *talk* | you *talk* |
| 3rd PERSON | she *talks* | they *talk* |
|  | he *talks* |  |
|  | it *rains* |  |

Notice: The verb after *she, he, it* (3rd person singular) has a final *-s*: *talks*.

| | |
|---|---|
| ( a ) I *eat* breakfast **every morning**. <br> ( b ) Ann *speaks* English **every day**. <br> ( c ) We *sleep* **every night**. <br> ( d ) They *go* to the beach **every weekend**. | The simple present tense expresses habits. In (a): Eating breakfast is a habit, a usual activity. *Every morning* = Monday morning, Tuesday morning, Wednesday morning, Thursday morning, Friday morning, Saturday morning, and Sunday morning. |

**■ EXERCISE 1:** What do you do every morning?  On the left, there is a list of habits.  On the right, make a list of _your_ habits every morning.  Put them in order.  What do you do first, second, third, etc.?

| HABITS | MY HABITS EVERY MORNING |
|---|---|
| 17 (a)  eat breakfast | 1. *The alarm clock rings.* |
| 22 (b)  go to class | 2. _I turn off the alarm clock._ |
| 12 (c)  put on my clothes | 3. |
| 16 (d)  drink a cup of coffee/tea | 4. |
| 10 (e)  shave | 5. |
| 14 (f)  put on my make-up | 6. |
| 11 (g)  take a shower/bath | 7. |
| 4 (h)  get up | 8. |
| 19 (i)  pick up my books | 9. |
| 5 (j)  walk to the bathroom | 10. |
| 18 (k)  watch TV | 11. |
| 6 (l)  look in the mirror | 12. |
| ✔ 2 (m)  turn off the alarm clock | 13. |
| 15 (n)  go to the kitchen/the cafeteria | 14. |
| 13 (o)  brush/comb my hair | 15. |
| 21 (p)  say good-bye to my roommate/ wife/husband | 16. |
| 8 (q)  brush my teeth | 17. |
| 9 (r)  do exercises | 18. |
| 7 (s)  wash my face | 19. |
| 3 (t)  stretch, yawn, and rub my eyes | 20. |
| 20 (u)  *other habits* | 21. |
| | 22. |

## 2-2 USING FREQUENCY ADVERBS: *ALWAYS, USUALLY, OFTEN, SOMETIMES, SELDOM, RARELY, NEVER*

| *always* | *usually* | *often* | *sometimes* | *seldom* | *rarely* | *never* |
|----------|-----------|---------|-------------|----------|----------|---------|
| 100% | 99%–90% | 90%–75% | 75%–25% | 25%–10% | 10%–1% | 0% |

| | | FREQUENCY | | SIMPLE | *Always, usually, often, sometimes, seldom, rarely* and *never* are called "frequency adverbs." They come between the subject and the simple present verb.* |
|---|---|---|---|---|---|
| | SUBJECT + | ADVERB | + | PRESENT VERB | |
| (a) | **Bob** | *always* | | *comes* to class. | |
| (b) | **Mary** | *usually* | | *comes* to class. | |
| (c) | **We** | *often* | | *watch* TV at night. | SUBJECT + { *always* *usually* *often* *sometimes* *seldom* *rarely* *never* } + VERB |
| (d) | **I** | *sometimes* | | *drink* tea with dinner. | |
| (e) | **They** | *seldom* | | *go* to the movies. | |
| (f) | **Anna** | *rarely* | | *makes* a mistake. | |
| (g) | **I** | *never* | | *eat* paper. | |

*Some frequency adverbs can also come at the beginning or at the end of a sentence. For example:
   **Sometimes** *I get up at seven.*   *I* **sometimes** *get up at seven.*   *I get up at seven* **sometimes.**
Also: See Chart 2-3 for the use of frequency adverbs with **be**.

| | Sun. | Mon. | Tues. | Wed. | Thurs. | Fri. | Sat. |
|---|---|---|---|---|---|---|---|
| Ann **always** drinks tea with lunch. | ☕ | ☕ | ☕ | ☕ | ☕ | ☕ | ☕ |
| Bob **usually** drinks tea with lunch. | | ☕ | ☕ | ☕ | ☕ | ☕ | ☕ |
| Maria **often** drinks tea with lunch. | | | ☕ | ☕ | ☕ | ☕ | ☕ |
| Gary **sometimes** drinks tea with lunch. | | | | | ☕ | ☕ | ☕ |
| Ali **seldom** drinks tea with lunch. | | | | | | ☕ | ☕ |
| Georgia **rarely** drinks tea with lunch. | | | | | | | ☕ |
| Joy never **drinks** tea with lunch. | | | | | | | |

■ **EXERCISE 2—ORAL:**   Find the SUBJECTS and VERBS in the sentences. Then add the FREQUENCY ADVERBS in italics to the sentences.

1. *always*      I eat breakfast.   → *I always eat breakfast.*
2. *usually*     I get up at 7:00.
3. *often*       I drink two cups of coffee in the morning.
4. *never*       I eat carrots for breakfast.
5. *seldom*      I watch TV in the morning.
6. *sometimes*   I have tea with dinner.
7. *usually*     Bob eats lunch at the cafeteria.
8. *rarely*      Ann drinks tea.

9. *always*      I do my homework.
10. *often*      We listen to music after dinner.
11. *never*      John and Sue watch TV in the afternoon.
12. *always*     The students speak English in the classroom.

■ **EXERCISE 3—ORAL:**  Use *always*, *usually*, *often*, *sometimes*, *seldom*, *rarely*, and
   *never* to talk about your activities (your habits) after 5:00 P.M. every day.

1. eat dinner
2. eat dinner at six o'clock
3. eat dinner at eight o'clock
4. watch TV
5. listen to music
6. go to a movie
7. go shopping
8. go dancing
9. go swimming
10. spend time with my friends
11. talk on the phone
12. speak English
13. write a letter
14. read a newspaper
15. study
16. study English grammar
17. drink milk
18. play with my children
19. kiss my husband/wife
20. have a snack
21. go to bed
22. go to bed at eleven o'clock
23. go to bed after midnight
24. go to bed early
25. go to bed late
26. turn off the lights
27. dream
28. dream in English

## 2-3  USING FREQUENCY ADVERBS WITH *BE*

| | |
|---|---|
| SUBJECT + *BE* + FREQUENCY ADVERB | |
| Tom + *is* + { *always* *usually* *often* *sometimes* *seldom* *rarely* *never* } + late for class. | Frequency adverbs follow *be*. |
| SUBJECT + FREQUENCY ADVERB + OTHER SIMPLE PRESENT VERBS | |
| Tom + { *always* *usually* *often* *sometimes* *seldom* *rarely* *never* } + *comes* late. | Frequency adverbs come before all simple present verbs except *be*. |

■ **EXERCISE 4:** Add the FREQUENCY ADVERB in *italics* to the sentence.

1. *always*      *always* Ann is, on time for class.

2. *always*      *always* Ann, comes to class on time.

3. *often*      Sue is, late for class.

4. *often*      Sue, comes to class late.

5. *never*      Ron is, happy.

6. *never*      Ron, smiles.

7. *usually*      Bob is, at home in the evening.

8. *usually*      Bob, stays at home in the evening.

9. *seldom*      Tom, studies at the library in the evening.

10. *seldom*      Tom is, at the library in the evening.

11. *rarely*      I, eat breakfast.

12. *often*      I, take the bus to school.

13. *usually*      The weather is, hot in July.

14. *never*      Sue, drinks coffee.

15. *sometimes*      She, drinks tea.

■ **EXERCISE 5—WRITTEN:** Describe a typical day in your life, from the time you get up in the morning until you go to bed. Use the following words to show the order of your activities: ***then, next, at . . . o'clock, after that, later.***

*Example:*      I usually get up at seven-thirty. I shave, brush my teeth, and take a shower. Then I put on my clothes and go to the student cafeteria for breakfast. After that I go back to my room. I sometimes watch the news on TV. At 8:15 I leave the dormitory. I go to class. My class begins at 8:30. I'm in class from 8:30 to 11:30. After that I eat lunch. I usually have a sandwich and a cup of tea for lunch. *(Continue until you complete your day.)*

## 2-4 PRONUNCIATION OF FINAL -S: /Z/ AND /S/

| | VOICED | | | VOICELESS | | |
|---|---|---|---|---|---|---|
| (a) | /b/ | rub | (b) | /p/ | sleep | Some sounds are "voiced." You use your voice box to make voiced sounds. For example, the sound /b/ comes from your voice box. The final sounds in (a) are voiced. |
| | /d/ | ride | | /t/ | write | |
| | /v/ | drive | | /f/ | laugh | |
| | | | | | | Some sounds are "voiceless." You don't use your voice box. You push air through your teeth and lips. For example, the sound /p/ comes from air through your lips. The final sounds in (b) are voiceless. |
| (c) | rubs = *rub*/z/ | | (d) | sleeps = *sleep*/s/ | | Final **-s** is pronounced /z/ after voiced sounds, as in (c). |
| | rides = *ride*/z/ | | | writes = *write*/s/ | | Final **-s** is pronounced /s/ after voiceless sounds, as in (d). |
| | drives = *drive*/z/ | | | laughs = *laugh*/s/ | | |

I can feel my voice box. It vibrates.

■ **EXERCISE 6:** The final sounds of the VERBS in these sentences are "voiced." Final **-s** is pronounced /z/. Read the sentences aloud.

1. Cindy  rides  the bus to school.
   ride/z/
2. Jack usually  drives  his car to school.
   drive/z/
3. Rain  falls.
   fall/z/  c?er
4. Sally often  dreams  about her boyfriend.
   dream/z/  soñdr
5. Sometimes Jim  runs  to class.
   run/z/
6. Tina  wears  blue jeans every day.
   wear/z/
7. Ann always  sees  Mr. Lee at the market.
   see/z/

Find the VERB in each sentence.  Pronounce it.  Then read the sentence aloud.

8. The teacher often stands in the front of the room.
/z/ parar

9. George lives in the dormitory.
/z/

10. Jean rarely smiles.
/z/

11. Sam always comes to class on time.
/z/

12. It rains a lot in Seattle.
/z/ llover

13. Jack always remembers his wife's birthday.
/z/

14. It snows in New York City in the winter.
/z/

■ **EXERCISE 7:**   The final sounds of the VERBS in these sentences are "voiceless."  Final *-s* is pronounced /s/.  Read the sentences aloud.

1. Mike  sleeps  for eight hours every night.
sleep/s/

2. Our teacher always  helps  us.
help/s/

3. Jack  writes  a letter to his girlfriend every day.
write/s/

4. Sara never  laughs.
laugh/s/

5. Sue usually  drinks  a cup of coffee in the morning.
drink/s/

6. Kate  walks  to school every day.
walk/s/  caminar

Find the VERB in each sentence.  Pronounce it.  Then read the sentence aloud.

7. My child often claps her hands.
aplaudir

8. Olga always bites her pencil in class.

9. Maria usually gets up at seven-thirty.
levantar

10. Yoko asks a lot of questions in class.

11. Ahmed always talks in class.

12. Sue coughs because she smokes.
toser

cough cough

## 2-5 SPELLING AND PRONUNCIATION OF FINAL -ES

|  |  | SPELLING | PRONUNCIATION |  |
|---|---|---|---|---|
| -sh | (a) push → | pushes | push/əz/ | Ending of verb: -sh, -ch, -ss, -x. |
| -ch | (b) teach → | teaches | teach/əz/ | Spelling: add -es. |
| -ss | (c) kiss → | kisses | kiss/əz/ | Pronounciation: /əz/. |
| -x | (d) fix → | fixes | fix/əz/ |  |

■ **EXERCISE 8:** Use the VERBS in *italics* to complete the sentences.

1. *brush*     Anita _____ *brushes* _____ her hair every morning.

2. *teach*     Alex _____ English.

3. *fix*     A mechanic _____ cars.

4. *drink*     Sonya _____ tea every afternoon.

5. *watch*     Joon–Kee often _____ television at night.

6. *kiss*     Peter always _____ his children goodnight.

7. *wear*     Tina usually _____ jeans to class.

8. *wash*     Eric seldom _____ dishes.

9. *walk*     Jessica _____ her dog twice each day.

10. *stretch,*     When Don gets up in the morning, he _____
    *yawn*
             and _____.

## 2-6 ADDING FINAL -S/-ES TO WORDS THAT END IN -Y

| (a) cry → cries<br>try → tries | End of verb: consonant + -y.<br>Spelling: change y to i, add -es. |
|---|---|
| (b) pay → pays<br>enjoy → enjoys | End of verb: vowel + -y.<br>Spelling: add -s. |

■ **EXERCISE 9:** Use the words in *italics* to complete the sentences.

1. *pay, always*    Boris _____*always pays*_____ his bills on time.

2. *cry, seldom*    Our baby _____ at night.

3. *study*    Paul _____ at the library every day.

4. *stay, usually*    Jean _____ home at night.

5. *fly*    Kunio is a pilot.  He _____ a plane.

6. *carry, always*    Carol _____ her books to class.

7. *pray*    Jack _____ every day.

8. *buy, seldom*    Ann _____ new clothes.

9. *worry*    Tina is a good student, but she _____ about her grades.

10. *enjoy*    Don _____ good food.

## 2-7    IRREGULAR SINGULAR VERBS:  *HAS, DOES, GOES*

| | | |
|---|---|---|
| ( a )  I *have* a book.<br>( b )  He *has* a book. | she<br>he } + *has* /hæz/<br>it | **Have, do,** and *go* have irregular forms for third person singular:<br><br>*have*  →  *has*<br>*do*  →  *does*<br>*go*  →  *goes* |
| ( c )  I *do* my work.<br>( d )  She *does* her work. | she<br>he } + *does* /dəz/<br>it | |
| ( e )  They *go* to school.<br>( f )  She *goes* to school. | she<br>he } + *goes* /gowz/<br>it | |

■ **EXERCISE 10:** Use the given VERBS to complete the sentences.

1. *do*      Pierre always _____*does*_____ his homework.

2. *do*      We always _____*do*_____ our homework.

3. *have*    Yoko and Kunio _____ their books.

4. *have*    Ali _____ a car.

5. *go*      Bill _____ to school every day.

6. *go*      My friends often _____ to the beach.

7. *do*      Anna seldom _____ her homework.

8. *do*      We _____ exercises in class every day.

9. *go, go*  Roberto _____ downtown every weekend.  He  and his wife

            _____ shopping.

10. *have*   Jessica _____ a snack every night around ten.

## 2-8 SUMMARY: SPELLING AND PRONUNCIATION OF -S AND -ES

| | SPELLING | PRONUNCIATION | |
|---|---|---|---|
| (a) | rub → rubs<br>ride → rides<br>smile → smiles<br>dream → dreams<br>run → runs<br>wear → wears<br>drive → drives<br>see → sees<br>snow → snows | rub/z/<br>ride/z/<br>smile/z/<br>dream/z/<br>run/z/<br>wear/z/<br>drive/z/<br>see/z/<br>snow/z/ | To form a simple present verb in 3rd person singular, you usually add only **-s**, as in (a) and (b).<br><br>In (a): **-s** is pronounced /z/. The final sounds in (a) are *voiced*. |
| (b) | drink → drinks<br>sleep → sleeps<br>write → writes<br>laugh → laughs | drink/s/<br>sleep/s/<br>write/s/<br>laugh/s/ | In (b): **-s** is pronounced /s/. The final sounds in (b) are *voiceless*. |
| (c) | push → pushes<br>teach → teaches<br>kiss → kisses<br>fix → fixes | push/əz/<br>teach/əz/<br>kiss/əz/<br>fix/əz/ | End of verb: **-sh, -ch, -ss, -x**<br>  Spelling: add **-es**<br>Pronunciation: /əz/ |
| (d) | cry → cries<br>study → studies | cry/z/<br>study/z/ | End of verb: consonant + **-y**<br>  Spelling: change **y** to **i**, add **-es** |
| (e) | pay → pays<br>buy → buys | pay/z/<br>buy/z/ | End of verb: vowel + **-y**<br>  Spelling: add **-s** |
| (f) | have → **has**<br>go → **goes**<br>do → **does** | /hæz/<br>/gowz/<br>/dəz/ | The 3rd person singular forms of *have*, *go*, and *do* are irregular. |

■ **EXERCISE 11—ORAL (BOOKS CLOSED):**  Talk about everyday activities using the given VERB.

*Example:*

| | |
|---|---|
| TEACHER: | eat |
| STUDENT A: | I eat breakfast every morning. |
| TEACHER: | What does ( . . . ) do every morning? |
| STUDENT B: | He/She eats breakfast. |

| | |
|---|---|
| TEACHER: | eat |
| STUDENT A: | I always eat dinner at the student cafeteria. |
| TEACHER: | What does ( . . . ) always do? |
| STUDENT B: | He/She always eats dinner at the student cafeteria. |

| | | |
|---|---|---|
| 1. eat | 6. study | 11. listen to |
| 2. go | 7. get up | 12. wash |
| 3. drink | 8. watch | 13. put on |
| 4. brush | 9. speak | 14. carry |
| 5. have | 10. do | 15. kiss |

■ **EXERCISE 12—ORAL (BOOKS CLOSED):** Tell a classmate about your usual habits in the morning. (Look at the list you made for Exercise 1 if you wish.) Your classmate will then write a summary of your daily morning habits.

Directions:

STUDENT A: *Tell Student B ten to fifteen things you do every morning.*

STUDENT B: *Take notes while Student A is talking. (You will use these notes later to write a paragraph about Student A's usual morning habits.)*

Then switch roles.

STUDENT B: *Tell Student A ten to fifteen things you do every morning.*

STUDENT A: *Take notes while Student B is talking.*

When you finish talking, each of you should write a paragraph about the other person's daily morning activities. Pay special attention to final **-s/-es.**

■ **EXERCISE 13:** Complete the sentences. Use the words in parentheses. Use the SIMPLE PRESENT TENSE. Pay special attention to singular and plural, to spelling, and to pronunciation of final **-s/-es**.

1. The students *(ask, often)* _____*often ask*_____ questions in class.

2. Pablo *(study, usually)* _____ at the library every evening.

3. Olga *(bite)* _____ her fingernails when she is nervous.

4. Don *(cash)* _____ a check at the bank once a week.

5. Sometimes I *(worry)* _____ about my grades at school.

   Sonya *(worry, never)* _____ about her grades.

   She *(study)* _____ hard.

6. Ms. Jones and Mr. Anderson *(teach)* _____ at the local high school. Ms. Jones *(teach)* _____ math.

7. Birds *(fly)* _____. They *(have)* _____ wings.

8. A bird *(fly)* _____. It *(have)* _____ wings.

9. Jason *(do, always)* _____ his homework. He

   *(go, never)* _____ to bed until his homework is finished.

10. Mr. Cook *(say, always)*\* _____ hello to his neighbor in the morning.

11. Ms. Chu *(pay, always)*\* _____ attention in class. She *(answer)* _____ questions. She *(listen)* _____ to the teacher. She *(ask)* _____ questions.

12. Sam *(enjoy)* _____ cooking. He *(try, often)* _____ to make new recipes. He *(like)* _____ to have company for dinner. He *(invite)* _____ me to dinner once a month. When I arrive, I *(go)* _____ to the kitchen and *(watch)* _____ him cook. He *(have, usually)* _____ three or four pots on the stove. He *(watch)* _____ the pots carefully. He *(make)* _____ a big mess in the kitchen when he cooks. After dinner, he *(wash, always)* _____ all the dishes and *(clean)* _____ the kitchen. I *(cook, never)* _____. It *(be)* _____ too much trouble. But my friend Sam *(love)* _____ to cook.

*Pronunciation of **says** = /sɛz/. Pronunciation of **pays** = /peyz/.

## 2-9 THE SIMPLE PRESENT: NEGATIVE

| | | | |
|---|---|---|---|
| (a) | **I** | **do not** | drink coffee. |
| | **We** | **do not** | drink coffee. |
| | **You** | **do not** | drink coffee. |
| | **They** | **do not** | drink coffee. |
| (b) | **She** | **does not** | drink coffee. |
| | **He** | **does not** | drink coffee. |
| | **It** | **does not** | drink coffee. |

NEGATIVE:  *I*, *we*, *you*, *they* } + **do not** + main verb

*she*, *he*, *it* } + **does not** + main verb

**Do** and **does** are called "helping verbs."

Notice in (b):  In 3rd person singular, there is no **-s** on the main verb; the final **-s** is part of **does**.
INCORRECT:  *She does not drink**s** coffee.*

| | |
|---|---|
| (c) | I **don't** drink tea. |
| | They **don't** have a car. |
| (d) | He **doesn't** drink tea. |
| | Mary **doesn't** have a car. |

CONTRACTIONS:  **do not = don't**
**does not = doesn't**
People usually use contractions when they speak.
People often use contractions when they write.

■ **EXERCISE 14:**  Use the words in *italics* to make NEGATIVE SENTENCES.

1. *like, not*   Ingrid _____ *doesn't like* _____ tea.

2. *like, not*   I _____ *don't like* _____ tea.

3. *know, not*   Mary and Jim are strangers.  Mary _____ Jim.

4. *need, not*   It's a nice day today.  You _____ your umbrella.

5. *snow, not*   It _____ in Bangkok in the winter.

6. *speak, not*   I _____ French.

7. *be, not*   I _____ hungry.

8. *live, not*   Butterflies _____ long.

9. *have, not*   A butterfly _____ a long life.

10. *be, not*   A butterfly _____ large.

11. *be, not*   Butterflies _____ large.

12. *have, not*   We _____ class every day.

13. *have, not*   This city _____ nice weather in the summer.

14. *be, not*   It _____ cold today.

15. *rain, not*   It _____ every day.

■ **EXERCISE 15:**   Complete the sentences.  Use the words in parentheses.  Use the SIMPLE PRESENT TENSE.

1. Alex *(like)* _____*likes*_____ tea, but he *(like, not)* _____*doesn't like*_____ coffee.

2. Sara *(know)* _____ Ali, but she *(know, not)* _____

   _____ Hiroshi.

3. Pablo and Maria *(want)* _____ to stay home tonight.  They *(want, not)*

   _____ to go to a movie.

4. Robert *(be, not)* _____ hungry.  He *(want, not)* _____

   _____ a sandwich.

5. Mr. Smith *(drink, not)* _____ coffee, but Mr. Jones

   *(drink)* _____ twelve cups every day.

6. I *(be, not)* _____ rich.  I *(have, not)* _____
   a lot of money.

7. This pen *(belong, not)* _____ to me.  It *(belong)*

   _____ to Pierre.

8. My friends *(live, not)* _____ in the dorm.  They *(have)*

   _____ an apartment.

9. It *(be)* _____ a nice day today.  It *(be, not)* _____ cold.  You

   *(need, not)* _____ your coat.

10. Today *(be)* _____ a holiday.  We *(have, not)* _____
    class today.

■ **EXERCISE 16:** Use verbs from the list to complete the sentences. Make all of the sentences NEGATIVE by using *does* + *not* or *do* + *not*.

> | | | |
> |---|---|---|
> | *carry* - carga, | *go* ir | *smoke* = fumar |
> | *do* - hacer | *shave* -resurar | *speak* - habla |
> | *drink* tomar | *make* - hacer | |
> | *eat* comer | *put on* - poner | |

1. Bob _____ *doesn't go* _____ to school every day.

2. My roommates are from Japan. They _____ Spanish.

3. Fred has a beard. He _____ in the morning.

4. Sue has a briefcase. She _____ a bookbag to class.

5. We _____ to class on Sunday.

6. Sally takes care of her health. She _____ cigarettes.

7. Jane and Alex always have lunch at home. They _____ at the cafeteria.

8. Sometimes I _____ my homework in the evening. I watch TV instead.

9. Jack is a careful writer. He _____ mistakes in spelling when he writes.

10. My sister likes tea, but she _____ coffee.

11. I'm lazy. I _____ exercises in the morning.

12. Sometimes Ann _____ her shoes when she goes outside. She likes to walk barefoot in the grass.

■ **EXERCISE 17—ORAL (BOOKS CLOSED):** Use *not*.

TEACHER: eat breakfast every day
STUDENT A: I don't eat breakfast every day.
TEACHER: Tell me about (Student A).
STUDENT B: She/He doesn't eat breakfast every day.

1. walk to school every day
2. shave every day
3. read a newspaper every day
4. go shopping every day
5. study grammar every day
6. watch TV every day
7. write a letter every day
8. go dancing every day
9. drink coffee every day
10. eat lunch every day
11. listen to music every day
12. come to class every day

■ **EXERCISE 18—ORAL:** Use the given words to make truthful sentences.

1. Grass \ be blue. → *Grass isn't blue.*
2. Grass \ be green. → *Grass is green.*
3. Dogs \ have tails. → *Dogs have tails.*
4. People* \ have tails. → *People don't have tails.*
5. A restaurant \ sell shoes.
6. A restaurant \ serve food.
7. People \ wear clothes.
8. Animals \ wear clothes.
9. A child \ need love, food, care, and toys.
10. A child \ need a driver's license.
11. Refrigerators \ be hot inside.
12. Refrigerators \ be cold inside.
13. Electricity \ be visible.
14. Light \ be visible.
15. Fresh vegetables \ be good for you.
16. Junk food** \ be good for you.
17. Cats \ have whiskers.
18. Birds \ have whiskers.
19. An architect \ design buildings.
20. Doctors \ design buildings.
21. Doctors \ take care of sick people.
22. A bus \ carry people from one place to another.
23. The weather \ be very hot today.
24. It \ be very cold today.
25. Glass \ break.
26. Rubber \ be flexible.
27. Rubber \ break.
28. English \ be an easy language to learn.
29. People in this city \ be friendly.
30. It \ rain a lot in this city.
31. Apples \ have seeds.
32. Scientists \ have all the answers to the mysteries of the universe.

---

*\*People* is a plural noun. It takes a plural verb.
*\*\*Junk food* is food that has a lot of fat and/or sugar, but little nutritional value.

## 2-10 THE SIMPLE PRESENT: YES/NO QUESTIONS

| | | | | QUESTION FORMS, SIMPLE PRESENT |
|---|---|---|---|---|
| | *DO/DOES* + | SUBJECT + | MAIN VERB | **Do I** |
| | | | | **Do you** ⎫ |
| (a) **Do** | **you** | *like* | coffee? | **Do we** ⎬ + *main verb (simple form)* |
| | | | | **Do they** ⎭ |
| | | | | **Does she** ⎫ |
| (b) **Does** | **Bob** | *like* | coffee? | **Does he** ⎬ + *main verb (simple form)* |
| | | | | **Does it** ⎭ |

| | |
|---|---|
| | Notice in (b): The main verb in the question does not have a final **-s**. The final **-s** is part of **does**. INCORRECT: *Does Bob likes coffee?* |

| | | |
|---|---|---|
| (c) **Are you** a student? | | When the main verb is a form of **be, do** is NOT used. See Chart 1-9 for question forms with **be**. |
| (d) INCORRECT: *Do you be a student?* | | |

| QUESTION | SHORT ANSWER + (LONG ANSWER) | **Do, don't, does,** and **doesn't** are used in the short answers to yes/ no questions in the simple present. |
|---|---|---|
| (e) *Do* you *like* tea? | → Yes, I **do**. (I *like* tea.) No, I **don't**. (I *don't like* tea.) | |
| (f) *Does* Bob *like* tea? | → Yes, he **does**. (He *likes* tea.) No, he **doesn't**. (He *doesn't like* tea.) | |

■ **EXERCISE 19:** Make questions. Give short answers.

1. A: ___*Do you like tea?*___

   B: ___*Yes, I do.*___ (I like tea.)

2. A: ___*Do you like coffee?*___

   B: ___*No, I don't.*___ (I don't like coffee.)

3. A: _____

   B: _____ (I don't speak Japanese.)

4. A: _____

   B: _____ (Ann speaks French.)  *she*

5. A: _____

   B: _____ (Ann and Tom don't speak Arabic.)  *They*

6. A: _____

   B: _____ (I do exercises every morning.)

7. A: _____

   B: _____ (I don't have a Spanish-English dictionary.)

8. A: _____

   B: _____ (Sue has a cold.)

9. A: _____

   B: _____ (The teacher comes to class every day.)

10. A: _____

    B: _____ (Jim and Sue don't do their homework every day.)

11. A: _____

    B: _____ (It rains a lot in April.)

12. A: _____

    B: _____ (My parents live in Baghdad.)

■ **EXERCISE 20—ORAL (BOOKS CLOSED):** Ask and answer questions.

TEACHER:     walk to school every day
STUDENT A:   Do you walk to school every day?
STUDENT B:   Yes, I do.   OR:   No, I don't.
STUDENT A:   Does *(Student B)* walk to school every day?
STUDENT C:   Yes, he/she does.   OR:   No, he/she doesn't.

1. walk to school every day
2. watch TV every day
3. eat breakfast every day
4. speak English every day
5. come to class every day
6. get up at seven o'clock every day
7. talk on the phone every day
8. go to the bank every day
9. wear blue jeans every day
10. have a car
11. have a bicycle
12. like ice cream
13. like *(name of city)*
14. live in *(name of a hotel)*
15. live in an apartment
16. go shopping every day

■ **EXERCISE 21:** Make questions. Give short answers. Use the names of your classmates in the questions.

1. A:   *Does (Carlos) speak English?* _____

   B:   *Yes, he does.* _____ (He speaks English.)

2. A: _____Does (Yoko) speak Spanish?_____

   B: _____No, she doesn't.____ (She doesn't speak Spanish.)

3. A: _____Is (Ali) in class today?_____

   B: _____No, he isn't._____ (He isn't in class today.)

4. A: _____

   B: _____ (He comes to class every day.)

5. A: _____

   B: _____ (They're in class today.)

6. A: _____

   B: _____ (She sits in the same seat every day.)

7. A: _____

   B: _____ (He has a mustache.)

8. A: _____

   B: _____ (She doesn't have a bicycle.)

9. A: _____

   B: _____ (He's wearing blue jeans today.)

10. A: _____

    B: _____ (He wears blue jeans every day.)

11. A: _____

    B: _____ (They aren't from Indonesia.)

12: A: _____

    B: _____ (They don't have dictionaries on their desks.)

13. A: _____

    B: _____ (She's writing in her book right now.)

14. A: _____

    B: _____ (She studies hard.)

15. A: _____

    B: _____ (They speak English.)

## 2-11 THE SIMPLE PRESENT: ASKING INFORMATION QUESTIONS WITH *WHERE*

| (WHERE) + DO/DOES + SUBJECT + MAIN VERB | | | | | | SHORT ANSWER |
|---|---|---|---|---|---|---|
| (a) | | **Do** | they | **live** | in Tokyo? → | **Yes**, they do. / **No**, they don't. |
| (b) | **Where** | **do** | they | **live?** | → | **In Tokyo.** |
| (c) | | **Does** | Gina | **live** | in Rome? → | **Yes**, she does. / **No**, she doesn't. |
| (d) | **Where** | **does** | Gina | **live?** | → | **In Rome.** |

NOTE: (a) and (c) are called "yes/no questions." The answer to these questions can be *yes* or *no*. (b) and (d) are called "information questions." The answer gives information. *Where* asks for information about place.

Notice in the examples: The form of yes/no questions and information questions is the same:
DO/DOES + SUBJECT + MAIN VERB

■ **EXERCISE 22:** Make questions.

1. A: ___*Does Jean eat lunch at the cafeteria every day?*___
   B: Yes, she does. (Jean eats lunch at the cafeteria every day.)

2. A: ___*Where does Jean eat lunch every day?*___
   B: At the cafeteria. (Jean eats lunch at the cafeteria every day.)

3. A: _____
   B: At the post office. (Peter works at the post office.)

4. A: _____
   B: Yes, he does. (Peter works at the post office.)

5. A: _____
   B: Yes, I do. (I live in an apartment.)

6. A: _____
   B: In an apartment. (I live in an apartment.)

7. A: _____
   B: At a restaurant. (Bill eats dinner at a restaurant every day.)

8. A: _____
   B: In the front row. (I sit in the front row during class.)

9. A: _____
   B: At the University of Wisconsin. (Jessica goes to school at the University of Wisconsin.)

10. A: _____
    B: On my desk. (My book is on my desk.)

11. A: _____
    B: To class.  (I go to class every morning.)

12. A: _____
    B: In class.  (The students are in class right now.)

13. A: _____
    B: In Australia.  (Kangaroos live in Australia.)

■ **EXERCISE 23:—ORAL (BOOKS CLOSED):**  Ask a classmate a question.  Use ***where.***

*Example:*    live
STUDENT A:  Where do you live?
STUDENT B:  *(free response)*

1. live
2. eat lunch every day
3. sit during class
4. study at night
5. go to school
6. buy school supplies
7. buy your groceries
8. go on weekends

9. go after class
10. eat dinner
11. be *(name of a student in this room)*
12. be *(names of two students)*
13. be *(name of a country or city)*
14. be *(names of two countries or cities)*
15. be *(something a student owns)*
16. be *(some things a student owns)*

## 2-12 THE SIMPLE PRESENT: ASKING INFORMATION QUESTIONS WITH WHEN AND WHAT TIME

| Q-WORD* + | DOES/DO + | SUBJECT + | MAIN VERB | | | SHORT ANSWER |
|---|---|---|---|---|---|---|
| (a) **When** | do | you | go | to class? | → | **At nine o'clock.** |
| (b) **What time** | do | you | go | to class? | → | **At nine o'clock.** |
| (c) **When** | does | Anna | eat | dinner? | → | **At six P.M.** |
| (d) **What time** | does | Anna | eat | dinner? | → | **At six P.M.** |
| (e) What time *do you **usually** go to class?* | | | | The frequency adverb **usually** comes immediately after the subject in a question. QUESTION WORD + **DOES/DO** + SUBJECT + **USUALLY** + MAIN VERB | | |

*A "Q-word" is a "question word." *Where, when, what, what time, who,* and *why* are examples of question words.

■ **EXERCISE 24:** Make questions.

1. A: _____*When/What time do you eat breakfast?*_____
   B: At 7:30 (I eat breakfast at 7:30 in the morning.)

2. A: _____*When/What time do ~~os Alek~~ you usually eat breakfast?*_____
   B: At 7:00. (Alex usually eats breakfast at 7:00.)

3. A: _____
   B: At 6:45. (I get up at 6:45.)

4. A: _____
   B: At 6:30. (Maria usually gets up at 6:30.)

5. A: _____
   B: At 8:15. (The movie starts at 8:15.)

6. A: _____
   B: Around 11:00. (I usually go to bed around 11:00.)

7. A: _____
   B: At half-past twelve. (I usually eat lunch at half-past twelve.)

8. A: _____
   B: At 5:30. (The restaurant opens at 5:30.)

9. A: _____
   B: At 9:05. (The train leaves at 9:05.)

10. A: _____
    B: Between 6:30 and 8:00. (I usually eat dinner between 6:30 and 8:00.)

11. A: _____

    B: At 10:00 P.M.  (The library closes at 10:00 P.M. on Saturday.)

12. A: _____

    B: At a quarter past eight.  (My classes begin at a quarter past eight.)

■ **EXERCISE 25—ORAL (BOOKS CLOSED):**  Ask a classmate a question.  Use **when** or **what time.**

*Example:*      eat breakfast
STUDENT A:  When/What time do you eat breakfast?
STUDENT B:  *(free response)*

1. get up
2. usually get up
3. eat breakfast
4. leave home in the morning
5. usually get to class
6. eat lunch
7. go back home
8. get home
9. have dinner
10. usually study in the evening
11. go to bed

---

## 2-13  SUMMARY: INFORMATION QUESTIONS WITH *BE* AND *DO*

| Q-WORD | + | *BE* | + | SUBJECT | | LONG ANSWER |
|---|---|---|---|---|---|---|
| (a) Where | | *is* | | Thailand? | → | Thailand *is* in Southeast Asia. |
| (b) Where | | *are* | | your books? | → | My books *are* on my desk. |
| (c) When | | *is* | | the concert? | → | The concert *is* on April 3rd. |
| (d) What | | *is* | | your name? | → | My name *is* Yoko. |
| (e) What time | | *is* | | it? | → | It *is* ten-thirty. |

| Q-WORD | + | *DO* | + | SUBJECT | + | MAIN VERB | LONG ANSWER |
|---|---|---|---|---|---|---|---|
| (f) Where | | *do* | | you | | *live?* → | I *live* in Los Angeles. |
| (g) What time | | *does* | | the plane | | *arrive?* → | The plane *arrives* at six-fifteen. |
| (h) What | | *do* | | monkeys | | *eat?* → | Monkeys *eat* fruit, plants, and insects. |
| (k) When | | *does* | | Bob | | *study?* → | Bob *studies* in the evenings. |

NOTICE:  In questions with *be* as the main and only verb, the subject follows *be*.  In simple present questions with verbs other than *be*, the subject comes between *do/does* and the main verb.

■ **EXERCISE 26:** Complete the questions in the dialogues by using *is, are, does,* or *do.*

DIALOGUE ONE

(1) A: What time _____ the movie start?

(2) B: Seven-fifteen. _____ you want to go with us?

(3) A: Yes. What time _____ it now?

(4) B: Almost seven o'clock. _____ you ready to leave?
    A: Yes, let's go.

DIALOGUE TWO

(5) A: Where _____ my keys to the car?

(6) B: I don't know. Where _____ you usually keep them?
    A: In my purse. But they're not there.
    B: Are you sure?

(7) A: Yes. _____ you see them?

(8) B: No. _____ they in one of your pockets?
    A: I don't think so.

(9) B: _____ your husband have them?
    A: No. He has his own set of car keys.
    B: Well, I hope you find them.
    A: Thanks.

DIALOGUE THREE

(10) A: _____ you go to school?
     B: Yes.

(11) A: _____ your brother go to school too?
     B: No. He quit school last semester. He has a job now.

(12)  A:  _____ it a good job?

      B:  Not really.

(13)  A:  Where _____ he work?

      B:  At a restaurant.  He washes dishes.

(14)  A:  _____ he live with you?

      B:  No, he lives with my parents.

(15)  A:  _____ your parents unhappy that he quit school?

      B:  They're very unhappy about it.

(16)  A:  _____ they want him to return to school?

      B:  Of course.  They don't want him to be a dishwasher for the rest of his life.  They have many dreams for him and his future.


■ **EXERCISE 27:**  Complete the dialogues with appropriate questions.

1.  A:  ___*What time does the concert begin?*___
    B:  At eight.  (The concert begins at eight.)

2.  A:  ___*Is San Francisco foggy in the winter?*___
    B:  Yes, it is.  (San Francisco is foggy in the winter.)

3.  A:  *Does the weather start to get hot?*
    B:  In May.  (The weather starts to get hot in May.)

4.  A:  *Do you dream in color?*
    B:  Yes.  (I dream in color.)

5.  A:  *Does Igor come from Russia?*
    B:  Yes.  (Igor comes from Russia.)

6.  A:  *Where does Olga come from?*
    B:  Russia.  (Olga comes from Russia.)

7.  A:  *Is Ivan from Russia?*
    B:  Yes, he is.  (Ivan is from Russia.)

8.  A:  *Is Red Square in /*
    B:  In Moscow.  (Red Square is in Moscow.)

9.  A:  *Do birds sleep?*
    B:  Yes.  (Birds sleep.)

    A:  *Where do they sleep?*
    B:  In trees and bushes or in their nests.  (They sleep in trees and bushes or in their nests.)

Blue whale

10. A: _____
    B: The blue whale. (The biggest animal on earth is the blue whale.)

11. A: _____
    B: No, they aren't. (Whales aren't fish.)

    A: _____
    B: Yes, they are. (They are mammals.)

    A: _____
    B: Yes, they do. (They breathe air.)

12. A: _____
    B: No, it isn't. (A seahorse isn't a mammal.)

13. A: _____
    B: A very small fish that looks a little like a horse.
       (A seahorse is a very small fish that looks
       a little like a horse.)

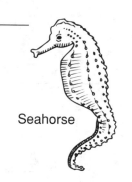

Seahorse

14. A: _____
    B: Yes. (A starfish has a mouth.)

    A: _____
    B: In the middle of its underside. (It is in the middle of its underside.)

    A: _____
    B: Clams, oysters, and shrimp. (A starfish eats clams, oysters, and shrimp.)

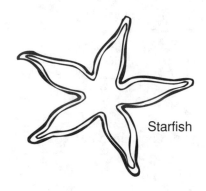

Starfish

■ **EXERCISE 28:** Complete the dialogues with your own words.

1. A: Do _____?
   B: No, I don't.

2. A: Where are _____?
   B: I don't know.

3. A: What time does _____?

   B: _____

4. A: When do _____?

   B: _____

5. A: Is _____?

   B: _____

6. A: What is _____?

   B: _____

7. A: Are _____?

   B: _____

8. A: What are _____?

   B: _____

9. A: What do _____?

   B: _____

10. A: What does _____?

    B: _____

■ **EXERCISE 29—ORAL/WRITTEN:** Interview someone (a friend, a roommate, a classmate, etc.) about her/his daily schedule. Use the information from the interview to write a composition.

*Some questions you might want to ask during the interview:*

What do you do every morning?
What do you do every afternoon?
What do you do every evening?

What time do you . . . ?
When do you . . . ?
Where do you . . . ?

## 2-14 USING *IT* TO TALK ABOUT TIME

| QUESTION | ANSWER | |
|---|---|---|
| (a) What day is it? | *It's* Monday. | In English, people use *it* to express (to talk about) time. |
| (b) What month is it? | *It's* September. | |
| (c) What year is it? | *It's* _____. | Look at Appendixes 2 and 3 in the back of the book for lists of days, months, and numbers. |
| (d) What's the date today? <br> *what date is it ?* | *It's* September 15th. <br> *It's* the 15th of September. | |
| (e) What time is it? | *It's* 9:00.* <br> *It's* nine. <br> *It's* nine o'clock. <br> *It's* nine (o'clock) A.M. | Look at Appendix 4 in the back of the book for ways of saying the time. |

*American English uses a colon (two dots) between the hour and the minutes: 9:00 A.M. British English uses one dot: 9.00 A.M.

■ **EXERCISE 30:** Make questions. Use *what* in your questions.

1. A: _____*What day is it?*_____
   B: It's Tuesday.

2. A: _____
   B: It's March 14th.

3. A: _____
   B: Ten-thirty.

4. A: _____
   B: March.

5. A: _____
   B: It's six-fifteen.

6. A: _____
   B: The 1st of April.

7. A: _____
   B: Wednesday.

8. A: _____
   B: July 3rd.

9. A: _____
   B: It's 6:05.

10. A: _____
    B: It's 10:55.

## 2-15 PREPOSITIONS OF TIME

| at | (a) We have class **at** one o'clock. <br> (b) I have an appointment with the doctor **at** 3:00. <br> (c) We sleep **at** night. | **at** + a specific time on the clock <br><br> **at** + *night* |
|---|---|---|
| in | (d) My birthday is **in** October. <br> (e) I was born **in** 1960. <br> (f) We have class **in** the morning. <br> (g) Bob has class **in** the afternoon. <br> (h) I study **in** the evening. | **in** + specific month <br> **in** + specific year <br> **in** + *the morning* <br> **in** + *the afternoon* <br> **in** + *the evening* |
| on | (i) I have class **on** Monday. <br> (j) I was born **on** October 31, 1975. | **on** + a specific day of the week <br> **on** + a specific date |
| from ... to | (k) We have class **from** 1:00 **to** 2:00. | **from** (a specific time) **to** (a specific time) |

■ **EXERCISE 31:** Complete the sentences with PREPOSITIONS OF TIME.

1. We have class _____*at*_____ ten o'clock.

2. We have class _____ ten _____ eleven.

3. I have class _____ the morning.

4. I work _____ the afternoon.

5. I study _____ the evening.

6. I sleep _____ night.

7. I was born _____ May.

8. I was born _____ 1979.

9. I was born _____ May 25.

10. I was born _____ May 25, 1979.

11. The post office isn't open _____ Sunday.

12. The post office is open _____ 8:00 A.M. _____ 5:00 P.M. Monday.

13. The post office closes _____ 5:00 P.M.

■ **EXERCISE 32:** Complete the sentences with PREPOSITIONS OF TIME.

1. Jane has an appointment with the dentist _____ ten-thirty.

2. We go to class _____ the morning.

3. The bank is open _____ Friday, but it isn't open _____ Saturday.

4. My birthday is _____ February.

5. I was born _____ February 14, 1973.

6. I watch television _____ the evening.

7. I go to bed _____ night.

8. The bank is open _____ 9:00 A.M. _____ 4:00 P.M.

9. I was in high school _____ 1988.

10. Our classes begin _____ January 10.

11. I study at the library _____ the afternoon.

12. We have a vacation _____ August.

## 2-16 USING *IT* TO TALK ABOUT THE WEATHER

| | |
|---|---|
| (a) *It's* sunny today.<br>(b) *It's* hot and humid today.<br>(c) *It's* a nice day today. | In English, people usually use *it* when they talk about the weather. |
| (d) *What's the weather like* in Istanbul in January?<br>(e) *How's the weather* in Moscow in the summer? | People commonly ask about the weather by saying: *What's the weather like?* OR: *How's the weather?* |

■ **EXERCISE 33—ORAL:** How's the weather today? Use these words to talk about today's weather.

*Example:* hot
*Response:* It's hot today.   OR:   It isn't / It's not hot today.

| | | |
|---|---|---|
| 1. hot | 7. cloudy | 13. gloomy |
| 2. warm | 8. partly cloudy | 14. humid |
| 3. cool | 9. clear | 15. muggy |
| 4. chilly – fresco | 10. nice | 16. stormy |
| 5. cold | 11. windy | 17. freezing |
| 6. sunny | 12. foggy | 18. below freezing |

■ **EXERCISE 34—ORAL:** Change the Fahrenheit temperatures to Celsius by choosing temperatures from the list. Then describe the temperature in words.

| | |
|---|---|
| 38° C | 0° C |
| 24° C | -18°C |
| ✔10° C | |

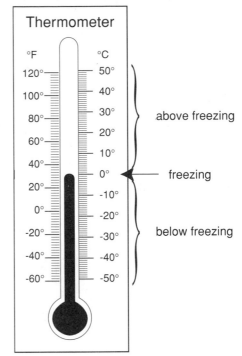

Thermometer

above freezing

freezing

below freezing

| FARENHEIT | CELSIUS | DESCRIPTION |
|---|---|---|
| 1. 50°F | _10°C_ | _cool, chilly_ |
| 2. 32°F | _____ | _____ |
| 3. 100°F | _____ | _____ |
| 4. 75°F | _____ | _____ |
| 5. 0°F | _____ | _____ |

■ **EXERCISE 35:** "Approximate" means "close but not exact." Here is a fast way to get an **approximate** number when you convert from one temperature system to another.*

> • To change **Celsius to Fahrenheit**: DOUBLE THE CELSIUS NUMBER AND ADD 30.
>
>     *Examples:* 12°C x 2 = 24 + 30 = 54°F. (Exact numbers: 12°C = 53.6°F.)
>                   20°C x 2 = 40 + 30 = 70°F. (Exact numbers: 20°C = 68°F.)
>                   35°C x 2 = 70 + 30 = 100°F. (Exact numbers: 35°C = 95°F.)
>
> • To change **Fahrenheit to Celsius**: SUBTRACT 30 FROM THE FAHRENHEIT NUMBER AND THEN DIVIDE BY 2.
>
>     *Examples:* 60°F - 30 = 30 ÷ 2 = 15°C. (Exact numbers: 60°F = 15.6°C.)
>                   80°F - 30 = 50 ÷ 2 = 25°C. (Exact numbers: 80°F = 26.7°C.)
>                   90°F - 30 = 60 ÷ 2 = 30°C. (Exact numbers: 90°F = 32.2°C.)

Change the following from Celsius to Fahrenheit and Fahrenheit to Celsius. Calculate the **approximate** numbers.

1. 22°C → *22°C = approximately 74°F (22°C x 2 = 44 + 30 = 74°F )*
2. 2°C                                      6. 45°F
3. 30°C                                   7. 70°F
4. 10°C                                   8. 58°F
5. 16°C                                   9. 100°F

*To get exact numbers, use these formulas: $C = 5/9 (°F -32)$ OR $F = 9/5 (°C) + 32$.

■ **EXERCISE 36—REVIEW:** Add *-s* or *-es* where necessary. Discuss the correct pronunciation: /s/, /z/, or /əz/.

### ABDUL AND PABLO

*S (lives = live + /z/)*

(1) My friend Abdul live▲ in an apartment near school. (2) He walk to school almost every day. (3) Sometimes he catch a bus, especially if it's cold and rainy outside. (4) Abdul share the apartment with Pablo. (5) Pablo come from Venezuela. (6) Abdul and Pablo go to the same school. (7) They take English classes. (8) Abdul speak Arabic as his first language, and Pablo speak Spanish. (9) They communicate in English. (10) Sometimes Abdul try to teach Pablo to speak a little Arabic, and Pablo give Abdul Spanish lessons. (11) They laugh a lot during the Arabic and Spanish lessons. (12) Abdul enjoy having Pablo as his roommate, but he miss his family back in Saudi Arabia.

### SNAKES

(13) Snakes eat all sorts of things. (14) Eggs are a favorite food of many snakes. (15) When a snake eat an egg, the snake first curl around the egg. (16) It don't want the egg to roll away. (17) Then the snake open its mouth and move the egg into its throat. (18) It squeeze the egg with muscles in its neck. (19) The egg break and go into the snake's stomach. (20) Then the snake spit out the eggshell. (21) Snakes love to eat eggs.

■ **EXERCISE 37—REVIEW:** Complete the sentences with the words in parentheses. Use the SIMPLE PRESENT of the verbs.

1. *(Anita, go)* _____*Does Anita go*_____ to her uncle's house every day?

2. *(monkeys, eat)* _____ insects?

3. A: I usually *(remember, not)* _____ my dreams.

   *(you, remember)* _____ your dreams?

B: Sometimes. I often (write) _____ my dreams down as soon as I wake up. I (like) _____ to think about my dreams. I (try) _____ to understand them.

4. I (understand, not) _____ my brother. He (have, not) _____ a job or a place to live. He (sleep) _____ at his friends' apartments. He (take, not) _____ care of himself. I (worry) _____ about him all the time.

5. Ocean waves (be) _____ interesting. In an ocean wave, water (move) _____ up and down, but the water (move, not) _____ _____ forward. This movement (be) _____ the same as the movement you can see in a rope. If you shake one end of a rope, waves (run) _____ along the rope, but the rope (move, not) _____ _____ forward. The water in an ocean wave (move) _____ forward only when a wave (reach) _____ land. Then an ocean wave (carry) _____ sand and other things forward when it (hit) _____ a sandy beach.

6. A: (you, study) _____ a lot?

B: I (study) _____ at least three hours every night. My roommate (study) _____ at least five hours. She's very serious about her education. How about you? (you, spend) _____ a lot of time studying?

A: No, I don't. I (spend) _____ as little time as possible. I

(like, not) _____ to study.

B: Then why (you, be) _____ a student?

A: My parents (want) _____ me to go to school. I (want, not)

_____ to be here.

B: In that case, I (think) _____ that you should drop out of school

and find a job until you figure out what you want to do with your life.

7. I (have) _____ two roommates. One of them, Sam, is always neat

and clean. He (wash) _____ his clothes once a week. (you, know)

_____ Matt, my other roommate? He (be) _____

the opposite of Sam. For example, Matt (change, not) _____ the

sheets on his bed. He (keep) _____ the same sheets week after

week. He (wash, never) _____ his clothes.

He (wear) _____ the same dirty jeans every day. Sam's side of the

room (be, always) _____ neat, and Matt's side

(be, always) _____ a mess. As my mother always

(say) _____ , it (take) _____ all kinds of people

to make a world.

■ **EXERCISE 38—REVIEW:**  Complete the dialogues with your own words by asking questions.

1. A: _____
   B: No, I don't.

2. A: _____
   B: Yes, I am.

3. A: _____
   B: In an apartment.

4. A: _____
   B: Six-thirty.

5. A: _____
   B: Monday.

6. A: _____
   B: At home.

7. A: _____
   B: No, he doesn't.

8. A: _____
   B: No, she isn't.

9. A: _____
   B: South of the United States.

10. A: _____
    B: Yes, it is.

11. A: _____
    B: Yes, they do.

12. A: _____
    B: In Southeast Asia.

13. A: _____
    B: Hot in the summer.

14. A: _____
    B: September.

15. A: _____
    B: Yes, I do.

■ **EXERCISE 39—REVIEW:**   Correct the mistakes in the following sentences.

                                *lives*

1. Yoko ~~live~~ in Japan.

2. Ann comes usually to class on time.

3. Peter watch TV every evening.

4. Anita carry a briefcase to work every day.

5. She enjoy her job.

6. I no know Joe.

7. Mike don't like milk.  He never drink it.

8. Tina doesn't speaks Chinese.  She speakes Spanish.

9. Do you are a student?

10. Does your roommate sleeps with the window open?

11. A:  Do you like strong coffee?

    B:  Yes, I like.

12. Where your parents live?

13. What time is your English class begins?

14. Olga isn't need a car.  She have a bicycle.

15. Do Pablo does his homework every day?

■ **EXERCISE 40—REVIEW:**   Choose the correct completion.

1. Alex _____ know French.
     A.  isn't         B.  doesn't         C.  don't

2. _____ Alex speak Russian?
     A.  Is            B.  Does          C.  Do

3. _____ Alex from Canada?
     A.  Is            B.  Does          C.  Do

4. When _____ you usually study?
     A.  are        B.  does         C.  do

5. Anita _____ a job.
   A. no have          B. no has          C. doesn't have

6. Omar _____ his new car every Saturday.
   A. wash             B. washs           C. washes

7. Where does Tina _____ to school?
   A. go               B. goes            C. to go

8. Fumiko _____ English at this school.
   A. study            B. studies         C. studys

9. Fumiko and Omar _____ students at this school.
   A. is               B. are             C. be

10. They _____ speak the same language.
    A. aren't          B. doesn't         C. don't

■ **EXERCISE 41—REVIEW:**  Complete the sentences.

1. A: Do you _____?

   B: Yes, I do.  How about you?  Do you _____?

   A: _____.

2. A: _____ don't _____.
   B: I know.

3. A: _____ doesn't _____.

   B: Really?  Does _____?
   A: I don't know.

4. A: Where is _____?
   B: At home.

   A: Where does _____?
   B: On Fifth Avenue.

5. A: _____?
   B: Yes, I do.

   A: _____?
   B: No, he doesn't.

   A: _____?
   B: Yes, I am.

   A: _____?
   B: No, he isn't.

6. A: Do you like _____?

 B: Yes, of course I _____. Everybody _____.

7. A: What _____ snakes?

 B: They _____ long, thin animals. They _____ have legs.

 A: _____ snakes reptiles?

 B: Yes, they _____.

 A: _____ snakes eat eggs?

 B: Yes, they _____.

8. A: _____ you usually _____ in the morning?

 B: _____.

 A: When _____?

 B: _____.

■ **EXERCISE 42—REVIEW:** Work in pairs. Follow the steps listed below.

1. STUDENT A: Say five things about Student B's physical appearance (for example, describe hair color, eye color, straight or curly hair, glasses, a mustache, a beard, etc.).
 STUDENT B: Agree or disagree with the description.

 *Example:*
 STUDENT A:  You have dark hair.
 STUDENT B:  *(Nods in agreement.)*
 STUDENT A:  You have black eyes.
 STUDENT B:  No, I have brown eyes.
 STUDENT A:  You have dark brown eyes.
 STUDENT B:  Okay. That's right.
 STUDENT A:  You wear glasses.
 STUDENT B:  Yes.
 Etc.

 *Then switch roles, with Student B saying five things about Student A's appearance.*

2. STUDENT A: Ask Student B five questions about things s/he has and doesn't have (for example, a car, a computer, a pet, children, a TV set, a briefcase, etc.).
 STUDENT B: Answer the questions.

 *Example:*
 STUDENT A:  Do you have a car?
 STUDENT B:  No.
 STUDENT A:  Do you have a computer.
 STUDENT B:  Yes, but it's not here. It's in my country.
 Etc.

*Then switch roles.*

3. STUDENT A:  Ask Student B five questions about things s/he likes and doesn't like (for example, kinds of food and drink, music, movies, books, etc.)

   STUDENT B:  Answer the questions.

*Example:*
STUDENT A:  Do you like pizza?
STUDENT B:  Yes.
STUDENT A:  Do you like the music of *(name of a group or singer)?*
STUDENT B:  No, I don't.
Etc.

*Then switch roles.*

4. Write about the other person.  Give a physical description.  Write about things this person has and doesn't have.  Write about things this person likes and doesn't like.

■ **EXERCISE 43—REVIEW:**  Find out information about your classmates' hometowns.  Use the information to write a report.  Ask questions about: *the name of the hometown, its location, its population, its weather and average temperature in a particular month (of your choosing).*

*Example:*
STUDENT A:  What's your hometown?
STUDENT B:  Athens.
STUDENT A:  Where is it located?
STUDENT B:  In southwestern Greece on the Aegean Sea.
STUDENT A:  What's the population of Athens?
STUDENT B:  3,507,000.
STUDENT A:  What's the weather like in Athens in May?
STUDENT B:  It's mild.  Sometimes it's a little rainy.
STUDENT A:  What's the average temperature in May?
STUDENT B:  The average temperature is around 8° Celsius.

*Chart for recording information about your classmates' hometowns.*

| Name | *Sypros* | | | |
|---|---|---|---|---|
| Hometown | *Athens* | | | |
| Location | *SW Greece on Aegean Sea* | | | |
| Population | *almost 4 million* | | | |
| Weather | *mild in May (around 8°C, in the mid-forties Fahrenheit)* | | | |

# CHAPTER 3

# Expressing Present Time (Part 2)

## 3-1 BE + ING: THE PRESENT PROGRESSIVE TENSE

| | | | | |
|---|---|---|---|---|
| *am* | + | *-ing* | (a) | I ***am sitting*** in class right now. |
| *is* | + | *-ing* | (b) | Rita ***is sitting*** in class right now. |
| *are* | + | *-ing* | (c) | You ***are sitting*** in class right now. |

In (a): When I say this sentence, I am in class. I am sitting. I am not standing. The action (sitting) is happening right now, and I am saying the sentence at the same time.

***am***, ***is***, ***are*** = helping verbs
***sitting*** = the main verb

***am***, ***is***, ***are*** + ***-ing*** = the present progressive tense*

*The present progressive is also called the "present continuous" or the "continuous present."

■ **EXERCISE 1—ORAL (BOOKS CLOSED):** Practice using the PRESENT PROGRESSIVE by using ***am/is/are*** + ***wearing***.

*PART I:* Answer questions about what you are wearing today and what your classmates are wearing.

*Example:*
TEACHER: Rosa, what are you wearing today?
STUDENT: I'm wearing a white blouse and a blue skirt.
TEACHER: What is Jin Won wearing?
STUDENT: He's wearing blue jeans and a sweat shirt.
TEACHER: What color is his sweat shirt?
STUDENT: It's gray with red letters.
TEACHER: What else is Jin Won wearing?
STUDENT: He's wearing sneakers, white socks, and a wristwatch. Etc.

*PART II:* Identify who is wearing particular articles of clothing.

*Example:* a (blue) shirt
*Response:* Marco is wearing a blue shirt.

*Example:* (blue) shirts
*Response:* Marco and Abdul are wearing blue shirts.

Suggestions:

| | | |
|---|---|---|
| 1. (gold) earrings | 4. a (red) blouse | 7. a (black) belt |
| 2. blue jeans | 5. (gray) slacks | 8. a necklace |
| 3. a blouse | 6. (brown) boots | 9. running shoes |

■ **EXERCISE 2—ORAL:** What are the animals in the following pictures doing?

■ **EXERCISE 3—ORAL (BOOKS CLOSED):** Act out the directions. Describe the actions using the PRESENT PROGRESSIVE. Sustain the action during the description.

> *Example:* Smile.
> TEACHER: (Student A), please smile. What are you doing?
> STUDENT A: I'm smiling.
> TEACHER: (Student A) and (Student B), please smile. (Student A), what are you and (Student B) doing?
> STUDENT A: We're smiling.
> TEACHER: (Student C), what are (Student A and Student B) doing?
> STUDENT C: They're smiling.
> TEACHER: (Student A), please smile. (Student B), what is (Student A) doing?
> STUDENT B: He/She is smiling.

1. Stand in the middle of the room.
2. Sit in the middle of the room.
3. Stand in the back of the room.
4. Smile.
5. Stand between ( . . . ) and ( . . . ).
6. Touch the floor.
7. Touch the ceiling.
8. Touch your toes.
9. Open/Close the door/window.
10. Close/Open the door/window.
11. Shake hands with ( . . . ).
12. Smile at ( . . . ).
13. Stand up and turn around in a circle.
14. Hold your book above your head.
15. Hold up your right hand.
16. Hold up your left hand.
17. Touch your right ear with your left hand.
18. Stand up.
19. Sit down.
20. Clap your hands.

■ **EXERCISE 4—ORAL (BOOKS CLOSED):** Practice using the PRESENT PROGRESSIVE by describing what your teacher and classmates are pantomiming, i.e., pretending to do. The pantomimist should sustain the action until the oral description is completed.

> *Example:* drink
> TEACHER: *(The teacher pantomimes drinking.)* What am I doing?
> STUDENT: You're drinking.

> *Example:* drive
> TEACHER: (Student A), drive. Pretend to drive.
> STUDENT A: *(The student pantomimes driving.)*
> TEACHER: What are you doing?
> STUDENT A: I'm driving.
> TEACHER: What is ( . . . ) doing?
> STUDENT B: He/She's driving.

1. eat
2. read
3. sleep
4. write
5. walk
6. run
7. fly
8. smile
9. laugh
10. cry
11. dance
12. wave
13. push
14. pull
15. clap
16. kick
17. count
18. stand in back of ( . . . )
19. touch ( . . . )
20. shake hands with ( . . . )
21. sit on the floor

## 3-2 SPELLING OF -ING

| | END OF VERB → -ING FORM | |
|---|---|---|
| Rule 1: | A CONSONANT★ + -e → smile → write → | DROP THE -e and ADD -ing smiling writing |
| Rule 2: | ONE VOWEL★ + ONE CONSONANT → sit → run → | DOUBLE THE CONSONANT and ADD -ing★★ sitting running |
| Rule 3: | TWO VOWELS + ONE CONSONANT → read → rain → | ADD -ing; DO NOT DOUBLE THE CONSONANT reading raining |
| Rule 4: | TWO CONSONANTS → stand → push → | ADD -ing; DO NOT DOUBLE THE CONSONANT standing pushing |

★ Vowels = a, e, i, o, u.
   Consonants = b, c, d, f, g, h, j, k, l, m, n, p, q, r, s, t, v, w, x, y, z.
★★ Exception to Rule 2: Do not double w, x, and y.
   snow → snowing   fix → fixing   say → saying

■ **EXERCISE 5:** Write the **-ing** forms for the following words.

1. stand _____*standing*_____
2. smile _____
3. run _____
4. rain _____
5. sleep _____
6. stop _____
7. write _____
8. eat _____
9. count _____
10. wear _____

11. ride _____
12. cut _____
13. dance _____
14. put _____
15. sneeze _____
16. plan _____
17. snow _____
18. fix _____
19. say _____
20. cry _____

■ **EXERCISE 6:** Write the *-ing* forms for the following words.

1. dream _____
2. come _____
3. look _____
4. take _____
5. bite _____

6. hit _____
7. hurt _____
8. clap _____
9. keep _____
10. camp _____

11. shine _____
12. win _____
13. join _____
14. sign _____
15. fly _____

16. pay _____
17. study _____
18. get _____
19. wait _____
20. write _____

■ **EXERCISE 7—ORAL:** Practice using the PRESENT PROGRESSIVE to describe actions.

STUDENT A: Act out the given directions. Sustain the action until Student B's description is completed.

STUDENT B: Describe Student A's action using the present progressive.

*Example:* erase the board
STUDENT A: *(Student A sustains the action of erasing the board.)*
STUDENT B: ( . . . )/He/She is erasing the board.

1. erase the board
2. draw a picture on the board
3. sneeze
4. cough
5. wave at your friends
6. sign your name on the board
7. clap your hands
8. walk around the room
9. count your fingers

10. bite your finger
11. hit your desk
12. drop your pen
13. tear a piece of paper
14. break a piece of chalk
15. fall down
16. sing, hum, or whistle
17. sleep
18. snore

19. chew gum
20. *(two students)* throw and catch *(something in the room)*
21. hold your grammar book between your feet
22. carry your book on the top of your head to the front of the room

■ **EXERCISE 8—WRITTEN (BOOKS CLOSED):** Practice spelling using *-ing.* As the teacher performs or pantomimes actions, write descriptions.

*Example:* wave
TEACHER: *(Acts out waving and asks, "What am I doing?")*
*Written:* *waving*

1. smile
2. cry
3. laugh
4. sit
5. stand
6. sleep
7. clap
8. write
9. eat
10. run
11. sing
12. read
13. drink
14. sneeze
15. fly
16. cut (a piece of paper)

## 3-3 THE PRESENT PROGRESSIVE: QUESTIONS

| | QUESTION | | | SHORT ANSWER + (LONG ANSWER) |
|---|---|---|---|---|
| | *BE* + | SUBJECT + | *-ING* | |
| (a) | *Is* | Mary | *sleeping* | → Yes, *she is*. (She's sleeping.) |
| | | | | → No, *she's not*. (She's not sleeping.) |
| | | | | → No, *she isn't*. (She isn't sleeping.) |
| (b) | *Are* | you | *watching* TV? | → Yes, *I am*. (I'm watching TV.) |
| | | | | → No, *I'm not*. (I'm not watching TV.) |
| | Q-WORD + *BE* + | SUBJECT + | *-ING* | |
| (c) *Where* | *is* | Mary | *sleeping*? | → *On the sofa*. (She's sleeping on the sofa.) |
| (d) *Why* | *are* | you | *watching* TV? | → *Because I like this program*. (I'm watching TV because I like this program.) |

■ **EXERCISE 9:** Make questions. Give short answers to yes/no questions.

1. A: What _____*are you writing?*_____
   B: A letter. (I'm writing a letter.)

2. A: _____*Is Ali reading a book?*_____

   B: No, _____*he isn't/he's not.*_____ (Ali isn't reading a book.)

3. A: _____

   B: Yes, _____ (Anna is eating lunch.)

4. A: Where _____
   B: At the Red Bird Cafe.   (She's eating lunch at the Red Bird Cafe.)

5. A: _____

   B: No, _____ (Mike isn't drinking a cup of coffee.)

6. A: What _____
   B: A cup of tea.   (He's drinking a cup of tea.)

7. A: _____

   B: No, _____.   (The girls aren't playing in the street.)

8. A: Where _____
   B: In the park.   (They're playing in the park.)

9. A: Why _____
   B: Because they don't have school today.   (They're playing in the park because they don't have school today.)

10. A: Hi, kids. _____

   B: No, _____. (We aren't drawing pictures with our crayons.)

   A: Oh? Then what _____

   B: Maps to our secret place in the woods. (We're drawing maps to our secret place in the woods.)

   A: Why _____

      Because we have a buried treasure at our secret place in the woods. (We're drawing maps because we have a buried treasure at our secret place in the woods.)

■ **EXERCISE 10—ORAL (BOOKS CLOSED):** Practice yes/no questions using the PRESENT PROGRESSIVE. The teacher will hand out slips of paper on which are written the directions in Exercise 4 on page 86.

   STUDENT A: Pantomime the directions on your slip of paper.
   STUDENT B: Ask Student A or another classmate a yes/no question using the present progressive.

   *Example:* drive *(written on a slip of paper)*
   STUDENT A: *(Student A pantomimes driving.)*
   STUDENT B: Are you driving?
   STUDENT A: Yes, I am.
               OR
   STUDENT B: (Student C), is (Student A) driving?
   STUDENT C: Yes, he/she is.

■ **EXERCISE 11:** Make questions with **where**, **why**, and **what**.

   1. A: _____*What are you writing?*_____
      B: A letter. (I'm writing a letter.)

   2. A: _____
      B: Because I'm happy. (I'm smiling because I'm happy.)

3. A: _____
   B: My grammar book.  (I'm reading my grammar book.)

4. A: _____
   B: Because we're doing an exercise.  (I'm reading my grammar book because we're doing an exercise.)

5. A: _____
   B: In the back of the room.  (Roberto is sitting in the back of the room.)

6. A: _____
   B: Downtown.  (I'm going downtown.)

7. A: _____
   B: Because I need to buy some shoes.  (I'm going downtown because I need to buy some shoes.)

8. A: _____
   B: Blue jeans and a sweatshirt.  (Akihiko is wearing blue jeans and a sweatshirt today.)

## 3-4  THE SIMPLE PRESENT vs. THE PRESENT PROGRESSIVE

| | |
|---|---|
| STATEMENTS: <br> (a) I **sit** in class *every day*. <br> (b) I **am sitting** in class *right now*. <br><br> (c) The teacher **writes** on the board on *every day*. <br> (d) The teacher **is writing** on the board *right now*. | • The SIMPLE PRESENT expresses habits or usual activities, as in (a), (c), and (e). <br> • The PRESENT PROGRESSIVE expresses actions that are happening right now, while the speaker is speaking, as in (b), (d), and (f). |
| QUESTIONS: <br> (e) **Do** you **sit** in class every day? <br> (f) **Are** you **sitting** in class right now? <br><br> (g) **Does** the teacher **write** on the board every day? <br> (h) **Is** the teacher **writing** on the board right now? | • The SIMPLE PRESENT uses **do** and **does** as helping verbs in questions. <br> • The PRESENT PROGRESSIVE uses **am**, **is**, and **are** in questions. |
| NEGATIVES: <br> (i) I **don't sit** in class every day. <br> (j) I**'m not sitting** in class right now. <br><br> (k) The teacher **doesn't write** on the board every day. <br> (l) The teacher **isn't writing** on the board right now. | • The SIMPLE PRESENT uses **do** and **does** as helping verbs in negatives. <br> • The PRESENT PROGRESSIVE uses **am**, **is**, and **are** in negatives. |

■ **EXERCISE 12:**   Complete the sentences with the words in parentheses.

1. I (walk) _____walk_____ to school every day.  I (take, not)

   _____don't take_____ the bus.

2. I (read) _____read_____ the newspaper every day.  I (read, not)

   _____don't read_____ my grammar book every day.

3. A:  What (you, read) _____are you reading_____ right now?

   B:  I (read) _____am reading_____ my grammar book.

4. Robert (cook) _____cooks_____ his own dinner every evening.

5. Right now Robert is in his kitchen.  He (cook) _____is cooking_____ rice
   and beans for dinner.

6. Robert is a vegetarian.  He (eat, not) _____doesn't eat_____ meat.

7. (you, cook) _____Do you cook_____ your own dinner every day?

8. A:  (you, want) _____Do you want_____ your coat?
   B:  Yes.

   A:  (be, this) _____Is this_____ your coat?

   B:  No, my coat (hang) _____is hanging_____ in the closet.

9. A:  (Tom, have) _____Does Tom have_____ a black hat?
   B:  Yes.

   A:  (he, wear) _____Does he wear_____ it every day?
   B:  No.

   A:  (he, wear) _____Is he wearing_____ it right now?

   B:  I (know, not) _____don't know_____.  Why do you care about
   Tom's hat?

   A:  I found a hat in my apartment.  Someone left it there.  I (think)

   _____think_____ that it belongs to Tom.

10. Ahmed (talk) _____talks_____ to his classmates every day in class.  Right now he

    (talk) _____is talking_____ to Yoko.

11. Yoko and Ahmed (sit) _____sit_____ next to each other in class every day, so they

    often (help) _____help_____ each other with their grammar exercises.  Right now

    Yoko (help) _____is helping_____ Ahmed with an exercise on present verb tenses.

12. It (rain) _____rains_____ a lot in this city, but it (rain, not)

_____isn't raining_____ right now.  The sun (shine)

_____is shining_____.  (it, rain) _____Does it rain_____ a lot

in your hometown?

13. A:  Hello?
    B:  Hello.  This is Mike.  Is Tony there?
    A:  Yes, but he can't come to the phone right now.  He (eat)

    _____is eating_____ dinner.  Can he call you back in about ten minutes?
    B:  Sure.  Thanks.  Bye.
    A:  Bye.

14. Tony's family (eat) _____eats_____ dinner at the same time every day.  During

    dinner time, Tony's mother (let, not) _____doesn't let_____ the children talk
    on the phone.

15. A:  What are you doing?  (you, work) _____Are you working_____ on
        your English paper?

    B:  No, I (study, not) _____am not studying_____.  I (write)

        _____am writing_____ a letter to my sister.

    A:  (you, write) _____Do you write_____ to her often?

    B:  I (write, not) _____don't write_____ a lot of letters to anyone.

    A:  (she, write) _____Does she write_____ to you often?

    B:  Yes.  I (get) _____get_____ a letter from her about once a week.  (you, write)

        _____Do you write_____ a lot of letters?

    A:  Yes.  I (like) _____like_____ to write letters.

16. Olga Burns is a pilot for an airline company in Alaska.  She (fly) _____flies_____

    almost every day.  Today she (fly) _____is flying_____ from Juno to Anchorage.

17. A:  Where (the teacher, stand, usually) _____Does the teacher usually stand_____ the teacher
        every day?

    B:  She usually (stand) _____stands_____ in the front of the room every day.

    A:  Where (she, stand) _____is she standing_____ today?

    B:  She (stand) _____standing_____ in the middle of the room.

18. A: Excuse me. *(you, wait)* _____Are you waiting_____ for the downtown bus?

B: Yes, I *(be)* ____am____. Can I help you?

A: Yes. What time *(the bus, stop)* ____is the bus stopping____ here?

B: Ten thirty-five.

19. A: *(animals, dream)* ____Do dream animals____?

B: I don't know. I suppose so. Animals *(be, not)* ____aren't____ very different from human beings in lots of ways.

A: Look at my dog. She *(sleep)* ____is sleeping____. Her eyes *(be)* ____is____ closed. At the same time, she *(yip)* ____is yipping____ and *(move)* ____is moving____ her head and her front legs. I *(be)* ____am____ sure that she *(dream)* ____is dreaming____ right now. I'm sure that animals *(dream)* ____dream____.

YIP, ZZZ, YIP, ZZZ, YIP, YIP, ZZZ, YIP.

## 3-5 NONACTION VERBS NOT USED IN THE PRESENT PROGRESSIVE

| | |
|---|---|
| (a) I'm hungry **right now**. **I want** an apple. (INCORRECT: *I am wanting an apple.*) | Some verbs are NOT used in the present progressive. They are called "nonaction verbs." In (a): *Want* is a nonaction verb. *Want* expresses a physical or emotional need, not an action. In (b): *Hear* is a nonaction verb. *Hear* expresses a sensory experience, not an action. |
| (b) **I hear** a siren. **Do you hear** it too? (INCORRECT: *I'm hearing a siren. Are you hearing it too?*) | |

NONACTION VERBS

| | | |
|---|---|---|
| want — querer | hear — escuchar | understand — entender |
| need — necesitar | see — ver | know — conocer, saber |
| like — gustar | smell — holer | believe — creer |
| love — amar | taste — provar | think (meaning *believe*)* — pensar |
| hate — odiar | | |

*Sometimes *think* is used in progressive tenses. See Chart 3-10 for a discussion of *think about* and *think that*.

■ **EXERCISE 13:** Use the words in parentheses to complete the sentences. Use the SIMPLE PRESENT or the PRESENT PROGRESSIVE.

1. Alice is in her room right now. She *(read)* _____ *is reading* _____ a book.

   She *(like)* _____ *likes* _____ the book.

2. It *(snow)* _____ is snowing _____ right now. It's beautiful! I *(like)*
   _____ like _____ this weather.

3. I *(know)* _____ know _____ Jessica Jones. She's in my class.

4. The teacher *(talk)* _____ is talking _____ to us right now. I *(understand)*
   _____ understand _____ everything she's saying.

5. Don is at a restaurant right now. He *(eat)* _____ is eating _____ dinner. He
   *(like)* _____ likes _____ the food. It *(taste)* _____ tastes _____ good.

6. (Sniff-sniff). I *(smell)* _____ smell _____ gas. *(you, smell)*
   _____ Do you smell _____ it too?

7. Jason *(tell)* _____ is telling _____ us a story right now. I *(believe)*
   _____ believe _____ his story. I *(think)* _____ think _____ that his story is true.

8. Ugh! That cigar *(smell)* _____ smells _____ terrible.

9. Look at the picture. Jane *(sit)* _____ is sitting _____ in
   a chair. A cat *(sit)* _____ is sitting _____ on her lap.
   Jane *(hate)* _____ hates _____ the cat.

10. Look at the picture. Mr. Allen *(hold)*
    _____ is holding _____ a cat. He *(love)*
    _____ loves _____ the cat. The cat *(lick)*
    _____ is licking _____ Mr. Allen's face.

## 3-6 SEE, LOOK AT, WATCH, HEAR, AND LISTEN TO

| | |
|---|---|
| SEE, LOOK AT, and WATCH<br>(a) I **see** many things in this room. | In (a): **see** = a nonaction verb. Seeing happens because my eyes are open. Seeing is a physical reaction, not a planned action. |
| (b) I'**m looking at** the clock. I want to know the time.<br>*mirar* | In (b): **look at** = an action verb. Looking is a planned or purposeful action. Looking happens for a reason. |
| (c) Bob **is watching** TV.<br>*ver* | In (c): **watch** = an action verb. I *watch* something for a long time, but I *look at* something for a short time. |
| HEAR and LISTEN TO<br>(d) I'm in my apartment. I'm trying to study. I *or* **hear** music from the next apartment. The music is loud.<br>*escuchar* | In (d): **hear** = a nonaction verb. Hearing is an unplanned act. It expresses a physical reaction. |
| (e) I'm in my apartment. I'm studying. I have a tape recorder. I'**m listening to** music. I like to listen to music when I study. | In (e): **listen (to)** = an action verb. Listening happens for a purpose. |

■ **EXERCISE 14—ORAL:** Answer the questions.

1. What do you see in this room?
   Now look at something. What are you looking at?

2. Turn to page 85 of this book. What do you see?
   Now look at one thing on that page. What are you looking at?

3. Look at the floor. What do you see?
   Now look the carpet

4. Look at the chalkboard. What do you see?

5. What programs do you like to watch on TV?

6. What sports do you like to watch?

7. What animals do you like to watch when you go to the zoo?

8. What do you hear right now?

9. What do you hear when you walk down the street?

10. What do you hear at night in the place where you live?

11. What do you listen to when you go to a concert?

12. What do you listen to when you go to a language laboratory?

## 3-7 *NEED* AND *WANT* + A NOUN OR AN INFINITIVE

| | | VERB | + | NOUN | | Need is stronger than want. Need gives the idea that something is *very important*. |
|---|---|---|---|---|---|---|
| (a) | We | need | | food. | | |
| (b) | I | want | | a sandwich. | | Need and want are followed by a noun or by an infinitive. |
| | | VERB | + | INFINITIVE | | |
| (c) | We | need | | to eat. | | An infinitive = to + the simple form of a verb.* |
| (d) | I | want | | to eat a sandwich. | | |

*The simple form of a verb = a verb without *-s, -ed,* or *-ing.*
Examples of the simple form of a verb: **come, help, answer, write.**
Examples of infinitives: **to come, to help, to answer, to write.**

■ **EXERCISE 15:** Use the words in the list or your own words to complete the sentences. Use an INFINITIVE *(to + verb)* in each sentence.

| | | | | |
|---|---|---|---|---|
| buy | do | listen to | play | walk |
| call | get | marry | take | wash |
| cash | go | pay | talk to | watch |

1. Anna is sleepy. She wants _____ *to go* _____ to bed.

2. I want _____ to go _____ downtown today because I need _____ to buy _____ a new coat.

3. Mike wants _____ to watch _____ TV. There's a good program on Channel 5.

4. Do you want _____ to play _____ soccer with us at the park this afternoon?

5. I need _____ to call _____ Jennifer on the phone.

6. I want _____ to go _____ to the bank because I need _____ to cash _____ a check.

7. James doesn't want _____ to do _____ his homework tonight.

8. My clothes are dirty. I need _____ to wash _____ them.

9. John loves Mary. He wants _____ to marry _____ her.

10. David's desk is full of overdue bills. He needs _____ to pay _____ his bills.

11. It's a nice day. I don't want _____ to take _____ the bus home today. I want _____ to walk _____ home instead.

12. Do you want _____ to listen to _____ some music on the radio?

13. Helen needs _____ to get _____ an English course.

14. Where do you want _____ to talk to _____ for lunch?

■ **EXERCISE 16:** Here are ten short conversations. Complete the sentences. Use the words in parentheses and other necessary words.

1. A: *(go \ you \ want )* ____Do you want to go____ downtown this afternoon?

   B: Yes, I do. *(I \ buy \ need)* ____I need to buy____ a winter coat.

2. A: Where *(you \ go \ want)* ____Do you want to go____ for dinner tonight?

   B: Rossini's Restaurant.

3. A: What time *(be \ need \ you)* ____Do you need to be____ at the airport?

   B: Around six. My plane leaves at seven.

4. A: *(want not \ Jean \ go)* ____Jean doesn't wants to go____ to the baseball game.

   B: Why not?

   A: Because *(she \ need \ study)* ____she needs to study____ for a test.

5. A: I'm getting tired. *(take \ I \ want)* ____I want to take____ a break for a few minutes.

   B: Okay. Let's take a break. We can finish the work later.

6. A: *(go back \ Peter \ want)* ____Peter wants to go back____ to his apartment.

   B: Why?

   A: Because *(he \ want \ change)* ____he wants to change____ his clothes before he goes to the party.

7. A: *(come \ we \ need not)* ____we don't need to come____ to class on Friday.

   B: Why not?

   A: It's a holiday.

8. A: Where *(you \ go \ want)* ____do you want to go____ for your vacation?

   B: *(I \ want \ visit)* ____I want to visit____ Niagara Falls, New York City, and Washington, D.C.

9. A: May I see your dictionary? *(I \ look up \ need)* ____I need to look up____ a word.

   B: Of course. Here it is.

   A: Thanks.

10. A: *(come \ want \ you)* ____Do you want to come____ with us to the park?

    B: Sure. Thanks. *(I \ get \ need)* ____I need to get____ some exercise.

*me da placer / me gusta*

## 3-8 WOULD LIKE

| | |
|---|---|
| (a) I'm thirsty. I **want** a glass of water. <br><br> (b) I'm thirsty. I **would like** a glass of water. | (a) and (b) have the same meaning, but **would like** is usually more polite than **want**. <br> *I would like* is a nice way of saying *I want*. |
| (c) *I would like* <br> *You would like* <br> *She would like* <br> *He would like*  } a glass of water. <br> *We would like* <br> *They would like* | Notice in (c): <br> There is not a final **-s** on **would**. <br> There is not a final **-s** on **like**. |
| (d) CONTRACTIONS <br> *I'd* = *I would* <br> *you'd* = *you would* <br> *she'd* = *she would* <br> *he'd* = *he would* <br> *we'd* = *we would* <br> *they'd* = *they would* | **Would** is usually contracted to **'d** in speaking. Contractions of **would** and pronouns are often used in writing. |
| (e) *WOULD LIKE* + *INFINITIVE* <br> I **would like** **to eat** a sandwich. | Notice in (e): **would like** can be followed by an infinitive. |
| (f) *WOULD* + SUBJECT + *LIKE* <br> **Would** you **like** some tea? | In a question, **would** comes before the subject. |
| (g) Yes, I **would**. (I would like some tea.) | **Would** is used alone in short answers to questions with **would like**. |

■ **EXERCISE 17—ORAL:** Change the sentences by using **would like**. Discuss the use of contracted speech with **would**.★

1. Tony wants a cup of coffee.
   → *Tony would like a cup of coffee.*
2. He wants some sugar in his coffee.
3. Ahmed and Anita want some coffee, too.
4. They want some sugar in their coffee, too.
5. A: Do you want a cup of coffee?
   B: Yes, I do. Thank you.
6. I want to thank you for your kindness and hospitality.
7. My friends want to thank you, too.
8. A: Does Robert want to ride with us?
   B: Yes, he does.

---

★**Would** is almost always contracted with pronouns in everyday speaking. The difference between *I'd like to go* and *I like to go* is sometimes difficult to hear. In addition, **would** is often contracted with nouns in speaking (but not in writing). There is a difference between *My friends'd like to come with us* and *My friends like to come with us*, but the difference is sometimes hard to hear.

■ **EXERCISE 18—ORAL (BOOKS CLOSED):** Answer the questions.

1. Who's hungry right now? ( . . . ), are you hungry? What would you like?
2. Who's thirsty? ( . . . ), are you thirsty? What would you like?
3. Who's sleepy? What would you like to do?
4. What would you like to do this weekend?
5. What would you like to do after class today?
6. What would you like to have for dinner tonight?
7. What countries would you like to visit?
8. What cities would you like to visit in *(the United States, Canada, etc.)*?
9. What languages would you like to learn?
10. You listened to your classmates. What would they like to do? Do you remember what they said?
11. Pretend that you are a host at a party at your home and your classmates are your guests. Ask them what they would like.
12. Think of something fun to do tonight or this weekend. Using *would you like*, invite a classmate to join you.

## 3-9 WOULD LIKE vs. LIKE

| | |
|---|---|
| (a)  I **would like to go** to the zoo. | In (a): *I would like to go to the zoo* means *I want to go to the zoo.* |
| (b)  I **like to go** to the zoo. | In (b): *I like to go to the zoo* means *I enjoy the zoo.* |
| | ***Would like*** indicates that I want to do something now or in the future. |
| | ***Like*** indicates that I always, usually, or often enjoy something. |

■ **EXERCISE 19—ORAL:** Answer the questions.

1. Do you like to go to the zoo?
2. Would you like to go to the zoo with me this afternoon?
3. Do you like apples?
4. Would you like an apple right now?
5. Do you like dogs?
6. Would you like to have a dog as a pet?
7. What do you like to do when you have free time?
8. What do you need to do this evening?
9. What would you like to do this evening?
10. What would you like to do in class tomorrow?

■ **EXERCISE 20:** Complete the sentences with your own words.

1. I need to _____ every day.

2. I want to _____ today.

3. I like to _____ every day.

4. I would like to _____ today.

5. I don't like to _____ every day.

6. I don't want to _____ today.

7. Do you like to _____?

8. Would you like to _____?

9. I need to _____ and

_____ today.

10. _____ would you like to _____ this evening?

## 3-10 THINK ABOUT AND THINK THAT

| | | | | |
|---|---|---|---|---|
| (a) I | THINK<br>**think** | + ABOUT<br>**about** | + A NOUN<br>**my family** every day. | In (a): Ideas about my family are in my mind every day. |
| (b) I *am* **thinking** | | **about** | **grammar** right now. | In (b): My mind is busy now. Ideas about grammar are in my mind right now. |
| (c) I | THINK<br>**think** | + THAT<br>**that** | + A STATEMENT<br>**Sue is lazy**. | In (c): In my opinion, Sue is lazy. I believe that Sue is lazy. |
| (d) Sue | **thinks** | **that** | **I am lazy**. | People use **think that** when they want to say (to state) their beliefs. |
| (e) I | **think** | **that** | **the weather is nice**. | The present progressive is often used with **think about.**<br>The present progressive is almost never used with **think that.**<br>INCORRECT: *I am thinking that Sue is lazy.* |
| (f) I **think that** Mike is a nice person.<br>(g) I **think** Mike is a nice person. | | | | (f) and (g) have the same meaning.<br>People often often omit **that** after **think**, especially in speaking. |

■ **EXERCISE 21:** Use **I think (that)** to give your opinion.

1. English grammar is easy / hard / fun / interesting.

_____*I think (that) English grammar is . . . .*_____

2. People in this city are friendly / unfriendly / kind / cold.

_____I think on Hammond are friendly_____

3. The food at *(name of a place)* is delicious / terrible / good / excellent / awful.

_I think at Michoacano's is delicious_

4. Baseball is interesting / boring / confusing / etc.

_I think baseball is boring._

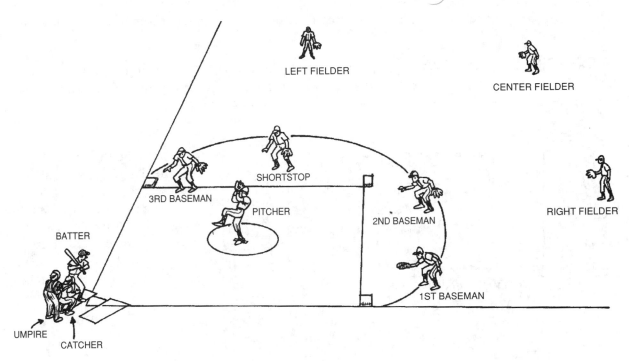

LEFT FIELDER

CENTER FIELDER

SHORTSTOP

3RD BASEMAN

PITCHER

2ND BASEMAN

RIGHT FIELDER

BATTER

1ST BASEMAN

UMPIRE

CATCHER

■ **EXERCISE 22:** Complete the sentences.

1. I think that the weather today is _nice._

2. I think my classmates are _friendly._

3. Right now I'm thinking about _grammar._

4. In my opinion, English grammar is _interesting_

5. In my opinion, soccer is _confusing_

6. I think that my parents are _good._

7. I think this school _is beautiful_

8. I think about _homework_

9. I think that _she is kind._

10. In my opinion, _the theache is a good person._

■ **EXERCISE 23—ORAL:** State an opinion about each of the following topics.

*Example:* books
*Response:* I think that *War and Peace* is an excellent novel.
In my opinion, *War and Peace* is an excellent novel.

1. this city
2. your English classes
3. music
4. movies
5. food
6. a current local, national, or international news story

■ **EXERCISE 24—REVIEW:** Complete the sentences. Use the words in parentheses. Use the SIMPLE PRESENT or the PRESENT PROGRESSIVE. Use an INFINITIVE where necessary.

|  |  |  |
|---|---|---|
| the baby | = | Bobby |
| the daughter | = | Ellen |
| the son | = | Paul |
| the mother | = | Mrs. Smith |
| the father | = | Mr. Smith |
| the cat | = | Pussycat |
| the bird | = | Tweetie |
| the mouse | = | Mickey |

(1)        The Smiths are at home. It is evening. Paul *(sit)* ____is sitting____ on

(2)    the sofa. He *(read)* ____is reading____ a newspaper. Ellen *(sit)*

(3)    ____is sitting____ at the desk. She *(study)* ____is studying____ .

(4)    While she is studying, she *(listen to)* ____is listening to____ music on her

(5)    radio. Paul *(hear)* ____hears____ the music, but he *(listen to, not)* ____isn't____

(6)    ____listen to____ it right now. He *(concentrate)* ____is concentrating____

(7)    on the weather report in the newspaper. He *(think about)* ____thinks____

(8)    ____about____ the weather report.

(9)        Ellen *(study)* ____is studying____ her chemistry text. She *(like)*

(10)    ____likes____ chemistry. She *(think)* ____is thinking____ that chemistry is easy.

(11) She *(think about)* __is thinking about__ chemical formulas. She

(12) *(understand)* __understands__ the formulas. She *(like)* __likes__

(13) her chemistry course, but she *(like, not)* __doesn't like__ her history course.

(14) Mrs. Smith is in the kitchen. She *(cook)* __is cooking__ dinner.

(15) She *(cut)* __is cutting__ up vegetables for a salad. Steam *(rise)*

(16) __is rising__ from the pot on the stove. Mrs. Smith *(like, not)*

(17) __doesn't cook__ to cook, but she *(know)* __knows__ that her family

(18) has to eat good food. While she *(make)* __is making__ dinner, Mrs. Smith

(19) *(think about)* __thinks about__ a vacation on the beach. Sometimes

(20) Mrs. Smith *(get)* __gets__ tired of cooking all the time, but she *(love)*

(21) __loves__ her family very much and *(want)* __want__ to take care

(22) of their health. Her husband *(know, not)* __doesn't know__ how to cook.

(23) Mr. Smith *(stand)* __'s standing__ near the front door. He *(take, off)*

(24) __is taking off__ his coat. Under his coat, he *(wear)* __is__

(25) __wearing__ a suit. Mr. Smith is happy to be home. He *(think about)*

(26) __is thinking about__ dinner. After dinner, he *(want)*

(27) __wants__ *(watch)* __to watch__ television. He *(need)*

(28) __needs__ *(go)* __to go__ to bed early tonight because he has a busy

(29) day at work tomorrow.

(30) In the corner of the living room, a mouse *(eat)* __is eating__ a piece

(31) of cheese. The mouse thinks that the cheese *(taste)* __taste__ good.

(32) Pussycat *(see, not)* __doesn't see__ the mouse. She *(smell, not)*

(33) __doesn't smell__ the mouse. Pussycat *(sleep)* __is sleeping__.

(34) She *(dream about)* __is dreaming about__ a mouse.

(35) Bobby is in the middle of the living room. He *(play)* __is playing__

(36) with a toy train. He *(see, not)* __doesn't see__ the mouse because he

(37) *(look at)* __is looking at__ his toy train. The bird, Tweetie, *(sing)*

(38) __is singing__. Bobby *(listen to, not)* __doesn't listen to__

(39) _____ the bird.  Bobby is busy with his toy train.  But Mrs.

(40) Smith can hear the bird.  She *(like)* _____*likes*_____ *(listen to)*

(41) _____*to listen to*_____ Tweetie sing.

---

## 3-11  THERE + BE

| | THERE + BE + SUBJECT + LOCATION | **There + be** is used to say that something exists in a particular location. |
|---|---|---|
| (a) | **There**   **is**   **a bird**   in the tree. | Notice:  The subject follows **be:** |
| (b) | **There**   **are**   **four birds**   in the tree. | there + is + singular noun<br>there + are + plural noun |
| (c) | **There's** a bird in the tree. | Contractions: |
| (d) | **There're** four birds in the tree. | there + is = there's<br>there + are = there're |

■ **EXERCISE 25:**  Complete the sentences with *is* or *are*.

1.  There _____*is*_____ a grammar book on Ahmed's desk.

2.  There _____*are*_____ many grammar books in this room.

3.  There _____*are*_____ two pens on Pierre's desk.

4.  There _____*is*_____ a pen on my desk.

5.  There _____*are*_____ thirty-one days in July.

6.  There _____*is*_____ only one student from Singapore in our class.

7.  There _____*are*_____ three students from Argentina.

8.  There _____*are*_____ ten sentences in this exercise.

9.  There _____*is*_____ a wonderful restaurant on 33rd Avenue.

10.  There _____*are*_____ many problems in the world today.

■ **EXERCISE 26—ORAL:** Make sentences with ***there is*** or ***there are***. Use the given phrases (groups of words) in your sentences.

1. a book \ on my desk
   → *There is (There's) a book on my desk.*

2. on Ali's desk \ some books
   → *There are (There're) some books on Ali's desk.*

3. on the wall \ a map
   *There is a map on the wall.*

4. some pictures \ on the wall
   *There are some pictures on the wall*

5. in this room \ three windows
   *There are three windows in this room,*

6. fifteen students \ in this room
   *There are feefteen students in this room*

7. in the refrigerator \ some milk
   *There is some milk in the refrigerator*

8. a bus stop \ at the corner of Main Street and 2nd Avenue
   *There is a bus stop at the corner of Main Street and 2nd Avenue*

9. in Canada \ ten provinces
   *There are ten provinces in Canada*

10. on television tonight \ a good program
    *There is a good program on television tonight*

■ **EXERCISE 27—ORAL:** After everybody puts one or two objects (e.g., a coin, some matches, a pen, a dictionary) on a table in the classroom, describe the items on the table by using ***there is*** and ***there are***.

*Examples:*
STUDENT A: There are three dictionaries on the table.
STUDENT B: There are some keys on the table.
STUDENT C: There is a pencil sharpener on the table.

■ **EXERCISE 28—ORAL/WRITTEN:** Describe your classroom. Use ***there is*** and ***there are***.

*Example:* I would like to describe this room. There are three windows.
There is a green chalkboard. Etc.

## 3-12 *THERE + BE:* YES/NO QUESTIONS

| QUESTION | SHORT ANSWER |
|---|---|
| *BE* + *THERE* + SUBJECT | |
| (a) **Is** **there** **any milk** in the refrigerator? | → Yes, **there is**.<br>→ No, **there isn't**. |
| (b) **Are** **there** **any eggs** in the refrigerator? | → Yes, **there are**.<br>→ No, **there aren't**. |

■ **EXERCISE 29—ORAL:** Ask a classmate a question about the contents of the refrigerator in the picture. Use the NOUNS in the list in your questions. Use "*Is there . . . ?*" or "*Are there . . . ?*"

*Example:*
STUDENT A: Is there any milk in the refrigerator?
STUDENT B: Yes, there is.

*Example:*
STUDENT A: Are there any onions in the refrigerator?
STUDENT B: No, there aren't.

| | | |
|---|---|---|
| 1. milk | 6. bread | 11. oranges |
| 2. onions | 7. apples | 12. fruit |
| 3. cheese | 8. potatoes | 13. meat |
| 4. butter | 9. orange juice | 14. roses |
| 5. eggs | 10. strawberries | 15. flour |

■ **EXERCISE 30—ORAL:** Ask and answer questions using *there + be*.

STUDENT A: Ask a classmate questions about this city. Use "*Is there . . . ?*" or "*Are there . . . ?*" Your book is open.
STUDENT B: Answer the questions. Your book is closed.

*Example:*
STUDENT A: Is there a zoo in *(name of this city)*?
STUDENT B: Yes, there is. OR: No, there isn't. OR: I don't know.

| | |
|---|---|
| 1. a zoo | 7. any good restaurants |
| 2. an airport | 8. a good (Vietnamese) restaurant |
| 3. an aquarium | 9. a botanical garden |
| 4. any lakes | 10. any swimming pools |
| 5. a train station | 11. an art museum |
| 6. a subway | 12. a good public transportation system |

■ **EXERCISE 31—ORAL:** Complete the sentences with your own words.

*Example:* There . . . in this building.
*Responses:* There are five floors in this building.
There are many classrooms in this building.
There is an elevator in this building. Etc.

1. There . . . in this building.

2. There . . . in this city.

3. There . . . in my country.

4. There . . . in the world.

5. There . . . in the universe.

# BANQUETE NAVIDEÑO

Estimado estudiante

Fairhaven Baptist Church cordialmente lo invita a Ud., y
su familia al banquete anual de Navidad que se llevará a
cabo ci día 17 de Diciembre de 1998 a las 6:30 pm.
Despues del banquetc habrá un servicio Biblico.

Por favor pagar su reservación antes del dia 14 de
Diciembre el costo será:

| | |
|---|---|
| Adultos | $4.00 |
| Ninos menores de 12 años | $ 3.50 |

Si desea asistir por favor llenar este pequeño questionario,
para poder brindarles una mejor atención.

1.___Si me gustaria asistir
2.___Lo siento, pero no puedo asistir al banquete.
3.___Por favor indicar el número de personas que asistirán
4.___Por favor indicar si desea asistir y necesita t
      transportación.
5.___Por favor indicar cuantos niños planea traer a la
      guardería.

Nombre_____No. de Teléfono_____

Si Ud., tiene alguna pregunta, por favor dirijase al Sr.
Ramos.

Atentamente

Sr. Ramos

NOTA: A los niños menores de 4 años., por favor
alimentenlos ántes de venir. Muchas Gracias

---

City, but there are

rks
ndonesia
oks

**NY**

ANSWER + (LONG ANSWER)

ve. (There are twelve
ers in this book.)
(There are ten
ces in Canada.)

stion with *how many*.

America
orld
m
ng

questions about this room.

is room.

1. windows     4. teachers     7. grammar books
2. doors        5. women        8. dictionaries
3. students     6. men          9. etc.

■ **EXERCISE 35—ORAL:** Pair up with a classmate. Ask and answer questions about the picture.

*Examples:*
STUDENT A: Are there any dogs in the picture?
STUDENT B: No, there aren't any dogs in the picture.
STUDENT A: Where are the boots?
STUDENT B: The boots are next to the picnic bench.
STUDENT A: How many trees are there?
STUDENT B: There's only one tree.

■ **EXERCISE 36—REVIEW:** Complete the sentences with your own words.

1. I need . . . because . . . .
2. I want . . . because . . . .
3. I would like . . . .
4. Would you like . . . ?
5. Do you like . . . ?
6. There is . . . .
7. There are . . . .
8. I'm listening to . . . , but I also hear . . . .
9. I'm looking at . . . , but I also see . . . .
10. I'm thinking about . . . .
11. I think that . . . .
12. In my opinion, . . . .
13. How many . . . are there . . . ?
14. Is there . . . ?

## 3-14 PREPOSITIONS OF LOCATION

| | |
|---|---|
| (a) My book is **on** my desk. | In (a): *on* = a preposition<br>*my desk* = object of the preposition<br>*on my desk* = a prepositional phrase |
| (b) Tom lives **in** the United States.<br>     He lives **in** New York City.<br>(c) He lives **on** Hill Street.<br>(d) He lives **at** 4472 Hill Street. | A person lives:  **in** a country and **in** a city<br>                 **on** a street, avenue, road, etc.<br>                 **at** an address<br>(See Chart 7-17 for more information about using **in** and **at**.) |

SOME PREPOSITIONS OF LOCATION★

| | | |
|---|---|---|
| above | far (away) from | inside |
| around | in | near |
| at | in back of | next to |
| behind | in the back of | on |
| below | in front of | on top of |
| beside | in the front of | outside |
| between | in the middle of | under |

★Prepositions of location are also called "prepositions of place."

A.

The book is **beside** the cup.
The book is **next to** the cup.
The book is **near** the cup.

B.

The book is **between** two cups.

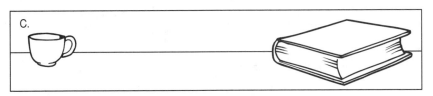

C.

In picture C, the book is **far away from** the cup.

D.

The cup is **on** the book.
The cup is **on top of** the book.

E.

The cup is **under** the book.

F.

The cup is **above** the book.

G.

A hand is **around** the cup.

H.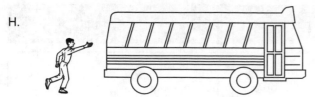

The man is **in back of** the bus.
The man is **behind** the bus.

I.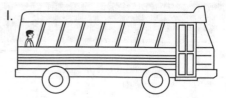

The man is **in the back of** the bus.

J.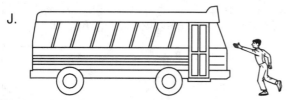

The man is **in front of** the bus.
In H and J, the man is **outside** the bus.

K.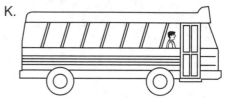

The man is **in the front of** the bus.
In I and K, the man is **inside** the bus.

L.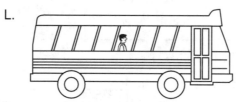

The man is **in the middle of** the bus.

■ **EXERCISE 37:** Describe the pictures by completing the sentences with prepositional expressions of location. There may be more than one possible completion.

1. 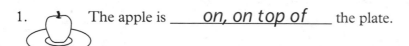 The apple is _____*on, on top of*_____ the plate.

2. 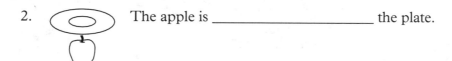 The apple is _____ the plate.

3.  The apple is _____ the plate.

4. 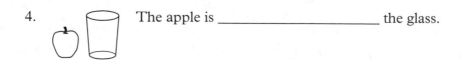 The apple is _____ the glass.

5.

The apple isn't near the glass.  It is _____ the glass.

6.  The apple is _____ the glass.

7. 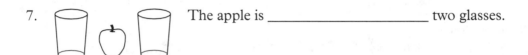 The apple is _____ two glasses.

8. 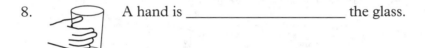 A hand is _____ the glass.

9.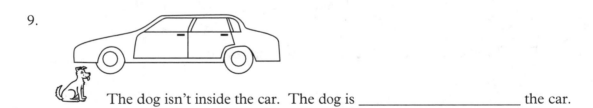

The dog isn't inside the car.  The dog is _____ the car.

10.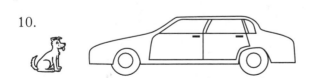

The dog is in _____ of the car.

11.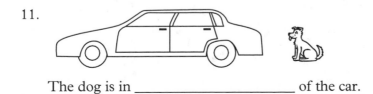

The dog is in _____ of the car.

12. The dog is in _____ of the car.

13. The dog is in _____ of the car.

■ **EXERCISE 38—ORAL:** Pair up with a classmate. Choose objects in the classroom (a book, a pen, an eraser, a cup, your hand, etc.) to demonstrate the meaning of the PREPOSITIONS in the list.

*Example:*
STUDENT A: Can you show me the meaning of "under"?
STUDENT B: Yes. The pen is under the book. Now it's your turn to demonstrate the meaning of "under."
STUDENT A: Okay. My hand is under this table.

| | | |
|---|---|---|
| 1. under | 7. in the middle of | 13. in back of |
| 2. above | 8. around | 14. in front of |
| 3. next to | 9. near | 15. in the back of |
| 4. between | 10. far (away) from | 16. in the front of |
| 5. inside | 11. behind | |
| 6. on top of | 12. below | |

■ **EXERCISE 39:** Complete the sentences with *in*, *on*, or *at*.

1. Pablo lives _____ Canada.

2. He lives _____ Toronto.

3. He lives _____ Lake Street.

4. He lives _____ 5541 Lake Street _____ Toronto, Canada.

*Complete the sentences:*

5. I live _____. *(name of country)*

6. I live _____. *(name of city)*

7. I live _____. *(name of street)*

8. I live _____. *(address)*

■ **EXERCISE 40—REVIEW:** Below are some pictures of John and Mary.

### A. VOCABULARY CHECKLIST

| | | |
|---|---|---|
| *eat dinner* | *a bowl* | *meat* |
| *hold a knife and a fork* | *a bowl of salad* | *a piece of meat* |
| *have a steak for dinner* | *a candle* | *a plate* |
| *burn* | *a cup* | *a restaurant* |
| | *a cup of coffee* | *a saucer* |
| | *a fork* | *a spoon* |
| | *a glass* | *a steak* |
| | *a glass of water* | *a table* |
| | *a knife* | *a waiter* |
| | *a vase of flowers* | |

### B. ANSWER THE QUESTIONS.

1. What is Mary doing?
2. What do you see on the table?
3. What is Mary holding in her right hand? in her left hand?
4. What is in the bowl?
5. What is on the plate?

6. What is in the cup?
7. What is burning?
8. Is Mary eating breakfast?
9. Is Mary at home? Where is she?
10. What is she cutting?

### C. COMPLETE THE SENTENCES.

11. Mary is sitting _____ a table.

12. There is a candle _____ the table.

13. There is coffee _____ the cup.

14. Mary _____ holding a knife

    _____ her right hand.

15. She's _____ a restaurant.

16. She _____ at home.

17. She _____ eating breakfast.

## A. VOCABULARY CHECKLIST

| | |
|---|---|
| *study at the library* | *the circulation desk* |
| *read a book* | *a librarian* |
| *take notes* | *a shelf (singular)* |
| | *shelves (plural)★* |

## B. ANSWER THE QUESTIONS.

1. What is John doing?
2. What do you see in the picture?
3. Is John at home? Where is he?
4. Is John reading a newspaper?
5. Where is the librarian standing?
6. Is John right-handed or left-handed?

## C. COMPLETE THE SENTENCES.

7. John is studying _____ the library.

8. He is sitting _____ a table.

9. He is sitting _____ a chair.

10. His legs are _____ the table.

11. There are books _____ the shelves.

12. John is writing _____ a piece of paper.

13. He's taking notes _____ a piece of paper.

14. He _____ reading a newspaper.

15. The librarian _____ standing _____ the circulation desk.

16. Another student is sitting _____ John.

---

★See Chart 4-5 for information about nouns with irregular plural forms.

## A. VOCABULARY CHECKLIST

| | | |
|---|---|---|
| write a check★ | a bank | name and address |
| sign a check | cash | first name/given name |
| sign her name | a check | middle initial |
| | the date | last name/family name/surname |

## B. ANSWER THE QUESTIONS.

1. What is Mary doing?
2. What is Mary's address?
3. What is Mary's full name?
4. What is Mary's middle initial?
5. What is Mary's last name?
6. How much money does Mary want?
7. What is in the upper left corner of the check?
8. What is in the lower left corner of the check?
9. What is the name of the bank?

## C. COMPLETE THE SENTENCES.

10. Mary is writing a _____.

11. She is signing _____ name.

12. The name _____ the bank is First National Bank.

13. Mary lives _____ 3471 Tree Street.

14. Mary lives _____ Chicago, Illinois.

15. Mary's name and address are _____ the upper left corner _____ the check.

---

**MARY S. JONES**
3471 TREE ST.
CHICAGO, IL 60565

212

May 3 19 95

PAY TO THE
ORDER OF ___Cash___ $ 25⁰⁰

Twenty five and ⁰⁰/₁₀₀ _____ DOLLARS

**FIRST NATIONAL BANK**
605 MICHIGAN AVE.
CHICAGO, IL 60503

Mary S. Jones

⑊021 200911 438 200

---

★*Check* (American English) is spelled *cheque* in British and Canadian English. The pronunciation of *check* and *cheque* is the same.

## A. VOCABULARY CHECKLIST

| | | |
|---|---|---|
| *cash a check* | *a bank teller* | *a man (singular)* |
| *stand in line* | *a counter* | *men (plural)★* |
| | *a line* | *a woman (singular)* |
| | | *women (plural)★* |
| | | *people (plural)★* |

## B. ANSWER THE QUESTIONS.

1. What is Mary doing?
2. Is Mary at a store? Where is she?
3. What do you see in the picture?
4. Who is standing behind Mary, a man or a woman?
5. Who is standing at the end of the line, a man or a woman?
6. How many men are there in the picture?
7. How many women are there in the picture?
8. How many people are there in the picture?
9. How many people are standing in line?

## C. COMPLETE THE SENTENCES.

10. Mary is _____ a bank.

11. Four people _____ standing in line.

12. Mary is standing _____ the counter.

13. The bank teller is standing _____ the counter.

14. A woman _____ standing _____ Mary.

15. Mary _____ standing _____ the end _____ the line.

16. A man _____ standing _____ the end _____ the line.

17. A businessman _____ standing _____ the woman with the big hat and the young man in jeans.

*See Chart 4-5 for information about nouns with irregular plural forms.

## A. VOCABULARY CHECKLIST

| | | |
|---|---|---|
| cook | a kitchen | bread |
| cook dinner | a list/a grocery list | coffee |
| make dinner | a pot | an egg |
| taste (food) | a refrigerator | butter |
| | a stove | milk |
| | a pepper shaker | pepper |
| | a salt shaker | salt |

## B. ANSWER THE QUESTIONS.

1. What is John doing?
2. What do you see in the picture?
3. Where is John?
4. Is John tasting his dinner?
5. Is John a good cook?

6. Where is the refrigerator?
7. What is on the refrigerator?
8. Is the food on the stove hot or cold?
9. Is the food in the refrigerator hot or cold?

## C. COMPLETE THE SENTENCES.

10. John is making dinner. He's _____ the kitchen.

11. There is a pot _____ the stove.

12. The stove is _____ the refrigerator.

13. There is a grocery list _____ the refrigerator door.

14. A salt shaker and a pepper shaker are _____ the stove.

15. There is hot food _____ top _____ the stove.

16. There is cold food _____ the refrigerator.

## A. VOCABULARY CHECKLIST

| | | |
|---|---|---|
| *watch TV / television* | *a cat* | *a living room* |
| *sit on a sofa* | *a dog* | *a rug* |
| *sing* | *a fish* | *a singer* |
| *sleep* | *a fishbowl* | *a sofa* |
| *swim* | *a floor* | *a TV set / a television set* |
| | *a lamp* | |

## B. ANSWER THE QUESTIONS.

1. What are John and Mary doing?
2. What do you see in the picture?
3. Are Mary and John in a kitchen? Where are they?
4. Where is the lamp?
5. Where is the rug?
6. Where is the dog?
7. Where is the cat?
8. Is the cat walking? What is the cat doing?
9. What is the dog doing?
10. What is on top of the TV set?
11. Is the fish watching TV?
12. What is on the TV screen? What are John and Mary watching?

## C. COMPLETE THE SENTENCES.

13. John and Mary _____ watching TV.

14. They _____ sitting _____ a sofa.

15. They _____ sleeping.

16. There is a rug _____ the floor.

17. A dog _____ sleeping _____ the rug.

18. A cat _____ sleeping _____ the sofa.

## A. VOCABULARY CHECKLIST

| | | |
|---|---|---|
| *talk to* (someone) | *an arrow* | *a piece of paper* |
| *talk on the phone* | *a calendar* | *a telephone book* |
| *talk to each other* | *a heart* | *a wall* |
| *smile* | *a phone/a telephone* | |
| *draw a picture* | *a picture* | |
| | *a picture of a mountain* | |

## B. ANSWER THE QUESTIONS.

1. What are John and Mary doing?
2. What do you see in the picture?
3. Is John happy? Is Mary happy?
   Are John and Mary smiling?
4. Are they sad?
5. Who is standing? Who is sitting?
6. Is John in his bedroom?
   Where is John?
7. What is Mary drawing?
8. What is on Mary's table?
9. What is on the wall next to the refrigerator?
10. Where is the clock?
11. What time is it?
12. What is on the wall above the table?

## C. COMPLETE THE SENTENCES.

14. John and Mary _____ talking _____ the phone.

15. John _____ talking _____ Mary. Mary _____ talking

    _____ John. They _____ talking to _____ other.

16. John is _____ the kitchen. He's standing _____ the refrigerator.

17. There is a calendar _____ the wall next to the refrigerator.

18. Mary _____ sitting _____ a table. She's _____ a picture.

19. There is a telephone book _____ the table.

20. There is picture _____ a mountain _____ the table.

## A. VOCABULARY CHECKLIST

| | |
|---|---|
| *sleep* | *a bed* |
| *dream* | *a dream* |
| *dream about* (someone/something) | *a head* |
| | *a pillow* |

## B. ANSWER THE QUESTIONS.

1. What is Mary doing?
2. What is John doing?
3. What are Mary and John doing?
4. What do you see in the picture?
5. Is Mary in her bedroom?
6. Is John in class? Where is he?
7. Is John standing or lying down?
8. Is Mary dreaming?
9. Are Mary and John dreaming about each other?
10. Are John and Mary in love?

## C. COMPLETE THE SENTENCES.

11. John and Mary _____ sleeping. They are _____ bed.

12. John _____ dreaming _____ Mary. Mary _____ dreaming _____ John. They _____ dreaming _____ each other.

13. Mary's head is _____ a pillow.

14. John and Mary _____ in the living room.

15. They _____ asleep. They _____ awake.

16. John and Mary love each other. They are _____ love.

■ **EXERCISE 41—REVIEW:** Complete the sentences with the words in parentheses. Use the
SIMPLE PRESENT or the PRESENT PROGRESSIVE.

1. I (sit) _____*am sitting*_____ in class right now. I (sit, always)

_____*always sit*_____ in the same seat every day.

2. Ali (speak) _____ Arabic, but right now he (speak)

_____ English.

3. Right now we (do) _____ an exercise in class. We (do)

_____ exercises in class every day.

4. I'm in class now. I (look) _____ at my classmates. Kim

(write) _____ in his book. Francisco (look)

_____ out the window. Yoko (bite) _____

her pencil. Abdullah (smile) _____. Maria (sleep)

_____. Jung-Po (chew) _____ gum.

5. The person on the bench in the picture below is Barbara. She's an accountant. She

(work) _____ for the government. She (have) _____

an hour for lunch every day. She (eat, often) _____ lunch in

the park. She (bring, usually) _____ a sandwich and

some fruit with her to the park. She (sit, usually) _____

on a bench, but sometimes she (sit) _____ on the grass. While she's at the

park, she (watch) _____ people and animals. She (watch)

_____ joggers and squirrels.  She *(relax)* _____

when she eats at the park.

6. Right now I *( look)* _____ at a picture of Barbara.  She

*(be, not)* _____ at home in the picture.  She *(be)* _____ at the

park.  She *(sit)* _____ on a bench.  She *(eat)*

_____ her lunch.  Some joggers *(run)* _____

_____ on a patch through the park.  A squirrel *(sit)*

_____ on the ground in front of Barbara.  The squirrel *(eat)*

_____ a nut.  Barbara *(watch)* _____

_____ the squirrel.  She *(watch, always)* _____

_____ squirrels when she eats lunch in the park.  Some ducks *(swim)*

_____ in the pond in the picture, and some birds *(fly)*

_____ in the sky.  A police officer *(ride)* _____

a horse.  He *(ride)* _____ a horse through the park every day.

Near Barbara, a family *(have)* _____ a picnic.  They *(go)*

_____ on a picnic every week.

■ **EXERCISE 42—ORAL:**  Bring to class one or two pictures of your country (or any interesting picture).  Ask your classmates to describe the picture(s).

■ **EXERCISE 43—WRITTEN:**  Choose one of the pictures your classmates brought to class.  Describe the picture in a composition.

■ **EXERCISE 44—REVIEW:**  Choose the correct completion.

1. Jack lives _____ China.
   A. in                      B. at                      C. on

2. Anita and Pablo _____ TV right now.
   A. watch                   B. watching               C. are watching

3. "_____ you writing a letter to your parents?"
   "No.  I'm studying."
   A. Do                      B. Are                    C. Don't

4. I _____ like to write letters.
   A. no                      B. am not                 C. don't

5. "Jack has six telephones in his apartment."

"I _____ you. No one needs six telephones in one apartment."
    A. am not believing    B. believe         C. don't believe

6. When I want to know the time, I _____ a clock.
    A. see              B. watch           C. look at

7. I need _____ a new notebook.
    A. buy              B. to buy          C. buying

8. "_____ a cup of tea?"
    "Yes, thank you."
    A. Would you like   B. Do you like     C. Like you

9. "Do you know Fatima?"

"Yes, I do. I _____ she is a very nice person."
    A. am thinking      B. thinking        C. think

10. There _____ twenty-two desks in this room.
    A. be               B. is              C. are

11. Pilots sit _____ an airplane.
    A. in front of      B. in the front of C. front of

12. I live _____ 6601 Fourth Avenue.
    A. in               B. on              C. at

■ **EXERCISE 45—REVIEW:** Correct the mistakes.

1. It's rainning today. I am needing my umbrella.

2. Do you want go downtown with me?

3. There's many problems in big cities today.

4. I like New York City. I am thinking that it is a wonderful city.

5. Does Abdul be sleeping right now?

6. Why you are going downtown today?

7. I'm listening you.

8. Are you hearing a noise outside the window?

9. I'd like see a movie tonight.

10. Kunio at a restaurant right now.  He usually eat at home, but today he eatting dinner at a restaurant.

11. I am liking flowers.  They are smelling good.

12. Mr. Rice woulds likes to have a cup of tea.

13. How many students there are in your class?

14. Alex is siting at his desk.  He writting a letter.

15. Yoko and Ivan are study grammar right now.  They want learn English.

16. Where do they are sitting today?

# CHAPTER 4
# Nouns and Pronouns

■ **EXERCISE 1:** Name things that belong to each category. Make a list. Compare your list with your classmates' lists. All of the words you use in this exercise are called "nouns."

1. Name clothing you see in this room. *(shirt)*
2. Name kinds of fruit. *(apple)*
3. Name things you drink. *(coffee)*
4. Name parts of the body. *(head)*
5. Name kinds of animals. *(horse)*
6. Name cities in the United States and Canada. *(New York, Montreal . . . )*
   NOTE: The names of cities begin with capital letters.
7. Name languages. *(English)* NOTE: The names of languages begin with capital letters.
8. Name school subjects. *(history)*

## 4-1 NOUNS: SUBJECTS AND OBJECTS

| | |
|---|---|
| (a)    NOUN <br> **Birds** \| fly. <br> subject   verb <br><br> (b)    NOUN        NOUN <br> **John** \| is holding \| a **pen**. <br> subject    verb     object | A NOUN is used as the **subject** of a sentence. A NOUN is used as the **object** of a verb.★ <br> In (a): *Birds* is a NOUN. It is used as the subject of the sentence. <br> In (b): *pen* is a NOUN. It has the article *a* in front of it; *a pen* is used as the object of the verb *is holding*. |
| (c)    NOUN           NOUN <br> **Birds** \| fly \| in \| the **sky**. <br> subject   verb   prep.   object of prep. <br><br> (c)    NOUN      NOUN      NOUN <br> **John** \| is holding \| a **pen** \| in \| his **hand**. <br> subject    verb     object   prep.   object of prep. | A NOUN is also used as the **object of a preposition.** <br> In (c): *in* is a **preposition** (prep.). The noun *sky* (with the article *the* in front) is the OBJECT of the preposition *in*. <br> Examples of some common prepositions: *about, across, at, between, by, for, from, in, of, on, to, with*. |

★Some verbs are followed by an object. These verbs are called transitive verbs (*v.t.* in a dictionary). Some verbs are not followed by an object. These verbs are called intransitive verbs (*v.i.* in a dictionary).

■ **EXERCISE 2:**   Describe the grammatical structure of the sentences as shown in items 1 and 2.
Then identify each NOUN.  Is the noun used as:
   • the subject of the sentence?
   • the object of the verb?
   • the object of a preposition?

1.  Marie studies chemistry.

| Marie | studies | chemistry | (none) | (none) |
|---|---|---|---|---|
| subject | verb | object | preposition | object of prep. |

→  *Marie = a noun, subject of the sentence*
   *chemistry = a noun, object of the verb "studies"*

2.  The children are playing in the park.

| The children | are playing | (none) | in | the park |
|---|---|---|---|---|
| subject | verb | object | preposition | object of prep. |

→  *children = a noun, subject of the sentence*
   *park = a noun, object of the preposition, "in"*

3.  Children like candy.

| | | | | |
|---|---|---|---|---|
| subject | verb | object | preposition | object of prep. |

4.  The teacher is erasing the board with her hand.

| | | | | |
|---|---|---|---|---|
| subject | verb | object | preposition | object of prep. |

5.  Mike lives in Africa.

| | | | | |
|---|---|---|---|---|
| subject | verb | object | preposition | object of prep. |

6.  The sun is shining.

| | | | | |
|---|---|---|---|---|
| subject | verb | object | preposition | object of prep. |

7.  Robert is reading a book about butterflies.

| | | | | |
|---|---|---|---|---|
| subject | verb | object | preposition | object of prep. |

8.  Tom and Ann live with their parents.

| | | | | |
|---|---|---|---|---|
| subject | verb | object | preposition | object of prep. |

9. Monkeys eat fruit and insects.

| | | | | |
|---|---|---|---|---|
| subject | verb | object | preposition | object of prep. |

10. Mary and Bob help Sue with her homework.

| | | | | |
|---|---|---|---|---|
| subject | verb | object | preposition | object of prep. |

11. Ships sail across the ocean.

| | | | | |
|---|---|---|---|---|
| subject | verb | object | preposition | object of prep. |

12. Water contains hydrogen and oxygen.

| | | | | |
|---|---|---|---|---|
| subject | verb | object | preposition | object of prep. |

## 4-2 ADJECTIVE + NOUN

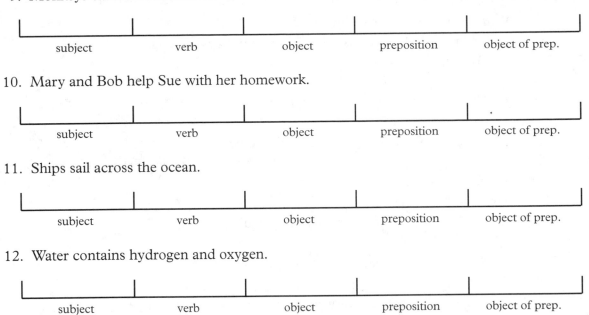

| | |
|---|---|
| (a) I don't like **cold** *weather*.<br>    (adj) + (noun) | Adjectives describe nouns. In grammar, we say that adjectives "modify" nouns. The word "modify" means "change a little." Adjectives give a little different meaning to a noun: *cold weather, hot weather, nice weather, bad weather.* |
| (b) Alex is a **happy** *child*.<br>    (adj) + (noun) | |
| (c) The **hungry** *boy* has a **fresh** *apple*.<br>    (adj)+(noun)    (adj) + (noun) | Adjectives come in front of nouns. |
| (d) The *weather*   is    **cold**.<br>    (noun) + (*be*) + (adj) | Reminder: An adjective can also follow **be**; the adjective describes the subject of the sentence. (See Chart 1-6.) |

COMMON ADJECTIVES

| | | | | Nationalities |
|---|---|---|---|---|
| beautiful–ugly | good–bad | angry | important | **American** |
| big–little | happy–sad | bright | intelligent | Canadian |
| big–small | large–small | busy | interesting | Chinese |
| cheap–expensive | long–short | delicious | kind | Egyptian |
| clean–dirty | noisy–quiet | famous | lazy | Indonesian |
| cold–hot | old–new | favorite | nervous | Italian |
| dangerous–safe | old–young | free | nice | Japanese |
| dry–wet | poor–rich | fresh | ripe | Korean |
| easy–hard | sour–sweet | honest | serious | Malaysian |
| easy–difficult | strong–weak | hungry | wonderful | Mexican |
| | | | | Saudi Arabian |

■ **EXERCISE 3:** Find the ADJECTIVES and NOUNS in the following sentences.

   1. Jim has an expensive bicycle.
     → *Jim = a noun; expensive = an adjective; bicycle = a noun*
   2. My sister has a beautiful house.

   3. We often eat at an Italian restaurant.

   4. Maria sings her favorite songs in the shower.

   5. Olga likes American hamburgers.

   6. You like sour apples, but I like sweet fruit.

   7. Political leaders make important decisions.

   8. Heavy traffic creates noisy streets.

   9. Poverty causes serious problems in the world.

  10. Young people have interesting ideas about modern music.

■ **EXERCISE 4:** Add ADJECTIVES to the sentences. Use any adjectives that make sense. Think of at least three possible adjectives to complete each sentence.

   1. I don't like ___cold / hot / wet / rainy / bad / etc.___ weather.

   2. Do you like _____ food?

   3. I admire _____ people.

   4. _____ people make me angry.

   5. Pollution is a/an _____ problem in the modern world.

   6. I had a/an _____ experience yesterday.

■ **EXERCISE 5:** Find each NOUN. Is the noun used as:
     • the subject of the sentence?
     • the object of the verb?
     • the object of a preposition?

   1. Bob and his wife like coffee with their breakfast.
     → *Bob = a noun, used as a subject of the sentence*
      *wife = a noun, used as a subject of the sentence*
      *coffee = a noun, object of the verb "like"*
      *breakfast = a noun, object of the preposition "with"*

2. Jack doesn't have a radio in his car.

3. Monkeys and apes have thumbs.

4. Scientists don't agree on the origin of the earth.

5. Does Janet work in a large office?

6. Egypt has hot summers and mild winters.

7. Many Vietnamese farmers live in small villages near their fields.

8. Large cities face many serious problems.

9. These problems include poverty, pollution, and crime.

10. An hour consists of sixty minutes. Does a day consist of 1440 minutes?

## 4-3 SUBJECT PRONOUNS AND OBJECT PRONOUNS

| SUBJECT PRONOUNS | OBJECT PRONOUNS | SUBJECT – OBJECT |
|---|---|---|
| (a) *I* speak English. | (b) Bob knows *me*. | *I* – *me* |
| (c) *You* speak English. | (d) Bob knows *you*. | *you* – *you* |
| (e) *She* speaks English. | (f) Bob knows *her*. | *she* – *her* |
| (g) *He* speaks English. | (h) Bob knows *him*. | *he* – *him* |
| (i) *It* starts at 8:00. | (j) Bob knows *it*. | *it* – *it* |
| (k) *We* speak English. | (l) Bob talks to *us*. | *we* – *us* |
| (m) *You* speak English. | (n) Bob talks to *you*. | *you* – *you* |
| (o) *They* speak English. | (p) Bob talks to *them*. | *they* – *them* |

| | |
|---|---|
| (q) I know *Tony*. *He* is a friendly person. | A pronoun has the same meaning as a noun. In (q): *he* has the same meaning as *Tony*. In (r): *him* has the same meaning as *Tony*. In grammar, we say that a pronoun "refers to" a noun. The pronouns *he* and *him* refer to the noun *Tony*. |
| (r) I like *Tony*. I know *him* well. | |
| (s) I have *a red book*. *It* is on my desk. | Sometimes a pronoun refers to a "noun phrase." In (s): *it* refers to the whole phrase *a red book*. |

■ **EXERCISE 6:** Complete the sentences. Use PRONOUNS (**I**, **me**, **he**, **him**, etc.).

1. Rita has a book. _____She_____ bought _____it_____ last week.

2. I know the new students, but Tony doesn't know _____ yet.

3. I wrote a letter, but I can't send _____ because I don't have a stamp.

4. Tom is in Canada. _____ is studying at a university.

5. Bill lives in my dorm. I eat breakfast with _____ every morning.

6. Ann is my neighbor. I talk to _____ every day. _____

   and _____ have interesting conversations together.

7. I have two pictures on my bedroom wall. I like _____.

   _____ are beautiful.

8. Ann and I have a dinner invitation. Mr. and Mrs. Brown want _____
   to come to dinner at their house.

9. Judy has a new car. _____ is a Toyota.

10. My husband and I have a new car. _____ got _____ last
    month.

■ **EXERCISE 7:** Complete the sentences. Use PRONOUNS.

1. A: Do you know Kate and Jim?

   B: Yes, _____I_____ do. I live near _____them_____.

2. A: Is the chemical formula for water $H_3O$?

   B: No, _____ isn't. _____ is $H_2O$.

3. A: Would Judy and you like to come to the movie with us?

   B: Yes, _____ would. Judy and _____ would enjoy

   going to the movie with _____.

4. A: Do Mr. and Mrs. Kelly live in the city?

   B: No, _____ don't. _____ live in the suburbs. I

   visited _____ last month.

5. A: Do you know how to spell "Mississippi"?

   B: Sure! I can spell _____. _____ is easy to spell.

6. A: Is Paul Cook in your class?

   B: Yes, _____ is.  I sit next to _____.

7. A: Yoko and I are going to go downtown this afternoon.  Do you want to come with
   _____?

   B: I don't think so, but thanks anyway.  Chris and _____ are going to
   go to the library.  _____ need to study for our test.

8. A: Do you and Jack want to join me for dinner tonight at a Chinese restaurant?

   B: Jack and _____ usually eat at home.  _____ need to
   save our money.

   A: _____ is not an expensive restaurant, and the food is really good.

   B: Okay.  Can you meet Jack and _____ there around six?
   A: Great!  See you then.

9. A: Do George and Mike come over to your house often?

   B: Yes, _____ do.  I invite _____ to my house often.
   We like to play cards together.
   A: Who usually wins your card games?

   B: Mike.  _____ is a really good card player.  We can't beat _____.

10. A: Hi, Ann.  How do you like your new apartment?

B: _____ is very nice.

A: Do you have a roommate?

B: Yes.  Maria Hall is my roommate.  Do you know _____?

_____ is from Miami.

A: No, I don't know _____.  Do you get along with _____?

B: Yes, _____ enjoy living together.  You must visit

_____ sometime.  Maybe _____ can come over for
dinner sometime soon.

A: Thanks.  I'd like that.

## 4-4  NOUNS: SINGULAR AND PLURAL

|  | SINGULAR | PLURAL |  |
|---|---|---|---|
| (a) | one pen<br>one apple<br>one cup<br>one elephant | two pens<br>three apples<br>four cups<br>five elephants | To make the plural form of most nouns:  add -s. |
| (b) | baby<br>city | babies<br>cities | End of noun:  *consonant* + -y<br>Plural form:  change y to i, add -es. |
| (c) | boy<br>key | boys<br>keys | End of noun:  *vowel* + -y<br>Plural form:  add -s. |
| (d) | wife<br>thief | wives<br>thieves | End of noun:  -fe or -f<br>Plural form:  change f to v, add -es. |
| (e) | dish<br>match<br>class<br>box | dishes<br>matches<br>classes<br>boxes | End of noun:  -sh, -ch, -ss, -x<br>Plural form:  add -es.<br>Pronunciation:  /əz/ |
| (f) | tomato<br>potato<br><br>zoo<br>radio | tomatoes<br>potatoes<br><br>zoos<br>radios | End of noun:  *consonant* + -o<br>Plural form:  add -es.<br>End of noun:  *vowel* + -o<br>Plural form  add -s. |

■ **EXERCISE 8:** Complete the sentences. Use the plural form of the words in the lists. Use each word only one time.

**LIST A:**

| | | |
|---|---|---|
| baby | cowboy | lady |
| ✔ boy | dictionary | party |
| city | key | tray |
| country | | |

1. Mr. and Mrs. Parker have one daughter and two sons. They have one girl and two

   _____*boys*_____.

2. The students in my class come from many _____.

3. Women give birth to _____.

4. My money and my _____ are in my pocket.

5. I know the names of many _____ in the United States and Canada.

6. I like to go to _____ because I like to meet and talk to people.

7. People carry their food on _____ at a cafeteria.

8. We always use our _____ when we write compositions.

9. Good evening, _____ and gentlemen.

10. _____ ride horses.

## LIST B:

| | | |
|---|---|---|
| *knife* | *life* | *wife* |
| *leaf* | *thief* | |

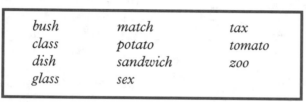

11. Please put the _____, forks, and spoons on the table.

12. Sue and Ann are married. They are _____. They have husbands.

13. We all have some problems in our _____.

14. Police officers catch _____.

15. It is fall. The _____ are falling from the trees.

## LIST C:

| | | |
|---|---|---|
| *bush* | *match* | *tax* |
| *class* | *potato* | *tomato* |
| *dish* | *sandwich* | *zoo* |
| *glass* | *sex* | |

16. Bob drinks eight _____ of water every day.

17. There are two _____: male and female.

18. Please put the _____ and the silverware on the table.

19. All citizens pay money to the government every year. They pay their

    _____.

20. I can see trees and _____ outside the window.

21. I want to light the candles. I need some _____.

22. When I make a salad, I use lettuce and _____.

23. Sometimes Sue has a hamburger and French-fried _____ for dinner.

24. Some animals live all of their lives in _____.

25. Mehmet is a student. He likes his

    _____.

26. We often eat _____ for lunch.

## ■ EXERCISE 9: Practice the pronunciation of -s/-es.*

**GROUP A:** Final **-s** is pronounced /z/ after voiced sounds.

| | |
|---|---|
| 1. taxicabs | 7. years |
| 2. beds | 8. lives |
| 3. dogs | 9. trees |
| 4. balls | 10. cities |
| 5. rooms | 11. boys |
| 6. coins | 12. days |

**GROUP B:** Final **-s** is pronounced /s/ after voiceless sounds.

| | |
|---|---|
| 13. books | 16. groups |
| 14. desks | 17. cats |
| 15. cups | 18. students |

**GROUP C:** Final **-s/-es** is pronounced /əz/

• after "s" sounds:
19. classes
20. glasses
21. horses
22. places
23. sentences
24. faces
25. offices
26. pieces
27. boxes
28. sexes

• after "z" sounds:
29. sizes
30. exercises
31. roses
32. noises

• after "sh" sounds:
33. dishes
34. bushes

• after "ch" sounds:
35. matches
36. sandwiches

• after "ge/dge" sounds:
37. pages
38. ages
39. oranges
40. bridges
41. edges

---

*For more information, see Chart 2-8.

■ **EXERCISE 10:**  Practice the pronunciation of *-s/-es*. Find the plural NOUN(S) in each sentence.  Pronounce the noun(s).  Then read the sentence aloud.

1. There are twenty desks in the room.

2. Oranges are usually sweet.

3. Roses are beautiful flowers.  Rose bushes are beautiful.

4. The weather is terrible.  It's raining cats and dogs.

5. We are reading sentences aloud.

6. I like to visit new places.

7. We do exercises in class.

8. I need two pieces of paper.

9. Don wants three sandwiches for lunch.

10. At the zoo you can see tigers, monkeys,

    birds, elephants, bears, and snakes.

11. Department stores sell many sizes of clothes.

12. The students are carrying books and bookbags.

13. The teachers have their offices in this building.

14. Engineers build bridges.

15. People have two ears, two eyes, two arms, two hands,

    two legs, and two feet.

16. Square tables and rectangular tables have four edges.

17. My dictionary has 350 pages.

18. I like apples, bananas, strawberries,

    and peaches.

19. There are three colleges in this city.

20. My apartment has cockroaches in the kitchen.

## 4-5 NOUNS: IRREGULAR PLURAL FORMS

| SINGULAR | PLURAL | EXAMPLES |
|---|---|---|
| (a) *child* | **children** | Mr. Smith has one *child*. Mr. Cook has two **children**. |
| (b) *foot* | **feet** | I have a right *foot* and a left *foot*. I have two **feet**. |
| (c) *man* | **men** | I see a *man* on the street. I see two **men** on the street. |
| (d) *mouse* | **mice** | My cat sees a *mouse*. Cats like to catch **mice**. |
| (e) *tooth* | **teeth** | My *tooth* hurts. My **teeth** are white. |
| (f) *woman* | **women** | There's one *woman* in our class. There are ten **women** in your class. |
| (g) *fish* | **fish** | Bob has an aquarium. He has one *fish*. Sue has an aquarium. She has seven **fish**. |
| (h) *(none)** | **people** | There are fifteen **people** in this room. (Notice: *people* does not have a final **-s**.) |

*__People__ is always plural. It has no singular form.

■ **EXERCISE 11—ORAL (BOOKS CLOSED):** Use *two* and the plural form of the NOUN.

*Example:* one child
*Response:* two children

1. one child
2. one woman
3. one tooth
4. one foot
5. one man
6. one mouse
7. one fish
8. one page
9. one place
10. one banana
11. one child
12. one desk
13. one sentence
14. one man
15. one orange
16. one foot
17. one knife
18. one sex
19. one girl
20. one exercise
21. one tooth
22. one woman
23. one boy and one woman

■ **EXERCISE 12:** The object of the game on the following page is to fill in each list with NOUNS. Write one noun that begins with each letter of the alphabet if possible. The nouns must belong to the category of the list. When you finish one list, count the number of nouns in your list. That is your score.

| List 1 Things in nature | List 2 Things you eat and drink | List 3 Animals and insects | List 4 Things for sale at (name of a local store) |
|---|---|---|---|
| A _____air_____ | A _____ | A _____ | A _____ |
| B _____bushes_____ | B _____ | B _____ | B _____ |
| C _____ | C _____ | C _____ | C _____ |
| D _____ | D _____ | D _____ | D _____ |
| E _____earth_____ | E _____ | E _____ | E _____ |
| F _____fish_____ | F _____ | F _____ | F _____ |
| G _____grass_____ | G _____ | G _____ | G _____ |
| H _____ | H _____ | H _____ | H _____ |
| I _____ice_____ | I _____ | I _____ | I _____ |
| J _____ | J _____ | J _____ | J _____ |
| K _____ | K _____ | K _____ | K _____ |
| L _____leaves_____ | L _____ | L _____ | L _____ |
| M _____ | M _____ | M _____ | M _____ |
| N _____ | N _____ | N _____ | N _____ |
| O _____oceans_____ | O _____ | O _____ | O _____ |
| P _____plants_____ | P _____ | P _____ | P _____ |
| Q _____ | Q _____ | Q _____ | Q _____ |
| R _____rain_____ | R _____ | R _____ | R _____ |
| S _____stars_____ | S _____ | S _____ | S _____ |
| T _____trees_____ | T _____ | T _____ | T _____ |
| U _____ | U _____ | U _____ | U _____ |
| V _____ | V _____ | V _____ | V _____ |
| W _____water_____ | W _____ | W _____ | W _____ |
| X _____ | X _____ | X _____ | X _____ |
| Y _____ | Y _____ | Y _____ | Y _____ |
| Z _____ | Z _____ | Z _____ | Z _____ |
| Score: _____13_____ | Score: _____ | Score: _____ | Score: _____ |

## 4-6 NOUNS: COUNT AND NONCOUNT

|  | SINGULAR | PLURAL |
|---|---|---|
| COUNT NOUN | *a book* *one book* | *books* *two books* *some books* *a lot of books* *many books* *a few books* |

**A COUNT NOUN**

| SINGULAR: | PLURAL: |
|---|---|
| *a* + *noun* *one* + *noun* | *noun* + *-s* |

| NONCOUNT NOUN | *money* *some money* *a lot of money*  (none) *much money* *a little money* |
|---|---|

**A NONCOUNT NOUN**

| SINGULAR: | PLURAL: |
|---|---|
| Do not use *a*. Do not use *one*. | A noncount noun does not have a plural form. |

COMMON NONCOUNT NOUNS

| | | | |
|---|---|---|---|
| *advice* | *mail* | *bread* | *pepper* |
| *furniture* | *money* | *cheese* | *rice* |
| *help* | *music* | *coffee* | *salt* |
| *homework* | *peace* | *food* | *soup* |
| *information* | *traffic* | *fruit* | *sugar* |
| *jewelry* | *weather* | *meat* | *tea* |
| *luck* | *work* | *milk* | *water* |

■ **EXERCISE 13:**   Look at the italicized words.  Underline the noun.  Is the noun COUNT or NONCOUNT?

1. (COUNT)   NONCOUNT     He sits on *a <u>chair</u>*.

2. COUNT   (NONCOUNT)     He sits on <u>*furniture*</u>.

3. COUNT   NONCOUNT     She has *a coin*.

4. COUNT   NONCOUNT     She has *some money*.

5. COUNT   NONCOUNT     She has *some letters*.

6. COUNT   NONCOUNT     She has *some mail*.

7. COUNT   NONCOUNT     The street is full of *traffic*.

8. COUNT   NONCOUNT     There are *a lot of cars* in the street.

9. COUNT   NONCOUNT     I know *a fact* about bees.

10. COUNT   NONCOUNT     I have *some information* about bees.

11. COUNT   NONCOUNT     The teacher gives us *homework*.

| | | |
|---|---|---|
| 12. COUNT | NONCOUNT | We have *an assignment*. |
| 13. COUNT | NONCOUNT | I like *music*. |
| 14. COUNT | NONCOUNT | Would you like *some coffee?* |
| 15. COUNT | NONCOUNT | Our school has *a library*. |
| 16. COUNT | NONCOUNT | People want *peace* in the world. |
| 17. COUNT | NONCOUNT | I need *some advice*. |
| 18. COUNT | NONCOUNT | Tom has *a good job*. |
| 19. COUNT | NONCOUNT | He likes *his work*. |
| 20. COUNT | NONCOUNT | Would you like *some water* with your food? |
| 21. COUNT | NONCOUNT | Maria wears *a lot of jewelry*. |
| 22. COUNT | NONCOUNT | She wears *earrings, rings, necklaces,* and *bracelets*. |

■ **EXERCISE 14—ORAL:** Most nouns are COUNT NOUNS. Complete the following by naming things you see in the classroom.

1. I see a _____. I see a _____.

   I see a _____ and a _____.

2. I see two _____.

3. I see three / four / five / six / etc. _____.

4. I see some _____.

5. I see a lot of _____.

6. I see many _____.

| | |
|---|---|
| (a) *A* dog is *an* animal. | *A* and *an* are used in front of singular count nouns. In (a): *dog* and *animal* are singular count nouns. |
| (b) I work in *an* office.<br><br>(c) Mr. Lee is *an* old man. | Use *an* in front of words that begin with the vowels *a, e, i,* and *o*: *an apartment, an elephant, an idea, an ocean.*<br>In (c): Notice that *an* is used because the adjective *(old)* begins with a vowel and comes in front of a singular count noun *(man)*. |
| (d) I have *an* uncle.<br>COMPARE:<br>(e) He works at *a* university. | Use *an* if a word that begins with "*u*" has a vowel sound: *an uncle, an ugly picture.*<br>Use *a* if a word that begins with "*u*" has a /yu/ sound: *a university, a usual event.* |
| (f) I need *an* hour to finish my work.<br><br>COMPARE:<br>(g) I live in *a* house. He lives in *a* hotel. | In some words that begin with "*h*," the "*h*" is not pronounced. Instead, the word begins with a vowel sound and *an* is used: *an hour, an honor.*<br>In most words that begin with "*h*," the "*h*" is pronounced. Use *a* if the "*h*" is pronounced. |

■ **EXERCISE 15:** Complete the sentences. Use *a* or *an*.

1. Bob is eating _____ apple.

2. Tom is eating _____ banana.

3. Alice works in _____ office.

4. I have _____ idea.

5. I have _____ good idea.

6. Sue is talking to _____ man.

7. Sue is talking to _____ old man.

8. I need to see _____ doctor.

9. Cuba is _____ island.

10. Mary is reading _____ article in the newspaper.

11. Bill is _____ uncle. He has _____ niece and two nephews.

12. _____ hour has sixty minutes.

13. _____ horse has hooves.

14. Miss Anderson has _____ job.

15. She has _____ unusual job.

16. _____ university is _____ educational institution.

■ **EXERCISE 16:** Complete the sentences. Use ***a*** or ***an***.

1. Carol is _____ nurse.

2. I live in _____ apartment building.

3. I live in _____ noisy apartment building.

4. Jake has _____ honest face.

5. Does Mark own _____ horse?

6. A fly is _____ insect.

7. Sonya's English class lasts _____ hour.

8. I had _____ interesting experience.

9. My father has _____ office downtown. It's _____ insurance office.

10. Gary and Joel are having _____ argument in the cafeteria. It is _____ unpleasant situation.

11. Are you _____ responsible person?

12. _____ angry woman is complaining to the store's manager.

13. _____ healthy person gets regular exercise.

14. Janet is _____ honorable person.

15. My uncle Jake has never said _____ unkind word. He is _____ very special man.

## 4-8 USING A/AN vs. SOME

| | |
|---|---|
| (a) I have ***a*** pen. | ***A/An*** is used in front of ***singular*** count nouns.<br>In (a): the word *pen* is a singular count noun.<br><br>***Some*** is used in front of ***plural*** count nouns.<br>In (b): the word *pens* is a plural count noun. |
| (b) I have ***some*** pens. | |
| (c) I have ***some*** rice. | ***Some*** is used in front of noncount nouns.*<br>In (c): the word *rice* is a noncount noun. |

*Reminder: Noncount nouns do not have a plural form. Noncount nouns are grammatically singular.

■ **EXERCISE 17:** Use *a*/*an* or **some** with the COUNT NOUNS in the following sentences. Are the nouns singular or plural?

1. Bob has _____*a*_____ book on his desk. → *book = a singular count noun*

2. Bob has _____*some*_____ books on his desk. → *books = a plural count noun*

3. I see _____ desk in this room.

4. I see _____ desks in this room.

5. Are _____ students standing in the front of the room?

6. Is _____ student standing in the middle of the room?

7. I'm hungry. I would like _____ apple.

8. The children are hungry. They would like _____ apples.

9. _____ children are playing in the street.

10. _____ child is playing in the street.

11. We are doing _____ exercise in class.

12. We are doing _____ exercises in class.

■ **EXERCISE 18:** Use *a*, *an*, or **some** with the nouns in the following sentences. Are they singular count nouns or noncount nouns?

1. I need _____*some*_____ money. → *money = a noncount noun*

2. I need _____*a*_____ dollar. → *dollar = a singular count noun*

3. Alice has _____ mail in her mailbox.

4. Alice has _____ letter in her mailbox.

5. I'm hungry. I would like _____ fruit.

6. I would like _____ apple.

7. Jane is hungry. She would like _____ food.

8. She would like _____ sandwich.

9. I'm thirsty. I'd like _____ water.

10. I'd like _____ glass of water.

11. Ann would like _____ milk.

12. I need _____ sugar for my coffee. Please hand me the sugar. Thanks.

13. I want to make _____ sandwich.

14. I need _____ bread and _____ cheese.

15. I'd like to have _____ soup with my sandwich.

■ **EXERCISE 19:** Use *a/an* or *some*.

1. Sonya is wearing ____*some*____ silver jewelry. She's wearing

   ____*a*____ necklace and ____*some*____ earrings.

2. We have _____ table, _____ sofa, and

   _____ chairs in our living room.

3. We have _____ furniture in our living room.

4. Sue has a CD player. She is listening to _____ music.

5. I'm busy. I have _____ homework to do.

6. Jane is very busy. She has _____ work to do.

7. Jane has _____ job. She is _____ teacher.

8. I'm hungry. I would like _____ orange.

9. The children are hungry. They would like _____ oranges. They

   would like _____ fruit.

10. I need _____ information about the bus schedule.

11. I'm confused. I need _____ advice.

12. I'm looking out the window. I see _____ cars, _____

    bus, and _____ trucks on the street. I see _____ traffic.

13. Bob is having _____ beans, _____ meat, and

    _____ bowl of soup for dinner.

■ **EXERCISE 20:** Use the word in *italics* to complete the sentence. Add *-s* to a COUNT NOUN
   (or give the irregular plural form). Do not add *-s* to a NONCOUNT NOUN.

1. *money*     I need some ____*money*____.

2. *desk*      I see some ____*desks*____ in this room.

3. *man*       Some ____*men*____ are working in the street.

4. *music*     I want to listen to some _____.

5. *flower*     Don wants to buy some _____ for his girlfriend.

6. *information*     I need some _____.

7. *jewelry*     Fred wants to buy some _____.

8. *furniture*     We need to buy some _____.

9. *chair*     We need to buy some _____.

10. *child*     Some _____ are playing in the park.

11. *homework*     I can't go to the movie because I have some _____ to do.

12. *advice*     Could you please give me some _____?

13. *suggestion*     I have some _____ for you.

14. *help*     I need some _____ with my homework.

15 *tea*     I'm thirsty.  I would like some _____.

16. *food*     I'm hungry.  I would like some _____.

17. *sandwich*     We're hungry.  We want to make some _____.

18. *animal*     I see some _____ in the picture.

19. *banana*     The monkeys are hungry. They would like some _____.

20. *fruit*     I'm hungry.  I would like some _____.

21. *weather*   We're having some hot _____ right now.

22. *picture*   I have some _____ of my family in my wallet.

23. *rice, bean*   I usually have some _____ and

_____ for dinner.

■ **EXERCISE 21:** Change the italicized noun to its PLURAL FORM if possible, changing *a* to *some*.  Make other changes in the sentence as necessary.

1. There is *a chair* in this room.  PLURAL FORM →  *There are some chairs in this room.*

2. There is *some furniture* in this room.   PLURAL FORM →  *(none)*

3. I have *a coin* in my pocket.

4. I have *some money* in my wallet.

5. There is *some mail* in my mailbox.

6. There is *a letter* in my mailbox.

7. There's *a lot of traffic* on Main Street.

8. There's *a car* on Main Street.

9. Our teacher assigns *a lot of homework*.

10. I like rock *music*.

11. Hong Kong has hot *weather*.

12. I need *some information* and *some advice* from you.

13. There's *a dictionary* on the shelf.

14. I'd like to put *some cheese* on my *bread*.

15. I hope you do well on your exam.  Good *luck!*

■ **EXERCISE 22—ORAL (BOOKS CLOSED):** Use *a, an,* or *some* with the given word.

*Example:* book    *Example:* books    *Example:* money
*Response:* a book    *Response:* some books    *Response:* some money

| | | | |
|---|---|---|---|
| 1. desk | 14. apple | 27. window | 40. bread |
| 2. desks | 15. man | 28. horse | 41. office |
| 3. animal | 16. old man | 29. hour | 42. food |
| 4. animals | 17. men | 30. dishes | 43. table |
| 5. chair | 18. bananas | 31. women | 44. cheese |
| 6. chairs | 19. banana | 32. oranges | 45. matches |
| 7. furniture | 20. fruit | 33. orange | 46. adjective |
| 8. child | 21. island | 34. place | 47. advice |
| 9. children | 22. jewelry | 35. places | 48. house |
| 10. music | 23. university | 36. water | 49. people |
| 11. homework | 24. uncle | 37. mail | 50. potatoes |
| 12. flower | 25. rice | 38. letter | 51. potato |
| 13. information | 26. boys | 39. letters | 52. sugar |

■ **EXERCISE 23:** Make the nouns PLURAL where necessary.

1. Toronto and Bangkok are big ~~city.~~ → *cities*

2. I need some information. → *(no change)*

3. Horse are large animals.

4. I like to listen to music when I study.

5. I have two small child.

6. I like to tell them story.

7. There are sixty minute in an hour.

8. Korea and Japan are country in Asia.

9. Children like to play with toy.

10. Our teacher gives us a lot of homework.

11. My bookcase has three shelf.

12. There are five woman and seven man in this class.

13. Bangkok has a lot of hot weather.

14. Are you hungry?  Could I get you some food?

15. Taiwan and Cuba are island.

16. I drink eight glass of water every day.

17. Tomato are red when they are ripe.

18. There is a lot of traffic at five o'clock.

19. Before dinner, I put dish, spoon, fork, knife, and napkin on the table.

20. I have many friend.  I don't have many enemy.

## 4-9  MEASUREMENTS WITH NONCOUNT NOUNS

| | |
|---|---|
| (a)  I'd like **some** water.<br>(b)  I'd like **a glass of** water.<br>(c)  I'd like **a cup of** coffee.<br>(d)  I'd like **a piece of** fruit. | Units of measure are used with noncount nouns to express a specific quantity, for example:  *a glass of, a cup of, a piece of.*<br>In (a):  *some water* = an unspecific quantity.<br>In (b):  *a glass of water* = a specific quantity. |

COMMON EXPRESSIONS OF MEASURE

| | | |
|---|---|---|
| *a bag of rice* | *a bunch of bananas* | *a jar of pickles* |
| *a bar of soap* | *a can of corn** | *a loaf of bread* |
| *a bottle of beer* | *a carton of milk* | *a piece of cheese* |
| *a bowl of cereal* | *a glass of water* | *a sheet of paper* |
| *a box of candy* | *a head of lettuce* | *a tube of toothpaste* |

*In British English:  *a tin of corn.*

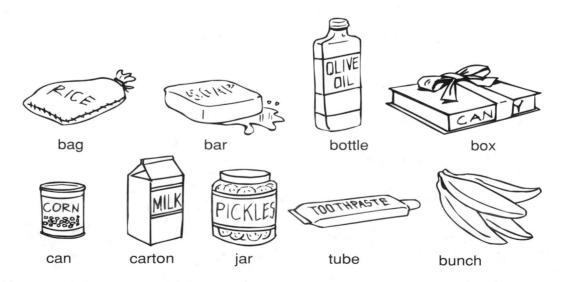

bag      bar      bottle      box

can      carton      jar      tube      bunch

■ **EXERCISE 24:** Complete the following. Use *a piece of*, *a cup of*, *a glass of*, or *a bowl of*.

You are hungry and thirsty. What would you like?

1. ___*a cup of / a glass of*___ tea

2. _____ bread

3. _____ water

4. _____ coffee

5. _____ cheese

6. _____ soup

7. _____ meat

8. _____ wine

9. _____ fruit

10. _____ rice

■ **EXERCISE 25:** Complete the sentences with NOUNS.

1. At the store, I bought a carton of ___*orange juice / milk / etc.*___

2. I also bought a tube of _____ and two bars of

   _____.

3. I got a can of _____ and a jar of _____.

4. I also got a loaf of _____ and a box of _____.

5. I wanted to get a head of _____, but none of it looked fresh.

6. I got a couple of bottles of _____ and a jar of _____.

■ **EXERCISE 26—ORAL (BOOKS CLOSED):** Use *I would like*. Use *a/an* or *some*.

*Example:* coffee
*Response:* I would like some coffee. OR: I would like a cup of coffee.

*Example:* new pen
*Response:* I'd like a new pen.

| | | | |
|---|---|---|---|
| 1. coffee | 9. apple | 17. sandwich | 25. new shirt/blouse |
| 2. money | 10. oranges | 18. meat | 26. new shoes |
| 3. dollar | 11. water | 19. roast beef | 27. tea |
| 4. paper | 12. new pencil | 20. soup | 28. cheese |
| 5. new book | 13. information | 21. salt | 29. rice |
| 6. new books | 14. help | 22. sugar | 30. bread |
| 7. fruit | 15. advice | 23. fish | 31. chicken |
| 8. banana | 16. food | 24. new car | 32. new furniture |

■ **EXERCISE 27—ORAL:** Change *a lot of* to *many* or *much* in the following sentences. Use *many* with COUNT NOUNS. Use *much* with NONCOUNT NOUNS.* (See Chart 4-6.)

1. I don't have a lot of money. → *I don't have much money.*

2. Tom has a lot of problems.

3. I want to visit a lot of cities in the United States and Canada.

4. I don't put a lot of sugar in my coffee.

5. I have a lot of questions to ask you.

6. Sue and John have a small apartment. They don't have a lot of furniture.

7. You can see a lot of people at the zoo on Sunday.

8. Dick doesn't get a lot of mail because he doesn't write a lot of letters.

9. Chicago has a lot of skyscrapers. Montreal has a lot of tall buildings too.

10. Mary is lazy. She doesn't do a lot of work.

11. I don't drink a lot of coffee.

12. Don is a friendly person. He has a lot of friends.

13. Do you usually buy a lot of fruit at the market?

14. Does Don drink a lot of coffee?

15. Do you write a lot of letters?

■ **EXERCISE 28:** Complete the questions with *many* or *much*.

1. How _____*much*_____ money do you have in your wallet?

2. How _____*many*_____ roommates do you have?

3. How _____ languages do you speak?

4. How _____ homework does your teacher usually assign?

5. How _____ tea do you drink in a day?

6. How _____ sugar do you put in your tea?

7. How _____ sentences are there in this exercise?

8. How _____ water is there in an Olympic-size swimming pool?

---

*Much* is usually used only in negative sentences and in questions. *Much* is rarely used in statements.

■ **EXERCISE 29—ORAL:** Ask questions with *how many* or *how much* and *are there* or *is there*.

> *Example:* students in this room
> *Question:* How many students are there in this room?
>
> *Example:* coffee in that pot
> *Question:* How much coffee is there in that pot?

1. restaurants in this city
2. desks in this room
3. furniture in this room
4. letters in your mailbox today
5. mail in your mailbox today
6. cheese in the refrigerator
7. bridges in this city
8. traffic on the street right now
9. cars on the street
10. people in this room

■ **EXERCISE 30:** Change *some* to *a few* or *a little*. Use *a few* with COUNT NOUNS. Use *a little* with NONCOUNT NOUNS. (See Chart 4-6.)

1. I need some paper. → *I need a little paper.*

2. I usually add some salt to my food.

3. I have some questions to ask you.

4. Bob needs some help. He has some problems. He needs some advice.

5. I need to buy some clothes.

6. I have some homework to do tonight.

7. I usually get some mail every day.

8. I usually get some letters every day.

9. When I'm hungry in the evening, I usually eat some cheese.

10. We usually do some oral exercises in class every day.

■ **EXERCISE 31:** Use these words in the sentences. If necessary, use the plural form. Use each word only once.

| | | | |
|---|---|---|---|
| bush | foot | information | page |
| child | fruit | knife | paper |
| city | furniture | ✔ match | piece |
| country | help | money | sex |
| edge | homework | monkey | traffic |

1. I want to light a candle. I need some _____*matches*_____.

2. I have a lot of _____ in my wallet. I'm rich.

3. There are two _____ : male and female.

4. I would like to visit many _____ in the United States. I'd like to visit Chicago, Los Angeles, Dallas, Miami, and some others.

5. There are some _____ , forks, and spoons on the table.

6. I want to take the bus downtown, but I don't know the bus schedule. I need some

   _____ about the bus schedule.

7. I want to write a letter. I have a pen, but I need some _____.

8. There are three _____ in North America: Canada, the United States, and Mexico.

9. There are a lot of trees and _____ in the park.

10. Bob is studying. He has a lot of _____ to do.

11. I like to go to the zoo. I like to watch animals. I like to watch elephants, tigers, and

    _____.

12. There is a lot of _____ on the street during rush hour.

13. My dictionary has 437 _____.

14. This puzzle has 200 _____.

15. Barbara has four suitcases.  She can't carry all of them.  She

    needs some _____.

16. Susie and Bobby are seven years old.  They aren't adults.

    They're _____.

17. A piece of paper has four _____.

18. We need a new bed, a new sofa, and some new chairs.

    We need some new _____.

19. People wear shoes on their _____.

20. I like apples, oranges, and bananas.  I eat a lot of _____.

■ **EXERCISE 32:**   Use these words in the sentences.  Use the plural form if necessary.

| | | | |
|---|---|---|---|
| *advice* | *glass* | *potato* | *tray* |
| *centimeter* | *horse* | *sentence* | *valley* |
| *dish* | *inch* | *size* | *weather* |
| *fish* | *leaf* | *strawberry* | *woman* |
| *foot* | *man* | *thief* | *work* |

1. _____ fall from the trees in autumn.

2. Sometimes I have a steak, a salad, and French-fried _____
   for dinner.

3. When the temperature is around 35°C (77°F), I'm comfortable.  But I don't like

   very hot _____.

4. Cowboys ride _____.

5. Plates and bowls are called _____.

6. Married _____ are called wives.

7. _____ steal things:  money, jewelry, cars, etc.

8. _____ are small, red, sweet, and delicious.

9. People carry their food on _____ at a cafeteria.

10. I'm not busy today.  I don't have much _____ to do.

11. Sweaters in a store often have four _____ :  small, medium,
    large, and extra large.

12. I have a problem. I need your help. I need some _____ from you.

13. Some _____ have mustaches.

14. Mountains are high, and _____ are low.

15. Ann has five _____ in her aquarium.

16. In some countries, people use cups for their tea. In other countries, they usually use

_____ for their tea.

17. There are 100 _____ in a meter.

18. There are 12 _____ in a foot.★

19. There are 3 _____ in a yard.★

20. There are twenty-five _____ in this exercise.

## 4-10 USING THE

| | |
|---|---|
| (a) A: Where's David?<br>   B: He's in **the** *kitchen*. | A speaker uses **the** when the speaker and the listener have the same thing or person in mind. **The** shows that a noun is specific.<br>In (a): Both A and B have the same kitchen in mind.<br>In (b): When B says "the apple," both A and B have the same apple in mind. |
| (b) A: I have two pieces of fruit for us, an apple and a banana. Which do you want?<br>   B: I'd like **the** *apple*, thank you. | |
| (c) A: It's a nice summer day today. **The** *sky* is blue. **The** *sun* is hot.<br>   B: Yes, I really like summer. | In (c): Both A and B are thinking of the same sky (there is only one sky for them to think of) and the same sun (there is only one sun for them to think of). |
| (d) Mike has **a** *pen* and **a** *pencil*.<br>**The** *pen* is blue.<br>**The** *pencil* is yellow. | **The** is used with:<br>  • singular count nouns, as in (d).<br>  • plural count nouns, as in (e).<br>  • noncount nouns, as in (f).<br>In other words, **the** is used with each of the three kinds of nouns. |
| (e) Mike has **some** *pens* and *pencils*.<br>**The** *pens* are blue.<br>**The** *pencils* are yellow. | |
| (f) Mike has **some** *rice* and **some** *cheese*.<br>**The** *rice* is white.<br>**The** *cheese* is yellow. | Notice in the examples: the speaker is using **the** for the **second** mention of a noun. When the speaker mentions a noun for a second time, both the speaker and listener are now thinking about the same thing.<br>       First mention:   I have **a** *pen*.<br>       Second mention: **The** *pen* is blue. |

---

★1 inch = 2.54 centimeters.  1 foot = 30.48 centimeters.  1 yard = 0.91 meters.

■ **EXERCISE 33:** Complete the sentences with *the* or *a/an*.

1. I have ____*a*____ notebook and _____ grammar book. _____ notebook is brown. _____ grammar book is red.

2. Right now Pablo is sitting in class. He's sitting between _____ woman and _____ man. _____ woman is Graciela. _____ man is Mustafa.

3. Susan is wearing _____ ring and _____ necklace. _____ ring is on her left hand.

4. Tony and Sara are waiting for their plane to depart. Tony is reading _____ magazine. Sara is reading _____ newspaper. When Sara finishes _____ newspaper and Tony finishes _____ magazine, they will trade.

5. In the picture below, there are four figures: _____ circle, _____ triangle, _____ square, and _____ rectangle. _____ circle is next to _____ triangle. _____ square is between _____ triangle and _____ rectangle.

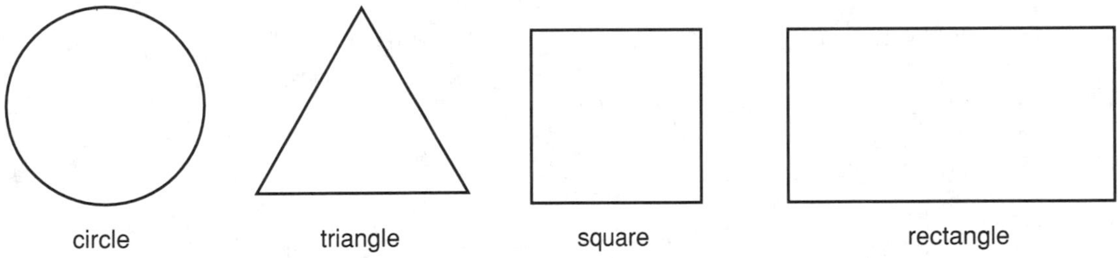

circle      triangle      square      rectangle

6. Linda and Anne live in _____ apartment in _____ old building. They like _____ apartment because it is big. _____ building is very old. It was built more than one hundred years ago.

7. I gave my friend _____ card and _____ flower for her birthday. _____ card wished her "Happy Birthday." She liked both _____ card and _____ flower.

8. We stayed at _____ hotel in New York. _____ hotel was very expensive.

■ **EXERCISE 34:** Complete the sentences with *the* or *a/an*.

(1) A: Look at the picture on this page of your grammar book. What do you see?

(2) B: I see _____ chair, _____ desk, _____ window, _____ plant.

(3) A: Where is _____ chair?

(4) B: _____ chair is under _____ window.

(5) A: Where is _____ plant?

(6) B: _____ plant is beside _____ chair.

(7) A: Do you see any people?

(8) B: Yes. I see _____ man and _____ woman. _____ man is standing. _____ woman is sitting down.

(9) A: Do you see any animals?

(10) B: Yes. I see _____ dog, _____ cat, and _____ bird in _____ cage.

(11) A: What is _____ dog doing?

(12) B: It's sleeping.

(13) A: How about _____ cat?

(14) B: _____ cat is watching _____ bird.

■ **EXERCISE 35:** Complete the sentences with *the* or *a/an*.

1. A: I need to go shopping. I need to buy _____ coat.

   B: I'll go with you. I need to get _____ umbrella.

2. A: Hi! Come in!

   B: Hi! _____ weather is terrible today! It's cold and wet outside.
   A: Well, it's warm in here.
   B: What should I do with my coat and umbrella?

   A: You can put _____ coat in that closet. I'll take _____ umbrella and

   put it in _____ kitchen where it can dry.

3. My cousin Jane has _____ good job. She works in _____ office. She

   uses _____ computer.

4. A: How much longer do you need to use _____ computer?
   B: Why?
   A: I need to use it too.
   B: Just five more minutes, then you can have it.

5. A: I need _____ stamp for this letter. Do you have one?
   B: Yes. Here.
   A: Thanks.

6. A: Would you like _____ egg for breakfast?

   B: No thanks. I'll just have _____ glass of juice and some toast.

7. A: Do you see my pen? I can't find it.

   B: There it is. It's on _____ floor.
   A: Oh. I see it. Thanks.

8. A: Be sure to look at _____ moon tonight.
   B: Why?

   A: _____ moon is full now, and it's beautiful.

9. A: Can I call you tonight?

   B: No. I don't have _____ telephone in my apartment yet. I just moved in
   yesterday.

10. A: Could you answer _____ telephone? Thanks.
    B: Hello?

## 4-11  USING Ø (NO ARTICLE) TO MAKE GENERALIZATIONS

| | |
|---|---|
| (a) Ø *Apples* are good for you. <br> (b) Ø *Students* use Ø *pens* and Ø *pencils*. <br> (c) I like to listen to Ø *music*. <br> (d) Ø *Rice* is good for you. | No article (symbolized by Ø) is used to make generalizations with: <br> • plural count nouns, as in (a) and (b), and <br> • noncount nouns, as in (c) and (d). |
| (e) Tom and Ann ate some fruit. ***The*** *apples* were very good, but ***the*** *bananas* were too ripe. <br><br> (f) We went to a concert last night. ***The*** *music* was very good. | COMPARE: In (a), the word *apples* is general. It refers to all apples, any apples. No article (Ø) is used. <br> In (e), the word *apples* is specific, so *the* is used in front of it. It refers to the specific apples that Tom and Ann ate. <br> COMPARE: In (c), *music* is general. In (f), *the music* is specific. |

■ **EXERCISE 36:**  Complete the sentences with ***the*** or Ø (no article).

1. _____Ø_____ sugar is sweet.

2. Could you please pass me _____*the*_____ sugar?

3. Oranges are orange, and _____ bananas are yellow.

4. There was some fruit on the table. I didn't eat _____ bananas because they were soft and brown.

5. Everybody needs _____ food to live.

6. We ate at a good restaurant last night. _____ food was excellent.

7. _____ salt tastes salty, and _____ pepper tastes hot.

8. Could you please pass me _____ salt? Thanks. And could I have _____ pepper too?

9. _____ coffee is brown.

10. Steven made some coffee and some tea. _____ coffee was very good. I didn't taste _____ tea.

11. I like _____ fruit. I also like _____ vegetables.

12. There was some food on the table. The children ate _____ fruit, but they didn't want _____ vegetables.

13. _____ pages in this book are full of grammar exercises.

14. _____ books consist of _____ pages.

## 4-12 USING SOME AND ANY

| STATEMENT: | (a) Alice has **some money**. | Use *some* in a statement. |
|---|---|---|
| NEGATIVE: | (b) Alice doesn't have **any money**. | Use *any* in a negative sentence. |
| QUESTION: | (c) Does Alice have **any money**?<br>(d) Does Alice have **some money**? | Use either *some* or *any* in a question. |
| (e) I don't have **any money**. (noncount noun)<br>(f) I don't have **any matches**. (plural count noun) || *Any* is used with noncount nouns and plural count nouns. |

■ **EXERCISE 37:** Use **some** or **any** to complete the sentences.

1. Sue has _____ some _____ money.

2. I don't have _____ any _____ money.

3. Do you have _____ some/any _____ money?

4. Do you need _____ help?

5. No, thank you. I don't need _____ help.

6. Ken needs _____ help.

7. Anita usually doesn't get _____ mail.

8. We don't have _____ fruit in the apartment. We don't have

_____ apples, _____ bananas, or _____

oranges.

9. The house is empty. There aren't _____ people in the house.

10. I need _____ paper. Do you have _____ paper?

11. Heidi can't write a letter because she doesn't have _____ paper.

12. Steve is getting along fine. He doesn't have _____ problems.

13. I need to go to the grocery store. I need to buy _____ food. Do you

need to buy _____ groceries?

14. I'm not busy tonight. I don't have _____ homework to do.

15. I don't have _____ money in my purse.

16. There are _____ beautiful flowers in my garden this year.

■ **EXERCISE 38—ORAL (BOOKS CLOSED):**  Ask a classmate a question about what he or she sees in this room.  Use *any* in the question.

*Example:*     desks
STUDENT A:  Do you see any desks in this room?
STUDENT B:  Yes, I do.  I see some desks / a lot of desks / twenty desks.

*Example:*     monkeys
STUDENT A:  Do you see any monkeys in this room?
STUDENT B:  No, I don't.  I don't see any monkeys.

| | | | |
|---|---|---|---|
| 1. books | 6. food | 11. hats | 16. red sweaters |
| 2. flowers | 7. curtains | 12. signs on the wall | 17. dogs or cats |
| 3. dictionaries | 8. paper | 13. bicycles | 18. bookshelves |
| 4. birds | 9. bookbags | 14. erasers | 19. women |
| 5. furniture | 10. children | 15. pillows | 20. light bulbs |

■ **EXERCISE 39:**  Use *any* or *a*.  Use *any* with NONCOUNT NOUNS and PLURAL COUNT NOUNS. Use *a* with SINGULAR COUNT NOUNS.

1. I don't have _____*any*_____ money.

2. I don't have _____*a*_____ pen.

3. I don't have _____*any*_____ brothers or sisters.

4. We don't need to buy _____ new furniture.

5. Mr. and Mrs. Kelly don't have _____ children.

6. I can't make _____ coffee.  There isn't _____ coffee in the house.

7. Ann doesn't want _____ cup of coffee.

8. I don't like this room because there aren't _____ windows.

9. Amanda is very unhappy because she doesn't have _____ friends.

10. I don't need _____ help.  I can finish my homework by myself.

11. I don't have _____ comfortable chair in my dormitory room.

12. I'm getting along fine.  I don't have _____ problems.

13. Joe doesn't have _____ car, so he has to take the bus to school.

14. I don't have _____ homework to do tonight.

15. I don't need _____ new clothes.★

16. I don't need _____ new suit.

_____

★*Clothes* is always plural.  The word "clothes" does not have a singular form.

## 4-13 INDEFINITE PRONOUNS: *SOMETHING, SOMEONE, ANYTHING, ANYONE*

| STATEMENT: | (a) Mary bought **something** at the store.<br>(b) Jim talked to **someone** after class. | In a statement, use *something* or *someone*. |
|---|---|---|
| NEGATIVE: | (c) Mary didn't buy **anything** at the store.<br>(d) Jim didn't talk to **anyone** after class. | In a negative sentence, use *anything* or *anyone*. |
| QUESTION: | (e) Did Mary buy **something** at the store?<br>Did Mary buy **anything** at the store?<br>(f) Did Jim talk to **someone** after class?<br>Did Jim talk to **anyone** after class? | In a question, use either *something/someone* or *anything/anyone*. |

■ **EXERCISE 40:** Complete the sentences. Use **something**, **someone**, **anything**, or **anyone**.★

1. I have ____*something*____ in my pocket.

2. Do you have _____ in your pocket?

3. Ken doesn't have _____ in his pocket.

4. I bought _____ when I went shopping yesterday.

5. Rosa didn't buy _____ when she went shopping.

6. Did you buy _____ when you went shopping?

7. My roommate is speaking to _____ on the phone.

8. Yuko didn't tell _____ her secret.

9. I talked to _____ at the phone company about my bill.

10. Did you talk to _____ about your problem?

11. Kim gave me _____ for my birthday.

12. Paul didn't give me _____ for my birthday.

13. Did Paul give you _____ for your birthday?

14. My brother is sitting at his desk. He's writing a letter to _____.

15. The hall is empty. I don't see _____.

───────────

★*Someone* and *somebody* have the same meaning. *Anyone* and *anybody* have the same meaning. You may also wish to include practice with *somebody* and *anybody* in this exercise.

16. A: Listen. Do you hear a noise?

    B: No, I don't. I don't hear _____.

17. A: Did you talk to Jim on the phone last night?

    B: No. I didn't talk to _____.

18. A: Where's your bicycle?

    B: _____ stole it.

19. A: Does _____ have some change? I need to use the pay phone.
    B: Here.
    A: Thanks. I'll pay you back later.

20. A: What did you do last weekend?

    B: I didn't do _____. I stayed home.


## 4-14 INDEFINITE PRONOUNS: *NOTHING* AND *NO ONE*

| | |
|---|---|
| (a) I **didn't say anything**.<br>(b) I **said nothing**. | (a) and (b) have the same meaning.<br>*Anything* is used when the verb is negative.<br>*Nothing* is used when the verb is affirmative.★ |
| (c) Bob **didn't see anyone** at the park.<br>(d) Bob **saw no one** at the park. | (c) and (d) have the same meaning.<br>*Anyone* is used when the verb is negative.<br>*No one* is used when the verb is affirmative.★ |

★INCORRECT:  *I didn't say nothing.*
 INCORRECT:  *Bob didn't see no one at the park.*


■ **EXERCISE 41:**  Complete the sentences by using *anything*, *nothing*, *anyone*, or *no one*.

1. Jim doesn't know _____ about butterflies.

2. Jim knows _____ about butterflies.

3. Jean didn't tell _____ about her problem.

4. Jean told _____ about her problem.

5. There's _____ in my pocket. It's empty.

6. There isn't _____ in my pocket.

7. Liz went to a shoe store, but she didn't buy _____.

8. Liz bought _____ at the shoe store.

9. I got _____ in the mail today. My mailbox was empty.

10. George sat quietly in the corner. He didn't speak to _____.

11. The office is closed from 12:00 to 1:00. _____ is there during the lunch hour.

12. I know _____ about nuclear physics.

13. _____ was at home last night. Both my roommate and I were out.

14. Joan has a new apartment. She doesn't know _____ in her apartment building yet.

15. A: Do you know _____ about Iowa?

    B: Iowa? I know _____ about Iowa.
    A: It's an agricultural state that is located between the Mississippi and Missouri rivers.

■ **EXERCISE 42—REVIEW:** Describe the grammatical structure of the sentences as shown in item 1.

1. Mr. Cook is living in a hotel.

| Mr. Cook | is living | (none) | in | a hotel |
|---|---|---|---|---|
| subject | verb | object | preposition | object of prep. |

2. Anita carries her books in her bookbag.

| | | | | |
|---|---|---|---|---|
| subject | verb | object | preposition | object of prep. |

3. Snow falls.

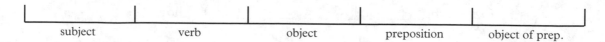

| subject | verb | object | preposition | object of prep. |

4. Monkeys sleep in trees.

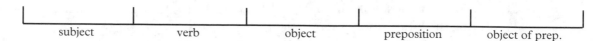

| subject | verb | object | preposition | object of prep. |

5. The teacher is writing words on the chalkboard.

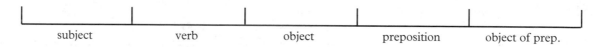

| subject | verb | object | preposition | object of prep. |

6. I like apples.

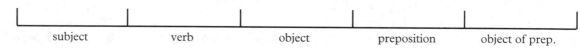

| subject | verb | object | preposition | object of prep. |

■ **EXERCISE 43—REVIEW:** A *complete sentence* has a subject and a verb. An *incomplete sentence* is a group of words that does not have a subject and a verb.

    If the words are a complete sentence, change the first letter to a capital letter (a big letter) and add final punctuation (a period or a question mark). If the words are an incomplete sentence, write "*Inc.*" to mean "*Incomplete.*"

1. monkeys like bananas → *Monkeys like bananas.*

2. in my garden → *Inc.*

3. do you like sour apples → *Do you like sour apples?*

4. rain falls

5. teaches English

6. this class ends at two o'clock

7. do the students go to class on Saturdays

8. in the classroom

9. my mother works in an office

10. my father to foreign countries on business every month

11. in Spain this month

12. does your brother have a job

13. does not work

14. where do you work

15. my brother lives in an apartment

16. has a roommate

17. the apartment has two bedrooms

18. a small kitchen and a big living room

19. on the third floor

20. pays the rent on the first day of every month

■ **EXERCISE 44—REVIEW:** Choose the correct completion.

1. My sister and I live together. Our parents call _____*A*_____ on the telephone often.
   A. us        B. them        C. we        D. they

2. Tom has a broken leg. I visit _____ in the hospital every day.
   A. he        B. him        C. them        D. it

3. Sue and I are good friends. _____ spend a lot of time together.
   A. They        B. You        C. We        D. She

4. Our children enjoy the zoo. We take _____ to the zoo often.
   A. it        B. they        C. them        D. him

5. Mary drives an old car. She takes good care of _____.
   A. her        B. them        C. it        D. him

6. Jack and _____ don't know Mr. Bush.
   A. I        B. me        C. us        D. them

7. Ms. Gray is a lawyer in Chicago. Do you know _____?
   A. them        B. it        C. him        D. her

8. Ahmed lives near Yoko and _____.
   A. I        B. me        C. him        D. her

9. My sister and a friend are visiting me. _____ are visiting here for two days.
   A. She        B. They        C. We        D. Them

10. Do _____ have the correct time?
    A. you        B. them        C. him        D. her

# ■ EXERCISE 45—REVIEW: Correct the errors in the following.

1. Omar a car has.  →  *Omar has a car.*

2. Our teacher gives tests difficult.

3. I need an advice from you.

4. Alex helps Mike and I.

5. I like rock musics.  I listen to them every day.

6. Babys cry.

7.  Mike and Tom in an apartment live.

8. There are seven woman in this class.

9. I don't like hot weathers.

10. I usually have a egg for breakfast.

11. There are nineteen peoples in my class.

12. Sun rises every morning.

13. Olga and Ivan has three childrens.

14. The students in this class do a lot of homeworks every day.

15. How many language do you know?

16. I don't have many money.

17. There is twenty classroom in this building.

18. I don't know nothing about ancient history.

■ **EXERCISE 46—REVIEW:** In pairs, pretend that tomorrow you are moving into a new apartment together. What do you need? Ask each other questions. Discuss your needs.

In writing, list the things you need and indicate quantity (*two, some, a lot of, a little, etc.*). List twenty to thirty things. Be sure to write down the <u>quantity</u>. You are completing this sentence: "***We need . . . .***"

*Example:* We need . . .
1. a sofa.
2. two beds.
3. a can opener.
4. some spaghetti.
5. a little fruit.
6. some bookcases. etc.

■ **EXERCISE 47—REVIEW:** Make a list of everything in the picture by completing the sentence "***I see . . . .***" Try to use numbers (e.g., ***three*** spoons) or other units of measure (e.g., ***a box of*** candy). Use ***a*** for singular count nouns (e.g., ***a*** fly).

*Example:* I see three spoons, a box of candy, a fly, etc.

■ **EXERCISE 48—REVIEW:** In pairs, ask and answer questions about the things and people in the picture on the following page.

*Example:*
STUDENT A: How many boys are there in the picture?
STUDENT B: There are three boys in the picture.
STUDENT A: Are there any flowers?
STUDENT B: No, there aren't any flowers in the picture.
STUDENT A: Are you sure?
STUDENT B: Well, hmmm. I don't see any flowers.
STUDENT A: Oh?

## CHAPTER 5
# Expressing Past Time

---

### 5-1 USING *BE*: PAST TIME

| PRESENT TIME | PAST TIME |
|---|---|
| (a) I *am* in class *today.* | (b) I *was* in class *yesterday.* |
| (c) Alice *is* at the library *today.* | (d) Alice *was* at the library *yesterday.* |
| (e) My friends *are* at home *today.* | (f) My friends *were* at home *yesterday.* |

SIMPLE PAST TENSE OF *BE*

| *Singular* | *Plural* |
|---|---|
| *I was* | *we were* |
| *you were* (one person) | *you were* (more than one person) |
| *she was* | *they were* |
| *he was* | |
| *it was* | |

$$\left. \begin{array}{l} I \\ she \\ he \\ it \end{array} \right\} + was$$

$$\left. \begin{array}{l} we \\ you \\ they \end{array} \right\} + were$$

■ **EXERCISE 1—ORAL:** Change the sentences to the past.

1. Bob is in class today. → *He was in class yesterday too.*

2. I'm in class today. → *I was in class yesterday too.*

3. Mary is at the library today.

4. We're in class today.

5. You're busy today.

6. I'm happy today.

7. The classroom is hot today.

8. Ann is in her office today.

9. Tom is in his office today.

10. Ann and Tom are in their offices today.

■ **EXERCISE 2—ORAL (BOOKS CLOSED):** Talk about today and yesterday.

> *Example:* I'm in class.
> *Response:* I'm in class **today**. I was in class **yesterday too**.
> *Example:* ( . . . ) is in class.
> *Response:* ( . . . ) is in class **today**. She/He was in class **yesterday too**.

1. We're in class.
2. I'm in class.
3. ( . . . ) is in class
4. ( . . . ) and ( . . . ) are in class.
5. ( . . . ) is here.

6. ( . . . ) is absent.
7. I'm tired.
8. ( . . . ) and ( . . . ) are (in the front row).
9. The door is open/closed.
10. It's hot/cold.

## 5-2 PAST OF *BE:* NEGATIVE

| | | |
|---|---|---|
| (a) I | ***was not*** in class yesterday. | NEGATIVE CONTRACTIONS:    ***was + not = wasn't*** |
| (b) I | ***wasn't*** in class yesterday. | ***were + not = weren't*** |

| | |
|---|---|
| (c) They ***were not*** at home last night. | $\left.\begin{array}{l} I \\ she \\ he \\ it \end{array}\right\}$ + *wasn't*     $\left.\begin{array}{l} we \\ you \\ they \end{array}\right\}$ + *weren't* |
| (d) They ***weren't*** at home last night. | |

■ **EXERCISE 3:** Study the time expressions. Then complete the sentences. Use ***wasn't*** or ***weren't***. Use a past time expression.

| PRESENT | | PAST |
|---|---|---|
| *today* | → | *yesterday* |
| *this morning* | → | *yesterday morning* |
| *this afternoon* | → | *yesterday afternoon* |
| *tonight* | → | *last night* |
| *this week* | → | *last week* |

1. Ken is here today, but _____ *he wasn't here yesterday.* _____

2. I'm at home tonight, but _____ *I wasn't at home last night.* _____

3. Olga is busy today, but _____

4. We're in class this morning, but _____

5. Tom is at the library tonight, but _____

6. It's cold this week, but _____

7. Alex and Rita are at work this afternoon, but _____

8. Mr. and Mrs. Jones are at home tonight, but _____

9. You're in class today, but _____

10. Dr. Ruckman is in her office this afternoon, but _____

## 5-3 PAST OF *BE:* QUESTIONS

| YES/NO QUESTIONS | SHORT ANSWER + (LONG ANSWER) |
|---|---|
| (a) **Were  you**      in class yesterday?<br>   *(be)* + *(subject)* | → **Yes, I was.**  (I was in class yesterday.)<br>→ **No, I wasn't.**  (I wasn't in class yesterday.) |
| (b) **Was  Carlos**    at home last night?<br>   *(be)* + *(subject)* | → **Yes, he was.**  (He was at home last night.)<br>→ **No, he wasn't.**  (He wasn't at home last night.) |
| INFORMATION QUESTIONS | SHORT ANSWER + (LONG ANSWER) |
| (c) **Where  were  you**      yesterday?<br>   *Where* + *(be)* + *(subject)* | → **In class.**  (I was in class yesterday.) |
| (d) **Where  was  Jennifer** last night?<br>   *Where* + *(be)* + *(subject)* | → **At home.**  (She was at home last night.) |

■ **EXERCISE 4:**   Make questions and give short answers.

1. *(you \ at home \ last night)*

   A: _____*Were you at home last night?*_____

   B: No, _____*I wasn't.*_____

2. *(Mr. Yamamoto \ absent from class \ yesterday)*

   A: _____

   B: Yes, _____

3. *(Alex and Sue \ at home \ last night)*

   A: _____

   B: Yes, _____

4. *(you \ nervous \ the first day of class)*

   A: _____

   B: No, _____

5. *(Ahmed \ at the library \ last night)*

A: _____

B: Yes, _____

6. *(Mr. Shin \ in class \ yesterday)*

A: _____

B: No, _____

A: Where _____

B: At home.

7. *(you and your wife \ in Canada \ last year)*

A: _____

B: No, _____

A: Where _____

B: In Ireland.

■ **EXERCISE 5:** Make questions and give short answers.

1. *(you \ in class \ yesterday)*

A: ___*Were you in class yesterday?*_____

B: Yes, ___*I was.*_____

2. *(Anita \ in class \ today)*

A: ___*Is Anita in class today?*_____

B: No, ___*she isn't.*_____ She's absent.

3. *(you \ tired \ last night)*

A: _____

B: Yes, _____. I went to bed early.

4. *(you \ hungry \ right now)*

A: _____

B: No, _____, but I'm thirsty.

5. *(the weather \ hot in New York City \ last summer)*

    A: _____

    B: Yes, _____. It was very hot.

6. *(the weather \ cold in Alaska \ in the winter)*

    A: _____

    B: Yes, _____. It's very cold.

7. *(Yoko and Mohammed \ here \ yesterday afternoon)*

    A: _____

    B: Yes, _____

8. *(the students in this class \ intelligent)*

    A: _____

    B: Of course _____! They are very intelligent!

9. *(Mr. Tok \ absent \ today)*

    A: _____

    B: Yes, _____

    A: Where _____

    B: _____

10. *(Tony and Benito \ at the party \ last night)*

    A: _____

    B: No, _____

    A: Where _____

    B: _____

11. *(Mr. and Mrs. Rice \ in town \ this week)*

    A: _____

    B: No, _____. They're out of town.

    A: Oh? Where _____

    B: _____

12. (Anna \ out of town \ last week)

A: _____

B: Yes, _____

A: Where _____

B: _____

■ **EXERCISE 6—ORAL (BOOKS CLOSED):** Pair up with a classmate and ask questions. If Student B answers **yes**, the exercise item is finished. If Student B answers **no**, Student A should follow with a **where**-question.

*Example:*   in class \ now
STUDENT A:   ( . . . ), are you in class now? *(Student A's book is open.)*
STUDENT B:   Yes, I am. *(Student B's book is closed.)*

*Example:*   at the library \ last night
STUDENT A:   ( . . . ), were you at the library last night?
STUDENT B:   No, I wasn't.
STUDENT A:   Where were you?
STUDENT B:   I was (at home / in my room / at a party, etc.)

1. at home \ now
2. at home \ yesterday morning
3. at home \ last night
4. in class \ two days ago
5. in *(name of a place in this city)* \ now
6. in *(name of this city)* \ last year
7. *(name of your teacher)* \ in class \ yesterday
8. *(names of two classmates)* \ here \ yesterday

*Change roles. Student B should now ask Student A questions.*

9. in *(name of this country)* \ two weeks ago
10. in *(name of this country)* \ two years ago
11. in *(name of a city)* \ now
12. at *(name of a park in this city)* \ yesterday afternoon
13. at *(name of a famous place in this city)* \ this morning*
14. at *(name of a popular place where students like to go)* \ last night
15. *(name of the teacher)* \ at home \ last night
16. *(names of two students)* \ *(name of this building)* \ yesterday afternoon

---

*Student B: If you are asking this question in the morning, use a present verb. If it is now afternoon or evening, use a past verb.

## 5-4 THE SIMPLE PAST TENSE: USING -ED

| | | | |
|---|---|---|---|
| SIMPLE PRESENT: | (a) I **walk** to school *every day*. | verb + **-ed** = the simple past tense | |
| SIMPLE PAST: | (b) I **walked** to school *yesterday*. | | |
| | | *I* | |
| SIMPLE PRESENT: | (c) Ann **walks** to school *every day*. | *you* | |
| SIMPLE PAST: | (d) Ann **walked** to school *yesterday*. | *she* *he* *it* *we* *they* } + *walked (verb + -ed)* | |

■ **EXERCISE 7:** Complete the sentences. Use the words in the list; use the SIMPLE PRESENT or the SIMPLE PAST.

| | | |
|---|---|---|
| ask | ✔ rain | wait |
| cook | shave | walk |
| dream | smile | watch |
| erase | stay | work |

1. It often _____*rains*_____ in the morning. It _____*rained*_____ yesterday.

2. I _____ to school every morning. I _____ to school yesterday morning.

3. Sue often _____ questions. She _____ a question in class yesterday.

4. I _____ a movie on television last night. I usually

    _____ TV in the evening because I want to improve my English.

5. Mike _____ his own dinner yesterday evening. He

    _____ his own dinner every evening.

6. I usually _____ home at night because I have to study. I

    _____ home last night.

7. I have a job at the library. I _____ at the library every evening. I

    _____ there yesterday evening.

8. When I am asleep, I often _____. I _____ about my family last night.★

---
★The past of *dream* can be *dreamed* or *dreamt*.

9. Linda usually _____ for the bus at a bus stop in front of her

apartment building. She _____ for the bus there yesterday morning.

10. The teacher _____ some words from the board a couple of minutes ago. He used his hand instead of an eraser.

11. Our teacher is a warm, friendly person. She often _____ when she is talking to us.

12. Rick doesn't have a beard anymore. He _____ five days ago.

Now he _____ every morning.

## 5-5 PAST TIME WORDS: *YESTERDAY, LAST,* AND *AGO*

NOTICE:

In (a): *yesterday* is used with *morning, afternoon,* and *evening.*

In (b): *last* is used with *night,* with long periods of time *(week, month, year),* with seasons *(spring, summer, etc.),* and with days of the week.

In (c): *ago* means "in the past." It follows specific lengths of time (e.g., *two minutes + ago, five years + ago*).

| *YESTERDAY* | *LAST* | *AGO* |
|---|---|---|
| (a) Bob was here . . . <br>      *yesterday*. <br>      *yesterday morning*. <br>      *yesterday afternoon*. <br>      *yesterday evening*. | (b) Sue was here . . . <br>      *last night*. <br>      *last week*. <br>      *last month*. <br>      *last year*. <br><br>      *last spring*. <br>      *last summer*. <br>      *last fall*. <br>      *last winter*. <br><br>      *last Monday*. <br>      *last Tuesday*. <br>      *last Wednesday*. <br>      *etc.* | (c) Tom was here . . . <br>      *five minutes ago*. <br>      *two hours ago*. <br>      *three days ago*. <br>      *a (one) week ago*. <br>      *six months ago*. <br>      *a (one) year ago*. |

■ **EXERCISE 8:**  Use *yesterday* or *last*.

1. I dreamed about you _____*last*_____ night.

2. I was downtown _____ morning.

3. Two students were absent _____ Friday.

4. Ann wasn't at home _____ night.

5. Ann wasn't at home _____ evening.

6. Carmen was out of town _____ week.

7. I visited my aunt and uncle _____ fall.

8. Roberto walked home _____ afternoon.

9. My sister arrived in Miami _____ Sunday.

10. We watched TV _____ night.

11. Ali played with his children _____ evening.

12. Yoko arrived in Los Angeles _____ summer.

13. I visited my relatives in San Francisco _____ month.

14. My wife and I moved into a new house _____ year.

15. Mrs. Porter washed the kitchen floor _____ morning.

■ **EXERCISE 9:**  Complete the sentences.  Use *ago* in your completion.

1. I'm in class now, but I was at home ___*ten minutes ago/two hours ago/etc.*___

2. I'm in class today, but I was absent from class _____

3. I'm in this country now, but I was in my country _____

4. I was in *(name of a city)* _____

5. I was in elementary school _____

6. I arrived in this city _____

7. There is a nice park in this city.  I was at the park _____

8. We finished EXERCISE 2 _____

9. I was home in bed _____

10. It rained in this city _____

## 5-6 PRONUNCIATION OF -ED: /t/, /d/, AND /əd/

Final -ed has three pronunciations: /t/, /d/, and /əd/.

| END OF VERB | SIMPLE FORM | SIMPLE PAST | PRONUNCIATION | |
|---|---|---|---|---|
| VOICELESS★ | (a) help<br>laugh<br>guess | helped →<br>laughed →<br>guessed → | help/t/<br>laugh/t/<br>guess/t/★★ | • Final -ed is pronounced /t/ if a verb ends in a voiceless sound, as in (a). |
| VOICED★ | (b) rub<br>live<br>seem | rubbed →<br>lived →<br>seemed → | rub/d/<br>liv/d/<br>seem/d/ | • Final -ed is pronounced /d/ if the simple form of the verb ends in a voiced sound, as in (b). |
| -d or -t | (c) need<br>want | needed →<br>wanted → | need/əd/<br>want/əd/ | • Final -ed is pronounced /əd/ if a verb ends in the letters "d" or "t," as in (c). |

  ★  See Chart 2-4 for information about voiced and voiceless sounds.
★★  The words *guessed* and *guest* have the same pronunciation.

■ **EXERCISE 10:** Read the words aloud. Then use the words to complete the sentences.

**GROUP A:** Final -ed is pronounced /t/ after voiceless sounds:

| | | | |
|---|---|---|---|
| 1. walked | ✔ 5. watched | 9. kissed | 13. laughed |
| 2. worked | 6. touched | 10. erased | 14. coughed |
| 3. cooked | 7. washed | 11. helped | |
| 4. asked | 8. finished | 12. stopped | |

15. I _____*watched*_____ TV last night.

16. Anna _____ to class yesterday instead of taking the bus.

17. I _____ the dirty dishes after dinner last night.

18. Jim _____ the board with an eraser.

19. Robert loves his daughter. He _____ her on the forehead.

20. The joke was funny. We _____ at the funny story.

21. The rain _____ a few minutes ago. The sky is clear now.

22. I worked for three hours last night. I _____ my homework about nine o'clock.

23. Steve _____ my shoulder with his hand to get my attention.

24. Mr. Wilson _____ in his garden yesterday morning.

25. Judy _____ because she was sick. She had the flu.

26. Don is a good cook. He _____ some delicious food last night.

27. Linda _____ a question in class yesterday.

28. I had a problem with my homework. The teacher _____ me before class.

**GROUP B:** Final *-ed* is pronounced /d/ after voiced sounds:

| | | |
|---|---|---|
| 1. rained | 5. smiled | 9. remembered |
| 2. signed | 6. killed | 10. played |
| 3. shaved | 7. sneezed | 11. enjoyed |
| 4. arrived | 8. closed | 12. snowed |

13. It's winter. The ground is white because it _____ yesterday.

14. Anita _____ in this city three weeks ago. She

_____ at the airport on September 3rd.★

15. The girls and boys _____ baseball after school yesterday.

16. When Ali got a new credit card, he _____ his name in ink on the back of the card.

17. Rick used to have a beard, but now he doesn't. He _____ this morning.

18. The students' test papers were very good. The teacher, Mr. Jackson, was very

pleased. He _____ when he returned the test papers.

19. I _____ the party last night. It was fun. I had a good time.

20. The window was open. Mr. Chan _____ it because it was cold outside.

21. The streets were wet this morning because it _____ last night.

22. "Achoo!" When Judy _____, Ken said, "Bless you." Oscar said, "Gesundheit!"

---

★Notice preposition usage after *arrive*:
   I arrive *in* a country or *in* a city.
   I arrive *at* a particular place (a building, an airport, a house, an apartment, a party, etc.)
  *Arrive* is followed by either *in* or *at*. *Arrive* is not followed by *to*.
    INCORRECT: *She arrived to the United States.*
    INCORRECT: *She arrived to the airport.*

23. I have my books with me. I didn't forget them today. I

_____ to bring them to class.

24. Mrs. Lane was going crazy because there was a fly
in the room. The fly was buzzing all around

the room. Finally, she _____
it with a rolled up newspaper.

**GROUP C:** Final **-ed** is pronounced /əd/ after /t/ and /d/:

| | |
|---|---|
| 1. waited | 5. invited |
| 2. wanted | 6. needed |
| 3. counted | 7. added |
| 4. visited | 8. folded |

9. The children _____ some candy after dinner.

10. Mr. Miller _____ to stay in the hospital for two weeks after he had
an operation.

11. I _____ the number of students in the room.

12. Mr. and Mrs. Johnson _____ us to come to their house last
Sunday.

13. Last Sunday we _____ the Johnsons.

14. I _____ the letter before I put it in the envelope.

15. Kim _____ for the bus at the corner of 5th Avenue and Main
Street.

16. The boy _____ the numbers on
the chalkboard in arithmetic class yesterday.

■ **EXERCISE 11—ORAL (BOOKS CLOSED):** Practice pronouncing *-ed*.

*Example:*    walk to the front of the room
STUDENT A:   *(Student A walks to the front of the room.)*
TEACHER:   What did ( . . . ) do?
STUDENT B:   She/He walked to the front of the room.
TEACHER:   What did you do?
STUDENT A:   I walked to the front of the room.

| | |
|---|---|
| 1. smile | 11. wash your hands *(pantomime)* |
| 2. laugh | 12. touch the floor |
| 3. cough | 13. point at the door |
| 4. sneeze | 14. fold a piece of paper |
| 5. shave *(pantomime)* | 15. count your fingers |
| 6. erase the board | 16. push *(something in the room)* |
| 7. sign your name | 17. pull *(something in the room)* |
| 8. open the door | 18. yawn |
| 9. close the door | 19. pick up your pen |
| 10. ask a question | 20. add two and two on the board |

## 5-7 SPELLING OF -ED VERBS

| | END OF VERB | → | -ED FORM |
|---|---|---|---|
| Rule 1: | END OF VERB: A CONSONANT + *-e*<br>smi*le*<br>era*se* | → | ADD *-d*<br>smi*led*<br>era*sed* |
| Rule 2: | ONE VOWEL + ONE CONSONANT★<br>st*op*<br>r*ub* | → | DOUBLE THE CONSONANT, ADD *-ed*<br>st*opped*<br>r*ubbed* |
| Rule 3: | TWO VOWELS + ONE CONSONANT<br>r*ain*<br>n*eed* | → | ADD *-ed*; DO NOT DOUBLE THE CONSONANT<br>r*ained*<br>n*eeded* |
| Rule 4: | TWO CONSONANTS<br>cou*nt*<br>he*lp* | → | ADD *-ed*; DO NOT DOUBLE THE CONSONANT<br>cou*nted*<br>he*lped* |
| Rule 5: | CONSONANT + *-y*<br>stu*dy*<br>car*ry* | → | CHANGE *-y* TO *-i*, ADD *-ed*<br>stu*died*<br>car*ried* |
| Rule 6: | VOWEL + *-y*<br>pl*ay*<br>enj*oy* | → | ADD *-ed*; DO NOT CHANGE *-y* TO *-i*<br>pl*ayed*<br>enj*oyed* |

★EXCEPTIONS: Do not double *x* (*fix* + *-ed* = *fixed*). Do not double *w* (*snow* + *-ed* = *snowed*).
NOTE: For two-syllable verbs that end in a vowel and a consonant (e.g., *visit, open*), see Chart 5-8.

■ **EXERCISE 12:** Give the *-ed* and *-ing* forms of these words.*

|  | -ED | -ING |
|---|---|---|
| 1. count | counted | counting |
| 2. stop | | |
| 3. smile | | |
| 4. rain | | |
| 5. help | | |
| 6. dream | | |
| 7. clap | | |
| 8. erase | | |
| 9. rub | | |
| 10. yawn | | |
| 11. study | | |
| 12. stay | | |
| 13. worry | | |
| 14. enjoy | | |

■ **EXERCISE 13:** Use the correct form of the words in the list to complete the sentences.

| carry | ✔ finish | stay |
|---|---|---|
| clap | learn | stop |
| cry | rub | taste |
| enjoy | smile | wait |
| fail | | |

1. I _____ *finished* _____ my homework at nine last night.

2. We _____ some new vocabulary yesterday.

3. I _____ the soup before dinner last night. It was delicious.

4. Linda _____ for the bus at the corner yesterday.

5. The bus _____ at the corner. It was on time.

_____

*See Chart 5-8 for the spelling of *-ing* forms.

6. We _____ the play at the theater last night.  It was very good.

7. At the theater last night, the audience _____ when the play was over.

8. Ann _____ her suitcases to the bus station yesterday.  They weren't heavy.

9. The baby _____ her eyes because she was sleepy.

10. I _____ home and watched a sad movie on TV last night.  I _____ at the end of the movie.

11. Mike _____ his examination last week.  His grade was "F."

12. Jane _____ at the children.  She was happy to see them.

■ **EXERCISE 14:**  Write the correct spelling of the **-ed** form.  Then write the correct pronunciation of the **-ed** form: /t/, /d/, or /əd/.

| | | -ED FORM | PRONUNCIATION | | |
|---|---|---|---|---|---|
| 1. | wait | _waited_ | wait | + | /əd/ |
| 2. | spell | _spelled_ | spell | + | /d/ |
| 3. | kiss | _kissed_ | kiss | + | /t/ |
| 4. | plan | _____ | plan | + | _____ |
| 5. | join | _____ | join | + | _____ |
| 6. | hope | _____ | hope | + | _____ |
| 7. | drop | _____ | drop | + | _____ |
| 8. | add | _____ | add | + | _____ |
| 9. | point | _____ | point | + | _____ |
| 10. | pat | _____ | pat | + | _____ |
| 11. | shout | _____ | shout | + | _____ |
| 12. | reply | _____ | reply | + | _____ |
| 13. | play | _____ | play | + | _____ |
| 14. | touch | _____ | touch | + | _____ |
| 15. | end | _____ | end | + | _____ |

You may not know the meanings of the following words. Figure out the spelling and pronunciation of the **-ed** forms even if you don't know the meanings of the words.

16. mop   _____       mop  + _____

17. droop   _____       droop  + _____

18. cope   _____       cope  + _____

19. rant   _____       rant  + _____

20. date   _____       date  + _____

21. heat   _____       heat  + _____

22. bat   _____       bat  + _____

23. trick   _____       trick  + _____

24. fool   _____       fool  + _____

25. reward   _____       reward  + _____

26. grab   _____       grab  + _____

27. dance   _____       dance  + _____

28. paste   _____       paste  + _____

29. earn   _____       earn  + _____

30. grin   _____       grin  + _____

31. mend   _____       mend  + _____

## 5-8   SPELLING OF *-ED* AND *-ING:* TWO-SYLLABLE VERBS

| | VERB | SPEAKING STRESS | | Some verbs have two syllables. In (a): *visit* has two syllables: *vis + it*. In the word *visit*, the stress is on the first syllable. In (b): the stress is on the second syllable in the word *admit*. |
|---|---|---|---|---|
| (a) | visit | **VIS** · it | | |
| (b) | admit | ad · **MIT** | | |

| | VERB | STRESS | *-ED* FORM | *-ING* FORM | For two-syllable verbs that end in a vowel and a consonant: |
|---|---|---|---|---|---|
| (c) | visit | **VIS** · it | visited | visiting | • The consonant is not doubled if the stress is on the first syllable, as in (c) and (d). |
| (d) | open | **O** · pen | opened | opening | |
| (e) | admit | ad · **MIT** | admitted | admitting | • The consonant is doubled if the stress is on the second syllable, as in (e) and (f). |
| (f) | occur | oc · **CUR** | occurred | occurring | |

■ **EXERCISE 15:** Write the *-ed* and *-ing* forms of the given VERBS.

| | VERB | STRESS | -ED FORM | -ING FORM |
|---|---|---|---|---|
| 1. | answer | **AN** · swer★ | *answered* | *answering* |
| 2. | prefer | pre · **FER** | _____ | _____ |
| 3. | happen | **HAP** · pen | _____ | _____ |
| 4. | visit | **VIS** · it | _____ | _____ |
| 5. | permit | per · **MIT** | _____ | _____ |
| 6. | listen | **LIS** · ten★★ | _____ | _____ |
| 7. | offer | **OF** · fer | _____ | _____ |
| 8. | occur | oc · **CUR** | _____ | _____ |
| 9. | open | **O** · pen | _____ | _____ |
| 10. | enter | **EN** · ter | _____ | _____ |
| 11. | refer | re · **FER** | _____ | _____ |
| 12. | begin | be · **GIN** | ___*(none)*★★★___ | _____ |

■ **EXERCISE 16:** Complete the sentences with the VERBS in the list. Use the *-ed* forms. Use each verb only one time.

| | | |
|---|---|---|
| admit | listen | open |
| ✔ answer | occur | permit |
| happen | offer | visit |

1. The teacher ____*answered*____ a question for me in class.

2. Yesterday I _____ my aunt and uncle at their home.

3. We _____ to some music after dinner last night.

4. It was okay for the children to have some candy after lunch. Mrs. King

    _____ them to have a little candy.

5. I _____ the window because the room was hot.

_____

★ The "w" is not pronounced in *answer*.
★★ The "t" is not pronounced in *listen*.
★★★ The verb *begin* does not have an *-ed* form. Its past form is irregular: *began*.

6. A car accident _____ at the corner of 5th Street and Main yesterday.

7. A bicycle accident _____ on Forest Avenue yesterday.

8. My friend poured a glass of water and held it toward me.  She asked me if I wanted it.

   She _____ me a glass of water.

9. A man unlocked the gate and _____ the sports fans into the stadium.

ENTRANCE TO MEMORIAL STADIUM

ADMISSION TICKETS

■ **EXERCISE 17—ORAL/WRITTEN (BOOKS CLOSED):**  This is a spelling test.  Give the *-ed* form of each word.

| | | | |
|---|---|---|---|
| 1. stop | 6. rain | 11. carry | 16. occur |
| 2. wait | 7. permit | 12. open | 17. stay |
| 3. study | 8. listen | 13. fold | 18. help |
| 4. smile | 9. rub | 14. offer | 19. drop |
| 5. enjoy | 10. visit | 15. happen | 20. count |

■ **EXERCISE 18:**  Complete the sentences.  Use the words in parentheses.  Use the SIMPLE PRESENT, PRESENT PROGRESSIVE, or SIMPLE PAST.  Pay attention to spelling and pronunciation.

1. I *(walk)* _____*walked*_____ to school yesterday.

2. I *(sit)* _____*am sitting*_____ in class right now.

3. I usually *(go)* _____*go*_____ to bed at eleven o'clock every night.

4. Sally *(finish)* _____ her homework at ten o'clock last night.

5. I (study) _____ at the library yesterday.

6. I (study) _____ English every day.

7. I am in class right now. I (study) _____ English.

8. I need an umbrella because it (rain) _____ right now.

9. It (rain) _____ yesterday morning.

10. My roommate (help) _____ me with my homework last night.

11. We can go outside now. The rain (stop) _____ a few minutes ago.

12. The children are in the park. They (play) _____ baseball.

13. I (play) _____ soccer last week.

14. Yesterday morning I (brush) _____ my teeth, (wash) _____ my face, and (shave) _____.

15. Ann is in her living room right now. She (watch) _____ television.

16. Ann usually (watch) _____ TV in the evening.

17. She (watch) _____ a good program on TV last night.

18. We (do) _____ an exercise in class right now. We (use) _____ verb tenses in sentences.

19. I (arrive) _____ in this city a month ago.

20. Matt (listen) _____ to music every morning while he's getting ready to go to school.

21. A: Where's Matt?
    B: He's in his room?

    A: What (do, he) _____?

    B: He (listen) _____ to music.

22. A: (you, listen) _____ to the news every day?

    B: Yes. I (like) _____ to know about events in the world.

    I usually (listen) _____ to the news on TV before I go

    to sleep at night, but last night I (listen) _____ to the news on the radio.

Some verbs do not have **-ed** forms. The past form is irregular.

| PRESENT | PAST |
|---------|------|
| *come* | *– came* |
| *do* | *– did* |
| *eat* | *– ate* |
| *get* | *– got* |
| *go* | *– went* |
| *have* | *– had* |
| *put* | *– put* |
| *see* | *– saw* |
| *sit* | *– sat* |
| *sleep* | *– slept* |
| *stand* | *– stood* |
| *write* | *– wrote* |

(a) I **come** to class **every day**.
(b) I *came* to class **yesterday**.

(c) I **do** my homework **every day**.
(d) I *did* my homework **yesterday**.

(e) Ann **eats** breakfast **every morning**.
(f) Ann *ate* breakfast **yesterday morning**.

■ **EXERCISE 19—ORAL:** Change the sentences to the past.

1. Tom gets some mail every day.
   → *Tom got some mail yesterday.*
2. They go downtown every day.
3. We have lunch every day.
4. I see my friends every day.
5. Hamid sits in the front row every day.
6. I sleep for eight hours every night.
7. The students stand in line at the cafeteria.
8. I write a letter to my parents every week.
9. Wai-Leng comes to class late every day.
10. We do exercises in class every day.
11. I eat breakfast every morning.
12. I get up at seven every day.
13. Robert puts his books in his briefcase every day.

■ **EXERCISE 20—ORAL (BOOKS CLOSED):** Change the sentences to the past.

*Example:* I come to class every day.
*Response:* I came to class yesterday.

1. I eat lunch every day.
2. I see you every day.
3. I sit in class every day.
4. I write a letter every day.
5. I do my homework every day.
6. I have breakfast every day.
7. I go downtown every day.
8. I get up at eight every day.
9. I stand at the bus stop every day.
10. I sleep for eight hours every night.
11. I come to school every day.
12. I put my pen in my pocket every day.

■ **EXERCISE 21:** Complete the sentences. Use the words in parentheses. Use SIMPLE PRESENT, PRESENT PROGRESSIVE, or SIMPLE PAST. Pay attention to spelling and pronunciation.

1. I *(get)* _____got_____ up at eight o'clock yesterday morning.

2. Mary *(talk)* _____ to John on the phone last night.

3. Mary *(talk)* _____ to John on the phone right now.

4. Mary *(talk)* _____ to John on the phone every day.

5. Jim and I *(eat)* _____ lunch at the cafeteria two hours ago.

6. We *(eat)* _____ lunch at the cafeteria every day.

7. I *(go)* _____ to bed early last night.

8. My roommate *(study)* _____ Spanish last year.

9. Sue *(write)* _____ a letter to her parents yesterday.

10. Sue *(write)* _____ a letter to her parents every week.

11. Sue is in her room right now. She *(sit)* _____ at her desk.

12. Maria *(do)* _____ her homework last night.

13. Yesterday I *(see)* _____ Fumiko at the library.

14. I *(have)* _____ a dream last night. I *(dream)* _____ about my friends. I *(sleep)* _____ for eight hours.

15. A strange thing *(happen)* _____ to me yesterday. I couldn't remember my own telephone number.

16. My wife *(come)* _____ home around five every day.

17. Yesterday she *(come)* _____ home at 5:15.

18. Our teacher *(stand)* _____ in the middle of the room right now.

19. Our teacher *(stand)* _____ in the front of the room yesterday.

20. Tom *(put)* _____ the butter in the refrigerator yesterday.

21. He *(put)* _____ the milk in the refrigerator every day.

22. Pablo usually *(sit)* _____ in the back of the room, but yesterday he *(sit)* _____ in the front row. Today he *(be)* _____ absent. He *(be)* _____ absent two days ago too.

## 5-10 THE SIMPLE PAST: NEGATIVE

| SUBJECT | + | DID | + | NOT | + | MAIN VERB | | |
|---------|---|-----|---|-----|---|-----------|---|---|
| (a) I | | **did** | | **not** | | **walk** | to school yesterday. | |
| (b) You | | **did** | | **not** | | **walk** | to school yesterday. | |
| (c) Tom | | **did** | | **not** | | **eat** | lunch yesterday. | |
| (d) They | | **did** | | **not** | | **come** | to class yesterday. | |

$\left.\begin{array}{l} I \\ you \\ she \\ he \\ it \\ we \\ they \end{array}\right\}$ + **did not** + *main verb★* (simple form)

| | |
|---|---|
| (e) INCORRECT: I *did not walked* to school yesterday. <br> (f) INCORRECT: Tom *did not ate* lunch yesterday. | Notice that the simple form of the main verb is used with **did not**. |
| (g) I **didn't walk** to school yesterday. <br> (h) Tom **didn't eat** lunch yesterday. | Negative contraction: <br> **did** + **not** = **didn't** |

*EXCEPTION: **did** is NOT used when the main verb is **be**. See Charts 5-2 and 5-3.
INCORRECT: Joe *didn't be* here yesterday.
CORRECT: Joe *wasn't* here yesterday.

■ **EXERCISE 22—ORAL (BOOKS CLOSED):** Use "**I don't . . . every day**" and "**I didn't . . . yesterday**."

*Example:* walk to school
*Response:* I don't walk to school every day. I didn't walk to school yesterday.

1. eat breakfast
2. watch TV
3. go shopping
4. read the newspaper
5. study
6. go to the library
7. visit my friends
8. see ( . . . )
9. do my homework
10. shave

■ **EXERCISE 23—ORAL (BOOKS CLOSED):** Practice present and past negatives.
STUDENT A: Use **I don't** and **I didn't**. Use an appropriate past time expression with **didn't**.
STUDENT B: Report what Student A said. Use **she/he doesn't** and then **she/he didn't** with an appropriate past time expression.

*Example:* walk to school every morning
STUDENT A: I don't walk to school every morning. I didn't walk to school yesterday morning.
TEACHER: Tell me about (Student A).
STUDENT B: She/He doesn't walk to school every morning. She/He didn't walk to school yesterday morning.

1. eat breakfast every morning
2. watch TV every night
3. talk to ( . . . ) every day
4. play soccer every afternoon
5. study grammar every evening
6. dream in English every night
7. visit my aunt and uncle every year
8. write to my parents every week
9. read the newspaper every morning
10. pay all of my bills every month

■ **EXERCISE 24:** Complete the sentences. Use the words in parentheses. Use SIMPLE PRESENT, SIMPLE PAST, or PRESENT PROGRESSIVE.

1. I *(go, not)* _____*didn't go*_____ to a movie last night. I *(stay)*

_____*stayed*_____ home.

2. Mike *(come, not)* _____*doesn't come*_____ to class every day.

3. I *(finish, not)* _____ my homework last night. I *(go)*

_____ to bed early.

4. Jane *(stand, not)* _____ up right now. She *(sit)*

_____ down.

5. It *(rain, not)* _____ right now. The rain *(stop)*

_____ a few minutes ago.

6. The weather *(be, not)* _____ cold today, but it *(be)* _____
cold yesterday.

7. Tina and I *(go, not)* _____ shopping yesterday. We *(go)*

_____ shopping last Monday.

8. I *(go)* _____ to a movie last night, but I *(enjoy, not)* _____

it. It *(be, not)* _____ very good.

9. I *(write)* _____ a letter to my girlfriend yesterday, but I *(write, not)*

_____ a letter to her last week.

10. Sue *(read)* _____ a magazine right now. She *(watch, not)*

_____ TV.

11. My husband *(come, not)* _____ home for dinner last night.

12. The children *(go)* _____ to bed a half an hour ago. They *(sleep)*

_____ now.

13. We *(be)* _____ late for the movie last night. The movie *(start)*

_____ at seven, but we *(arrive, not)* _____

until seven-fifteen.

14. Olga *(ask)* _____ Hamid a question a few minutes ago, but he

*(answer, not)* _____ her question.

15. Toshi is a busy student. He usually *(eat, not)* _____

lunch because he *(have, not)* _____ enough time
between classes.

16. He *(eat)* _____ lunch the day before yesterday, but he *(eat, not)*

_____ lunch yesterday.

## 5-11 THE SIMPLE PAST: *YES/NO* QUESTIONS

| *DID* + SUBJECT + MAIN VERB | SHORT ANSWER + (LONG ANSWER) |
|---|---|
| (a) **Did** **Mary** **walk** to school? → <br> → | **Yes, she did**. (She walked to school.) <br> **No, she didn't**. (She didn't walk to school.) |
| (b) **Did** **you** **come** to class? → <br> → | **Yes, I did**. (I came to class.) <br> **No, I didn't**. (I didn't come to class.) |

■ **EXERCISE 25:** Make questions. Give short answers.

1. A: _____ *Did you walk downtown yesterday?* _____

   B: _____ *Yes, I did.* _____ (I walked downtown yesterday.)

2. A: _____ *Did it rain last week?* _____

   B: _____ *No, it didn't.* _____ (It didn't rain last week.)

3. A: _____

   B: _____ (I ate lunch at the cafeteria.)

4.  A: _____

    B: _____ (Mr. Kwan didn't go out of town last week.)

5.  A: _____

    B: _____ (I had a cup of tea this morning.)

6.  A: _____

    B: _____ (Benito and I went to a party last night.)

7.  A: _____

    B: _____ (Olga studied English in high school.)

8.  A: _____

    B: _____ (Yoko and Ali didn't do their homework last night.)

9.  A: _____

    B: _____ (I saw Gina at dinner last night.)

10. A: _____

    B: _____ (I didn't dream in English last night.)

■ **EXERCISE 26:**  Complete the sentences with *was*, *were*, or *did*.

1.  I _____*did*_____ not go to work yesterday.  I _____*was*_____ sick, so I stayed home from the office.

2.  Tom _____ not in his office yesterday.  He _____ not go to work.

3.  A: _____ Mr. Chan in his office yesterday?
    B: Yes.

    A: _____ you see him about your problem?

    B: Yes.  He answered all my questions.  He _____ very helpful.

4.  A: _____ you at the meeting yesterday?
    B: What meeting?

    A: _____ you forget about the meeting?
    B: I guess so.  What meeting?
    A: The meeting with the president of the company about employee benefits.

    B: Oh.  Now I remember.  No, I _____ not there.  _____ you?
    A: Yes.  I can tell you all about it.
    B: Thanks.

5. A: Where _____ you yesterday?

   B: I _____ at the zoo.

   A: _____ you enjoy it?

   B: Yes, but the weather _____ very hot. I tried to stay out of the sun. Most

   of the animals _____ in their houses or in the shade. The sun

   _____ too hot for them, too. They _____ not want to be
   outside in the hot sun.

■ **EXERCISE 27:** Make questions. Give short answers.

   1. A: _____*Were you at home last night?*_____

      B: _____*No, I wasn't.*_____ (I wasn't at home last night.)

      A: _____*Did you go to a movie?*_____

      B: _____*Yes, I did.*_____ (I went to a movie.)

   2. A: _____

      B: _____ (It isn't cold today.)

   3. A: _____

      B: _____ (I come to class every day.)

   4. A: _____

      B : _____ (Roberto was absent yesterday.)

   5. A: _____

      B: _____ (Roberto stayed home yesterday.)

   6. A: _____

      B: _____ (I don't watch television every day.)

   7. A: _____

      B: _____ (Mohammed isn't in class today.)

      A: _____

      B: _____ (He was here yesterday.)

      A: _____

      B: _____ (He came to class the day before yesterday.)

      A: _____

      B: _____ (He usually comes to class every day.)

8. A: _____

   B: _____ (I live in an apartment.)

   A: _____

   B: _____ (I don't have a roommate.)

   A: _____

   B: _____ (I don't want a roommate.)

   A: _____

   B: _____ (I had a roommate last year.)  It didn't work out.

   A: _____

   B: _____ (He was difficult to live with.)
   A: What did he do?
   B: He never picked up his dirty clothes.  He never washed his dirty dishes.  He was always late with his share of the rent.

   A: _____

   B: _____ (I asked him to keep the apartment clean.)  He always agreed, but he never did it.

   A: _____

   B: _____ (I was glad when he left.)  I like living alone.

■ **EXERCISE 28—ORAL (BOOKS CLOSED):**   Ask a classmate a question about her/his activities this morning.

*Example:*    walk to school
STUDENT A:  Did you walk to school this morning?
STUDENT B:  Yes, I did.   OR:  No, I didn't.

   1. get up at seven          7. smoke a cigarette
   2. eat breakfast            8. go shopping
   3. study English            9. have a cup of coffee
   4. walk to class           10. watch TV
   5. talk to ( . . . )       11. listen to the radio
   6. see ( . . . )           12. read a newspaper

■ **EXERCISE 29—ORAL (BOOKS CLOSED):** Ask questions about the present and the past.

*Example:* walk to school
STUDENT A: Do you walk to school every day?
STUDENT B: Yes, I do.  OR:  No, I don't.
STUDENT A: Did you walk to school this morning?
STUDENT B: Yes, I did.  OR:  No, I didn't.

1. go downtown
2. dream in color
3. talk to ( . . . ) on the phone
4. come to (grammar) class
5. sing in the shower
6. eat at least two pieces of fresh fruit
7. think about your family
8. cook your own dinner
9. wear *(an article of clothing)*
10. laugh out loud at least two times
11. speak *(name of a language)*
12. go to *(name of a place in this city)*
13. read at least one book
14. go swimming
15. go shopping

■ **EXERCISE 30—ORAL (BOOKS CLOSED):** Review of irregular verbs. Answer all the questions "yes." Give both a short answer and a long answer.

*Example:* Did you come to class today?
*Response:* Yes, I did.  I came to class today.

1. Did you eat dinner last night?
2. Did ( . . . ) come to class today?
3. Did you get a letter yesterday?
4. Did ( . . . ) go shopping yesterday?
5. Did ( . . . ) do his/her homework last night?
6. Did you sleep well last night?
7. Did you have a cup of coffee this morning?
8. Did ( . . . ) go to a movie last night?
9. Did ( . . . ) sit in that chair yesterday?
10. Did you write a letter yesterday.?
11. *(Tell a student to stand up.)* Did ( . . . ) stand up?  *(Tell him/her to sit down.)* Did ( . . . ) sit down?
12. Did ( . . . ) put his/her books on his/her desk this *(morning / afternoon / evening)?*

## 5-12  MORE IRREGULAR VERBS

| | | |
|---|---|---|
| ***bring - brought*** | ***drive - drove*** | ***run - ran*** |
| ***buy - bought*** | ***read - read\**** | ***teach - taught*** |
| ***catch - caught*** | ***ride - rode*** | ***think - thought*** |
| ***drink - drank*** | | |

★The past form of *read* is pronounced the same as the color red.

■ **EXERCISE 31—ORAL (BOOKS CLOSED):** Practice using irregular verbs.

*Example:*  teach-taught
TEACHER:  teach, taught. I teach class every day. I taught class yesterday. What did I do yesterday?
STUDENTS:  teach, taught. You taught class.

1. *bring-brought*  I bring my book to class every day. I brought my book to class yesterday. What did I do yesterday?

2. *buy-bought*  I buy books at the bookstore. I bought a book yesterday. What did I do yesterday?

3. *teach-taught*  I teach class every day. I taught class yesterday. What did I do yesterday?

4. *catch-caught*  I catch the bus every day. I caught the bus yesterday. What did I do yesterday?

5. *think-thought*  I often think about my family. I thought about my family yesterday. What did I do yesterday?

6. REVIEW:  What did I bring to class yesterday? What did you bring yesterday?
   What did I buy yesterday? What did you buy yesterday?
   Did you teach class yesterday? Who did?
   Did I walk to class yesterday or did I catch the bus?
   What did I think about yesterday? What did you think about yesterday?

7. *run-ran*  Sometimes I'm late for class, so I run. Yesterday I was late, so I ran. What did I do yesterday?

8. *read-read*  I like to read books. I read every day. Yesterday I read a book. What did I do yesterday? What did you read yesterday?

9. *drink-drank*  I usually drink a cup of coffee in the morning. I drank a cup of coffee this morning. What did I do this morning? Did you drink a cup of coffee this morning?

10. *drive-drove*  I usually drive my car to school. I drove my car to school this morning. What did I do this morning? Who has a car? Did you drive to school this morning?

11. *ride-rode*  Sometimes I ride the bus to school. I rode the bus yesterday morning. What did I do yesterday morning? Who rode the bus to school this morning?

12. REVIEW:  I was late for class yesterday morning, so what did I do?
   What did I read yesterday? What did you read yesterday?
   Did you read a newspaper this morning?
   What did I drink this morning? What did you drink this morning?
   I have a car. Did I drive to school this morning? Did you?
   Did you ride the bus to school this morning?

■ **EXERCISE 32:** Complete the sentences. Use the words in parentheses.

1. A: Why are you out of breath?

   B: I *(run)* _____ to class because I was late.

2. A: *(Ms. Carter, teach)* _____ class
   yesterday?

   B: No, she didn't. Mr. Adams *(teach)* _____ our class.

3. A: I *(ride)* _____ the bus to school yesterday. How did you
   get to school?

   B: I *(drive)* _____ my car.

4. A: Did you decide to change schools?

   B: I *(think)* _____ about it, but then I decided to stay here.

5. A: *(you, go)* _____ shopping yesterday?

   B: Yes. I *(buy)* _____ a new pair of shoes.

6. A: *(you, study)* _____ last night?

   B: No, I didn't. I was tired. I *(read)* _____ a magazine and then

   *(go)* _____ to bed early.

7. A: Do you like milk?

   B: No. I *(drink)* _____ milk when I *(be)* _____ a child,
   but I don't like milk now.

8. A: Did you leave your dictionary at home?

   B: No. I *(bring)* _____ it to class with me.

9. A: Did you enjoy your fishing trip?

   B: I had a wonderful time! I *(catch)* _____ a lot of fish.

■ **EXERCISE 33:** Complete the sentences. Use the verbs in parentheses.

1. Ann and I *(go)* _____ to the bookstore yesterday. I *(buy)*

   _____ some stationery and a T-shirt.

2. I had to go downtown yesterday. I *(catch)* _____ the bus in front

   of my apartment and *(ride)* _____ to Grand Avenue. Then I

   *(get off)* _____ the bus and transferred to another one. It *(be)*

   _____ a long trip.

3. Sue *(eat)* _____ popcorn and *(drink)* _____ a

   cola at the movie theater last night. I *(eat, not)* _____ anything.
   I'm on a diet.

4. Maria (ask) _____ the teacher a question in class yesterday. The

   teacher (think) _____ about the question for a few minutes and
   then said, "I don't know."

5. I (want) _____ (go) _____ to the basketball

   game last night, but I (stay) _____ home because I had to study.

6. Last night I (read) _____ an article in the newspaper. It (be)

   _____ about the snowstorm in Moscow.

7. Yesterday Yoko (teach) _____ us how to say "thank you" in

   Japanese. Kim (teach) _____ us how to say "I love you" in
   Korean.

8. When Ben and I (go) _____ to the department store yesterday, I

   (buy) _____ some new socks. Ben (buy, not) _____ anything.

9. Rita (pass, not) _____ the test yesterday. She (fail)

   _____ it.

10. Last summer we (drive) _____ to Colorado for our vacation. We

    (visit) _____ a national park, where we (camp) _____

    in our tent for a week. We (go) _____ fishing one morning. I

    (catch) _____ a

    very big fish, but my husband

    (catch, not) _____

    anything. We (enjoy) _____

    cooking and eating the fish for dinner.

    It (be) _____ delicious.

    I like fresh fish.

11. I almost *(have)* _____ an accident yesterday. A dog *(run)*

_____ into the street in front of my car. I *(slam)*

_____ on my brakes and just *(miss)* _____ the dog.

12. Yesterday I *(play)* _____ ball with my little boy. He *(catch)*

_____ the ball most of the time, but sometimes he *(drop)*

_____ it.

■ **EXERCISE 34—ORAL (BOOKS CLOSED):**  Ask and answer questions using the SIMPLE PAST.

STUDENT A: Ask a classmate a question. Use the given verb. Use the past tense.
STUDENT B: Answer the question. Give both a short answer and a long answer.

*Example:*  drink
STUDENT A: Did you drink a cup of coffee this morning?
STUDENT B: Yes, I did. I drank a cup of coffee this morning. OR: No, I didn't. I didn't drink a cup of coffee this morning.

| | | |
|---|---|---|
| 1. eat | 7. drink | 13. walk |
| 2. buy | 8. read | 14. watch |
| 3. get up | 9. drive | 15. listen to |
| 4. have | 10. sleep | 16. see |
| 5. go | 11. go | 17. think about |
| 6. study | 12. talk to | 18. rain |

■ **EXERCISE 35—WRITTEN:**  Use the expressions in the list below to write sentences about yourself. When did you do these things *in the past?* Use the SIMPLE PAST tense and past time expressions *(yesterday, two days ago, last week, etc.)* in all of your sentences.

*Example:* go downtown with *(someone)*
*Response:* I went downtown with Marco two days ago.

| | |
|---|---|
| 1. arrive in *(this city)* | 12. talk to *(someone)* on the phone |
| 2. write a letter to *(someone)* | 13. go shopping |
| 3. eat at a restaurant | 14. study English |
| 4. go to bed early | 15. read a newspaper |
| 5. buy *(something)* | 16. go on a picnic |
| 6. go to bed late | 17. go to a party |
| 7. get up early | 18. play *(soccer, a pinball machine, etc.)* |
| 8. be late for class | 19. see *(someone or something)* |
| 9. have a cold | 20. think about *(someone or something)* |
| 10. be in elementary school | 21. do my homework |
| 11. drink a cup of tea | 22. be born |

## 5-13 THE SIMPLE PAST: USING *WHERE, WHEN, WHAT TIME,* AND *WHY*

| QUESTION | | | | | | | SHORT ANSWER |
|---|---|---|---|---|---|---|---|
| (a) | | *Did* | you | *go* | downtown? | → | Yes, I did. / No, I didn't. |
| (b) | **Where** | *did* | you | *go?* | | → | **Downtown.** |
| (c) | | *Did* | you | *run* | because you were late? | → | Yes, I did. / No, I didn't. |
| (d) | **Why** | *did* | you | *run?* | | → | **Because I was late.** |
| (e) | | *Did* | Ann | *come* | at six? | → | Yes, she did. / No, she didn't. |
| (f) | **When** **What time** | *did* | Ann | *come?* | | → | **At six.** |

| | | |
|---|---|---|
| COMPARE: | | |
| (g) **What time** did Ann come? → **At six.** <br> → **Seven o'clock.** <br> → **Around 9:30.** | | **What time** usually asks specifically for time on a clock. |
| (h) **When** did Ann come? → **At six.** <br> → **Friday.** <br> → **June 15th.** <br> → **Last week.** <br> → **Three days ago.** | | The answer to **when** can be various expressions of time. |

■ **EXERCISE 36:** Make questions. Use *where, when, what time,* or *why.*

1. A: _____*Where did you go yesterday?*_____
   B: To the zoo. (I went to the zoo yesterday.)

2. A: _____
   B: Last month. (Jason arrived in Canada last month.)

3. A: _____
   B: At 7:05. (My plane arrived at 7:05.)

4. A: _____
   B: Because I was tired. (I stayed home last night because I was tired.)

5. A: _____
   B: At the library. (I studied at the library last night.)

6. A: _____
   B: Because it's dark in here. (I turned on the light because it's dark in here.)

7. A: _____
   B: To Greece. (Sara went to Greece for her vacation.)

8. A: _____
   B: Around midnight. (I finished my homework around midnight.)

9. A: _____
   B: Five weeks ago.  (I came to this city five weeks ago.)

10. A: _____
    B: Because Tony made a funny face.  (I laughed because Tony made a funny face.)

11. A: _____
    B: At Emerhoff's Shoe Store.  (I got my sandals at Emerhoff's Shoe Store.)

12. A: _____
    B: Upstairs. (Kate is upstairs.)

13. A: _____
    B: In the dormitory.  (Ben lives in the dormitory.)

14. A: _____
    B: To the park.  (I went to the park yesterday afternoon.)

15. A: _____
    B: Because he's sick.  (Bobby is in bed because he's sick.)

16. A: _____
    B: Because he was sick.  (Bobby stayed home because he was sick.)

17. A: _____
    B: 7:20.  (The movie starts at 7:20.)

18. A: _____
    B: Two days ago.  (Sara got back from Brazil two days ago.)

19. A: _____
    B: Because she wanted to talk to Joe.  (Tina called because she wanted to talk to Joe.)

20. A: _____
    B: Because he wants big muscles.  (Jim lifts weights because he wants big muscles.)

*Example:*   I got up at 7:30.
*Response:*   When/What time did you get up?

1.  I went to the zoo.
2.  I went to the zoo yesterday.
3.  I went to the zoo yesterday because I wanted to see the animals.
4.  ( . . . ) went to the park.
5.  ( . . . ) went to the park yesterday.
6.  ( . . . ) went to the park yesterday because the weather was nice.
7.  I am in class.
8.  I came to class (an hour) ago.
9.  ( . . . ) is in class.
10.  ( . . . ) came to class (an hour) ago.
11.  ( . . . ) studied at the library last night.
12.  ( . . . ) finished his/her homework around midnight.
13.  ( . . . ) went to bed at 7:30 last night.
14.  ( . . . ) went to bed early because he/she was tired.
15.  ( . . . ) went to the park.
16.  ( . . . ) went to the park yesterday.
17.  ( . . . ) went to the park yesterday because he/she wanted to jog.
18.  ( . . . ) is absent today because he/she is sick.
19.  ( . . . ) is at home.
20.  ( . . . ) stayed home because he/she is sick.

■ **EXERCISE 38:**   Complete the dialogues with questions that begin with ***why didn't***.

1.  A:  _____*Why didn't you come to class?*_____
    B:  Because I was sick.

2.  A:  _____
    B:  Because I didn't have enough time.

3.  A:  _____
    B:  Because I forgot your phone number.

4.  A:  _____
    B:  Because I had a headache.

5.  A:  _____
    B:  Because I wasn't hungry.

6.  A:  _____
    B:  Because I didn't want to.

■ **EXERCISE 39:** Use your own words to complete the dialogues with questions that begin with *why*, *when*, *what time*, and *where*.

1. A:  *Where do you want to go for your vacation?*
   B: Hawaii.

2. A: _____
   B: Ten o'clock.

3. A: _____
   B: Because I was tired.

4. A: _____
   B: Last week.

5. A: _____
   B: South America.

6. A: _____
   B: Because I forgot.

7. A: _____
   B: Downtown.

8. A: _____
   B: Several months ago.

9. A: _____
   B: At a Chinese restaurant.

## 5-14 QUESTIONS WITH *WHAT*

*What* is used in a question when you want to find out about a thing. *Who* is used when you want to find out about a person. (See Chart 5-15 for questions with *who*.)

| (QUESTION + WORD) | HELPING + VERB | SUBJECT + | MAIN VERB | | | ANSWER |
|---|---|---|---|---|---|---|
| (a) | *Did* | Carol | *buy* | a car? | → | *Yes, she did.* (She bought a car.) |
| (b) *What* | *did* | Carol | *buy*? | | → | *A car.* (She bought a car.) |
| (c) | *Is* | Fred | *holding* | a book? | → | *Yes, he is.* (He's holding a book.) |
| (d) *What* | *is* | Fred | *holding*? | | → | *A book.* (He's holding a book.) |

| | |
|---|---|
|      s     v     o<br>(e) Carol bought *a car*. | In (e): *a car* is the object of the verb. |
|      o    v    s    v<br>(f) *What* did Carol buy? | In (f): *what* is the object of the verb. |

■ **EXERCISE 40:** Make questions.

1. A:   *Did you buy a new tape recorder?*
   B: Yes, I did.  (I bought a new tape recorder.)

2. A:   *What did you buy?*
   B: A new tape recorder.  (I bought a new tape recorder.)

3. A: _____
   B: Yes, she is.  (Mary is carrying a suitcase.)

4. A: _____
   B: A suitcase.  (Mary is carrying a suitcase.)

5. A: _____
   B: Yes, I do.  (I see that airplane.)

6. A: _____
   B: An airplane.  (I see an airplane.)

7. A: _____
   B: A hamburger.  (Bob ate a hamburger for lunch.)

8. A: _____
   B: Yes, he did.  (Bob ate a hamburger for lunch.)

9. A: _____
   B: A sandwich.  (Bob usually eats a sandwich for lunch.)

10. A: _____
    B: No, he doesn't.  (Bob doesn't like salads.)

■ **EXERCISE 41:** Make questions.

1. A:   *What did John talk about?*
   B: His country.  (John talked about his country.)

2. A:   *Did John talk about his country?*
   B: Yes, he did.  (John talked about his country.)

3. A: _____
   B: A bird.  (I'm looking at a bird.)

4. A: _____
   B: Yes, I am.  (I'm looking at that bird.)

5. A: _____
   B: Yes, I am.  (I'm interested in science.)

6. A: _____
   B: Science.  (I'm interested in science.)

7. A: _____
   B: Nothing in particular.  (I'm thinking about nothing in particular.)

8. A: _____
   B: English grammar.  (I dreamed about English grammar last night.)

9. A: _____
   B: The map on the wall.  (The teacher is pointing at the map on the wall.)

10. A: _____
    B: No, I'm not.  (I'm not afraid of snakes.)  Are you?

■ **EXERCISE 42—ORAL (BOOKS CLOSED):**   Ask a classmate a question.  Use ***what*** and either a past or present verb.

*Example:*       eat
STUDENT A:   What did you eat for breakfast this morning? / What do you usually eat for dinner? / etc.
STUDENT A:   *(free response)*

1. eat                    6. be interested in
2. wear                   7. be afraid of
3. look at                8. dream about
4. study                  9. have
5. think about           10. need to buy

| QUESTION | | ANSWER | |
|---|---|---|---|
| (a) **What** did they see? | → | **A boat**. *(They saw a boat.)* | **What** is used to ask questions about things.<br>**Who** is used to ask questions about people. |
| (b) **Who** did they see? | → | **Jim**. *(They saw Jim.)* | |

| QUESTION | | ANSWER | |
|---|---|---|---|
| (c) **Who** did they see? | → | **Jim**. *(They saw Jim.)* | (c) and (d) have the same meaning.<br>**Whom** is used in formal English as the object of a verb or a preposition.<br>In (c): **who**, not **whom**, is usually used in everyday English.<br>In (d): **whom** is used in very formal English. **Whom** is rarely used in everyday spoken English. |
| (d) **Whom** did they see? | → | **Jim**. *(They saw Jim.)* | |

| QUESTION | | ANSWER | |
|---|---|---|---|
|          o<br>(e) **Who(m)** did they see? | → |          o<br>**Jim**. *(They saw **Jim**.)* | In (e): **who(m)** is the object of the verb. Usual question word order *(question word + helping verb + subject + main verb)* is used. |
|      s<br>(f) **Who** came? | → |      s<br>**Mary**. *(**Mary** came.)* | In (f), (g), and (h): **who** is the subject of the question. Usual question word order is NOT used. When **who** is the subject of a question, do NOT use **does**, **do**, or **did**. Do NOT change the verb in any way: the verb form in the question is the same as the verb form in the answer.<br>INCORRECT: *Who did come?* |
| (g) **Who** lives there? | → | **Ed**. *(**Ed** lives there.)* | |
| (h) **Who** saw Jim? | → | **Ann**. *(**Ann** saw Jim.)* | |

■ **EXERCISE 43:**   Make questions.

1. A: _____
   B: Mary.  (I saw Mary at the party.)

2. A: _____
   B: Mary.  (Mary came to the party.)

3. A: _____
   B: John.  (John lives in that house.)

4. A: _____
   B: John.  (I called John.)

5. A: _____
   B: My aunt and uncle. (I visited my aunt and uncle.)

6. A: _____
   B: My cousin.  (My cousin visited me.)

7. A: _____
   B: Bob.  (Bob helped Ann.)

8. A: _____
   B: Ann.  (Bob helped Ann.)

9. A: _____
   B: Yes, he did.  (Bob helped Ann.)

10. A: _____
    B: No, I'm not.  (I'm not confused.)

■ **EXERCISE 44:**   Make questions.

1. A: _____
   B: Ken.  (I saw Ken.)

2. A: _____
   B: Ken.  (I talked to Ken.)

3. A: _____
   B: Nancy.  (I visited Nancy.)

4. A: _____
   B: Mary.  (I'm thinking about Mary.)

5. A: _____
   B: Yuko.  (Yuko called.)

6. A: _____
   B: Ahmed.  (Ahmed answered the question.)

7. A: _____
   B: Mr. Lee.  (Mr. Lee taught the English class.)

8. A: _____
   B: Carlos.  (Carlos helped me.)

9. A: _____
   B. Gina.  (I helped Gina.)

10. A: _____
    B: My brother.  (My brother carried my suitcase.)

■ **EXERCISE 45:** Make questions. Use any appropriate question word: *where, when, what time, why, who, what*.

1. A: _____
   B: To the zoo. (Ann went to the zoo.)

2. A: _____
   B: Yesterday. (Ann went to the zoo yesterday.)

3. A: _____
   B: Ann. (Ann went to the zoo yesterday.)

4. A: _____
   B: Ali. (I saw Ali.)

5. A: _____
   B: At the zoo. (I saw Ali at the zoo.)

6. A: _____
   B: Yesterday. (I saw Ali at the zoo yesterday.)

7. A: _____
   B: Because the weather was nice. (I went to the zoo yesterday because the weather was nice.)

8. A: _____
   B: Dr. Jones. (I talked to Dr. Jones.)

9. A: _____
   B: Dr. Jones. (Dr. Jones called.)

10. A: _____
    B: Yesterday afternoon. (Dr. Jones called yesterday afternoon.)

11. A: _____
    B: At home. (I was at home yesterday afternoon.)

12. A: _____
    B: In an apartment. (I'm living in an apartment.)

13. A: _____
    B: Grammar. (The teacher is talking about grammar.)

14. A: _____
    B: A frog. (Annie has a frog in her pocket.)

## 5-16  ASKING ABOUT THE MEANING OF A WORD

| | |
|---|---|
| (a) **What does** "pretty" **mean**? | (a) and (b) have the same meaning. |
| (b) **What is the meaning of** "pretty"? | INCORRECT: *What means "pretty"?* |

■ **EXERCISE 46:**  Ask a classmate for the meaning of the following words:

| | | | |
|---|---|---|---|
| 1. muggy | 6. listen | 11. discover | 16. forest |
| 2. awful | 7. supermarket | 12. simple | 17. possess |
| 3. quiet | 8. crowd | 13. empty | 18. invite |
| 4. century | 9. lend | 14. enjoy | 19. modern |
| 5. finish | 10. murder | 15. ill | 20. pretty difficult |

■ **EXERCISE 47:**  Make questions.  Use your own words.

1. A: _____
   B: Yesterday.

2. A: _____
   B: My brother.

3. A: _____
   B: A new pair of sandals.

4. A: _____
   B: At 7:30.

5. A: _____
   B: At Rossini's Restaurant.

6. A: _____
   B: This afternoon.

7. A: _____
   B: In an apartment.

8. A: _____
   B: My roommate.

9. A: _____
   B: Because I wanted to.

10. A: _____
    B: Ann.

11. A: _____
    B: A bird.

12. A: _____
    B: The zoo.

■ **EXERCISE 48—ORAL (BOOKS CLOSED):**  Make questions that would produce the
following answers.

*Example:*  At 7 o'clock.
*Response:*  When did you get up this morning? / What time does the movie start? / etc.

1. In an apartment.
2. Yesterday.
3. It means "wonderful."
4. ( . . . ).
5. At seven-thirty.
6. A shirt.
7. A hamburger.
8. No.
9. Because I wanted to.
10. Grammar.
11. Yes.
12. Nothing.
13. In the dormitory.
14. Because I was tired.
15. ( . . . ).
16. At nine o'clock.
17. A new pair of shoes.
18. On (*name of a street in this city*).
19. In (*name of this state/province*).
20. Last night.

## 5-17   MORE IRREGULAR VERBS

| | | |
|---|---|---|
| *break - broke* | *meet - met* | *sing - sang* |
| *fly - flew* | *pay - paid* | *speak - spoke* |
| *hear - heard* | *ring - rang* | *take - took* |
| *leave - left* | *send - sent* | *wake up - woke up* |

■ **EXERCISE 49—ORAL (BOOKS CLOSED):**  Practice using IRREGULAR VERBS.

*Example:*   break-broke
TEACHER:   break, broke.  Sometimes a person breaks an arm or a leg.  I broke my arm
five years ago.  What happened five years ago?
STUDENTS:   break, broke.  You broke your arm.
TEACHER:   (to Student A)  Did you ever break a bone?
STUDENT A:   Yes.  I broke my leg ten years ago.

1. *fly-flew*   Sometimes I fly home in an airplane. I flew home in an airplane last
month.  What did I do last month?  When did you fly to this city?
2. *hear-heard*   I hear birds singing every morning.  I heard birds singing yesterday.
What did I do yesterday?  What did you hear when you woke up this
morning?
3. *pay-paid*   I pay the rent every month.  I paid the rent last month.  What did I do
last month?  Did you pay your rent last month?

4. *send-sent*   I send my mother a gift every year on her birthday. I sent my mother a gift last year on her birthday. What did I do last year? When did you send a gift to someone?

5. *leave-left*   I leave for school at 8:00 every morning. I left for school yesterday at 8:00 A.M. What did I do at 8:00 A.M. yesterday? What time did you leave for class this morning?

6. *meet-met*   I meet new people every week. Yesterday I met ( . . . )'s friend. What did I do yesterday? Do you know ( . . . )? When did you meet him/her?

7. *take-took*   I take my younger brother to the movies every month. I took my younger brother to the movies last month. What did I do last month? Who has a younger brother or sister? Where and when did you take him/her someplace?

8. *wake-woke*   I usually wake up at six. This morning I woke up at six-thirty. What time did I wake up this morning? What time did you wake up this morning?

9. *speak-spoke*   I speak to many students every day. Before class today, I spoke to ( . . . ). Who did I speak to? Who did you speak to before class today?

10. *ring-rang*   The phone in our apartment rings a lot. This morning it rang at six-thirty and woke me up. What happened at six-thirty this morning? Who had a telephone call this morning? What time did the phone ring?

11. *sing-sang*   I sing in the shower every morning. I sang in the shower yesterday. What did I do yesterday? Do you ever sing? When was the last time?

12. *break-broke*   Sometimes I break things. This morning I dropped a glass on the floor and it broke. What happened this morning? When did you break something?

■ **EXERCISE 50:**   Complete the sentences. Use the correct form of the words in the list.

| | | |
|---|---|---|
| *break* | *meet* | *sing* |
| *fly* | *pay* | *speak* |
| *hear* | *ring* | *take* |
| *leave* | *send* | *wake* |

1. A: What happened to your finger?

   B: I _____ it in a soccer game.

2. A: Who did you talk to at the director's office?

   B: I _____ to the secretary.

3. A: When did Jessica leave for Europe?

   B: She _____ for Europe five days ago.

4. A: Did you write Ted a letter?

   B: No, but I _____ him a postcard.

5. A: Do you know Meg Adams?

   B: Yes. I _____ her a couple of weeks ago.

6. A: Why did you call the police?

   B: Because I _____ a burglar!

7. A: Where did you go yesterday?

   B: I _____ the children to the zoo.

8. A: What time did you get up this morning?
   B: 6:15.
   A: Why did you get up so early?

   B: The telephone _____.

9. A: Did you enjoy the party?

   B: Yes, I had a good time. We _____ songs and danced. It was fun.

10. A: You look sleepy.

    B: I am. I _____ up before dawn this morning and couldn't get back to sleep.

11. A: Did you give the painter a check?

    B: No. I _____ him in cash.

12. A: A bird _____ into our apartment yesterday through an open window.
    B: Really? What did you do?
    A: I caught it and took it outside.

| | |
|---|---|
| (a)  $\overset{\text{s \ v}}{\text{\textit{I ate breakfast.}}}$ = a main clause | A clause is a group of words that has a subject and a verb. |
| (b)  $\overset{\quad\text{s \ v}}{\textbf{\textit{before}}\textit{ I went to class}}$ = a time clause | A main clause is a complete sentence. Example (a) is a complete sentence. Example (b) is an incomplete sentence. It must be connected to a main clause, as in (c) and (d). |
| (c)  $\boxed{\text{I ate breakfast}}$ $\boxed{\overset{\text{s \ v}}{\textbf{\textit{before}}\textit{ I went to class.}}}$ <br> main clause     time clause | |
| (d)  $\boxed{\overset{\text{s \ v}}{\textbf{\textit{Before}}\textit{ I went to class,}}}$ $\boxed{\text{I ate breakfast.}}$ <br> time clause     main clause | A time clause can begin with *before* or *after*: <br> *before* + s + v = a time clause <br> *after* + s + v = a time clause |
| (e)  $\boxed{\text{We took a walk}}$ $\boxed{\textbf{\textit{after}}\textit{ we finished our work.}}$ <br> main clause     time clause | A time clause can follow a main clause, as in (c) and (e). A time clause can come in front of a main clause, as in (d) and (f). There is no difference in meaning between (c) and (d) or between (e) and (f). |
| (f)  $\boxed{\textbf{\textit{After}}\textit{ we finished our work,}}$ $\boxed{\text{we took a walk.}}$ <br> time clause     main clause | |
| (g)  We took a walk $\boxed{\textit{after the movie.}}$ <br> prep. phrase | *Before* and *after* don't always introduce a time clause. They are also used as prepositions followed by a noun object, as in (g) and (h). See Charts 1-7 and 4-1 for information about prepositional phrases. |
| (h)  I had a cup of coffee $\boxed{\textit{before class.}}$ <br> prep. phrase | |

■ **EXERCISE 51:**   Find the main clauses and the time clauses.

1. Before I ate the banana, I peeled it.
   → *main clause = I peeled it*
   → *time clause = before I ate the banana*

2. We arrived at the airport before the plane landed.

3. I went to a movie after I finished my homework.

4. After the children got home from school, they watched TV.*

5. Before I moved to this city, I lived at home with my parents.

---

*NOTE: When a time clause comes before the main clause, a comma is used between the two clauses. A comma is not used when the time clause comes after the main clause.

■ **EXERCISE 52:** Add a capital letter and period to the complete sentences. Write "*Inc.*" to mean "*Incomplete*" if the group of words is a time clause and not a complete sentence.

1. we went home → ***W*** ~~w~~*e went home.*

2. after we left my uncle's house → *Inc.*

3. we went home after we left my uncle's house
   → ***W*** ~~w~~*e went home after we left my uncle's house.*

4. before we ate our picnic lunch

5. we went to the zoo

6. we went to the zoo before we ate our picnic lunch

7. the children played games after they did their work

8. the children played games

9. after they did their work

10. the lions killed a zebra

11. after the lions killed a zebra

12. they ate it

13. after the lions killed a zebra, they ate it

■ **EXERCISE 53:** Combine the two ideas into one sentence by using **before** and **after** to introduce time clauses.

*Example:* I put on my coat.  I went outside.
   → *Before I went outside, I put on my coat.*
   *I put on my coat before I went outside.*
   *After I put on my coat, I went outside.*
   *I went outside after I put on my coat.*

1. She ate breakfast.     She went to work.

2. He did his homework.     He went to bed.

3. We bought tickets.     We entered the theater.

■ **EXERCISE 54:** Use the given words to write sentences of your own. Use the SIMPLE PAST.

*Example:* after I
*Written:* I went to college after I graduated from high school.
After I finished dinner, I watched TV.
*Etc.*

1. before I came here
2. after I got home last night
3. I went . . . before I

4. after we
5. before they
6. Mr. . . . after he

## 5-19   *WHEN* IN TIME CLAUSES

| | |
|---|---|
| (a) ***When** the rain stopped,* we took a walk.  OR:<br>We took a walk ***when** the rain stopped.* | ***When*** can introduce a time clause.<br>      ***when*** + S + V = a time clause<br>In (a): ***when*** *the rain stopped* is a time clause. |
| (b) *When **Tom** was a child, **he** lived with his aunt.*  OR:<br>***Tom** lived with his aunt when **he** was a child.* | In (b):  Notice that the noun *(Tom)* comes<br>before the pronoun *(he).* |
| COMPARE:<br>(c) *When did the rain stop?*  = a question<br>(d) *when the rain stopped*  = a time clause | ***When*** is also used to introduce questions.\*  A<br>question is a complete sentence, as in (c).  A<br>time clause is not a complete sentence. |

\*See Charts 2-12 and 5-13 for information about using *when* in questions.

■ **EXERCISE 55:**   Choose the best completion.  Then change the position of the time clause.

*Example:* When the phone rang,
→ When the phone rang, I answered it.\*
I answered the phone when it rang.

1. When the phone rang,
2. When I was in Japan,
3. Maria bought some new shoes
4. I took a lot of photographs
5. When a stranger grabbed Ann's arm,
6. Jim was a wrestler
7. When the rain stopped,
8. The antique vase broke

A. she screamed.
B. when I dropped it.
C. I closed my umbrella.
D. when he was in high school.
✔ E. I answered it.
 F. when she went shopping
    yesterday.
G. I stayed in a hotel in Tokyo.
H. when I was in Hawaii.

------------

\*NOTE:  If a sentence with a *when*-clause talks about two actions, the action in the *when*-clause happens first.  In the sentence *When the phone rang, I answered it:* first the phone rang, and then I answered it. Not logically possible:  *When I answered the phone, it rang.*

■ **EXERCISE 56:** Add a capital letter and a question mark to complete the sentences. Write "*Inc.*" to mean "*Incomplete*" if the group of words is a time clause and not a question.

1. when did Jim arrive → *W when did Jim arrive?*

2. when Jim arrived → *Inc.*

3. when you were a child

4. when were you in Iran

5. when did the movie end

6. when the movie ended

7. when Mr. Wang arrived at the airport

8. when Khalid and Bakir went to a restaurant on First Street yesterday

9. when I was a high school student

10. when does the museum open

■ **EXERCISE 57:** Use the given words and your own words to create sentences. Don't change the order of the words.

1. When did . . . .     4. When were . . . .
2. When I . . . .     5. When the . . . .
3. I . . . when . . . .     6. The . . . when . . . .

■ **EXERCISE 58—REVIEW:** Complete the sentences. Use the words in parentheses.

(1)     Yesterday *(be)* _____ a terrible day. Everything *(go)*

(2)     _____ wrong. First, I *(oversleep)* _____.

(3)     My alarm clock *(ring, not)* _____. I *(wake)*

(4)     _____ up when I *(hear)*

(5)     _____ some noise outside my window.

(6)     It was 9:15. I *(get)* _____ dressed quickly.

(7)     I *(run)* _____ to class, but

(8)     I *(be)* _____ late. The teacher

(9) *(be)* _____ upset. After my classes in the morning,

(10) I *(go)* _____ to the cafeteria for lunch. I *(have)*

(11) _____ an embarrassing accident at the cafeteria. I accidentally

(12) *(drop)* _____ my tray of food. Some of the dishes *(break)*

(13) _____. When I *(drop)* _____ the tray,

(14) everyone in the cafeteria *(look)* _____ at me. I

(15) *(go)* _____ back to the cafeteria line and

(16) *(get)* _____ a second tray of food. I *(pay)*

(17) _____ for my lunch again. After I *(sit)*

(18) _____ down at a table in the corner by

(19) myself, I *(eat)* _____ my sandwich and

(20) *(drink)* _____ a cup of tea.

(21) After lunch, I *(go)* _____ outside. I *(sit)* _____

(22) under a tree near the classroom building. I *(see)* _____ a friend. I

(23) *(call)* _____ to him. He

(24) *(join)* _____ me on the grass.

(25) We *(talk)* _____ about our

(26) classes and *(relax)* _____.

Everything was fine. But when I *(stand)*

(27) _____ up, I *(step)*

(28) _____ in a hole and *(break)*

(29) _____ my ankle.

(30) My friend *(drive)* _____ me to

(31) the hospital. We *(go)* _____ to the

emergency ward. After the doctor *(take)*

(32) _____ X-rays of my ankle, he

(33) *(put)* _____ a cast on it. I

(34)  *(pay)* _____ my bill.  Then we *(leave)* _____

(35)  the hospital.  My friend *(take)* _____ me home and *(help)*

(36)  _____ me up the stairs to my apartment.

(37)  When we *(get)* _____ to the door of my apartment, I *(look)*

(38)  _____ for my key.  I *(look)* _____ in my

purse and in my pockets.  There was no key.  I *(ring)*

(39)  _____ the doorbell.  I *(think)*

(40)  _____ that my roommate might be

(41)  at home, but she *(be, not)* _____.  So I *(sit)*

(42)  _____ down on the floor outside my apartment

(43)  and *(wait)* _____ for my roommate to get

home.

(44)  Finally, my roommate *(come)* _____ home and I *(get)*

(45)  _____ into the apartment.  I *(eat)* _____

(46)  dinner quickly and *(go)* _____ to bed.  I *(sleep)*

(47)  _____ for ten hours.  I hope today is a better day than yesterday!

■ **EXERCISE 59—ORAL:**  The person in the story in Exercise 58 is named Sara.  Form small groups and tell the story of Sara's day.  The first person in the group should say a few things about Sara's day.  The next person should continue the story.  And then the next.  Pay special attention to the past form of the verbs.

Glance at your book if you need to remember the story, but don't look at your book when you are speaking.

*Example:*
STUDENT A: Sara had a terrible day yesterday. Everything went wrong for her.
STUDENT B: Yes, she had a terrible day. First she overslept and miss class.
STUDENT C: Missed. She *missed* class.
STUDENT B: Right. She *missed* class.
STUDENT C: She missed class because her alarm clock didn't rang.
STUDENT D: Didn't *ring*, not rang.
STUDENT C: Right! Her alarm clock didn't *ring*.
STUDENT D: She woke up when she heard some noise outside her window at 9:15. She got dressed quickly and run to class.
STUDENT A: Excuse me, but I think you should say that she got dressed quickly and . . . .

■ **EXERCISE 60—WRITTEN:** Write the story of Sara's day. Don't look at your textbook. Write from memory.

■ **EXERCISE 61—WRITTEN:** Choose one of the topics and write a composition about past events. Use time expressions (*first, next, then, at . . . o'clock, later, after, before, when, etc.*) to show the order of the activities.

*Topic 1:* Write about your activities yesterday, from the time you got up to the time you went to bed.
*Topic 2:* Write about one of the best days in your life. What happened?
*Topic 3:* Write about one of the worst days in your life. What happened?

■ **EXERCISE 62—WRITTEN:** Interview someone you know about his/her activities yesterday morning, yesterday afternoon, and last night. Then use this information to write a composition. Use time expressions (*first, next, then, at . . . o'clock, later, after, before, when, etc.*) to show the order of the activities.

■ **EXERCISE 63—REVIEW:** Give the past form of the verbs.

| | | | | |
|---|---|---|---|---|
| 1. visit | *visited* | | 10. pay | |
| 2. fly | *flew* | | 11. catch | |
| 3. go | | | 12. happen | |
| 4. worry | | | 13. listen | |
| 5. speak | | | 14. plan | |
| 6. ride | | | 15. rain | |
| 7. stand | | | 16. bring | |
| 8. turn | | | 17. take | |
| 9. hear | | | 18. write | |

| | | |
|---|---|---|
| 19. break _____ | | 25. ring _____ |
| 20. stop _____ | | 26. meet _____ |
| 21. hope _____ | | 27. leave _____ |
| 22. sing _____ | | 28. occur _____ |
| 23. think _____ | | 29. teach _____ |
| 24. drive _____ | | 30. read _____ |

■ **EXERCISE 64—REVIEW:** Ask and answer questions using the SIMPLE PAST. Use the given verbs.

> STUDENT A: Make up any question that includes the given verb. Use the SIMPLE PAST.
> STUDENT B: Answer the question. Give a short answer and a long answer.

*Example:* speak
STUDENT A: Did you speak to Mr. Lee yesterday?
STUDENT B: Yes, I did. I spoke to him yesterday.

*Example:* finish
STUDENT A: What time did you finish your homework last night?
STUDENT B: Around nine o'clock. I finished my homework around nine o'clock.

*Switch roles.*

| | | | |
|---|---|---|---|
| 1. drink | 5. fly | 9. see | 13. buy |
| 2. eat | 6. talk | 10. sleep | 14. send |
| 3. study | 7. wake up | 11. work | 15. watch |
| 4. take | 8. come | 12. have | 16. read |

■ **EXERCISE 65—REVIEW:** Correct the mistakes in the following.

1. Did you went downtown yesterday?

2. Yesterday I speak to Ken before he leaves his office and goes home.

3. I heared a good joke last night.

4. When Pablo finished his work.

5. I visitted my relatives in New York City last month.

6. Where you did go yesterday afternoon?

7. Ms. Wah was flew from Singapore to Tokyo last week.

8. When I see my friend yesterday, he didn't spoke to me.

9. Why Mustafa didn't came to class last week?

10. Where were you bought those shoes? I like them.

11. Mr. Adams teached our class last week.

12. I writed a letter last night.

13. Who you wrote a letter to?

14. Who did open the door? Jack openned it.

■ **EXERCISE 66—REVIEW:** Complete the sentences with the words in parentheses. Use the SIMPLE PRESENT, PRESENT PROGRESSIVE, or SIMPLE PAST. The sentence may require STATEMENT, NEGATIVE, or QUESTION FORMS.

1. Tom *(walk)* _____*walks*_____ to work almost every day.

2. I can see Tom from my window. He's on the street below. He *(walk)*

    _____ to work right now.

3. *(Tom, walk)* _____ to work every day?

4. *(you, walk)* _____ to work every day?

5. I usually take the bus to work, but yesterday I *(walk)* _____ to my office.

6. On my way to work yesterday, I *(see)* _____ an accident.

7. Alex *(see, not)* _____ the accident.

8. *(you, see)* _____ the accident yesterday?

9. Tom *(walk, not)* _____ to work when the weather is cold. He

    *(take)* _____ the bus.

10. I *(walk, not)* _____ to work in cold weather either.

■ **EXERCISE 67—REVIEW:** Complete the sentences with the words in parentheses.

(1)    Yesterday Fish *(be)* _____ in the river. He *(see)* _____

Bear on the bank of the river. Here is their conversation.

BEAR: Good morning, Fish.

(2) FISH: Good morning, Bear. How *(you, be)* _____ today?

(3) BEAR: I *(do)* _____ fine, thank you. And you?

FISH: Fine, thanks.

(4) BEAR: *(you, would like)* _____ to get out of the river and *(sit)*

(5) _____ with me? I *(need)* _____ someone to talk to.

(6) FISH: I *(need, not)* _____ to get out of the river for us to talk.

We can talk just the way we are now.

BEAR: Hmmm.

(7) FISH: Wait! What *(you, do)* _____?

(8) BEAR: I *(get)* _____ in the river to join you.

(9) FISH: Stop! This *(be)* _____ my river! I *(trust, not)* _____

(10) _____ you. What *(you, want)* _____?

(11) BEAR: Nothing. Just a little conversation. I *(want)* _____ to tell you about

(12) my problems. I *(have)* _____ a bad day yesterday.

FISH: Oh? What happened?

(13) BEAR: While I was walking through the woods, I *(see)* _____ a beehive. I

(14) *(love)* _____ honey. So I *(stop)* _____ at the

beehive. When I *(reach)*

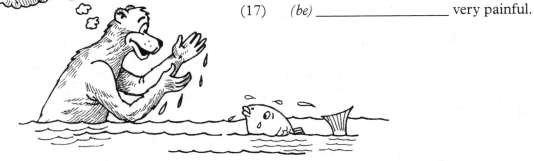

(15) _____ inside to get

some honey, a great big bee *(come)*

(16) _____ up behind

me and stung★ my ear. The sting

(17) *(be)* _____ very painful.

(18) FISH: I *(believe, not)* _____ you. Bees can't hurt bears. I

(19) *(believe, not)* _____ your story about a great big bee.

(20) All bees *(be)* _____ the same size, and they *(be, not)* _____ big.

(21) BEAR: But it *(be)* _____ true! Here. Come a little closer and look at

my ear. I'll show you where the big bee stung it.

(22) FISH: Okay. Where *(it, be)* _____? Where *(the bee, sting)*

(23) _____ you?

BEAR: Right here. See?

(24) FISH: Stop! What *(you, do)* _____? Let go of me! Why

(25) *(you, hold)* _____ me?

★*Stung* is the past form of the verb *sting*, which means "to cause sharp pain."

(26) BEAR: I *(hold)* _____ you because I'm going to eat you for dinner.

(27) FISH: Oh no! You *(trick)* _____ me! Your story about the great big bee

(28) never *(happen)* _____!

(29) BEAR: That's right. I *(get)* _____ in the river because I *(want)*

(30) _____ *(catch)* _____ you for dinner. And I

(31) did. I *(catch)* _____ you for dinner.

FISH: Watch out! Behind you! Oh no! Oh no! It's a very, very big bee. It's huge! It

(32) *(look)* _____ really angry!

(33) BEAR: I *(believe, not)* _____ you!

(34) FISH: But it *(be)* _____ true! A great big bee *(come)* _____

toward you. It's going to attack you and sting you!

(35) BEAR: What? Where? I *(see, not)* _____ a big bee! Oh no, Fish, you

(36) are getting away from me. Oh no! I *(drop)* _____ you! Come

back! Come back!

(37) FISH: Ha! I *(fool)* _____ you too, Bear. Now you must find your

dinner in another place.

(38) BEAR: Yes, you *(trick)* _____ me too. We *(teach)* _____

each other a good lesson today: Don't believe everything you hear.

FISH: Thank you for teaching me that lesson. Now I will live a long and happy life.

(39)    BEAR:   Yes, we *(learn)* _____ a good lesson today, and that's good.  But

(40)            I *(be)* _____ still hungry.  Hmmm.  I *(have)* _____

(41)            a gold tooth in my mouth.  *(you, would like)* _____ to

        come closer and look at it?

## CHAPTER **6**
# Expressing Future Time

---

### 6-1  FUTURE TIME: USING *BE GOING TO*

| | |
|---|---|
| (a)  I  **am going to go**  downtown tomorrow.<br>(b)  Sue  **is going to be**  here tomorrow afternoon.<br>(c)  We  **are going to come**  to class tomorrow morning. | **Be going to** expresses (talks about) the future.<br>FORM:  **am**<br>　　　 **is**  } + **going** + *infinitive**<br>　　　 **are** |
| (d)  I**'m not going to go** downtown tomorrow.<br>(e)  Ann **isn't going to study** tonight. | NEGATIVE: **be** + **not** + **going to** |
| (f)  "**Are** you **going to come** to class tomorrow?"<br>　　　"No, I'm not."<br>(g)  "**Is** Jim **going to be**  at the meeting tomorrow?"<br>　　　"Yes, he is."<br>(h)  "What time **are** you  **going to eat** dinner tonight?"<br>　　　"Around six." | QUESTION:  **be** + *subject* + **going to**<br>A form of **be**  is used in the short answer to a yes/no question with **be going to**, as in (f) and (g).  (See Chart 1-9 for information about short answers with **be**.) |

*Infinitive = **to** + the simple form of a verb (*to come, to go, to see, to study, etc.*).

■ **EXERCISE 1—ORAL:**  Some activities are listed on the next page.  Which of these activities are you going to do tomorrow?  Which ones are you not going to do tomorrow? Pair up with a classmate.

STUDENT A: Your book is open.  Ask a question.  Use *"Are you going to . . . tomorrow?"*

STUDENT B: Your book is closed.  Answer the question. Give  both a short answer and a long answer.  Use *"I'm going to . . . tomorrow"* or *"I'm not going to . . . tomorrow"* in the long answer.

*Example:*     go downtown
STUDENT A: Are you going to go downtown tomorrow?
STUDENT B: Yes, I am.  I'm going to go downtown tomorrow.  OR:
                 No, I'm not.  I'm not going to go downtown tomorrow.

*Switch roles.*

1. get up before eight o'clock
2. come to class
3. stay home all day
4. eat lunch
5. eat lunch with *(someone)*
6. get a haircut
7. watch TV in the evening
8. do something interesting in the evening
9. go to bed early
10. go to bed late

11. get up early
12. get up late
13. walk to school
14. study grammar
15. get some physical exercise
16. eat dinner
17. eat dinner alone
18. listen to music after dinner
19. go shopping
20. do something interesting and unusual

■ **EXERCISE 2—ORAL (BOOKS CLOSED):**  Answer the questions.

*Example:*     tomorrow?
TO STUDENT A:  What are you going to do tomorrow?
   STUDENT A:  I'm going to (go shopping).
TO STUDENT B:  What is ( . . . ) going to do tomorrow?
   STUDENT B:  He's/She's going to go shopping.

What are you going to do:
1. tomorrow?
2. tomorrow morning?
3. tomorrow afternoon?
4. tomorrow night?
5. at 7:00 tomorrow morning?
6. at 9:00 tomorrow morning?
7. at noon tomorrow?
8. at 5:00 tomorrow afternoon?
9. around 6:30 tomorrow evening?
10. after 8:00 tomorrow night?

■ **EXERCISE 3:**  Complete the sentences.  Use **be going to** + the following expressions (or your own words).

| | | |
|---|---|---|
| call the landlord | ✔ go to the bookstore | see a dentist |
| call the police | go to an Italian restaurant | stay in bed today |
| get something to eat | lie down and rest for a while | take a long walk in the park |
| go to the beach | look it up in my dictionary | take it to the post office |
| go to bed | major in psychology | take them to the laundromat |

1. I need to buy a book.  I ____ *am going to go to the bookstore* ____.

2. It's midnight now.  I'm sleepy.  I _____.

3. Sue is hungry. She _____.

4. My clothes are dirty. I _____.

5. I have a toothache. My wisdom tooth hurts. I _____.

6. I'm writing a composition. I don't know how to spell a word. I _____

_____.

7. George has to mail a package. He _____.

8. Rosa lives in an apartment. There's a problem with the plumbing. She _____

_____.

9. Sue and I want to go swimming. We _____.

10. I have a headache. I _____.

11. It's late at night. I hear a burglar! I _____.

12. I want to be a psychologist. When I go to the university, I _____

_____.

13. I feel terrible. I think I'm getting the flu. I _____.

14. Ivan and Natasha want to go out to eat. They _____.

15. It's a nice day today. Mary and I _____.

■ **EXERCISE 4—ORAL (BOOKS CLOSED):** Listen to the common activities that are described. Picture these activities in your mind. Use **be going to** to tell what you think your classmates are going to do.

*Example:* ( . . . ) is carrying his/her textbooks and notebooks. He/She is walking toward the library. What is ( . . . ) going to do?

*Response:* ( . . . ) is going to study at the library.

1. ( . . . ) is standing next to the chalkboard. He/She is picking up a piece of chalk. What is ( . . . ) going to do?
2. ( . . . ) has some letters in his/her hand. He/She is walking toward the post office. What is ( . . . ) going to do?
3. ( . . . ) is standing by a telephone. He/She is looking in the telephone book for ( . . . )'s name. What is ( . . . ) going to do?
4. ( . . . ) put some water on the stove to boil. She got a cup and saucer out of the cupboard and some tea. What is ( . . . ) going to do?
5. ( . . . ) is putting on his/her coat. He/She is walking toward the door. What is ( . . . ) going to do?
6. ( . . . ) has a basket full of dirty clothes. He/She is walking toward a laundromat. What is ( . . . ) going to do?
7. ( . . . ) bought some meat and vegetables at the market. He/She is holding a bag of rice. He/She just turned on the stove. What is ( . . . ) going to do?
8. ( . . . ) and ( . . . ) are walking into *(name of a local restaurant).* It's seven o'clock in the evening. What are ( . . . ) and ( . . . ) going to do?
9. ( . . . ) gave ( . . . ) a diamond engagement ring. What are ( . . . ) and ( . . . ) going to do?
10. ( . . . ) and ( . . . ) have airplane tickets. They're putting clothes in their suitcases. Their clothes include swimming suits and sandals. What are ( . . . ) and ( . . . ) going to do?

■ **EXERCISE 5—ORAL:** Ask a classmate a question. Use **be going to**.

*Example:* when / go downtown
STUDENT A: When are you going to go downtown?
STUDENT B: Tomorrow afternoon. / In a couple of days. / I don't know. / etc.

1. where / go after class today
2. what time / get home tonight
3. when / eat dinner
4. where / eat dinner
5. what time / go to bed tonight
6. what time / get up tomorrow morning
7. where / be tomorrow morning
8. when / see your family again
9. where / live next year
10. when / get married

■ **EXERCISE 6—ORAL:** Answer the questions. Use **be going to**.

*Example:*     You want to buy some tea. What are you going to do? What is ( . . . ) going to do and why?

To STUDENT A:    You want to buy some tea. What are you going to do?
STUDENT A:    I'm going to go to the grocery store.
To STUDENT B:    What is (Student A) going to do and why?
STUDENT B:    He/She's going to go to the grocery store because he/she wants to buy some tea.

1. You have a toothache. What are you going to do? What is ( . . . ) going to do and why?
2. You need to mail a package. Where are you going to go? Where is ( . . . ) going to go and why?
3. Your clothes are dirty.
4. It's midnight. You're sleepy.
5. It's late at night. You hear a burglar.
6. You need to buy some groceries.
7. You want to go swimming.
8. You want to go fishing.
9. You want to buy a new coat.
10. You're hungry.
11. You have a headache.
12. It's a nice day today.
13. You need to cash a check.
14. You want some *(pizza)* for dinner.
15. You're reading a book. You don't know the meaning of a word.

## 6-2  WORDS USED FOR PAST TIME AND FUTURE TIME

| PAST | FUTURE | |
|---|---|---|
| yesterday | tomorrow | PAST: It *rained* **yesterday**.<br>FUTURE: It's *going to rain* **tomorrow**. |
| yesterday morning<br>yesterday afternoon<br>yesterday evening<br>last night | tomorrow morning<br>tomorrow afternoon<br>tomorrow evening<br>tomorrow night | PAST: I *was* in class **yesterday morning**.<br>FUTURE: I'm *going to be* in class **tomorrow morning**. |
| last week<br>last month<br>last year<br>last weekend<br>last spring<br>last summer<br>last fall<br>last winter<br>last Monday, etc. | next week<br>next month<br>next year<br>next weekend<br>next spring<br>next summer<br>next fall<br>next winter<br>next Monday, etc. | PAST: Mary *went* downtown **last week**.<br>FUTURE: Mary *is going to go* downtown **next week**.<br><br>PAST: Bob *graduated* from high school **last spring**.<br>FUTURE: Ann *is going to graduate* from high school **next spring**. |
| . . . minutes ago<br>. . . hours ago<br>. . . days ago<br>. . . weeks ago<br>. . . months ago<br>. . . years ago | in . . . minutes (from now)<br>in . . . hours (from now)<br>in . . . days (from now)<br>in . . . weeks (from now)<br>in . . . months (from now)<br>in . . . years (from now) | PAST: I *finished* my homework **five minutes ago**.<br>FUTURE: Pablo *is going to finish* his homework **in five minutes**. |

■ **EXERCISE 7:** Complete the sentences. Use *yesterday*, *last*, *tomorrow*, or *next*.

1. I went swimming _____*yesterday*_____ morning.

2. Ken is going to go to the beach _____*tomorrow*_____ morning.

3. I'm going to take a trip _____ week.

4. Alice went to Miami _____ week for a short vacation.

5. We had a test in class _____ afternoon.

6. _____ afternoon we're going to go on a picnic.

7. My sister is going to arrive _____ Tuesday.

8. Sam bought a used car _____ Friday.

9. My brother is going to enter the university _____ fall.

10. _____ spring I took a trip to San Francisco.

11. Ann is going to fly to London _____ month.

12. Rick lived in Tokyo _____ year.

13. I'm going to study at the library _____ night.

14. _____ night I watched TV.

15. _____ evening I'm going to go to a baseball game.

16. Matt was at the laundromat _____ evening.

■ **EXERCISE 8:** Complete the sentences. Use the given time expression with *ago* or *in*.

1. *ten minutes*   Class is going to end _____*in ten minutes.*_____

2. *ten minutes*   Ann's class ended _____*ten minutes ago.*_____

3. *an hour*   The post office isn't open. It closed _____

4. *an hour*   Jack is going to call us _____

5. *two more months*   I'm studying abroad now, but I'm going to be back home

   _____

6. *two months*   My wife and I took a trip to Morocco _____

7. *a minute*   Karen left _____

8. *half an hour*   I'm going to meet David at the coffee shop _____

9. *one more week*   The new highway is going to open _____

10. *a year*   I was living in Korea _____

■ **EXERCISE 9:** Complete the sentences. Use *yesterday*, *last*, *tomorrow*, *next*, *in*, or *ago*.

1. I went to the zoo _____*last*_____ week.

2. Yolanda went to the zoo a week _____.

3. Peter Nelson is going to go to the zoo _____ Saturday.

4. We're going to go to the zoo _____ two more days.

5. My children went to the zoo _____ morning.

6. My cousin is going to go to the zoo _____ afternoon.

7. Kim Yang-Don graduated from Sogang University _____ spring.

8. I'm going to take a vacation in Canada _____ summer.

9. We're going to have company for dinner _____ night.

10. We had company for dinner three days _____.

11. We're going to have dinner at our friends' house _____ two days.

12. _____ evening we're going to go to a concert.

13. _____ Friday I went to a party.

14. _____ morning the students took a test.

15. I took a test two days _____.

16. The students are going to have another test _____ Thursday.

17. Are you going to be home _____ afternoon around three?

18. My little sister arrived here _____ month.

19. She is going to leave _____ two weeks.

20. _____ year Yuko is going to be a freshman in college.

## 6-3 USING *A COUPLE OF* OR *A FEW* WITH *AGO* (PAST) AND *IN* (FUTURE)

| | |
|---|---|
| (a) Sam arrived here **one** (OR: *a*) *year ago.*<br>(b) Jack is going to be here *in* **two** *minutes.*<br>(c) I talked to Ann **three** *days ago.* | Numbers are often used in time expressions with *ago* and *in*. |
| (d) I saw Carlos *a couple of* months ago.<br>(e) He's going to return to Mexico *in* **a couple of** *months.*<br>(f) I got a letter from Gina *a few* weeks ago.<br>(g) I got a letter to see Gina *in* **a few** *weeks.* | *A couple of* and *a few* are also commonly used. *A couple of* means "two." *A couple of months ago* = two months ago.<br><br>*A few* means "a small number, not a large number." *A few weeks ago* = three, four, or five weeks ago. |
| (h) I began college last year. I'm going to graduate *in* **two more** *years.* My sister is almost finished with her education. She's going to graduate *in* **a few more** *months.* She's going to graduate *in* **three more** *months.* | Frequently the word ***more*** is used in future time expressions that begin with *in*. |

■ **EXERCISE 10:** Complete the sentences, using information from your own life. Use the words in *italics*. Use **ago** or **in**. Use numbers (*one, two, three, ten, sixteen, etc.*) or the expressions **a couple of** or **a few**.

1. *days*     We studied Chapter 5 ___*a couple of days ago/three days ago/etc.*___

2. *days*     We're going to finish this chapter ___*in a few more days /*___
   ___*in three or four days / etc.*___

3. *hours*    I ate breakfast _____

4. *hours*    I'm going to eat lunch/dinner _____

5. *minutes*  We finished Exercise 9 _____

6. *minutes*  This class is going to end _____

7. *years*  I was born _____

8. *years*  My parents got married _____

9. *years*  I got/am going to get married _____

10. *weeks*  I arrived in this city _____, and I'm
    *months*
    *years*  going to leave this city _____

■ **EXERCISE 11:**  Complete the sentences.  Use your own words.  Write about your life.  For
example, what did you do a few days ago?  What are you going to do in a few days?

1. _____ a few days ago.

2. _____ in a few days *(from now)*.

3. _____ in a few more minutes.

4. _____ three hours ago.

5. _____ in four more hours.

6. _____ a couple of days ago.

7. _____ in a couple of months *(from now)*.

8. _____ a few minutes ago.

9. _____ many years ago.

10. _____ in a couple of minutes *(from now)*.

---

## 6-4  USING *TODAY, TONIGHT,* AND *THIS* + MORNING, AFTERNOON, EVENING, WEEK, MONTH, YEAR

| PRESENT | Right now it's 10 A.M.  We are in our English class.<br>(a) We **are studying** English **this morning**. | *today*<br>*tonight*<br>*this morning*<br>*this afternoon*<br>*this evening*<br>*this week*<br>*this weekend*<br>*this month*<br>*this year* | These words can express present, past, or future time. |
|---|---|---|---|
| PAST | Right now it's 10 A.M.  Nancy left home at 9 A.M. to go downtown.  She isn't at home right now.<br>(b) Nancy **went** downtown **this morning**. | | |
| FUTURE | Right now it's 10 A.M.  Class ends at 11 A.M.  After class today, I'm going to go to the post office.<br>(c) I**'m going to go** to the post office **this morning**. | | |

■ **EXERCISE 12:**   Answer the questions.  Use your own words.

1. What is something you did earlier this year?

   → I _____*came to this city*_____ this year.

2. What is something you are doing this year?

   → I _____*am studying English*_____ this year.

3. What is something you are going to do this year?

   → I _____*am going to visit my relatives in Cairo*_____ this year.

4. What is something you did earlier today?

   → I _____ today.

5. What is something you are doing today, right now?

   → I _____ today.

6. What is something you are going to do later today?

   → I _____ today.

7. What is something you did earlier this morning / afternoon / evening?

   → I _____ this _____.

8. What is something you are going to do later this morning / afternoon / evening?

   → I _____ this _____.

■ **EXERCISE 13:**   Complete the sentences.  Discuss the different VERB TENSES that are possible.

1. _____ today.

2. _____ this morning.

3. _____ this afternoon.

4. _____ this evening.

5. _____ tonight.

6. _____ this week.

7. _____ this month.

8. _____ this year.

■ **EXERCISE 14—ORAL:** In groups of three, ask classmates questions about future activities.
　STUDENT A: Begin your question with "***When are you going to . . . ?***"
　STUDENT B: Answer Student A's question.
　STUDENT A: Ask Student C a question that begins with "***When is ( . . . ) going to . . . ?***"
　STUDENT C: Answer in a complete sentence.

*Example:*　go downtown
STUDENT A: When are you going to go downtown?
STUDENT B: This weekend.  (Tomorrow morning. / In a couple of days. / Etc.)
STUDENT A: When is ( . . . ) going to go downtown?
STUDENT C: He/She is going to go downtown this weekend.

1. study at the library
2. go shopping
3. go to *(name of a class)*
4. have dinner
5. do your grammar homework
6. get married
7. go on a picnic
8. visit *(name of a place in this city)*

9. call ( . . . ) on the phone
10. go to *(name of restaurant)* for dinner
11. see your family again
12. quit smoking
13. buy a car
14. see ( . . . )
15. go to *(name of a place in this city)*
16. take a vacation


■ **EXERCISE 15—ORAL:** In pairs, ask a classmate a question.  Use the given words in your question.

*Example:*　tomorrow morning
STUDENT A: Are you going to come to class tomorrow morning?
STUDENT B: Yes, I am.　OR:　No, I'm not.
*Example:*　yesterday morning
STUDENT A: Did you eat breakfast yesterday morning?
STUDENT B: Yes, I did.　OR:　No, I didn't.

*Switch roles.*

1. last night
2. tomorrow night
3. tonight
4. tomorrow afternoon
5. yesterday afternoon
6. this afternoon
7. last Friday
8. next Friday
9. next week

10. last week
11. this week
12. yesterday morning
13. tomorrow morning
14. this morning
15. later today
16. a couple of hours ago
17. in a couple of hours *(from now)*
18. this evening

## 6-5 FUTURE TIME: USING *WILL*

| STATEMENT | (a) Mike **will go** to the library tomorrow.<br>(b) Mike **is going to go** to the library tomorrow. | (a) and (b) have basically the same meaning. |
|---|---|---|
| | (c) INCORRECT: *Mike will* **goes** *there.* | The simple form of a verb follows **will**. In (c): *goes* is NOT correct. |
| | (d) INCORRECT: *Mike will***s** *go there.* | There is never a final **-s** on **will** for future time. |
| | (e) INCORRECT: *Mike will* **to** *go there.* | **Will** is not followed by an infinitive with **to**. |
| CONTRACTIONS | (f) I will come.  =  **I'll** come.<br>You will come.  =  **You'll** come.<br>She will come.  =  **She'll** come.<br>He will come.  =  **He'll** come.<br>It will come.  =  **It'll** come.<br>We will come  =  **We'll** come.<br>They will come.  =  **They'll** come. | **Will** is contracted to **'ll** with subject pronouns.★ These contractions are common in both speaking and writing. |
| NEGATIVE | (g) Bob **will not be** here tomorrow.<br>(h) Bob **won't be** here tomorrow. | Negative contraction:<br>**will** + **not** = **won't** |

★**Will** is also often contracted with nouns in speaking (but not in writing).
  WRITTEN: *Tom will be here at ten.*
  SPOKEN: *"Tom'll" be here at ten.*

■ **EXERCISE 16—ORAL:**  Change the sentences by using **will** to express future time.

1. I'm going to arrive around six tomorrow.
   → *I'll arrive around six tomorrow.*
2. Fred isn't going to come to our party.
3. He's going to be out of town next week.
4. Sue is going to be in class tomorrow.
5. She has a cold, but she isn't going to stay home.
6. Jack and Peggy are going to meet us at the movie theater.
7. They're going to be there at 7:15.
8. Tina is going to stay home and watch TV tonight.★
9. This is an important letter.  I'm going to send this letter by express mail.

---

★When two verbs are connected by *and*, the helping verbs **be going to** and **will** are usually not repeated.  For example:
    *I'm going to lock the doors and* ~~am going to~~ *turn out the lights.*
    *I'll lock the doors and* ~~will~~ *turn out the lights.*

10. My parents are going to stay at a hotel in Honolulu.
11. Hurry up, or we're going to be late for the concert.
12. I'm not going to be at home this evening.
13. I'm going to wash the dishes and clean the kitchen after dinner.
14. Be careful with those scissors!  You're going to hurt yourself!

## 6-6  ASKING QUESTIONS WITH *WILL*

| QUESTION | | | | | | ANSWER |
|---|---|---|---|---|---|---|
| (QUESTION + WORD) | *WILL* + | SUBJECT + | MAIN VERB | | | |
| (a) | *Will* | *Tom* | *come* | tomorrow? | → | *Yes, he will.*★ *No, he won't.* |
| (b) | *Will* | *you* | *be* | at home tonight? | → | *Yes, I will.*★ *No, I won't.* |
| (c) When | *will* | *Ann* | *arrive?* | | → | *Next Saturday.* |
| (d) What time | *will* | *the plane* | *arrive?* | | → | *Three-thirty.* |
| (e) Where | *will* | *you* | *be* | tonight? | → | *At home.* |

★NOTE: *will* is not contracted with a pronoun in a short answer.  See Chart 1-9 for information about the use of contractions in short answers.

■ **EXERCISE 17:**  Make questions.

1. A: _____*Will you be at home tomorrow night?*_____

   B: Yes, _____*I will.*_____ (I'll be at home tomorrow night.)

2. A: _____*Will Ann be in class tomorrow?*_____

   B: No, _____*she won't.*_____ (Ann won't be in class tomorrow.)

3. A: ___*When will you see Mr. Pong?*___

   B: Tomorrow afternoon.  (I'll see Mr. Pong tomorrow afternoon.)

4. A: _____

   B: Yes, _____ (The plane will be on time.)

5. A: _____

   B: Yes, _____ (Dinner will be ready in a few minutes.)

6. A: _____

   B: In a few minutes.  (Dinner will be ready in a few minutes.)

7. A: _____

   B: Next year.  (I'll graduate next year.)

8. A: _____

   B: At the community college.  (Mary will go to school at the community college next year.)

9. A: _____

   B: No, _____ (Jane and Mark won't be at the party.)

10. A: _____

    B: Yes, _____ (Mike will arrive in Chicago next week.)

11. A: _____

    B: In Chicago.  (Mike will be in Chicago next week.)

12. A: _____

    B: No, _____ (I won't be home early tonight.)

13. A: _____

    B: In a few minutes.  (Dr. Smith will be back in a few minutes.)

14. A: _____

    B: Yes, _____ (I'll be ready to leave at 8:15.)

    A: Are you sure?

## 6-7 VERB SUMMARY: PRESENT, PAST, AND FUTURE

| | STATEMENT | NEGATIVE | QUESTION |
|---|---|---|---|
| SIMPLE PRESENT | I *eat* lunch every day.<br>He *eats* lunch every day. | I *don't eat* breakfast.<br>She *doesn't eat* breakfast. | *Do* you *eat* breakfast?<br>*Does* she *eat* lunch? |
| PRESENT PROGRESSIVE | I *am eating* an apple right now.<br>She *is eating* an apple.<br>They *are eating* apples. | I'*m not eating* a pear.<br><br>She *isn't eating* a pear.<br>They *aren't eating* pears. | *Am* I *eating* a banana?<br><br>*Is* he *eating* a banana?<br>*Are* they *eating* bananas? |
| SIMPLE PAST | He *ate* lunch yesterday. | He *didn't eat* breakfast. | *Did* you *eat* breakfast? |
| *BE GOING TO* | I *am going to eat* lunch at noon.<br>She *is going to eat* lunch at noon.<br>They *are going to eat* lunch at noon. | I'*m not going to eat* breakfast tomorrow.<br>She *isn't going to eat* breakfast tomorrow.<br>They *aren't going to eat* breakfast tomorrow. | *Am* I *going to see* you tomorrow?<br>*Is* she *going to eat* lunch tomorrow?<br>*Are* they *going to eat* lunch tomorrow? |
| *WILL* | He *will eat* lunch tomorrow. | He *won't eat* breakfast tomorrow. | *Will* he *eat* lunch tomorrow? |

■ **EXERCISE 18—VERB REVIEW:**  Complete the sentences with the verbs in parentheses.

1. Right now, Anita *(sit)* _____*is sitting*_____ at her desk.

2. She *(do, not)* _____ homework.  She *(write)*

    _____ a letter to her parents.

3. She *(write)* _____ to her parents every week.

4. She *(write, not)* _____ a letter every day.

5. Her parents *(expect, not)* _____ to get a letter every day.

6. Last night Anita *(write)* _____ a letter to her brother.  Then she *(start)* _____ to write a letter to her sister.

7. While Anita was writing a letter to her sister last night, her phone *(ring)* _____ .  It *(be)* _____ her sister!

8. Anita *(finish, not)* _____ the letter to her sister last night. After she *(talk)* _____ to her sister, she *(go)* _____ to bed.

9. Tomorrow she *(write)* _____ a letter to her cousin in Brazil.

10. Anita *(write, not)* _____ a letter to her parents tomorrow.

11. *(you, write)* _____ a letter to someone every day?

12. *(you, write)* _____ a letter to someone yesterday?

13. *(you, write)* _____ a letter to someone tomorrow?

## 6-8  VERB SUMMARY: FORMS OF *BE*

|  | STATEMENT | NEGATIVE | QUESTION |
|---|---|---|---|
| SIMPLE PRESENT | I *am* from Korea.<br>He *is* from Egypt.<br>They *are* from Venezuela. | I *am not* from Jordan.<br>She *isn't* from China.<br>They *aren't* from Italy. | *Am* I in the right room?<br>*Is* she from Greece?<br>*Are* they from Kenya? |
| SIMPLE PAST | Ann *was* late yesterday.<br>They *were* late yesterday. | She *wasn't* on time.<br>They *weren't* on time. | *Was* she in class?<br>*Were* they in class? |
| *BE GOING TO* | I *am going to be* late.<br>She *is going to be* late.<br>They *are going to be* late. | I'm *not going to be* on time.<br>She *isn't going to be* on time.<br>They *aren't going to be* on time. | *Am* I *going to be* late?<br>*Is* she *going to be* late?<br>*Are* they *going to be* late tomorrow? |
| *WILL* | He *will be* at home tomorrow. | He *won't be* at work tomorrow. | *Will* he *be* at work next week? |

■ **EXERCISE 19—REVIEW OF BE:** Complete the sentences with the VERBS in parentheses.

1. I *(be)* _____ in class right now. I *(be, not)* _____

   _____ here yesterday. I *(be)* _____ absent

   yesterday. *(you, be)* _____ in class yesterday? *(Carmen, be)*

   _____ here yesterday?

2. Carmen and I *(be)* _____ absent from class yesterday. We

   *(be, not)* _____ here.

3. My friends *(be)* _____ at Fatima's apartment tomorrow

   evening. I *(be)* _____ there too. *(you, be)* _____

   there? *(Yuko, be)* _____ there?

4. A whale *(be, not)* _____ a fish. It *(be)* _____ a

   mammal. Dolphins *(be, not)* _____ fish either. They

   *(be)* _____ mammals.

   DOLPHIN

■ **EXERCISE 20—VERB REVIEW:** Complete the sentences with the verbs in parentheses. Give short answers to questions where necessary.

1. A: *(you, have)* _____*Do you have*_____ a bicycle?

   B: Yes, I *(do)* _____*do*_____. I *(ride)* _____*ride*_____ it to work every day.

2. A: *(you, walk)* _____ to work yesterday?

   B: No, I _____. I *(ride)* _____ my bicycle.

3. A: *(you, know)* _____ Mr. Park?

   B: Yes, I _____.

   A: Where *(you, meet)* _____ him?

   B: I *(meet)* _____ him at a dinner party at my uncle's house.

4. A: What time *(you, get up)* _____ every day?
   B: Between six and seven.

   A: What time *(you, get up)* _____ tomorrow?
   B: Six-thirty.

5. A: Where *(you, study, usually)* _____?
   B: In my room.

   A: *(you, go)* _____ to the library to study sometimes?

   B: No. I *(like, not)* _____ to study at the library.

6. A: *(you, be)* _____ in class tomorrow?

   B: Yes, I _____. But I *(be, not)* _____ in class
   the day after tomorrow.

7. A: *(Yuko, call)* _____ you last night?

   B: Yes, she _____. We *(talk)* _____ for a few minutes.

   A: *(she, tell)* _____ you about her brother?

   B: No, she _____. She *(say, not)* _____
   anything about her brother. Why?

   A: Her brother *(be)* _____ in an accident.
   B: That's too bad. What happened?

A: A dog *(run)* _____ in front of his bicycle. Her brother *(want, not)*

_____ to hit the dog. When he *(try)* _____

to avoid the dog, his bike *(run)* _____ into a truck. It was an
unfortunate accident.

B: *(he, be)* _____ in the hospital now?

A: No, he _____. He *(be)* _____ at home.

8. A: *(whales, breathe)* _____ air?

B: Yes, they _____.

A: *(a whale, have)* _____ lungs?

B: Yes, it _____.

A: *(a whale, be)* _____ a fish?

B: No, it _____. It *(be)* _____ a mammal.

9. A: *(you, watch)* _____ *Star Trek* on TV last night?
   B: What's *Star Trek*?

A: It *(be)* _____ a TV show about

the future. It *(be)* _____ a
science fiction show. *(you, like)*

_____
science fiction?

B: Yes, I _____. I *(read)* _____ science fiction books

often. When *(Star Trek, be)* _____
on TV again?
A: Next week, on Thursday at nine o'clock.

B: I *(try)* _____ to watch it. I might like it. What *("trek," mean)*

_____?

A: "Trek" *(mean)* _____ a long and difficult journey.

B: What *("journey," mean)* _____?

A: "Journey" *(mean)* _____ that you travel from one place to another
place. *Star Trek* is the story of people who travel in outer space among the stars.

■ **EXERCISE 21—REVIEW (ORAL/WRITTEN):** The name of the person in the pictures is Alex. What is he doing? Why? Make up probable reasons. Give three different descriptions of his activities according to the given directions.

1. DESCRIPTION #1: Assume the pictures show things that Alex is doing right now and/or does every day. Use the pictures to describe some of Alex's activities, using present tenses.
2. DESCRIPTION #2: Assume the pictures show things that Alex is going to do tomorrow. Describe these activities.
3. DESCRIPTION #3: Assume the pictures show things that Alex did yesterday. Describe these activities.

| | | | |
|---|---|---|---|
| PRESENT<br>(a) *What* **do** you **do** every day? | → | I *work* every day. | ***What*** + *a form of* **do**<br>is used to ask about<br>activities. |
| (b) *What* **are** you **doing** right now? | → | I'm *studying English*. | |
| PAST<br>(c) *What* **did** you **do** yesterday? | → | I *went to school* yesterday. | |
| FUTURE<br>(d) *What* **are** you **going to do** tomorrow? | → | I'm *going to go downtown* tomorrow. | |
| (e) *What* **will** we **do** if it rains tomorrow? | → | We'll *stay home* if it rains tomorrow. | |

■ **EXERCISE 22:** Complete the sentences with the words in parentheses.

1. A: What (*you, do*) _____do you do_____ every Friday?

   B: I (*come*) _____come_____ to class.

2. A: What (*you, do*) _____ last Friday?

   B: I (*come*) _____ to class.

3. A: What (*you, do*) _____ next Friday?

   B: I (*come*) _____ to class.

4. A: What (*you, do*) _____ yesterday evening?

   B: I (*watch*) _____ TV.

5. A: What (*you, do*) _____ every evening?

   B: I (*watch*) _____ TV.

6. A: What (*you, do*) _____ tomorrow evening?

   B: I (*watch*) _____ TV.

7. A: What (*you, do*) _____ right now?

   B: I (*do*) _____ a grammar exercise.

8. A: What (*Maria, do*) _____ every morning?

   B: She (*go*) _____ to work.

9. A: What *(the students, do)* _____ right now?

   B: They *(work)* _____ on this exercise.

10. A: What *(they, do)* _____ in class tomorrow?

    B: They *(take)* _____ a test.

11. A: What *(Boris, do)* _____ last night?

    B: He *(go)* _____ to a movie.

12. A: What *(the teacher, do)* _____ every day at the beginning
    of class?

    B: She *(put)* _____ her books on her desk, *(look)* _____

    at the class, and *(say)* _____, "Good morning."

■ **EXERCISE 23—ORAL:** Ask a classmate a question. Use **What** + a form of **do** with the
given time expression.

*Example:* yesterday
STUDENT A: What did you do yesterday?
STUDENT B: *(free response)*

1. last night
2. every day
3. right now
4. tomorrow
5. yesterday afternoon
6. tomorrow morning
7. every morning

*Switch roles.*
8. right now
9. last Saturday
10. next Saturday
11. this morning
12. this afternoon
13. tonight
14. next week

| | |
|---|---|
| (a) It **may rain** tomorrow. <br> (b) Anita **may be** at home *now*. | **May** + *verb* (simple form) expresses a possibility in the future, as in (a), or a present possibility, as in (b). |
| (c) It **might rain** tomorrow. <br> (d) Anita **might be** at home *now*. | **Might** has the same meaning as **may**. (a) and (c) have the same meaning. |
| (e) Tom **will be** at the meeting tomorrow. <br><br> (f) Ms. Lee **may/might be** at the meeting tomorrow. | In (e): The speaker uses **will** because he feels sure about Tom's presence at the meeting tomorrow. <br> In (f): The speaker uses **may/might** to say, "I don't know if Ms. Lee will be at the meeting, but it is possible." |
| (g) Ms. Lee **may/might not be** at the meeting tomorrow. | Negative form: **may/might** + **not** <br> NOTE: (f) and (g) have essentially the same meaning: Ms. Lee may or may not be at the meeting tomorrow. |
| (h) INCORRECT: *Ms. Lee **may will** be at the meeting tomorrow.* <br> INCORRECT: *Ms. Lee **might will** be at the meeting tomorrow.* | **May** and **might** are not used with **will**. |

■ **EXERCISE 24:** Complete the sentences. Use **will** or **won't** if you're sure. Use **may/might** if you're not sure.

1. I _____ be in class next Monday.
   - → *I **will be** in class next Monday.* = You're sure.
   - → *I **will not (won't) be** in class next Monday.* = You're sure.
   - → *I **may/might be** in class next Monday (or I **may/might not be** in class next Monday).* = It's possible, but you're not sure.

2. I _____ eat breakfast tomorrow morning.

3. I _____ be in class tomorrow.

4. I _____ get a letter from a friend of mine tomorrow.

5. I _____ watch TV for a little while after dinner tonight.

6. We _____ have a grammar test in class tomorrow.

7. I _____ eat dinner at a restaurant tonight.

8. It _____ be cloudy tomorrow.

9. The sun _____ rise tomorrow morning.

10. I _____ choose a career in music after I finish school.

11. There _____ be another earthquake in Japan in the next few months.

12. The population of the earth _____ continue to grow.

13. Cities _____ become more and more crowded.

14. We _____ communicate with beings from outer space before the end of the 21st century.

15. Do you think we _____ communicate with other beings through music?

■ **EXERCISE 25—WRITTEN:** Complete the sentences. Write about your activities *tomorrow*. Use *be going to* and *may/might*.

1. I'm going to get up at . . . tomorrow morning.
2. Then . . . .
3. After that . . . .
4. Around . . . o'clock . . . .
5. Later . . . .
6. At . . . o'clock . . . .
7. Then . . . .
8. After that . . . .
9. Next . . . .
10. Then at . . . o'clock . . . .

■ **EXERCISE 26—WRITTEN:** Complete the sentences. Write about your activities *yesterday*.

1. I got up at . . . yesterday morning.
2. I . . . and . . . .
3. Then I . . . .
4. I didn't . . . because . . . .
5. Later . . . .
6. Around . . . o'clock . . . .
7. Then . . . .
8. After that . . . .
9. At . . . o'clock . . . .
10. I didn't . . . because . . . .
11. At . . . I . . . .
12. . . . after that.
13. Then at . . . .

## 6-11 MAYBE (ONE WORD) vs. MAY BE (TWO WORDS)

| | | |
|---|---|---|
| (a) | "Will Abdullah be in class tomorrow?"<br>"I don't know. **Maybe. Maybe Abdullah will be** in class tomorrow, and **maybe he won't.**" | The adverb **maybe** (one word) means "possibly." |
| (b) | ⎡**Maybe**⎤ ⎡Abdullah⎤ ⎡will be⎤ here.<br>  adverb     subject     verb | **Maybe** comes in front of a subject and verb. |
| (c) | ⎡Abdullah⎤ ⎡**may be**⎤ here tomorrow.<br>  subject     verb | **May be** (two words) is used as the verb of a sentence. |

■ **EXERCISE 27:** Find the sentences where **maybe** is used as an adverb and where **may** is used as part of the verb.

1. Maybe it will rain tomorrow. → **maybe** = *an adverb*

2. It may rain tomorrow. → **may rain** = *a verb;* **may** *is part of the verb*

3. We may go to the art museum tomorrow.

4. Maybe Ann would like to go to the museum with us.

5. She may like to go to art museums.

6. It's cold and cloudy today. It may be cold and cloudy tomorrow. Maybe the weather will be warm and sunny this weekend.

■ **EXERCISE 28:** Use **maybe** or **may/might**.

1. A: Is David going to come to the party?

   B: I don't know. _____*Maybe*_____.

2. A: What are you going to do tomorrow?

   B: I don't know. I _____*may/might*_____ go swimming.

3. A: What are you going to do tomorrow?

   B: I don't have any plans. _____ I'll go swimming.

4. A: Where is Robert?

   B: I don't know. He _____ be at his office.

5. A: Where is Robert?

   B: I don't know. _____ he's at his office.

6. A: Are Kate and Steve going to get married?

   B: _____. Who knows?

7. A: Are you going to move to Portland or to Seattle?

   B: I don't know. I _____ move to San Francisco.

8. A: Where are you planning to go on your vacation?

   B: _____ we'll go to Mexico. We haven't decided yet. We

      _____ go to Florida.

9. A: Is Amanda married?

   B: Hmmm. I'm not sure. _____ she is, and

      _____ she isn't.

10. A: Do you think it will rain tomorrow?

    B: I have no idea. _____ it will, and _____ it
       won't.

11. A: Are you going to study English next semester?

    B: _____. Are you?

12. A: I'd like to have a pet.

    B: Oh? What kind of pet would you like to get?

    A: Oh, I don't know. I haven't decided yet. _____ I'll get a

       canary. Or _____ I'll get a snake. I'm not sure. I

       _____ get a frog. Or I _____ get a turtle.

    B: What's wrong with a cat or dog?

■ **EXERCISE 29:** Complete the sentences with *maybe* or *may be*.

1. A: I _____ *may be* _____ a little late tonight.
   B: That's okay. I won't worry about you.

2. A: Will you be here by seven o'clock?

   B: It's hard to say. _____ *Maybe* _____ I'll be a little late.

3. A: It _____ cold tomorrow.
   B: That's okay. Let's go to the beach anyway.

4. A: Will the plane be on time?

   B: I think so, but it _____ a few minutes late.

5. A: Do you want to go to the park tomorrow?
   B: Sure.  That sounds like fun.

   A: Let's talk to Carlos too.  _____ he would like to go with us.

6. A: Where's Mr. Chu?

   B: Look in Room 506 down the hall.  I think he _____ there.

   A: No, he's not there.  I just looked in Room 506.

   B: _____ he's in Room 508.

## ■ EXERCISE 30—ORAL (BOOKS CLOSED):  Answer the question by using *I don't know* + *maybe* or *may/might*.

*Example:*     What are you going to do tonight?
*Response:*     I don't know.  Maybe I'll watch TV. / I may watch TV. / I might watch TV.

1. What are you going to do tonight?
2. What are you going to do tomorrow?
3. What are you going to do after class today?
4. What are you going to do this weekend?
5. What are you going to do this evening?
6. Who is going to go shopping tomorrow?  What are you going to buy?
7. Who is going to go out to eat tonight?  Where are you going to go?
8. Who is going to get married?  When?
9. Who is going to watch TV tonight?  What are you going to watch?
10. Who is absent today?  Where is he/she?
11. Is it going to rain tomorrow?  What is the weather going to be like tomorrow?
12. Who is planning to go on a vacation?  Where are you going to go?
13. Who wants to have a pet?  What kind of pet are you going to get?

## ■ EXERCISE 31—ORAL (BOOKS CLOSED):  Use the given information to make guesses.
Include *may/might* and *maybe* in some of your guesses.

*Example:*     ( . . . ) is absent today.  Why?  Do you have any possible explanations?
     →  *He/She **may be** sick.  He/She **might be** out of town today.  **Maybe** he/she*
        *is late today and will come soon.*

1. What is ( . . . ) going to do after class today?
2. ( . . . ) said, "I have very exciting plans for this weekend."  What is he/she going to do this weekend?
3. ( . . . ) has an airplane ticket in his pocket.  I saw it.  Do you know where he/she is going to go?

4. ( . . . ) said, "I don't like it here in this city." Why doesn't ( . . . ) like it here? Do you have any idea?

5. ( . . . ) doesn't like it here. What is he/she going to do?

6. ( . . . ) has something very special in his/her pocket, but he/she won't show anyone what it is. What do you suppose is in his/her pocket?

7. Can you think of some good things that may happen to you this year?

8. What are some good things that might happen to ( . . . ) this year or next year?

9. Can you think of some bad things that might happen in this world this year or next?

10. What are some good things that may happen in the world this year?

11. What new inventions do you think we may have in the future to make our lives easier?

## 6-12 FUTURE TIME CLAUSES WITH *BEFORE*, *AFTER*, AND *WHEN*

| | |
|---|---|
| (a) *Before Ann **goes** to work tomorrow,* she will eat breakfast. | In (a): *Before Ann goes to work tomorrow* is a future time clause.* A future time clause uses the SIMPLE PRESENT TENSE, not ***will*** or ***be going to.*** |
| (b) INCORRECT: *Before Ann **will go** to work tomorrow, she will eat breakfast.* INCORRECT: *Before Ann **is going to go** to work tomorrow, she will eat breakfast.* | |
| (c) I'm going to finish my homework *after I **eat** dinner tonight.* | In (c): *after I eat dinner tonight* = a future time clause. |
| (d) *When I **go** to New York next week,* I'm going to stay at the Hilton Hotel. | In (d): *When I go to New York next week* = a future time clause. |

*See Chart 5-18 for information about time clauses.

■ **EXERCISE 32:** Find the time clauses.

1. When we go to the park tomorrow, we're going to go to the zoo.
   → *When we go to the park tomorrow = a time clause*

2. After I get home tonight, I'm going to make an overseas call to my parents.

3. Mr. Kim will finish his report before he leaves the office today.

4. I'll get some fresh fruit when I go to the market tomorrow.

5. Before I go to bed tonight, I'm going to write a letter to my brother.

6. I'm going to look for a job at a computer company after I graduate next year.

■ **EXERCISE 33:** Complete the sentences with the words in parentheses.

1. Before I *(go)* _____go_____ to bed tonight, I *(watch)*

   _____am going to watch/will watch_____ my favorite show on TV.

2. I *(buy)* _____ a new coat when I *(go)* _____
   shopping tomorrow.

3. After I *(finish)* _____ my homework this evening, I *(take)*

   _____ a walk.

4. When I *(see)* _____ Eduardo tomorrow, I *(ask)* _____
   him to join us for dinner this weekend.

5. When I *(go)* _____ to Australia next month, I *(meet)*

   _____ my Aunt Emily for the first time.

6. Mrs. Polanski *(change)* _____ her clothes before she *(work)*

   _____ in her garden this afternoon.

■ **EXERCISE 34—ORAL (BOOKS CLOSED):** Give complete answers to the questions. Use time clauses.

*Example:* Who's going to go shopping later today? What are you going to do after you go shopping?
TEACHER: Who's going to go shopping later today?
STUDENT A: (*Student A raises his/her hand.*)
TEACHER: What are you going to do after you go shopping?
STUDENT A: After I go shopping, I'm going to go home. OR:
I'm going to go home after I go shopping.
TEACHER: What is ( . . . ) going to do after he/she goes shopping?
STUDENT B: After ( . . . ) goes shopping, he/she is going to go home. OR:
( . . . ) is going to go home after he/she goes shopping.

1. Who's going to study tonight? What are you going to do after you study tonight?
2. Who else is going to study tonight? What are you going to do before you study?
3. Who's going to watch TV tonight? What are you going to do before you watch TV?
4. Who's going to watch TV tonight? What are you going to do after you watch TV?
5. Who's going to go shopping tomorrow? What are you going to buy when you go shopping tomorrow?
6. ( . . . ), what are you going to do tonight? What are you going to do before you . . . ? What are you going to do after you . . . tonight?
7. ( . . . ), what are you going to do tomorrow? What are you going to do before you . . . tomorrow? What are you going to do after you . . . tomorrow?
8. Who's going out of town soon? Where are you going? What are you going to do when you go to *(name of place)*?
9. Who's going to eat dinner tonight? What are you going to do before you eat dinner? What are you going to do after you eat dinner? What are you going to have when you eat dinner?
10. ( . . . ), what time are you going to get home today? What are you going to do before you get home? What are you going to do when you get home? What are you going to do after you get home?

## 6-13 CLAUSES WITH *IF*

| | | |
|---|---|---|
| (a) | **If it rains tomorrow,** *if-clause*  we will stay home. *main clause* | An *if*-clause begins with **if** and has a subject and a verb. |
| (b) | We will stay home *main clause*  **if it rains tomorrow.** *if-clause* | An *if*-clause can come before or after a main clause. |
| (c) | **If** it **rains** tomorrow, we won't go on a picnic. | The SIMPLE PRESENT (not **will** or **be going to**) is used in an *if*-clause to express future time. |
| (d) | I'm going to buy a new car next year **if I have** enough money. **If I don't have** enough money for a new car next year, I'm going to buy a used car. | |

■ **EXERCISE 35:** Complete the sentences with the words in parentheses.

1. If Ali *(be)* _____*is*_____ in class tomorrow, I *(ask)*

   ____*am going to/will ask*____ him to join us for coffee after class.

2. If the weather *(be)* _____ nice tomorrow, I *(go)*

   _____ to Central Park with my friends.

3. I *(stay, not)* _____ home tomorrow if the weather *(be)*

   _____ nice.

4. If I *(feel, not)* _____ well tomorrow, I *(go, not)*

   _____ to work.

5. Masako *(stay)* _____ in bed tomorrow if she *(feel, not)*

   _____ well.

6. I *(stay)* _____ with my aunt and uncle if I *(go)*

   _____ to Miami next week.

7. If my friends *(be)* _____ busy tomorrow, I *(go)*

   _____ to a movie by myself.

8. If we *(continue)* _____ to pollute the land and oceans with poisons

   and waste, future generations *(suffer)* _____.

■ **EXERCISE 36—ORAL (BOOKS CLOSED):**   In pairs, ask and answer questions.

STUDENT A:   Your book is open.  Ask a question that begins with "***What are you going to do . . . ?***"

STUDENT B:   Your book is closed.  Answer the question.  Include the ***if***-clause in your answer.

*Example:*      . . . if the weather is nice tomorrow?
STUDENT A:   What are you going to do if the weather is nice tomorrow?
STUDENT B:   If the weather is nice tomorrow, I'm going to sit outside in the sun.  OR:   I'm going to sit outside in the sun if the weather is nice tomorrow.

1. . . . if the weather is cold tomorrow?
2. . . . if the weather is hot tomorrow?
3. . . . if you don't understand a question that I ask you?
4. . . . if class is canceled tomorrow?
5. . . . if you don't feel well tomorrow?
6. . . . if you go to *(name of a place in this city)* tomorrow?

*Switch roles.*
7. . . . if it rains tonight?
8. . . . if you're hungry after class today?
9. . . . if you go to *(name of a place in this city)* tomorrow?
10. . . . if you don't study tonight?
11. . . . if you lose your grammar book?
12. . . . if someone steals your *(name of a thing: bicycle, wallet, etc.)?*

■ **EXERCISE 37:**   Pair up with a classmate.

STUDENT A:   Fill out the calendar with your activities for next week.  (If you don't have many planned activities, invent some interesting ones.)  Then give the calendar to Student B.

STUDENT B:   In writing, describe Student A's activities next week.  Try to include some time clauses beginning with ***when***, ***after***, and ***before***.  Ask Student A questions about the activities on his/her calendar to get more information or clarification.

*Example:*      *(Student A is Ali.)*

**SUNDAY**

7:00 tennis with Talal
9:00 breakfast with Talal
1:00 meet Ivan at Cozy's before game
2:00 Memorial Stadium

7-9 Study

*Student B interviews Student A about his calendar and then writes:*  On Sunday, Ali is going to play tennis with Talal early in the morning.  They're going to play on the tennis courts here at this school.  After they play tennis, they're going to have breakfast.  In the afternoon, Ali is going to meet Ivan at Cozy's.  Cozy's is a cafe.  They're going to have a sandwich and a cup of coffee before they go to the soccer game at Memorial Stadium.  Ali will study in the evening before he watches TV and goes to bed.

Fill out this calendar with your activities for next week.

| MONDAY | THURSDAY |
|--------|----------|
|        |          |
| TUESDAY | FRIDAY |
|        |          |
| WEDNESDAY | SATURDAY |
|        |          |

## 6-14 EXPRESSING HABITUAL PRESENT WITH TIME CLAUSES AND *IF*-CLAUSES

| | | | |
|---|---|---|---|
| (a) | FUTURE | After Ann **gets** to work today, she **is going to have** a cup of coffee. | (a) expresses a specific activity in the future. The SIMPLE PRESENT is used in the time clause. *Be going to* is used in the main clause. |
| (b) | HABITUAL PRESENT | After Ann **gets** to work (every day), she always **has** a cup of coffee. | (b) expresses habitual activities, so the SIMPLE PRESENT is used in both the time clause and the main clause. |
| (c) | FUTURE | If it **rains** tomorrow, I **am going to** wear my raincoat to school. | (c) expresses a specific activity in the future. The SIMPLE PRESENT is used in the *if*-clause. *Be going to* is used in the main clause. |
| (d) | HABITUAL PRESENT | If it **rains**, I **wear** my raincoat. | (d) expresses habitual activities, so the SIMPLE PRESENT is used in both the *if*-clause and the main clause. |

■ **EXERCISE 38:** Complete the sentences with the words in parentheses.

1. When I *(go)* _____ to Miami, I *(stay, usually)* _____ with my aunt and uncle.

2. When I *(go)* _____ to Miami next week, I *(stay)* _____ with my aunt and uncle.

3. Before I *(go)* _____ to class today, I *(have)* _____ a cup of tea.

4. Before I *(go)* _____ to class, I *(have, usually)* _____ a cup of tea.

5. I'm often tired in the evening after a long day at work. If I *(be)* _____ tired

   in the evening, I *(stay, usually)* _____ home and *(go)*

   _____ to bed early.

6. If I *(be)* _____ tired this evening, I *(stay)* _____

   home and *(go)* _____ to bed early.

7. After I *(get)* _____ home in the evening, I *(sit, usually)* _____

   in my favorite chair and *(read)* _____ the newspaper.

8. After I *(get)* _____ home tonight, I *(sit)* _____

   in my favorite chair and *(read)* _____ the newspaper.

9. We *(go)* _____ swimming tomorrow if the weather *(be)*

   _____ warm.

10. My friends and I *(like)* _____ to go swimming if the weather *(be)*

    _____ warm.

11. People *(yawn, often)* _____ and *(stretch)*

    _____ when they *(wake)* _____ up.

12. I *(buy)* _____ some stamps when I *(go)* _____ to the post office this afternoon.

13. Before the teacher *(walk)* _____ into the room every day, there *(be)*

    _____ a lot of noise in the classroom.

14. When I (go) _____ to Taiwan next month, I (stay) _____

    with my friend Mr. Chu. After I (leave) _____ Taiwan, I (go)

    _____ to Hong Kong.

15. Ms. Wah (go) _____ to Hong Kong often. When she (be)

    _____ there, she (like) _____ to take the ferry across

    the bay, but sometimes she (take) _____ the subway under the bay.

■ **EXERCISE 39—ORAL (BOOKS CLOSED):**   Answer the questions in complete sentences.

   1. What do you do when you get up in the morning?
   2. What are you going to do when you get up tomorrow morning?
   3. What do you usually do before you go to bed?
   4. What are you going to do before you go to bed tonight?
   5. What are you going to do after you eat dinner tonight?
   6. What do you usually do after you eat dinner?
   7. What do you like to do if the weather is nice?
   8. What are you going to do if the weather is nice tomorrow?

■ **EXERCISE 40:**   Complete the sentences with your own words.

   1. Before I go to bed tonight, . . . .
   2. Before I go to bed, I usually . . . .
   3. I'm going to . . . tomorrow after I . . . .
   4. When I go to . . . , I'm going to . . . .
   5. When I go to . . . , I always . . . .
   6. If the weather . . . tomorrow, I . . . .
   7. I will visit . . . when I . . . .
   8. I'll . . . if I . . . .
   9. If the weather . . . tomorrow, . . . you going to . . . ?
  10. Are you going to . . . before you . . . ?
  11. Do you . . . before you . . . ?
  12. After I . . . tonight, I . . . .

■ **EXERCISE 41—REVIEW (ORAL/WRITTEN):**   Pretend that you are going to start a self-improvement plan for this coming year. What are some things you are going to do/will do to improve yourself and your life this year? For example: *I will stop smoking. I am going to get more exercise. Etc.*

■ **EXERCISE 42—REVIEW (ORAL/WRITTEN):** What is going to happen in the lives of your classmates in the next 50 years? Make predictions about your classmates' futures. For example: *Heidi is going to become a famous research scientist. Ali will have a happy marriage and lots of children. Carlos will live in a quiet place and write poetry. Etc.*

■ **EXERCISE 43—REVIEW (ORAL/WRITTEN):** In the mail, you find a letter from a bank. In the envelope is a gift of a lot of money. (As a class, decide on the amount of money in the gift.) You can keep the money if you follow the directions in the letter. There are six different versions of the letter. Choose one (or more) of the letters and describe what you are going to do.

LETTER #1: You have to spend the money on a wonderful vacation. What are you going to do?

LETTER #2: You have to spend the money to help other people. What are you going to do?

LETTER #3: You have to spend the money to improve your school or place of work. What are you going to do?

LETTER #4: You have to spend the money on your family. What are you going to do?

LETTER #5: You have to spend the money to make the world a better place. What are you going to do?

LETTER #6: You have to spend the money to improve your country. What are you going to do?

---

## 6-15 MORE IRREGULAR VERBS

| | | |
|---|---|---|
| *begin – began* | *say – said* | *tell – told* |
| *find – found* | *sell – sold* | *tear – tore* |
| *lose – lost* | *steal – stole* | *wear – wore* |
| *hang – hung* | | |

---

■ **EXERCISE 44—ORAL (BOOKS CLOSED):** Practice using the IRREGULAR VERBS in the above list.

1. *begin–began*    Our class begins at (9:00) every day. Class began at (9:00 this morning). When did class begin (this morning)?
   → *It began at (9:00).*

2. *lose–lost*    Sometimes I lose things. Yesterday I lost my keys. What did I do yesterday?

3. *find–found*    Sometimes I lose things. And then I find them. Yesterday I lost my keys, but then I found them in my jacket pocket. What did I do yesterday?

4. *tear–tore*    If we make a mistake when we write a check, we tear the check up. Yesterday I made a mistake when I wrote a check, so I tore it up and wrote a new check. What did I do yesterday?

5. *sell–sold*    People sell things that they don't need anymore. ( . . . ) has a new bicycle, so he/she sold his/her old bicycle. What did ( . . . ) do?

6. *hang–hung*    I like to hang pictures on my walls. This morning I hung a new picture in my bedroom. What did I do this morning?

7. *tell–told*    The kindergarten teacher likes to tell stories to her students. Yesterday she told a story about a little red train. What did the teacher do yesterday?

8. *wear–wore*    I wear a sweater to class every evening. Last night I wore a jacket as well. What did I wear last night?

9. *steal–stole*    Thieves steal money and other valuables. Last month a thief stole my aunt's pearl necklace. What did a thief do last month?

10. *say–said*    People usually say "hello" when they answer a phone. When ( . . . ) answered his/her phone this morning, he/she said "hello." What did ( . . . ) do this morning?

■ **EXERCISE 45:** Complete the sentences. Use the words in parentheses.

| | | |
|---|---|---|
| *begin* | *say* | *tear* |
| *find* | *sell* | *tell* |
| *hang* | *steal* | *wear* |
| *lose* | | |

1. A: Did you go to the park yesterday?

   B: No. We stayed home because it _____ to rain.

2. A: Susie is in trouble.
   B: Why?

   A: She _____ a lie. Her mom and dad are upset.

3. A: Where did you get that pretty shell?

   B: I _____ it on the beach.

SHELLS

4. A: May I please have your homework?

   B: I don't have it. I _____ it.
   A: You what!?
   B: I can't find it anywhere.

5. A: Where's my coat?

   B: I _____ it up in the closet for you.

6. A: What happened to your sleeve?

   B: I _____ it on a nail.
   A: That's too bad.

7. A: Do you still have your bicycle?

   B: No. I _____ it because I
      needed some extra money.

8. A: It's hot in here.
   B: Excuse me?  What did you say?

   A: I _____ , "It's hot in here."

9. A: Why did you take the bus to work this morning?  Why didn't you drive?

   B: Because somebody _____ my car last night.
   A: Did you call the police?
   B: Of course I did.

10. A: Did you wear your blue jeans to the job interview?

    B: Of course not!  I _____ a suit.

■ **EXERCISE 46:**  Complete the sentences.  Use the words in parentheses.  Use any appropriate
verb form.

1. A: *(you, be)* _____ at home tomorrow morning around ten?

   B: No.  I *(be)* _____ out.

2. A: I *(lose)* _____ my sunglasses yesterday.
   B: Where?

   A: I *(think)* _____ that I *(leave)* _____ them on a table
      at the restaurant.

3. A: How are you getting along?

   B: Fine.  I'm making a lot of friends, and my English *(improve)* _____.

4. A: Sometimes children tell little lies.  You talked to Annie.  *(she, tell)* _____

   _____ the truth, or *(she, tell)* _____ a lie?

   B: She *(tell)* _____ the truth.  She's honest.

5. A: *(you, write)* _____ a letter to George yesterday?

   B: Yes, I did.  I *(send)* _____ him a letter yesterday.

6. A: May I see the classified section of the newspaper?
   B: Sure. Here it is.

   A: Thanks. I (want) _____ (look) _____ at the want ads. I

   (need) _____ (find) _____ a new apartment.

---

**APTS., UNFURN.**

2 BR. $725/mo. Lake St.
Near bus. All utils. incl.
No pets. 361-3663. eves.

---

7. A: Where (you, go) _____ yesterday?

   B: I (go) _____ to my cousin's house. I (see) _____

   Jean there and (talk) _____ to her for a while. And I (meet)

   _____ my cousin's neighbors, Mr. and Mrs. Bell. They're nice
   people. I like them.

8. A: What are you going to do tonight? (you, study) _____?

   B: No. I don't think so. I'm tired. I think I (watch) _____

   TV for a while, or maybe I (listen) _____ to some

   music. Or I might read a novel. But I (want, not, study) _____

   _____ tonight.

9. A: (you, do) _____ your homework last night?

   B: No. I (be) _____ too tired. I (go) _____ to bed early

   and (sleep) _____ for nine hours.

10. A: Good morning.
    B: Excuse me?

    A: I (say) _____, "Good morning."

    B: Oh! Good morning! I'm sorry. I (understand, not) _____
    you at first.

11. A: What did you do yesterday?

B: Well, I *(wake up)* _____ around nine and *(go)*

_____ shopping. While I was downtown, someone *(steal)*

_____ my purse. I *(take)* _____ a taxi home. When

I *(get)* _____ out of the taxi, I *(tear)* _____ my

blouse. I *(borrow)* _____ some money from my roommate to
pay the taxi driver.

A: Did anything good happen to you yesterday?

B: Hmmm. Let me think. Oh yes. I *(lose)* _____ my grammar book,

but I *(find)* _____ it later.

## 6-16  MORE IRREGULAR VERBS

| | | |
|---|---|---|
| *cost – cost* | *hit – hit* | *spend – spent* |
| *cut – cut* | *hurt – hurt* | *understand – understood* |
| *forget –forgot* | *lend – lent* | |
| *give – gave* | *make – made* | |

■ **EXERCISE 47—ORAL (BOOKS CLOSED):**  Practice using the IRREGULAR VERBS in the
above list.

1. *cost-cost*    I bought a hat yesterday. I paid (twenty dollars) for it. It cost (twenty
dollars). What did I buy yesterday? How much did it cost?
 → *You bought a hat. It cost (twenty dollars).*

2. *give-gave*    People give gifts when someone has a birthday. Last week, ( . . . ) had
a birthday. I gave him/her *(something)*. What did I do?

3. *make-made*    I make good chocolate cake. Last week I made a cake for ( . . . )'s
birthday. What did I do last week?

4. *cut-cut*    ( . . . ) cuts vegetables when he/she makes a salad. Two nights ago,
while he/she was making a salad, he /she cut his/her finger with the
knife. What happened two nights ago?

5. *hurt-hurt*    When I have a headache, my head hurts. Yesterday I had a headache.
My head hurt yesterday. How did my head feel yesterday? How
does your head feel when you have a headache?

6. *lend-lent*    I lend money to my friends if they need it. Yesterday I lent *(a certain
amount of money)* to ( . . . ). What did I do?

7. *forget-forgot*    Sometimes I forget my wallet. Last night, I forgot it at a restaurant.
What did I do last night?

8. *spend-spent*    I usually spend Saturdays with my parents. Last Saturday, I spent the
day with my friends instead. What did I do last Saturday?

9. *shut-shut*     I shut the garage door every night at 10:00 P.M.  I shut it early last
                    night.  What did I do last night?
10. *understand-*  I always understand ( . . . ) when he/she speaks.  He/She just
    *understood*    said something and I understood it.  What just happened?
11. *hit-hit*       ( . . . ) lives in an apartment.  His/Her neighbors are very noisy.
                    When they make too much noise, ( . . . ) hits the wall with his/her
                    hand.  Last night he/she couldn't get to sleep because of the noise,
                    so he/she hit the wall with his/her hand.  What did ( . . . ) do last
                    night?  What does he/she usually do when his/her neighbors make
                    too much noise?

■ **EXERCISE 48:**   Complete the sentences.  Use the words in parentheses.

1. A: How much *(a new car, cost)* _____?

   B: It *(cost)* _____ a lot!  New cars are expensive.

2. A: Did you get a ticket for the rock concert?

   B: Yes, and it was really expensive!  It *(cost)* _____ fifty dollars.

3. A: Where's your dictionary?

   B: I *(give)* _____ it to Robert.

4. A: I had a car accident yesterday morning.
   B: What happened?

   A: I *(hit)* _____ a telephone pole.

5. A: May I have your homework, please?

   B: I'm sorry, but I don't have it.  I *(forget)* _____ it.

   A: You *(forget)* _____ it!?

6. A: Did you eat breakfast?

   B: Yeah.  I *(make)* _____ some scrambled eggs and toast for myself.

7. Jack *(put)* _____ on his clothes every morning.

8. Jack *(put)* _____ on his clothes this morning after he got up.

9. A: Did you enjoy going into the city to see a show?

   B: Yes, but I *(spend)* _____ a lot of money.  I can't afford to do
      that very often.

10. A: May I see your dictionary?

    B: I don't have it.  I *(lend)* _____ it to George.

11. A: Is that knife sharp?

   B: It's very sharp. It *(cut)* _____ anything easily.

12. A: I went to a barber this morning. He *(cut)* _____ my hair too short.
   B: It looks fine.

■ **EXERCISE 49—ORAL (BOOKS CLOSED):** Give the past form. Spell the past form. Make sentences using the past form.

   *Example:* come
   *Response:* came . . . C–A–M–E . . . I came to class this morning.

| | | |
|---|---|---|
| 1. come | 19. meet | 37. forget |
| 2. eat | 20. speak | 38. drive |
| 3. stand | 21. take | 39. ride |
| 4. understand | 22. wear | 40. run |
| 5. drink | 23. write | 41. go |
| 6. break | 24. fly | 42. see |
| 7. hear | 25. leave | 43. sit |
| 8. lose | 26. pay | 44. cut |
| 9. find | 27. cost | 45. hit |
| 10. begin | 28. spend | 46. sing |
| 11. put | 29. sell | 47. bring |
| 12. shut | 30. buy | 48. read |
| 13. hang | 31. ring | 49. teach |
| 14. tell | 32. make | 50. think |
| 15. tear | 33. do | 51. have |
| 16. get | 34. say | 52. sleep |
| 17. wake up | 35. catch | 53. give |
| 18. steal | 36. send | 54. lend |

■ **EXERCISE 50—REVIEW:** Complete the sentences. Use the words in parentheses. Use any appropriate verb form.

1. A: I *(cut)* _____ class tomorrow.
   B: Why?
   A: Why not?
   B: That's not a very good reason.

2. A: How did you get here?

   B: I *(take)* _____ a plane. I *(fly)* _____ here from Bangkok.

3. A: How do you usually get to class?

   B: I *(walk, usually)* _____, but sometimes I *(take)*

   _____ the bus.

4. A: Where *(you, meet)* _____ your wife?

   B: I *(meet)* _____ her at a party ten years ago.

5. A: Did you see that?
   B: What?

   A: The man in the red shirt *(hit)* _____ the man in the blue shirt.
   B: Really?

6. A: Were you late for the movie?

   B: No. The movie *(begin)* _____ at 7:30, and we *(get)* _____
   to the theater at 7:26.

7. A: What time *(the movie, begin)* _____ last
   night?
   B: 7:30.

   A: *(you, be)* _____ late?

   B: No. We *(make)* _____ it in time.

8. A: Do you hear that noise?
   B: What noise?

   A: *(you, listen)* _____?

9. A: Where's your homework?

   B: I *(lose)* _____ it.
   A: Oh?

   B: I *(forget)* _____ it.
   A: Oh?

   B: I *(give)* _____ it to Roberto to give to you, but he *(lose)*

   _____ it.
   A: Oh?

   B: Someone *(steal)* _____ it.
   A: Oh?

   B: Well, actually I *(have, not)* _____ enough time to
   finish it last night.
   A: I see.

10.  A: Where's my book!  Someone *(steal)* _____ it!

   B: Take it easy.  Your book *(be)* _____ right here.
   A: Oh.

11.  A: *(you, stay)* _____ here during vacation next week?

   B: No.  I *(take)* _____ a trip to Miami.  I *(visit)*

   _____ my aunt and uncle.

   A: How long *(you, be)* _____ away?
   B: About five days.

12.  A: Why *(you, wear)* _____ a cast on your foot?

   B: I *(break)* _____ my ankle.
   A: How?

   B: I *(step)* _____ in a hole while I was running in the park.

13.  A: *(you, want, go)* _____ to the zoo this afternoon?
   B: I'd like to go, but I can't because I have to study.
   A: That's too bad.

   B: *(you, go)* _____ to the zoo?

   A: Yes.  The weather is perfect, and I *(want)* _____ *(get)*

   _____ outside and *(enjoy)* _____ it.

14.  A: *(you, see)* _____ Randy yesterday?

   B: No, but I *(speak)* _____ to him on the phone.  He *(call)*

   _____ me yesterday evening.
   A: Is he okay?
   B: Yes.  He still has a cold, but he's feeling much better.
   A: That's good.

15.  A: Is Carol here?

   B: No, she *(be, not)* _____.  She *(leave)* _____ a few minutes ago.

   A: *(she, be)* _____ back soon?
   B: I think so.

   A: Where *(she, go)* _____?

   B: She *(go)* _____ to the drugstore.

■ **EXERCISE 51—REVIEW:**   Choose the correct completions.

1. "Are you going to go to the baseball game tomorrow afternoon?"

   "I don't know.  I _____."
       A.  will          B.  am going to    C.  maybe        D.  might

2. "Are Jane and Eric going to be at the meeting?"

   "No, they're too busy.  They _____ be there."
       A.  don't        B.  won't        C.  will        D.  may

3. "Are you going to go to the market today?"

   "No.  I went there _____ Friday."
       A.  yesterday    B.  next        C.  last        D.  ago

4. "When are you going to go to the bank?"

   "I'll go there before I _____ to the post office tomorrow morning."
       A.  will go      B.  go        C.  went        D.  am going

5. "Why is the teacher late today?"

   "I don't know.  _____ he slept late."
       A.  May        B.  Did        C.  Maybe       D.  Was

6. "Do you like to go to New York City?"

   "Yes.  When I'm in New York, I always _____ new things to do and places to go."
       A.  found       B.  find       C.  will find    D.  am finding

7. "Is Ken going to talk to us this afternoon about our plans for tomorrow?"

   "No.  He'll _____ us this evening."
       A.  calls        B.  calling      C.  call        D.  called

8. "_____ are you going to do after class today?"
   "I'm going to go home."
       A.  When       B.  Where      C.  What       D.  What time

9. "Where _____ Ivonne live before she moved into her new apartment?"
   "She lived in a dormitory at the university."
       A.  did        B.  does      C.  is        D.  was

10. "What time _____ Olga and Boris going to arrive?"
    "Six."
        A.  is        B.  do        C.  will        D.  are

■ **EXERCISE 52—REVIEW (ERROR ANALYSIS):**   Correct the errors in the sentences.

1. Is Ivan will go to work tomorrow?

2. When you will call me?

3. Will Tom to meet us for dinner tomorrow?

4. We went to a movie yesterday night.

5. If it will be cold tomorrow morning, my car won't start.

6. We maybe late for the concert tonight.

7. Did you found your keys?

8. What time you are going to come tomorrow?

9. My sister is going to meet me at the airport.  My brother won't to be there.

10. Fatima will call us tonight when she will arrive home safely.

11. Mr. Wong will sells his business and retires next year.

12. Do you will be in Venezuela next year?

13. Emily may will be at the party.

14. I'm going to return home in a couple of month.

15. When I'll see you tomorrow, I'll return your book to you.

16. I saw Jim three day ago.

17. I may to don't be in class tomorrow.

18. Ahmed puts his books on his desk when he walked into his apartment.

19. A thief stoled my bicycle.

20. I'll see my parents when I will return home for a visit next July.

■ **EXERCISE 53—REVIEW:** Complete the sentences. Use the words in parentheses. Use any appropriate verb form.

(1)         *Peter and Rachel are brother and sister. Right now their parents* (be) _____

(2)   *abroad on a trip, so they* (stay) _____ *with their grandmother. They*

(3)   (like) _____ *to stay with her. She* (make, always) _____

(4)   *wonderful food for them. And she* (tell) _____ *them stories every night before they*

(5)   (go) _____ *to bed.*

(6)       *Before Peter and Rachel* (go) _____ *to bed last night, they* (ask)

(7)   _____ *Grandma to tell them a story. She* (agree) _____. *The*

(8)   *children* (put) _____ *on their pajamas,* (brush) _____ *their teeth, and*

(9)   (sit) _____ *with their grandmother in her big chair to listen to a story.*

GRANDMA:     That's good. Sit here beside me and get comfortable.

(10)   CHILDREN:    What *(you, tell)* _____ us about tonight,

      Grandma?

(11)   GRANDMA:    Before I *(begin)* _____ the story, I *(give)* _____

      each of you a kiss on the forehead because I love you very much.

(12)   CHILDREN:    We *(love)* _____ you, too, Grandma.

(13)  GRANDMA:  Tonight I *(tell)* _____ you a story about Rabbit and

Eagle.  Ready?

CHILDREN:  Yes!

GRANDMA:  Rabbit had light gray fur and a white tail.  He lived with his family in a hole

(14)  in a big, grassy field.  Rabbit *(be)* _____ afraid of many things, but he

(15)  *(be)* _____ especially afraid of Eagle.  Eagle liked to eat rabbits for dinner.

(16)  One day while Rabbit was eating grass in the field, he *(see)* _____ Eagle in

(17)  the sky above him.  Rabbit *(be)* _____ very afraid and *(run)* _____

(18)  home to his hole as fast as he could.  Rabbit *(stay)* _____ in his hole day

(19)  after day because he *(be)* _____ afraid to go outside.  He *(get)* _____

(20)  very hungry, but still he *(stay)* _____ in his hole.  Finally, he *(find)*

(21)  _____ the courage to go outside because he *(need)* _____

(22)  *(eat)* _____.

(23)  Carefully and slowly, he *(put)* _____ his little pink nose outside the

(24)  hole.  He *(smell, not)* _____ any dangerous animals.

(25)  And he *(see, not)* _____ Eagle anywhere, so he *(hop)*

(26)  _____ out and *(find)* _____ some delicious new

(27)  grass to eat.  While he was eating the grass, he *(see)* _____ a shadow on the

(28)  field and *(look)* _____ up.  It was Eagle!  Rabbit said, "Please don't eat

me, Eagle!  Please don't eat me, Eagle!'"

On this sunny afternoon, Eagle was on her way home to her nest when she

(29) *(hear)* _____ a faint sound below her. "What is that sound?" Eagle said

(30) to herself. She looked around, but she *(see, not)* _____

(31) anything. She *(decide)* _____ to ignore the sound and go home.

(32) She was tired and *(want)* _____ *(rest)* _____ in

her nest.

(33) Then below her, Rabbit *(say)* _____ again in a very loud voice,

"Please don't eat me, Eagle! Please don't eat me, Eagle." This time Eagle *(hear)*

(34) _____ Rabbit clearly. Eagle *(spot)* _____ Rabbit in

(35) the field, *(fly)* _____ down, and *(pick)* _____ Rabbit

up in her talons.

"Thank you, Rabbit," said Eagle. "I was hungry and *(know, not)*

(36) _____ where I could find my dinner. It's a good thing

(37) you called to me." Then Eagle *(eat)* _____ Rabbit for dinner.

(38) There's a lesson to learn from this story, children. If you *(be)* _____

afraid and expect bad things to happen, bad things will happen. The opposite is also

(39) true. If you *(expect)* _____ good things to happen, good things will happen.

(40) *(you, understand)* _____? Now it's time for bed.

CHILDREN:    Please tell us another story!

(41)    GRANDMA:    Not tonight. I'm tired.   After I *(have)* _____ a warm drink, I

(42)    *(go)* _____ to bed.  All of us need *(get)* _____ a

(43)    good night's sleep.  Tomorrow *(be)* _____ a busy day.

(44)    CHILDREN:    What *(we, do)* _____ tomorrow?

(45)    GRANDMA:    After we *(have)* _____ breakfast, we *(go)* _____

(46)    to the zoo at Woodland Park.  When we *(be)* _____ at the zoo, we

(47)    *(see)* _____ lots of wonderful animals.  Then in the afternoon

(48)    we *(see)* _____ a play at the Children's Theater.  But before we

(49)    *(see)* _____ the play, we *(have)* _____

a picnic lunch in the park.

(50)    CHILDREN:    Wow!  We *(have)* _____ a wonderful day tomorrow!

GRANDMA:    Now off to bed!  Goodnight, Rachel and Peter.  Sleep tight.★

CHILDREN:    Goodnight, Grandma.  Thank you for the story!

---

★"Sleep tight" means "sleep well; have a good night's sleep."

# CHAPTER 7
## Expressing Ability

### 7-1 USING *CAN*

| | |
|---|---|
| (a) I have some money. I **can buy** a book.<br>(b) We have time and money. We **can go** to a movie.<br>(c) Tom is strong. He **can lift** the heavy box. | **Can** expresses *ability* and *possibility*. |
| (d) CORRECT: Yuko can **speak** English. | The simple form of the main verb follows **can**. In (d): *speak* is the main verb. |
| (e) INCORRECT: *Yuko can **to** speak English.* | An infinitive with **to** does NOT follow **can**. In (e): *to speak* is incorrect. |
| (f) INCORRECT: *Yuko can speak**s** English.* | The main verb never has a final **-s**. In (f): *speaks* is incorrect. |
| (g) Alice **can not** come.<br>Alice **cannot** come.<br>Alice **can't** come. | NEGATIVE:<br>    **can** + **not** = **can not** OR: **cannot**<br>CONTRACTION:<br>    **can** + **not** = **can't** |

■ **EXERCISE 1—ORAL:** Make sentences from the given words. Use **can** or **can't**.

*Example:* A bird \ sing          *Example:* A horse \ sing
*Response:* A bird can sing.     *Response:* A horse can't sing.

1. A bird \ fly
2. A cow \ fly
3. A child \ drive a car
4. An adult \ drive a car
5. A newborn baby \ walk
6. A fish \ breathe air
7. A fish \ swim

8. A deaf person \ hear
9. A blind person \ see
10. An elephant \ swim
11. An elephant \ climb trees
12. A cat \ climb trees
13. A boat \ float on water
14. A rock \ float on water

■ **EXERCISE 2—ORAL:**   Make sentences about yourself using *I can* or *I can't*.

> *Example:*   speak Chinese
> *Response:*   I can speak Chinese.  OR:  I can't speak Chinese.

1. whistle
2. ride a bicycle
3. touch my ear with my elbow
4. play the piano*
5. play the guitar
6. lift a piano
7. drive a stick-shift car
8. fix a flat tire

9. swim
10. float on water
11. ski
12. do arithmetic
13. make a paper airplane
14. sew a button on a shirt
15. eat with chopsticks
16. wiggle my ears

## 7-2   USING *CAN:* QUESTIONS

| (QUESTION WORD) + | *CAN* + | SUBJECT + | MAIN VERB | | | ANSWER |
|---|---|---|---|---|---|---|
| (a) | *Can* | *you* | *speak* | Arabic? | → | *Yes, I can.* |
| | | | | | → | *No, I can't.* |
| (b) | *Can* | *Marge* | *come* | to the party? | → | *Yes, she can.* |
| | | | | | → | *No, she can't.* |
| (c) *Where* | *can* | *I* | *buy* | a hammer? | → | *At a hardware store.* |
| (d) *When* | *can* | *you* | *help* | me? | → | *Tomorrow afternoon.* |

■ **EXERCISE 3:**   Make yes/no questions.  Give short answers.

1. A: _____*Can Jean speak English?*_____

   B: _____*Yes, she can.*_____ (Jean can speak English.)

2. A: _____*Can you speak French?*_____

   B: _____*No, I can't.*_____ (I can't speak French.)

3. A: _____

   B: _____ (Jim can't play the piano.)

4. A: _____

   B: _____ (I can whistle.)

---

*In expressions with **play**, **the** is usually used with musical instruments: *play the piano, play the guitar, play the violin, etc.*

5. A: _____

   B: _____ (I can go shopping with you this afternoon.)

6. A: _____

   B: _____ (Carmen can't ride a bicycle.)

7. A: _____

   B: _____ (Elephants can swim.)

8. A: _____

   B: _____ (The students can finish this exercise quickly.)

9. A: _____

   B: _____
   (I can stand on my head.)

10. A: _____

    B: _____
    (The doctor can see you tomorrow.)

11. A: _____

    B: _____
    (We can't have pets in the dormitory.)

■ **EXERCISE 4—ORAL:** Pair up with a classmate.
   STUDENT A: Your book is open. Ask a question. Use *"Can you . . . ?"*
   STUDENT B: Your book is closed. Answer the question.

*Example:*   speak Arabic
STUDENT A:  Can you speak Arabic?
STUDENT B:  Yes, I can.  OR:  No, I can't.

*Switch roles.*

1.  ride a bicycle
2.  ride a motorcycle
3.  ride a horse
4.  play the piano
5.  play the guitar
6.  touch the ceiling of this room
7.  cook *(a nationality)* food
8.  sing
9.  whistle
10. float on water

11. spell Mississippi
12. see the back of ( . . . )'s head
13. count to five in *(a language)*
14. stand on your head
15. touch your knee with your nose
16. touch your ear with your elbow
17. play the violin
18. drive a stick-shift car
19. fix a flat tire
20. ski

■ **EXERCISE 5—ORAL:** Pair up with a classmate.

STUDENT A: Your book is open. Ask a question. Use "*Where can I . . . ?*"
STUDENT B: Your book is closed. Answer the question.

*Example:*     buy a notebook
STUDENT A:   Where can I buy a notebook?
STUDENT B.   At the bookstore. / At *(name of a local store)*. / Etc.

*Switch roles.*

| | |
|---|---|
| 1. buy a camera | 9. buy a diamond ring |
| 2. get a dozen eggs | 10. buy a hammer |
| 3. buy a window fan | 11. see a zebra |
| 4. get a good dinner | 12. get a newspaper |
| 5. go swimming | 13. find an encyclopedia |
| 6. play tennis | 14. get a taxi |
| 7. catch a bus | 15. get a sandwich |
| 8. mail a package | 16. cash a check |

## 7-3   USING *KNOW HOW TO*

| | |
|---|---|
| (a)  I can swim. | (a) and (b) have basically the same meaning. ***Know how to*** expresses ability. |
| (b)  I ***know how to swim***. | |
| (c)  Can you cook? | (c) and (d) have basically the same meaning. |
| (d)  ***Do*** you ***know how to cook***? | |

■ **EXERCISE 6—ORAL:**  Pair up with a classmate.

STUDENT A: Your book is open.  Ask a question.  Use ***know how to*** in your question.
STUDENT B: Your book is closed.  Answer the question.

*Example:*     swim
STUDENT A:   Do you know how to swim?
STUDENT B:   Yes, I do.   OR:   No, I don't.

*Switch roles.*

| | |
|---|---|
| 1. cook | 9. play the guitar |
| 2. dance | 10. get to the airport from here |
| 3. play the piano | 11. get to *(name of a store)* from here |
| 4. get to the post office from here | 12. use a hammer |
| 5. fix a flat tire | 13. use a screwdriver |
| 6. drive a stick-shift car | 14. count to five in *(a language)* |
| 7. wiggle your ears | 15. add, subtract, multiply, and divide |
| 8. sew | 16. find the square root of nine |

■ **EXERCISE 7—ORAL/WRITTEN:** Walk around and talk to your classmates. Ask them questions. Find people who have the abilities listed below. Ask them questions about their abilities. Write a report of the information you get from your classmates.

1. play a musical instrument
2. play a sport
3. speak three or four languages
4. cook
5. sing
6. sew
7. fix a car
8. draw
9. swim
10. eat with chopsticks

## 7-4 USING *COULD*: PAST OF *CAN*

| | |
|---|---|
| (a)  I am in Hawaii.  I can go to the beach every day.<br>(b)  I was in Hawaii **last month**.  I **could go** to the beach every day when I was there. | **could** = the past form of **can**. |
| (c)  I can't go to the movie today.  I have to study.<br>(d)  I $\begin{Bmatrix} \textbf{couldn't go} \\ \textbf{could not go} \end{Bmatrix}$ to the movie **last night**.  I had to study. | NEGATIVE:<br>**could** + **not** = **couldn't** |
| (e)  **Could** you **speak** English before you came here? | QUESTION:<br>**could** + *subject* + *main verb* |

■ **EXERCISE 8:** Complete the sentences by using **couldn't**. Use the expressions in the list or your own words.

> call you
> come to class
> ✔ do my homework
> get into my car
> go swimming
>
> go to the movie
> light the candles
> listen to music
> wash his clothes
> watch TV

1. I _____*couldn't do my homework*_____ last night because I was too tired.

2. I _____ yesterday because I lost your telephone number.

3. I _____ last night because my TV set is broken.

4. Tom _____ because he didn't have any matches.

5. The teacher _____ yesterday because he was sick.

6. I _____ last night because my radio doesn't work.

7. Ken _____ because he didn't have any laundry soap.

8. We _____ yesterday because the water was too cold.

9. I _____ yesterday because I locked all the doors and left the keys inside.

10. I _____ last night because I had to study.

■ **EXERCISE 9—ORAL (BOOKS CLOSED):** Answer the questions. Use *"No, I couldn't . . . because . . . ."*

*Example:* Did you finish your homework last night?
*Response:* No, I couldn't finish my homework because (I had a headache, etc.).

1. go shopping yesterday
2. study last night
3. go swimming yesterday
4. watch TV last night
5. go to ( . . . )'s party last night
6. come to class yesterday
7. go downtown yesterday afternoon
8. wash your clothes yesterday

■ **EXERCISE 10—ORAL (BOOKS CLOSED):** What are some negative results in the given situations? Use *can't* or *couldn't*.

*Example:* There's no chalk in the classroom.
*Response:* We can't write on the board.

*Example:* There was no chalk in the classroom yesterday.
*Response:* The teacher couldn't write on the board.

1. ( . . . ) has a broken leg.
2. ( . . . ) had the flu last week.
3. ( . . . ) has only *(a small amount of money)* in his pocket/in her purse today.
4. ( . . . ) doesn't know how to use a computer.
5. Your parents had rules for you when you were a child.
6. All of you are adults. You are not children.
7. You didn't know any English last year.
8. Millions of people in the world live in poverty.

■ **EXERCISE 11:**  Correct the errors in the following sentences.

1. Could you to drive a car when you were thirteen years old?

2. If your brother goes to the graduation party, he can meets my sister.

3. Mr. Lo was born in Hong Kong, but now he lives in Canada.  He cannot understand spoken English before he moved to Canada, but now he speak and understand English very well.

4. I couldn't opened the door because I didn't have a key.

5. When Ernesto arrived at the airport last Tuesday, he can't find the right gate.

6. Please turn up the radio.  I can't to hear it.

## 7-5  USING *VERY* AND *TOO* + ADJECTIVE

| | |
|---|---|
| (a) The box is ***very*** *heavy*, but Tom ***can*** *lift* it.<br>(b) The box is ***too*** *heavy*.  Bob ***can't*** *lift* it.<br>(c) The coffee is ***very*** *hot*, but I ***can*** *drink* it.<br>(d) The coffee is ***too*** *hot*.  I ***can't*** *drink* it. | ***Very*** and ***too*** come in front of adjectives; *heavy* and *hot* are adjectives.<br>***Very*** and ***too*** do NOT have the same meaning.<br>In (a): *very heavy* = It is difficult but possible for Tom to lift the box.<br>In (b): *too heavy* = It is impossible for Bob to lift it. |
| (e) The coffee is ***too*** hot.<br>    NEGATIVE RESULT:  I can't drink it.<br>(f) The weather is ***too*** cold.<br>    NEGATIVE RESULT:  We can't go to the beach. | In the speaker's mind, the use of ***too*** implies a negative result. |

TOM

BOB

■ **EXERCISE 12:** Complete the sentences. Use the expressions in the list or your own words.

| | |
|---|---|
| *buy it* | *lift it* |
| *do his homework* | *reach the cookie jar* |
| *eat it* | *sleep* |
| *go swimming* | *take a break* |

1. The soup is too hot. I can't _____

2. The diamond ring is too expensive. I can't _____

3. The weather is too cold. We can't _____

4. Peggy is too short.

   She can't _____

5. Ali is too tired.

   He can't _____

6. I am too busy.

   I can't _____

7. It's too noisy in the dorm at night.

   I can't _____

8. A piano is too heavy.

   I can't _____

■ **EXERCISE 13:** Complete the sentences. Use ***too***. Use ADJECTIVES in the list or your own words.

| | |
|---|---|
| *cold* | *small* |
| *expensive* | *tall* |
| *heavy* | *tired* |
| *noisy* | *young* |

1. You can't lift a car. A car is _____

2. Jimmy is ten. He can't drive a car. He's _____

3. I can't study in the dorm at night. It's _____

4. I don't want to go to the zoo. The weather is _____

5. Ann doesn't want to play tennis this afternoon. She's _____

6. I can't buy a new car. A new car is _____

7. John has gained weight. He can't wear his old shirt. It's _____

8. The basketball player can't stand up straight in the subway. He's _____

■ **EXERCISE 14:** Complete the sentences. Use *too* or *very*.

1. The tea is _____*very*_____ hot, but I can drink it.

2. The tea is _____*too*_____ hot. I can't drink it.

3. I can't put my dictionary in my pocket. My dictionary is _____ big.

4. An elephant is _____ big. A mouse is _____ small.

5. I can't buy a boat because it's _____ expensive.

6. A sports car is _____ expensive, but Anita can buy one if she wants to.

7. We went to the Rocky Mountains for our vacation. The mountains are

_____ beautiful.

8. I can't eat this food because it's _____ salty.

9. Amanda doesn't like her room in the dorm. She thinks it's _____ small.

10. I lost your dictionary. I'm _____ sorry. I'll buy you a new one.

11. A: Do you like your math course?

B: Yes. It's _____ difficult, but I enjoy it.

12. A: Do you like your math course?

   B: No. It's _____ difficult. I don't like it because I can't understand the math.

13. A: It's seven-thirty. Do you want to go to the movie?

   B: We can't. It's _____ late. The movie started at seven.

14. A: Did you enjoy your dinner last night?

   B: Yes. The food was _____ good!

15. A: Are you going to buy that dress?

   B: No. It doesn't fit. It's _____ big.

16. A: Do you think Carol is smart?

   B: Yes, I do. I think she's _____ intelligent.

17. A: My daughter wants to get married.

   B: What? But she can't! She's _____ young.

18. A: Can you read that sign across the street?

   B: No, I can't. It's _____ far away.

---

## 7-6 USING *TOO MANY* AND *TOO MUCH* + NOUN

| | |
|---|---|
| My stomach doesn't feel good. <br> (a) I ate *too many sandwiches*. <br> (b) I ate *too much food*. | *Too* is frequently used with *many* and *much*. <br> *Too many* is used in front of count nouns, as in (a). <br> *Too much* is used in front of noncount nouns, as in (b).* |

*See Chart 4-6 for more information about count nouns and noncount nouns.

■ **EXERCISE 15:** Complete the sentences. Use *too many* or *too much*. Use *too many* with plural COUNT NOUNS. Use *too much* with NONCOUNT NOUNS.

1. I can't go to the movie tonight. I have _____*too much*_____ homework to do.

2. Mr. and Mrs. Smith have six cars. They have _____*too many*_____ cars.

3. Alex is nervous and jumpy. He drinks _____ coffee.

4. There are _____ students in my chemistry class. I can't remember all of their names.

5. Fred is a commuter. He drives to and from work every day. Yesterday afternoon he

tried to get home early, but he couldn't because there was _____

traffic. There were _____ cars on the highway during
rush hour.

6. You use _____ salt on your food. A lot of salt isn't good for you.

7. It's not possible for a person to have _____ friends.

8. The restaurant was crowded, so we left. There were _____
people at the restaurant.

9. This food is too hot! I can't eat it. There's _____ pepper in it.

10. Mike is gaining weight because he eats _____ food.

11. I can't buy this watch. It costs _____ money.

12. Ann doesn't study because she's always busy. She has _____
boyfriends.

13. I have to study for eight hours every night. My teachers assign _____
homework.

14. I invited three friends to my house for lunch. I made twelve sandwiches for them, but

they ate only six. I made _____ sandwiches. I made

_____ food for my guests.

■ **EXERCISE 16—ORAL (BOOKS CLOSED):**   Think of possible answers to the questions.

*Example:*   You had too much homework last night.  What was the result?
*Response:*   I couldn't finish it. / I didn't get to bed until after midnight. / Etc.

1. ( . . . ) wants to buy *(something)*, but it costs too much money.  What's the result?

2. ( . . . ) tried to read an article in the newspaper about *(a current topic)*, but there was too much vocabulary that he didn't know.  What was the result?

3. ( . . . ) and ( . . . ) wanted to eat at *(name of a local restaurant)* last night, but there were too many people there.  What was the result?

4. ( . . . ) likes to study in peace and quiet.  His/Her roommate likes to listen to loud music and makes too much noise.  What's the result?

5. ( . . . ) wants to *(do something)* today, but the weather is too (hot / cold / humid / cloudy / wet / etc.).  What's the result?

6. ( . . . ) invited ( . . . ) to *(do something)* last night, but ( . . . ) was too busy.  He/She had too much homework.  What was the result?

7. Sometimes  ( . . . ) drinks too much coffee.  What's the result?

8. ( . . . ) wants to climb *(name of a mountain)*, but the mountain is too steep and too high.  The climb is too difficult for ( . . . ) because he/she is an inexperienced climber.  What is the result?

9. ( . . . ) took the bus yesterday.  He/She was very tired and needed to sit down, but there were too many people on the bus.  What was the result?

10. ( . . . ) made a cup of coffee for ( . . . ), but it was too strong.  It tasted bitter.  What was the result?

11. At the present rates of population growth, someday there will be too many people on earth.  What will be the result?

12. ( . . . )'s apartment is too small for him/her and his/her wife/husband (and their children).  What's the result?

13. ( . . . ) took a trip to *(name of a place)* last month.  He/She took six big suitcases.  In other words, he/she had too many suitcases.  What was the result?

## 7-7 USING *TOO* + ADJECTIVE + INFINITIVE

| | |
|---|---|
| (a) Susie can't go to school because she is too young. | (a) and (b) have the same meaning. |
| (b) Susie is ***too young to go*** to school. | |

|  *TOO* + ADJECTIVE + INFINITIVE | |
|---|---|
| (c) Susie is ***too***     ***young***     ***to go***    to school. | |
| (d) Peggy is ***too***     ***short***     ***to reach***   the cookie jar. | |
| (e) Bob is ***too***     ***tired***     ***to do***    his homework. | |

■ **EXERCISE 17:** Make sentences with the same meaning by using an infinitive after *too* +
ADJECTIVE.

1. Mr. Cook is old. He can't drive a car anymore.

   → Mr. Cook is  a car.
   
                         too     +     adjective     +     infinitive
   
   (*too* = too, *adjective* = old, *infinitive* = to drive)

2. Susie doesn't want to go to the party because she is tired.

   → Susie is  to the party.
   
             too    +    adjective   +   infinitive

3. Robert is short. He can't touch the ceiling.

   → Robert is  the ceiling.
   
           too    +   adjective   +   infinitive

4. I couldn't finish my work because I was sleepy.

   → I was  my work.
   
          too    +   adjective   +   infinitive

5. Jackie is young. She can't get married.

   → Jackie is too . . . .

6. Sam didn't want to go to the zoo because he was busy.

   → Sam . . . .

7. I'm full. I can't eat another sandwich.

   → I . . . .

8. I don't want to clean up my apartment today. I'm lazy.

   → I . . . .

## 7-8 USING *TOO* + ADJECTIVE + *FOR (SOMEONE)* + INFINITIVE

| | | | |
|---|---|---|---|
| (a) | Bob can't lift the box because it is too heavy. | | (a) and (b) have the same meaning. |
| (b) | The box is *too heavy for Bob to lift*. | | |

| | | TOO + | ADJECTIVE + | FOR (SOMEONE) + | INFINITIVE |
|---|---|---|---|---|---|
| (c) | The box is | *too* | *heavy* | *for* *Bob* | *to lift*. |
| (d) | The dorm is | *too* | *noisy* | *for* *me* | *to study*. |

■ **EXERCISE 18:** Make sentences with the same meaning by using *too* + ADJECTIVE + *for (someone)* + INFINITIVE.

1. Robert can't touch the ceiling because it's too high.

→ The ceiling is | __too__ | | __high__ | | __for Robert__ | | __to touch__ |.
                too   +   adjective   +   *for* (someone)   +   infinitive

2. I can't do the homework because it's too difficult.

→ The homework is | | | | | | | |.
            too   +   adjective   +   *for* (someone)   +   infinitive

3. Rosa can't drink this coffee because it's too hot.

→ This coffee is | | | | | | | |.
            too   +   adjective   +   *for* (someone)   +   infinitive

4. We can't go to the movie because it's too late.

→ It's | | | | | | | |.
            too   +   adjective   +   *for* (someone)   +   infinitive

5. Ann can't carry that suitcase because it's too heavy.

→ That suitcase is too . . . .

6. I can't buy this book because it's too expensive.

→ This book . . . .

7. We can't go swimming because the weather is too cold.

→

8. Mrs. Rivers can't swallow the pill. It's too big.

→

■ **EXERCISE 19—ORAL (BOOKS CLOSED):** Answer *no* and explain why in a complete sentence that uses *too* and an INFINITIVE.

*Example:* The coffee is too hot. Can you drink it? Can ( . . . ) drink it?
*Response:* No. The coffee is too hot (for me) to drink. I think it's also too hot for ( . . . ) to drink.

1. *(This desk / A piano)* is heavy. Can you lift it? Can ( . . . )?
2. ( . . . )'s shoe is small. Can you wear it? Can ( . . . ) wear it?
3. ( . . . )'s shoe is big. Can you wear it? Can ( . . . ) wear it?
4. Who wants to buy his or her own private airplane? How much does one cost? Can you buy one? Can ( . . . ) buy one?
5. Who is a parent? Has a son or daughter? How old? Can he/she walk/read/go to college/get a job/get married?
6. Antarctica is very, very cold. Do people live there?
7. There are many, many stars in the universe. Can we see all of them?
8. An elephant is a large animal. Can an elephant walk through that door?
9. The Sahara Desert is very dry. Do farmers grow (crops, rice, vegetables) there?
10. An apple is about the same size as my fist. Can you swallow a whole apple all at once? Can anyone swallow a whole apple all at once?

## 7-9 USING ADJECTIVE + *ENOUGH*

| | |
|---|---|
| (a) Peggy can't go to school. She is too young. <br> (b) Peggy can't go to school. She is not **old enough**. | (a) and (b) give the same meaning. Notice: ***enough*** follows an adjective. |
| (c) I can't hear the radio. It's not **loud enough**. <br> (d) Bobby can read. He's **old enough**. <br> (e) We can go swimming. The weather is **warm enough**. | ADJECTIVE + ***ENOUGH*** <br> old      enough <br> loud     enough <br> warm    enough <br> ***Enough*** is pronounced "enuf." |

■ **EXERCISE 20:** Complete the sentences. Use *too* or *enough*. Use the words in parentheses.

1. *(young, old)*    Susie can't go to school. She's _____*too young*_____. She's not

      _____*old enough*_____.

2. *(loud, soft)*    I can't hear the music. It's _____. It's not

      _____.

3. *(big, small)*    Jack is gaining weight. He can't wear his old coat. It's

      _____. It's not _____.

4. (short, tall)   Cindy can't reach the book on the top shelf.  She's

_____ . She's not _____ .

5. (cold, hot)   I don't want to finish my coffee because it's _____ .

It's not _____ .

6. (weak, strong)   Ron can't lift the heavy box.  He's not _____ .

He's _____ .

7. (sweet, sour)   I don't want to finish eating this orange.  It's _____ .

It's not _____ .

8. (old, fresh)   Don't buy that fruit.  It's _____ . It's not

_____ .

9. (young, old)   Jimmy is an infant.  He can't talk yet.  He's not _____ .

He's _____ .

10. (strong, weak)   This coffee looks like dirty water.  It's _____ . It's

not _____ .

11. (big, small)   I can put my dictionary in my shirt pocket.  My pocket is

_____ . It's not _____ .

12. (comfortable, uncomfortable)   I don't want to sit in that chair.  It's _____ .

It's not _____ .

13. (wide, narrow, large, small)   Anne and Sue can't carry the love seat through the door.  The door is

_____ . The door

isn't _____ . The

love seat is _____ . The

love seat isn't _____ .

14. *(warm, cold)*    We can go to the beach today.  The weather is _____.

It's not _____.

■ **EXERCISE 21—ORAL (BOOKS CLOSED):**    Answer the question *no* and explain why by using *enough*.

*Example:*  Can you touch the ceiling?
*Response:*  No, I'm not tall enough to touch the ceiling.

1. Can an elephant walk through that door?
2. Can ten-year-old children go to college?
3. Can you touch *(name of a student who is not close)* without standing up?
4. Can you put your grammar book in your shirt pocket?
5. Can a dog learn to read?
6. Can you eat *(four hamburgers)* right now?
7. Can you read a book by moonlight?
8. Can you understand every word an English-speaking TV newscaster says?
9. Can a turtle win a race with a rabbit?
10. *(Write something in very small letters on the board.)* Can you read these letters?
11. Can this room hold *(two hundred)* people?
12. Can you cut a piece of paper with your fingernail?

| 7-10 | USING *ENOUGH* + NOUN AND *MORE* + NOUN |
|---|---|

| | |
|---|---|
| (a)  I can't buy this book.  I need **more money**. <br> (b)  I can't buy this book.  I don't have **enough money**. | **more** = additional. <br> **enough** = sufficient. |
| (c)  I can't finish my work.  I need some **more time**. <br> (d)  I can't finish my work.  I don't have **enough time**. | Notice:  **more** comes in front of a noun. <br>     **MORE**   +   *NOUN* <br>     more      money <br>     more      time <br> Notice:  **enough** comes in front of a noun.* <br>     **ENOUGH**  +   *NOUN* <br>     enough    money <br>     enough    time |

*Enough* may also follow a noun: *I don't have money enough.*  In everyday English, *enough* usually comes in front of a noun.

■ **EXERCISE 22:**    Complete the sentences.  Use your own words.

1. I can't _____ because I don't have enough money.

2. I can't _____ because I don't have enough time.

3. I couldn't _____ because I didn't have enough money.

4. I couldn't _____ because I didn't have enough time.

5. I don't want to _____ because I don't have enough time.

6. I would like to _____, but I can't because I don't have enough money.

■ **EXERCISE 23:** Complete the sentences. Use *more* or *enough*. Use the words in the list; use the plural form if necessary.

| | | |
|---|---|---|
| ✔ bread | light | time |
| desk | minute | vocabulary |
| ✔ egg | sugar | |
| gas | tea | |

1. I'm hungry. I want to make a sandwich, but I can't. There isn't

   _____ **enough bread** _____.

2. According to the cake recipe I need three eggs, but I have only one. I need two

   _____ **more eggs** _____.

3. Ken isn't finished with his test. He needs ten _____.

4. I can't go skiing Saturday. I'm too busy. I don't have _____.

5. My tea isn't sweet enough. I need some _____.

6. There are fifteen students in the class, but there are only ten desks. We need five

   _____.

7. I can't understand the front page of the newspaper because I don't know

   _____.

8. It's too dark in here. I can't read my book. There isn't _____.

9. A: Do we have _____?
   B: No. We have to stop at a gas station.

10. A: Would you like _____?
    B: Yes, thank you. I'd like one more cup.

## 7-11  USING *ENOUGH* + INFINITIVE

| | |
|---|---|
| (a)  Peggy can go to school because she is old enough.<br><br>      ADJECTIVE  +  *ENOUGH*  +  INFINITIVE<br>(b)  Peggy is     **old**        **enough**      **to go**      to school. | (a) and (b) have the same meaning. |
| (c)  I can't buy this book because I don't have enough money.<br><br>      *ENOUGH*  +  NOUN  +  INFINITIVE<br>(d)  I don't have **enough**      **money**      **to buy**      this book. | (c) and (d) have the same meaning. |

■ **EXERCISE 24:**  Make sentences with the same meaning by using an INFINITIVE.

1. Ken can reach the top shelf because he's tall enough.
   → *Ken is tall enough to reach the top shelf.*

2. I can't finish my work because I don't have enough time.

3. Mustafa can buy a new car because he has enough money.

4. Johnny can't get married because he isn't old enough.

5. Mr. and Mrs. Forest can't feed their family because they don't earn enough money.

6. I can eat a horse.  I'm hungry enough.*

7. Sally bought enough food.  She can feed an army.

8. Did you finish your homework last night?  Did you have enough time?

9. Can you buy a ticket to the show?  Do you have enough money?

10. I can't understand this article in the newspaper because I don't know enough vocabulary.

---

*\*I'm hungry enough to eat a horse* is an English idiom.  The speaker is saying "I'm very hungry."  The speaker does not really want to eat a horse.
   Other examples of idioms:
      *I put my foot in my mouth.* = I said something stupid.  I said something to the wrong person at the wrong time.
      *Watch your step.* = Be careful.
      *It's raining cats and dogs.* = It's raining hard.
   Every language has idioms.  They are common expressions that have special meanings.

■ **EXERCISE 25:** Complete the sentences. Use your own words.

    1. I'm old enough to _____

    2. I'm strong enough to _____

    3. I'm not strong enough to _____

    4. I'm not hungry enough to _____

    5. I have enough money to _____

    6. I don't have enough money to _____

    7. I have enough time to _____

    8. I don't have enough time to _____

    9. I know enough English to _____

  10. I don't know enough English to _____

■ **EXERCISE 26—ORAL (BOOKS CLOSED):** Answer *no* and explain why. Use *too* or *enough*.

*Example:* Is the weather perfect today?
*Response:* No, it's too cold. / No, it's not warm enough. / Etc.

    1. I have a daughter. She's two years old. Can she go to school?
    2. I'm making a noise (a very soft noise). Can you hear it?
    3. Bobby is fifteen years old. He's in love. He wants to get married. Is that a good idea?
    4. Can you put my briefcase/purse/etc. in your pants pocket/handbag/etc.?
    5. Can you understand everything on the front page of a newspaper?
    6. Can an elephant sit in that chair?
    7. Do you like the weather (in this city) in the winter/summer?
    8. Did you finish your homework last night?
    9. Do you want to go on a picnic Saturday?
  10. Would you like to eat your lunch on the floor of this room?
  11. Can you buy a hotel?
  12. Here's an arithmetic problem. You have three seconds to solve it (without a calculator). Multiply 673 by 897. Could you solve it in three seconds?

## 7-12 USING *BE ABLE TO*

| PRESENT | (a) I *am able to touch* my toes.<br>(b) I *can touch* my toes. | (a) and (b) have basically the same meaning. |
|---|---|---|
| FUTURE | (c) I *will be able to go* shopping tomorrow.<br>(d) I *can go* shopping tomorrow. | (c) and (d) have basically the same meaning. |
| PAST | (e) I *wasn't able to finish* my homework last night.<br>(f) I *couldn't finish* my homework last night. | (e) and (f) have basically the same meaning. |

■ **EXERCISE 27—ORAL:** Make sentences with the same meaning by using *be able to.*

1. I can be here tomorrow at ten o'clock.
   → *I'll (I will) be able to be here tomorrow at ten o'clock.*
2. Two students couldn't finish the test.
   → *Two students weren't able to finish the test.*
3. Mark is bilingual. He can speak two languages.
4. Sue can get her own apartment next year.
5. Animals can't speak.
6. Can you touch your toes without bending your knees?
7. Jack couldn't describe the thief.
8. Could you do the homework?
9. I couldn't sleep last night because my apartment was too hot.
10. My roommate can speak four languages. He's multilingual.
11. I'm sorry that I couldn't call you last night.
12. I'm sorry, but I can't come to your party next week.
13. Can we take vacations on the moon in the 22nd century?

■ **EXERCISE 28:** Complete the sentences.

1. I wasn't able to _____ last night because

   _____.

2. We'll be able to _____ in the 22nd century.

3. I'm sorry, but I won't be able to _____.

4. Birds are able to _____.

5. My friend is multilingual. She's able to _____.

6. I'm bilingual. I'm able to _____.

7. The students weren't able to _____ in class

   yesterday because _____.

8. Will you be able to _____ tomorrow?

9. _____ wasn't able to _____ because

   _____.

10. _____ isn't able to _____

    because _____.

11. _____ won't be able to _____

    because _____.

---

## 7-13 POLITE QUESTIONS: MAY I, COULD I, AND CAN I

| | |
|---|---|
| (a) **May I borrow** your pen? <br> (b) **Could I borrow** your pen? <br> (c) **Can I borrow** your pen? | (a), (b), and (c) have the same meaning: I want to borrow your pen. I am asking politely to borrow your pen. |
| (d) May I **please** borrow your pen? <br> (e) Could I **please** borrow your pen? <br> (f) Can I **please** borrow your pen? | **Please** is often used in polite questions. |
| TYPICAL RESPONSES <br> (g) **Yes, of course.** <br> (h) **Of course.** <br> (i) **Certainly.** <br> (j) **Sure.** (informal)★ <br> (k) **No problem.** (informal)★ | TYPICAL CONVERSATION <br> A: *May I please borrow your pen?* <br> B: **Yes, of course.** *Here it is.* <br> A: *Thank you. / Thanks.* |

★Informal English is typically used between friends and family members.

■ **EXERCISE 29:** Look at the pictures. Complete the dialogues by using *May I, Can I,* or *Could I* and typical responses.

■ **EXERCISE 30—ORAL (BOOKS CLOSED):** Ask and answer polite questions using *May I*, *Can I*, or *Could I*.

*Example:* ( . . . ) has a pencil. You want to borrow it.
STUDENT A: ( . . . ), may I (please) borrow your pencil?
STUDENT B: Certainly. Here it is.
STUDENT A: Thank you.

1. ( . . . ) has a dictionary. You want to borrow it.
2. ( . . . ) has a pen. You want to use it for a minute.
3. ( . . . ) has an eraser. You want to use it for a minute.
4. ( . . . ) has a pencil sharpener. You want to borrow it.
5. ( . . . ) has a book. You want to see it.
6. ( . . . ) has a dictionary. You want to see it.
7. You are at ( . . . )'s home. You want to use the phone.
8. You are at ( . . . )'s home. You want a glass of water.
9. You are at a restaurant. ( . . . ) is a waiter/waitress. You want to have a cup of coffee.
10. ( . . . ) is a waiter/waitress. You want to have the check.

## 7-14 POLITE QUESTIONS: *COULD YOU* AND *WOULD YOU*

| | |
|---|---|
| (a) ***Could you (please) open*** the door?<br>(b) ***Would you (please) open*** the door? | (a) and (b) have the same meaning: I want you to open the door. I am politely asking you to open the door. |
| TYPICAL RESPONSES<br>(c) ***Yes, of course.***<br>(d) ***Certainly.***<br>(e) ***I'd be glad to.***<br>(f) ***I'd be happy to.***<br>(g) ***Sure.*** (informal)<br>(h) ***No problem.*** (informal) | TYPICAL CONVERSATION<br>A: *Could you please open the door?*<br>B: ***I'd be glad to.***<br>A: *Thank you. / Thanks.* |

■ **EXERCISE 31:** Use the given expressions to complete the dialogues. Use **Could you** or **Would you** and give typical responses.

1. A: Excuse me, sir. _____

   B: _____

   A: _____

2. A: _____

   B: Excuse me? I didn't understand what you said.

   A: _____

   B: _____

■ **EXERCISE 32—ORAL (BOOKS CLOSED):** Ask and answer polite questions using **Could you** or **Would you**.

*Example*: You want ( . . . ) to open the window.
STUDENT A: ( . . . ), could you (please) open the window?
STUDENT B: Certainly.
STUDENT A: Thank you.

1. You want ( . . . ) to close the door.
2. You want ( . . . ) to turn on the light.
3. You want ( . . . ) to turn off the light.
4. You want ( . . . ) to pass you the salt and pepper.
5. You want ( . . . ) to hand you that book.
6. You want ( . . . ) to translate a word for you.
7. You want ( . . . ) to tell you the time.
8. You want ( . . . ) to open the window.
9. You want ( . . . ) to hold your books for a minute.
10. You want ( . . . ) to lend you *(an amount of money)*.

■ **EXERCISE 33—ORAL:** With a partner, make up a polite question that someone might typically ask in each situation. Share your dialogues with the rest of the class.
STUDENT A: Ask a polite question.
STUDENT B: Answer the question.

*Example*: *Situation*: professor's office. Student A is a student. Student B is a professor.
STUDENT A: *(Knock, knock)*. May I come in?
STUDENT B: Certainly. Come in. How are you today?
STUDENT A: Fine, thanks.
   OR:
STUDENT A: Hello, Professor Alvarez. Could I talk to you for a few minutes? I have some questions about the last assignment.
STUDENT B: Of course. Have a seat.
STUDENT A: Thank you.

1. *Situation*: a restaurant. Student A is a customer. Student B is a waitress/waiter.
2. *Situation*: a classroom. Student A is a teacher. Student B is a student.
3. *Situation*: a kitchen. Student A is a visitor. Student B is at home.
4. *Situation*: a clothing store. Student A is the customer. Student B is a salesperson.
5. *Situation*: an apartment. Student A and B are roommates.
6. *Situation*: a car. Student A is a passenger. Student B is the driver.
7. *Situation*: an office. Student A is a boss. Student B is an employee.
8. *Situation*: a telephone conversation. Student B answers the phone. Student A wants to talk to *(someone)*.

## 7-15 IMPERATIVE SENTENCES

| | | |
|---|---|---|
| (a) | "***Close*** the door, Jimmy. It's cold outside." "Okay, Mom." | In (a): ***Close the door*** is an *imperative sentence*. The sentence means, "Jimmy, I want you to close the door. I am telling you to close the door." |
| (b) (c) | ***Sit*** down. ***Be*** careful! | An imperative sentence uses the simple form of a verb (*close, sit, be, etc.*). |
| (d) (e) | ***Don't open*** the window. ***Don't be*** late. | NEGATIVE: ***don't*** + *the simple form of a verb* |
| (f) (g) (h) (i) | ORDERS: ***Stop***, thief! DIRECTIONS: ***Open*** your books to page 24. ADVICE: ***Don't worry***. REQUESTS: ***Please close*** the door. | Imperative sentence give orders, directions, and advice. With the addition of ***please***, as in (i), imperative sentences are used to make polite requests. |

■ **EXERCISE 34:** Underline the IMPERATIVE VERBS in the following dialogues.

1. CINDY: We're leaving.
   BETH: <u>Wait</u> for me!
   CINDY: <u>Hurry</u> up! We'll be late.
   BETH: Okay. Okay. I'm ready. Let's go.

2. MICHELLE: *(Knock, knock.)* May I come in?
   PROFESSOR: Certainly. Come in. Please have a seat.
   MICHELLE: Thanks.
   PROFESSOR: How can I help you?
   MICHELLE: I need to ask you a question about yesterday's lecture.
   PROFESSOR: Okay. What's the question?

3. MARY: We need to leave soon.
   IVAN: I'm ready.
   MARY: Don't forget your house key.
   IVAN: I have it.
   MARY: Okay.

4. TOM: What's the matter?
   JIM: I have the hiccups.
   TOM: Hold your breath.
   BOB: Drink some water.
   JOE: Breathe into a paper bag.
   KEN: Eat a piece of bread.
   JIM: It's okay. The hiccups are gone.

5. STUDENT: Do we have any homework for tomorrow?
   TEACHER: Yes. Read pages 24 through 36, and answer the questions on page 37, in writing.
   STUDENT: Is that all?
   TEACHER: Yes.

6. YUKO: How do I get to the post office from here?
   ERIC: Walk two blocks to 16th Avenue. Then turn right on Forest Street. Go two more blocks to Market Street and turn left. The post office is halfway down the street on the right-hand side.
   YUKO: Thanks.

7. ANDY: Bye, Mom. I'm going over to Billy's house.
   MOM: Wait a minute. Did you clean up your room?
   ANDY: I'll do it later.
   MOM: No. Do it now, before you leave.
   ANDY: Do I have to?
   MOM: Yes.
   ANDY: What do I have to do?
   MOM: Hang up your clothes. Make your bed. Put your books back on the shelf. Empty the wastepaper basket. Okay?
   ANDY: Okay.

8. HEIDI: Please close the window, Mike. It's a little chilly in here.
   MIKE: Okay. Is there anything else I can do for you before I leave?
   HEIDI: Could you turn off the light in the kitchen?
   MIKE: No problem. Anything else?
   HEIDI: Ummm, please hand me the remote control for the TV. It's over there.
   MIKE: Sure. Here.
   HEIDI: Thanks.
   MIKE: I'll stop by again tomorrow. Take care of yourself. Take good care of that broken leg.
   HEIDI: Don't worry. I will. Thanks again.

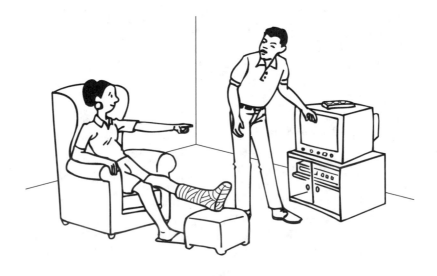

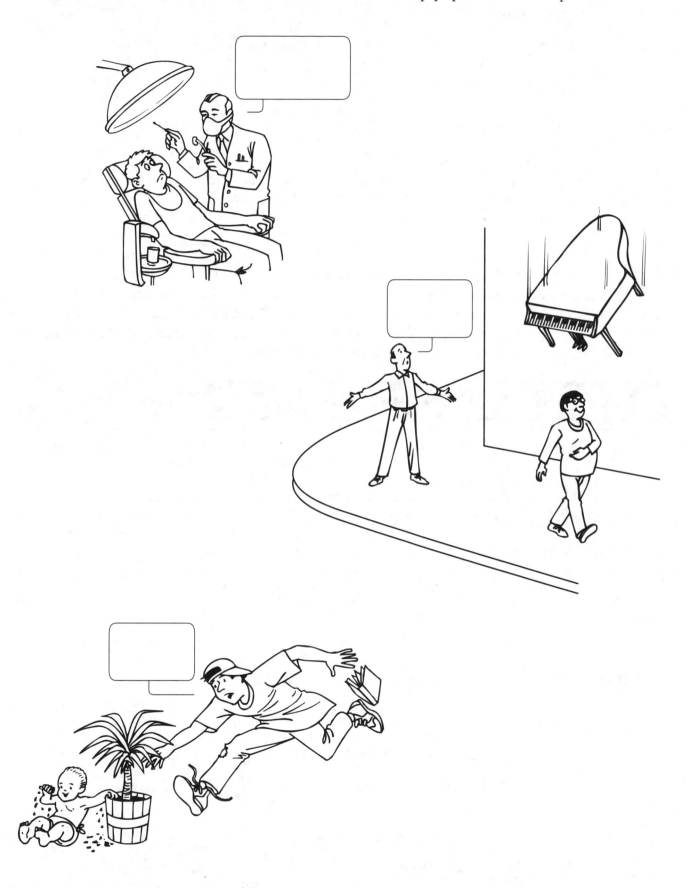

■ **EXERCISE 36—ORAL:** What are some typical IMPERATIVE SENTENCES you might hear in the given situations?

*Example:* ( . . . ) is your friend. He/She has a headache. What are some typical imperative sentences for this situation?

*Responses:* Take an aspirin.
Lie down and close your eyes for a little while.
Put a cold cloth across your forehead.
Take a hot bath and relax.
Etc.

1. You are the teacher of this class. You are assigning homework for tomorrow. What are some typical imperative sentences for this situation?
2. Your friend ( . . . ) has the hiccups. What are some typical imperative sentences for this situation?
3. ( . . . ) is your eight-year-old son/daughter. He/She is walking out the door to go to school. What are some typical imperative sentences for this situation?
4. ( . . . ) wants to improve his/her health. Tell him/her what to do and what not to do.
5. ( . . . ) is going to cook rice for the first time tonight. Tell him/her how to cook rice.
6. ( . . . ) is going to visit your country for the first time next month. Tell him/her what to do and what to see as a tourist in your country.

---

## 7-16    USING *TWO, TOO,* AND *TO*

| | | | |
|---|---|---|---|
| | | | **Two, too,** and **to** have the same pronunciation. |
| TWO | ( a ) | I have **two** children. | In (a): **two** = a number. |
| TOO | ( b ) | Timmy is **too** young. He can't read. | In (b): **too young** = **not old enough**. |
| | ( c ) | Ann saw the movie. I saw the movie **too**. | In (c): **too** = **also**. |
| TO | ( d ) | I talked **to** Jim. | In (d): **to** = a preposition. |
| | ( e ) | I want **to** watch television. | In (e): **to** = part of an infinitive. |

---

■ **EXERCISE 37:**    Complete the sentences. Use **two, too,** or **to.**

1. I'd like a cup of coffee. Bob would like a cup _____*too*_____.

2. I had _____ cups of coffee yesterday.

3. I can't drink my coffee. It's _____ hot. The coffee is _____ hot for me _____ drink.

4. I talked _____ Jim. Jane wants _____ talk _____ Jim _____.

5. I walked _____ school today. Alex walked _____ school today _____.

6. I'm going _____ take the bus _____ school tomorrow.

7. Shh.  I want _____ listen _____ the news broadcast.

8. I can't study.  The music is _____ loud.

9. The weather is _____ cold for us _____ go _____ the beach.

10. I have _____ apples.  Ken wants _____ have _____ apples _____.

---

## 7-17   MORE ABOUT PREPOSITIONS:  *AT* AND *IN* FOR LOCATIONS

| | |
|---|---|
| (a)  Olga is *at* home.<br>       Ivan is *at* work.<br>       Yoko is *at* school. | In (a):  *at* is used with *home*, *work*, and *school*. |
| (b)  Sue is *in* bed.<br>       Tom is *in* class.<br>       Paul is *in* jail/prison.<br>       Mr. Lee is *in (the)* hospital. | In (b):  *in* is used with *bed*, *class*, *jail/prison*, and *hospital*.<br>NOTE:  American English = *in the hospital*.<br>           British English = *in hospital*. |
| (c)  Ahmed is *in* the kitchen. | In (c):  *in* is used with rooms:  *in the kitchen, in the classroom, in the hall, in my bedroom,* etc. |
| (d)  David is *in* Mexico City. | In (d):  *in* is used with cities, states/provinces, countries, and continents:  *in Mexico City, in Florida, in Italy, in Asia,* etc. |
| (e)  A:  Where's Ivan?<br>       B:  He isn't here.  He's *at* the bank. | In (e):  *at* is usually used with locations in a city:  *at the post office, at the bank, at the library, at the bookstore, at the park, at the theater, at the restaurant, at the football stadium,* etc. |
| COMPARE<br>( f )  In Picture 2, Ivan is *in* the bank.<br>       He is not outside the bank. | In (f):  A speaker uses *in* with a building only when it is important to say that someone is inside, not outside, the building.  Usually a speaker uses *at* with a building.<br>*in the bank* = inside the bank building. |

Ivan is *at*  the bank.

Ivan is *at* the bank.
Ivan is *in (inside)* the bank.

■ **EXERCISE 38:**   Complete the sentences with **at** or **in**.  In some sentences, both prepositions
are correct.

1.  A:  Is Jennifer here?

    B:  No, she's _____*at*_____ the bookstore.*

2.  A:  Where's Jack?

    B:  He's _____*in*_____ his room.

3.  When I was _____ work yesterday, I had an interesting telephone call.

4.  Poor Anita.  She's _____ the hospital again for more surgery.

5.  Mr. Gow wasn't _____ class yesterday.  He was _____ home.  He wasn't
    feeling well.

6.  Last year at this time, Eric was _____ Korea.  This year he's _____ Spain.

7.  A:  Where's Donna?

    B:  She's _____ New York.  She's attending a conference.

8.  There's a fire extinguisher _____ the hall.

9.  The children are _____ home this morning.  They aren't _____ school.

10. A:  Where's Olga?  I was supposed to meet her here at five.

    B:  She's _____ the library.  She's studying for a test.
    A:   Oh.  Maybe she forgot that she was supposed to meet me here.

11. A:  Where's Robert?

    B:  He's _____ the computer room.

12. A:  Where's Fatima?

    B:  She's _____ the supermarket.

13. We ate _____ a good restaurant last night.  The food was delicious.

14. A thief broke the window of a jewelry store and stole some valuable jewelry.  The

    police caught him.  Now he's _____ jail.  He's going to be _____ prison for a
    long time.

15. Singapore is _____ Asia.

16. We had a good time _____ the zoo yesterday.

_____

*ALSO CORRECT: *She's **in** the bookstore,* but only if the speaker wants to say that she is inside, not outside, the
bookstore.  Usually a speaker uses **at** with a building to identify someone's location.

17. There are thirty-seven desks _____ our classroom.

18. A: Where can I get some fresh tomatoes?

    B: _____ the market on Waterfront Street.

19. A: Here's your hotel key, Ms. Fox.  You're _____ Room 609.
    B: Thank you.  Where are the elevators?

20. A: Is Mike up?

    B: No, he's _____ bed.
    A: Well, it's time to get up.  I'm going to wake him up. Hey, Mike!  You can't sleep all day!  Get up!
    C: Go away!

■ **EXERCISE 39—ORAL (BOOKS CLOSED):**  Complete the sentence *"I was . . . yesterday"* by using the given word and the correct preposition, *at* or *in*.

*Example:* work
*Response:*  I was at work yesterday.

| | |
|---|---|
| 1. class | 7. work |
| 2. the library | 8. Room 206 |
| 3. *(name of a city)* | 9. a hotel |
| 4. home | 10. *(name of a continent)* |
| 5. this room | 11. ( . . . )'s living room |
| 6. the bookstore | 12. *(name of a building)* |

■ **EXERCISE 40—ORAL (BOOKS CLOSED):**  Ask and answer questions about location.
    STUDENT A: Begin the question with *"Where were you . . . . ?"*
    STUDENT B: Use *at* or *in* in the answer.

*Example:*    yesterday afternoon
STUDENT A: Where were you yesterday afternoon?
STUDENT B: I was in class.

1. at nine o'clock last night
2. at two o'clock yesterday afternoon
3. after class yesterday
4. this morning at six o'clock
5. six weeks ago
6. five years ago
7. on your last vacation
8. when you were ten years old

■ **EXERCISE 41—REVIEW:**   What *can* or *can't* the following people/animals/things do?  Why or why not?  Discuss the topics in small groups and report to the rest of the class.

*Example:*   a tiger
*Responses:*   A tiger can kill a water buffalo because a tiger is very strong and powerful.
A tiger can sleep in the shade of a tree all day if it wants to.  It doesn't have a job, and it doesn't go to school.
A tiger can't speak (a human language).  It's an animal.
A tiger can communicate with other tigers.  Animals can talk to each other in their own languages.

1. the students in this class
2. small children
3. a monkey
4. *(name of a classmate)*
5. international students who live in *(name of this country)*
6. teenagers
7. people who live in *(name of this city)*
8. people who are illiterate
9. money
10. computers
11. *(name of the teacher of this class)*
12. *(name of the leader of this country or your country)*

■ **EXERCISE 42—REVIEW:**   Choose the correct completion.

1. _____ play a musical instrument?
   A.  Do you can     B.  Can you     C.  Do you be able to    D.  Can you to

2. Jack was _____ sick to go to work yesterday morning.  He stayed home.
   A.  very         B.  enough       C.  too            D.  too much

3. I was too sleepy _____ last night.
   A.  to studying    B.  for studying   C.  to study         D.  for study

4. *(Knock, knock.)* Hello? _____ come in?  Thanks.
   A.  Could I to    B.  Will I       C.  Can I to        D.  May I

5. I don't know how _____ to the Palace Hotel from here.
   A.  do I get     B.  get        C.  getting       D.  to get

6. Gina _____ understand the speaker at the lecture last night.
   A.  couldn't     B.  might not   C.  isn't able to    D.  can't

7. In my life right now, I have _____ problems.  I can't solve all of them.
   A.  very much    B.  too many   C.  too much     D.  very

8. I can't reach the eraser on my friend's desk.  My arms aren't _____.
   A.  long enough   B.  too long    C.  enough long    D.  too much long

9. My uncle can't _____ English.
    A. to speak        B. speaking        C. speaks           D. speak

10. I'm sorry. I can't hear what you're saying. _____ speak a little louder?
    A. May you        B. Could you       C. Don't            D. Can

11. An encyclopedia is too difficult _____.
    A. for to read a child        C. for a child to read
    B. to read a child           D. to for a child read

12. Rosa works for a computer company _____ Taipei.
    A. on           B. at          C. in             D. to

## ■ EXERCISE 43—REVIEW:   Correct the errors.

1. My brother wasn't able calling me last night.

2. Don't to interrupt. It's not polite.

3. May I please to borrow your dictionary? Thank you.

4. We will can go to the museum tomorrow afternoon.

5. We can't count all of the stars in the universe. There are to many.

6. The diamond ring was to buy too expensive for John.

7. Can you to stand on your head?

8. My son isn't enough old too go to school. He's only too years old.

9. I saw a beautiful vase at a store yesterday, but I couldn't bought it.

10. We have too many homeworks.

11. Closing the door please. Thank you.

12. Robert was to tired to go two his class at to o'clock.

■ **EXERCISE 44—REVIEW:** Complete the sentences. Use the words in parentheses. Use any appropriate verb form.

(1)     *Once upon a time there* (be) _____ *a mouse named Young Mouse. He lived near a river with his family and friends. Every day he and the other mice did the same things.*

(2)     *They* (hunt) _____ *for food and* (take) _____ *care of their*

(3)     *mouse holes. In the evening they* (listen) _____ *to stories around a fire. Young Mouse especially liked to listen to stories about the Far Away Land. He* (dream)

(4)     _____ *about the Far Away Land. It sounded wonderful. One day he*

(5)     (decide) _____ *to go there.*

YOUNG MOUSE:  Goodbye, Old Mouse.  I'm leaving now.

(6)     OLD MOUSE:  Why *(you, leave)* _____? Where

(7)         *(you, go)* _____?

(8)     YOUNG MOUSE:  I *(go)* _____ to a new and different place.  I *(go)*

(9)         _____ to the Far Away Land.

(10)    OLD MOUSE:  Why *(you, want)* _____ *(go)* _____ there?

(11)    YOUNG MOUSE:  I *(want)* _____ *(experience)* _____

(12)        all of life.  I *(need)* _____ *(learn)* _____ about everything.

(13)    OLD MOUSE:  You *(can learn)* _____ many things if you *(stay)*

(14)        _____ here with us.  Please *(stay)* _____ here with us.

(15)    YOUNG MOUSE:  No, I *(can stay, not)* _____ here by the

(16)        river for the rest of my life.  There *(be)* _____ too much to learn about in the world.  I must go to the Far Away Land.

OLD MOUSE:  The trip to the Far Away Land is a long and dangerous journey.  You *(have)*

(17)        _____ many problems before you *(get)* _____

(18)     there.  You *(face)* _____ many dangers.

YOUNG MOUSE:  I understand that, but I need to find out about the Far Away Land.

(19)     Goodbye, Old Mouse.  Goodbye, everyone!  I *(may see, never)* _____

(20)     any of you again, but I *(try)* _____ to return from the
Far Away Land someday.  Goodbye!

*So Young Mouse left to fulfill his dream of going to the Far Away Land.  His first problem
was the river.   At the river, he met a frog.*

(21)     MAGIC FROG:  Hello, Young Mouse.  I'm Magic Frog.  *(you, have)* _____
a problem right now?

(22)     YOUNG MOUSE:  Yes.  How *(I, can cross)* _____ this river?

(23)     I *(know, not)* _____ how to swim.  If I

(24)     *(can cross, not)* _____ this

(25)     river, I *(be, not)* _____

able to reach the Far Away Land.

(26)     MAGIC FROG:  I *(help)* _____

you to cross the river.  I *(give)*

(27)     _____ you

the power of my legs so you *(can jump)*

(28)     _____ across the river.  I *(give, also)* _____
you a new name.  Your new name will be Jumping Mouse.

JUMPING MOUSE:  Thank you, Magic Frog.

MAGIC FROG:  You are a brave mouse, Jumping Mouse, and you have a good heart.  If you

(29)     *(lose, not)* _____ hope, you *(reach)* _____
the Far Away Land.

*With his powerful new legs, Jumping Mouse jumped across the river.  He traveled fast for
many days across a wide grassland.  One day he met a buffalo.  The buffalo was lying on the
ground.*

JUMPING MOUSE:  Hello, Buffalo.  My name is Jumping Mouse.  Why *(you, lie\*)*

(30)     _____ on the ground?  *(you, be)* _____ ill?

---

\*The *-ing* form of *lie* is spelled *lying*.

(31)  BUFFALO:  Yes.  I *(can see, not)* _____.  I *(drink)*

(32)  _____ some poisoned water, and now I *(be)* _____

(33)  blind.  I *(die)* _____ soon because I *(can find, not)*

(34)  _____ food and water without my eyes.

(35)  JUMPING MOUSE:  When I started my journey, Magic Frog *(give)* _____
      me her powerful legs so I could jump across the river.  What *(I, can give)*

(36)  _____ you to help you?  I know!  I *(give)*

(37)  _____ you my sight so you can see to find food and water.

      BUFFALO:  Are you really going to do that?  Jumping Mouse, you are very kind!  Ah!  Yes,

(38)  I *(can see)* _____ again.  Thank you!  But now you

(39)  *(can see, not)* _____.  How *(you, find)* _____

(40)  _____ the Far Away Land?  I know.  *(jump)*

(41)  _____ onto my back.  I *(carry)* _____
      you across this land to the foot of the mountain.

      JUMPING MOUSE:  Thank you, Buffalo.

      *So Jumping Mouse found a way to reach the mountain.  When they reached the mountain,*
      *Jumping Mouse and Buffalo parted.*

(42)  BUFFALO:  I don't live in the mountains, so I *(can go, not)* _____
      any farther.

(43)  JUMPING MOUSE:  What *(I, do)* _____?  I *(have)*

(44)  _____ powerful legs, but I can't see.

(45)     BUFFALO: *(keep)* _____ your hope alive. You *(find)* _____

a way to reach the Far Away Land.

*Jumping Mouse was very afraid. He didn't know what to do. Suddenly he heard a wolf.*

(46)     JUMPING MOUSE: Hello? Wolf? I *(can see, not)* _____ you,

(47)     but I *(can hear)* _____ you.

(48)     WOLF: Yes, Jumping Mouse. I'm here, but I *(can help, not)* _____

(49)     you because I *(die★)* _____.

(50)     JUMPING MOUSE: What's wrong? Why *(you, die)* _____?

(51)     WOLF: I *(lose)* _____ my sense of smell many weeks ago, so now I

(52)     *(can find, not)* _____ food. I *(starve)*

(53)     _____ to death.

(54)     JUMPING MOUSE: Oh, Wolf, I *(can help)* _____ you. I *(give)*

(55)     _____ you my ability to smell.

(56)     WOLF: Oh, thank you, Jumping Mouse. Yes, I *(can smell)* _____
again. Now I'll be able to find food. That is a wonderful gift! How *(I, can help)*

(57)     _____ you?

(58)     JUMPING MOUSE: I *(try)* _____ to get to the Far Away Land.

(59)     I *(need)* _____ *(go)* _____ to the top of the mountain.

(60)     WOLF: *(come)* _____ over here. I *(put)* _____

(61)     you on my back and *(take)* _____ you to the top of the mountain.

_____

★The *-ing* form of *die* is spelled *dying*.

*So Wolf carried Jumping Mouse to the top of the mountain. But then Wolf left. Jumping*

(62)      *Mouse was all alone. He* (can see, not) _____

(63)      *and he* (can smell, not) _____ *, but he still had powerful legs.*

(64)      *He almost* (lose) _____ *hope. Then suddenly, he* (hear) _____ *Magic Frog.*

(65)      JUMPING MOUSE: Is that you, Magic Frog? Please *(help)* _____ me. I'm all alone and afraid.

(66)      MAGIC FROG: *(cry, not)* _____, Jumping Mouse. You have a

(67)      generous, open heart. You *(be, not)* _____ selfish. You help others. Your unselfishness caused you suffering during your journey, but you

(68)      *(lose, never)* _____ hope. Now you are in the Far

(69)      Away Land. *(jump)* _____, Jumping Mouse. *(use)* _____ your powerful legs to jump high in the air. Jump! Jump!

*Jumping Mouse jumped as high as he could, up, up, up.*
*He reached his arms out to his sides and started to fly.*
*He felt strong and powerful.*

JUMPING MOUSE: I can fly! I can fly! I *(fly)*

(70)      _____!

MAGIC FROG: Jumping Mouse, I am going to give you a new name. Now your name is Eagle!

*So Jumping Mouse became the powerful Eagle and fulfilled his dream of reaching the Far Away Land and experiencing all that life has to offer.* *

---

*This fable is based on a Native American story and has been adapted from *The Story of Jumping Mouse* by John Steptoe; © Lothrop, Lee & Shepard Books, 1984.

■ **EXERCISE 45:** In groups of six, create a play using the story of Jumping Mouse. There will be five characters in your play: Jumping Mouse, Old Mouse, Magic Frog, Buffalo, and Wolf. In addition, one person in the group will be the narrator. The narrator will tell the parts of the story that are in *italics* in Exercise 44. Rehearse your play in your group, and then present the play to the rest of the class.

## 7-18 MORE IRREGULAR VERBS

| | |
|---|---|
| *blow – blew* | *keep – kept* |
| *draw – drew* | *know - knew* |
| *fall – fell* | *swim – swam* |
| *feel – felt* | *throw – threw* |
| *grow – grew* | *win – won* |

■ **EXERCISE 46—ORAL (BOOKS CLOSED):** Practice using the IRREGULAR VERBS in the above list.

*Example:* *fall-fell* Rain falls. Leaves fall. Sometimes people fall. Yesterday I fell down. I hurt my knee. How did I hurt my knee yesterday?
*Response:* You fell (down).

1. *blow-blew* The sun shines. Rain falls. Wind blows. Last week we had a storm. It rained hard, and the wind blew hard. Tell me about the storm last week.

2. *draw-drew* I draw once a week in art class. Last week I drew a portrait of myself. What did I do in art class last week?

3. *feel-felt* You can feel an object. You can also feel an emotion or a sensation. Sometimes I feel sleepy in class. I felt tired all day yesterday. How did I feel yesterday? How did you feel yesterday?

4. *fall-fell* Sometimes I fall down. Yesterday I fell down. I felt bad when I fell down. What happened to me yesterday?

5. *grow-grew* Trees grow. Flowers grow. Vegetables grow. Usually I grow vegetables in my garden, but last year I grew only flowers. What did I grow in my garden last year?

6. *keep-kept* Now I keep my money in (*name of a local bank*). Last year I kept my money in (*name of another local bank*). Where did I keep my money last year?

7. *know-knew* ( . . . ) knows a lot about English grammar. On the grammar test last week, s/he knew all the answers. What did ( . . . ) know last week?

8. *swim-swam* I swim in (*name of a lake, sea, ocean, or local swimming pool*) every summer. I swam in (*name of a lake, sea, ocean, or local swimming pool*) last summer. What did I do last summer?

9. *throw-threw*   I can hand you this (piece of chalk) or I can throw it to you. I just threw this (piece of chalk) to ( . . . ). What did I just do?

10. *win-won*   You can win a game or lose a game. Last weekend *(name of a local sports team)* won a game/match against *(name of another team)*. How did *(name of the local sports team)* do last weekend? Did they win or lose?

■ **EXERCISE 47:**   Complete the sentences. Use the past form of the verbs in the list.

| | | |
|---|---|---|
| *blow* | *grow* | *swim* |
| *draw* | *hurt* | *throw* |
| *fall* | *keep* | *win* |
| *feel* | *know* | |

1. A: Did you enjoy your tennis game with Jackie?

   B: Yes, but I lost. Jackie _____.

2. A: How did you break your leg?

   B: I _____ down on the ice on the sidewalk.

3. A: Ouch!
   B: What's the matter?

   A: I _____ my finger.
   B: How?
   A: I pinched it in the door.

4. A: Did you give the box of candy to your girlfriend?

   B: No, I didn't. I _____ it and ate it myself.

5. A: That's a nice picture.

   B: I agree. Anna _____ it. She's a good artist.

6. A: Did you have a garden when you lived at home?

   B: Yes. I _____ vegetables and flowers.

7. A: Did you finish the test?

   B: No. I didn't have enough time. I _____ all of the answers but I ran out of time.

8. A: Did you have fun at the beach?

   B: Lots of fun. We sunbathed and _____ in the ocean.

9. A: I burned my finger.
   B: Did you put ice on it?

   A: No.  I _____ on it.

10. A: What's the matter?  You sound like you have a frog in your throat.

    B: I think I'm catching a cold.  I _____ okay yesterday, but I don't feel very good today.

11. A: How did you break the window, Tommy?

    B: Well, I _____ a ball to Annie, but I missed Annie and hit the window instead.

■ **EXERCISE 48:**   Complete the sentences.  Use the past form of the verbs in the list.

| | | | |
|---|---|---|---|
| *begin* | *fly* | *make* | *take* |
| *break* | *grow* | *meet* | *tell* |
| *catch* | *know* | *sing* | *throw* |
| *cost* | *leave* | *spend* | *wear* |
| *fall* | *lose* | *steal* | *win* |

1. When I went to the airport yesterday, I _____ a taxi.

2. I _____ my winter jacket yesterday because the weather was cold.

3. Tom bought a new tie.  It _____ a lot because it was a hand-painted silk tie.

4. Laurie doesn't feel good.  She _____ a cold a couple of days ago.

5. Leo could read the story easily.  The words in the story weren't new for him.  He

   _____ the vocabulary in the story.

6. I know Ronald Sawyer.  I _____ him at a party a couple of weeks ago.

7. My hometown is Ames, Iowa.  I _____ up there.

8. I dropped my book.  It _____ to the floor.

9. Ken couldn't get into his apartment because he _____ his keys.

10. We _____ a lot of money at the restaurant last night.  The food was good, but expensive.

11. The baseball player _____ the ball to the catcher.

12. I wrote a check yesterday. I _____ a mistake on the check, so I tore it up and wrote another one.

13. Someone _____ my bicycle, so I called the police.

14. Maggie didn't tell a lie. She _____ the truth.

15. Rick _____ his arm when he fell on the ice.

16. We were late for the movie. It _____ at 7:00, but we didn't get there until 7:15.

17. We _____ songs at the party last night and had a good time.

18. I _____ to Chicago last week. The plane was only five minutes late.

19. My plane _____ at 6:03 and arrived at 8:45.

20. We played a soccer game yesterday. The other team _____. We lost.

# CHAPTER 8
## Nouns, Adjectives, and Pronouns

■ **EXERCISE 1:** How are these words usually used, as NOUNS or ADJECTIVES? Use each word in a sentence.

1. busy     NOUN   (ADJ)
   → *I'm too busy to go to the zoo.*

2. computer   (NOUN)   ADJ
   → *Computers are machines.*

3. tall     NOUN   ADJ

4. apartment    NOUN   ADJ

5. Tom     NOUN   ADJ

6. intelligent    NOUN   ADJ

7. hand     NOUN   ADJ

8. good     NOUN   ADJ

9. monkey     NOUN   ADJ

10. young     NOUN   ADJ

11. music     NOUN   ADJ

12. expensive     NOUN   ADJ

13. grammar     NOUN   ADJ

## 8-1 MODIFYING NOUNS WITH ADJECTIVES AND NOUNS

| | |
|---|---|
|         ADJECTIVE + NOUN <br> (a) I bought an ***expensive***   book. | Adjectives can modify nouns, as in (a). See Chart 4-2 for a list of common adjectives. |
|         NOUN + NOUN <br> (b) I bought a ***grammar***   book | Nouns can modify other nouns. In (b): *grammar* is a noun that is used as an adjective to modify another noun *(book)*. |
|         NOUN + NOUN <br> (c) He works at a ***shoe***   store. <br> (d) INCORRECT: *He works at a shoes store.* | A noun that is used as an adjective is always in its singular form. In (c): the store sells shoes, but it is called a *shoe* (singular form) *store*. |
|         ADJECTIVE + NOUN + NOUN <br> (e) I bought an ***expensive***   ***grammar***   book. <br> (f) INCORRECT: *I bought a grammar expensive book.* | Both an adjective and a noun can modify a noun; the adjective comes first, the noun second. |

■ **EXERCISE 2:** Find the ADJECTIVES and identify the nouns they modify.

1. I drank some hot tea.

2. My grandmother is a wise woman.

3. English is not my native language.

4. The busy waitress poured coffee into the empty cup.

5. A young man carried the heavy suitcase for Fumiko.

6. I sat in an uncomfortable chair at the restaurant.

7. There is international news on the front page of the newspaper.

8. My uncle is a wonderful man.

■ **EXERCISE 3:** Find the NOUNS USED AS ADJECTIVES and identify the nouns they modify.

1. We sat at the kitchen table.

2. I bought some new CDs at the music store.

3. We met Jack at the train station.

4. Vegetable soup is nutritious.

5. The movie theater is next to the furniture store.

6. The waiter handed us a lunch menu.

7. The traffic light was red, so we stopped.

8. Ms. Bell gave me her business card.

■ **EXERCISE 4:** Complete the sentences. Use the information in the first part of the sentence. Use A NOUN THAT MODIFIES ANOTHER NOUN in the completion.

1. Vases that are used for flowers are called ____*flower vases.*____

2. A cup that is used for coffee is called ____*a coffee cup.*____

3. A story that appears in a newspaper is called _____

4. Rooms in hotels are called _____

5. Soup that is made of beans is called _____

6. A worker in an office is called _____

7. A room that contains computers is called _____

8. Seats on airplanes are called _____

9. A bench that is found in a park is called _____

10. A tag that gives the price of something is called _____

■ **EXERCISE 5:** Which noun in the list can be used with all three of the nouns used as modifiers? For example, in the first sentence below, the completion can be *a university education, a high school education,* and *a college education.*

| | | |
|---|---|---|
| class | official | soup |
| ✔ education | program | store |
| keys | race | tickets |
| number | room | trip |

1. Jane has a
   { university
   high school
   college }
   ___education._____

2. We went to a
   { furniture
   shoe
   clothing }
   _____

3. I took a
   { history
   math
   science }
   _____

4. We watched a
   { horse
   car
   foot }
   _____

5. I talked to a
   { government
   city
   school }
   _____

6. Mom made some
   { vegetable
   bean
   chicken }
   _____

7. He told me about a
   { radio
   television
   computer }
   _____

8. We took a/an
   { boat
   bus
   airplane }
   _____

9. I couldn't find my
   { car
   house
   door }
   _____

10. What is your
    { telephone
    apartment
    license plate }
    _____

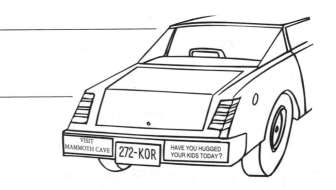

11. We bought some { theater  concert  airplane } _____

12. We visited Sue in her { hospital  hotel  dormitory } _____

■ **EXERCISE 6:** Each item lists two NOUNS and one ADJECTIVE. Put them in the correct order.

1. *homework*
   *long*
   *assignment*

   The teacher gave us a ___*long homework assignment.*___

2. *program*
   *good*
   *television*

   I watched a _____

3. *road*
   *mountain*
   *dangerous*

   We drove on a _____

4. *automobile*
   *bad*
   *accident*

   Janet was in a _____

5. *article*
   *magazine*
   *interesting*

   I read an _____

6. *delicious*
   *vegetable*
   *soup*

   Mrs. Green made some _____

7. *card*
   *funny*
   *birthday*

   My sister gave me a _____

8. *narrow*
   *seats*
   *airplane*

   People don't like to sit in _____

| | |
|---|---|
| (a)  a **large red** car <br> (b)  INCORRECT:  *a red large car* | In (a): two adjectives *(large* and *red)* modify a noun *(car).*  Adjectives follow a particular order.  In (a), an adjective describing **size** *(large)* comes before **color** *(red)* . |
| (c)  a **beautiful young** woman <br> (d)  a **beautiful red** car <br> (e)  a **beautiful Greek** island | The adjective *beautiful* expresses an opinion. Opinion adjectives usually come before all other adjectives. <br> In (c): opinion precedes age. <br> In (d): opinion precedes color. <br> In (e): opinion precedes nationality. |
| (f)  OPINION ADJECTIVES <br><br> *dangerous    favorite    important* <br> *difficult     good       interesting* <br> *dirty        happy      strong* <br> *expensive    honest     wonderful* | There are many opinion adjectives.  The words in (f) are examples of common opinion adjectives. |

### USUAL WORD ORDER OF ADJECTIVES

| (1) <br> **OPINION** | (2) <br> **SIZE** | (3) <br> **AGE** | (4) <br> **COLOR** | (5) <br> **NATIONALITY*** | (6) <br> **MATERIAL** |
|---|---|---|---|---|---|
| *beautiful* | *large* | *young* | *red* | *Greek* | *metal* |
| *delicious* | *tall* | *old* | *blue* | *Chinese* | *glass* |
| *kind* | *little* | *middle-aged* | *black* | *Mexican* | *plastic* |

| | |
|---|---|
| (g)  some **delicious Mexican** food <br> (h)  a **small glass** vase <br> (i)  a **kind old Chinese** man | A noun is usually modified by only one or two adjectives, although sometimes there are three. |
| (j)  RARE: <br> a *beautiful small old brown Greek metal coin* | It is very rare to find a long list of adjectives in front of a noun. |

*NOTE: Adjectives that describe nationality are capitalized:  **K**orean, **V**enezuelan, **S**audi Arabian, etc.

■ **EXERCISE 7:**  Put the *italicized* words in the correct order.

1. *glass*      a _____*tall glass*_____ vase
   *tall*

2. *delicious*  some _____ food
   *Thai*

3. *red*        some _____ tomatoes
   *small*

4. *old*
   *big*
   *brown*

   some _____ cows

5. *narrow*
   *dirt*

   a _____ road

6. *young*
   *serious*

   a _____ woman

7. *long*
   *black*
   *beautiful*

   _____ hair

8. *Chinese*
   *famous*
   *old*

   a/an _____ work of art

9. *leather*
   *brown*
   *thin*

   a _____ belt

10. *wonderful*
    *old*
    *Native American*

    a/an _____ story

■ **EXERCISE 8:**   Complete the sentences with words from the list below.

| | | |
|---|---|---|
| *Asian* | ✔ *cotton* | *polite* |
| *brick* | *important* | *soft* |
| *Canadian* | *leather* | *unhappy* |
| *coffee* | | |

1. Jack is wearing a white _____*cotton*_____ shirt.

2. Hong Kong is an important _____ city.

3. I'm wearing some comfortable old _____ shoes.

4. Tommy was a/an _____ little boy when he broke his favorite toy.

5. Ann has a/an _____ wool blanket on her bed.

6. Our dorm is a tall red _____ building.

7. The computer is a/an _____ modern invention.

8. My nephew has good manners. He is always a/an _____ ■ young man, especially to his elders.

9. Jack always carries a large blue _____ cup with him.

10. Ice hockey is a popular _____ sport.

■ **EXERCISE 9:**  Add ADJECTIVES or NOUNS USED AS ADJECTIVES to the sentences below.

1. We had some hot _____ food.

2. My dog, Rover, is a/an _____ old dog.

3. We bought a blue _____ blanket.

4. Alice has _____ gold earrings.

5. Tom has short _____ hair.

6. Mr. Lee is a/an _____ young man.

7. Jack lives in a large _____ brick house.

8. I bought a big _____ suitcase.

9. Sally picked a/an _____ red flower.

10. Ali wore an old _____ shirt to the picnic.

■ **EXERCISE 10—ERROR ANALYSIS:** Many, but not all, of the following sentences contain mistakes in the word order of modifiers. Find and correct the mistakes. Make changes in the use of *a* and *an* as necessary.

*an old wood*
1. Ms. Lane has ~~a wood old~~ desk in her office.

2. She put the flowers in a blue glass vase. *(no change)*

3. The Great Wall is a Chinese landmark famous.

4. I read a newspaper article interesting this morning.

5. Spiro gave me a wonderful small black Greek box as a birthday present.

6. Alice reached down and put her hand in the mountain cold stream.

7. Pizza is my favorite food Italian.

8. There was a beautiful flower arrangement on the kitchen table.

9. Jack usually wears brown old comfortable shoes leather.

10. Gnats are black tiny insects.

11. I used a box brown cardboard to mail a gift to my sister.

12. Tony has a noisy electric fan in his bedroom window.

13. James is a middle-aged handsome man with brown short hair.

14. When Jane was on her last business trip, she had a cheap rental car, but she stayed in a room expensive hotel.

■ **EXERCISE 11—ORAL:**   Practice modifying nouns.

STUDENT A:  Your book is open.  Say the words in each item.  Don't let your
                  intonation drop because Student B is going to finish the phrase.
STUDENT B:  Your book is closed.  Complete Student A's phrase with a noun.
                  Respond as quickly as you can with the first noun that comes to mind.

*Example:*      a dark . . .
STUDENT A:  a dark
STUDENT B:  night (room, building, day, cloud, etc.)

*Example:*      some ripe . . .
STUDENT A:  some ripe
STUDENT B:  soup
STUDENT A:  some ripe soup??  I don't think soup can be called ripe.
STUDENT B:  Okay.  How about "some ripe fruit"?  OR: "some ripe bananas"?
STUDENT A:  That's good.  Some ripe fruit or some ripe bananas.

| | |
|---|---|
| 1. a kitchen . . . | 11. a birthday . . . |
| 2. a busy . . . | 12. a computer . . . |
| 3. a public . . . | 13. a baby . . . |
| 4. a true . . . | 14. a soft . . . |
| 5. some expensive . . . | 15. an easy . . . |
| 6. an interesting old . . . | 16. a government . . . |
| 7. an airplane . . . | 17. some hot . . . |
| 8. a dangerous . . . | 18. a flower . . . |
| 9. a beautiful Korean . . . | 19. a bright . . . |
| 10. some delicious Mexican . . . | 20. some small round . . . |

*Switch roles.*

| | |
|---|---|
| 21. a telephone . . . | 31. some great old . . . |
| 22. a fast . . . | 32. a television . . . |
| 23. some comfortable . . . | 33. a very deep . . . |
| 24. a foreign . . . | 34. an office . . . |
| 25. a famous Italian . . . | 35. a gray wool . . . |
| 26. a bus . . . | 36. an afternoon . . . |
| 27. a history . . . | 37. an empty . . . |
| 28. a rubber bicycle . . . | 38. a wonderful South American . . . |
| 29. a hospital . . . | 39. a bedroom . . . |
| 30. a movie . . . | 40. a science . . . |

## 8-3 EXPRESSIONS OF QUANTITY: *ALL OF, MOST OF, SOME OF*

| | |
|---|---|
| (a) Rita ate **all of** the food on her plate.<br>(b) Mike ate **most of** his food.<br>(c) Susie ate **some of** her food. | *All of*, *most of*, and *some of* express quantities.<br> *all of* = 100%<br> *most of* = a large part, but not all<br> *some of* = a small or medium part |
| (d) Matt ate **almost all of** his food.<br>(e) INCORRECT: *Matt ate almost of his food.* | *all of* = 100%<br>*almost all of* = 95%–99%<br>**Almost** is used with **all**; **all** cannot be omitted. |

■ **EXERCISE 12:** Complete the sentences with *(almost) all of*, *most of*, or *some of*.

1. 2, 4, 6, 8: _____*All of*_____ these numbers are even.

2. 1, 3, 5, 7: _____these numbers are odd.

3. 1, 3, 4, 6, 7, 9: _____ these numbers are odd.

4. 1, 3, 4, 6, 7, 8: _____ these numbers are odd.

5. 1, 3, 4, 5, 7, 9: _____ these numbers are odd.

6. _____ the birds in Picture A are flying.

7. _____ the birds in Picture B are flying.

8. _____ the birds in Picture C are flying.

9. _____ the birds in Picture D are flying.

PICTURE A

PICTURE B

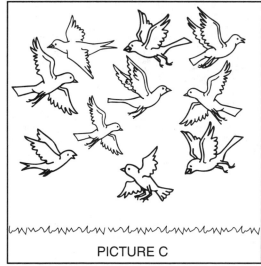

PICTURE C

PICTURE D

10. _____ the students in this class have dark hair.

11. _____ the students in this class are using pens rather than pencils to do this exercise.

12. _____ the students in this class wear glasses.

13. _____ the students in this class can speak English.

## 8-4 EXPRESSIONS OF QUANTITY: SUBJECT–VERB AGREEMENT

| | |
|---|---|
| (a) *All of my **work is** finished.*<br>(b) *All of my **friends are** kind.*<br>(c) *Some of my **homework is** finished.*<br>(d) *Some of my **friends are** coming to my birthday party.* | In (a): *all of* + **singular** noun + **singular** verb.<br>In (b): *all of* + **plural** noun + **plural** verb.<br>In (c): *some of* + **singular** noun + **singular** verb.<br>In (d): *some of* + **plural** noun + **plural** verb. |
| | When a subject includes an expression of quantity, the verb agrees with the noun that immediately follows *of*. |

COMMON EXPRESSIONS OF QUANTITY

| | | |
|---|---|---|
| *all of* | *most of* | *half of* |
| *almost all of* | *a lot of* | *some of* |

■ **EXERCISE 13:** Choose the correct VERB.

1. All of that money ____*is*____ mine.
   (is \ are)

2. All of the windows _____ open.
   (is \ are)

3. We saw one movie. Some of the movie _____ interesting.
   (was \ were)

4. We saw five movies. Some of the movies _____ interesting.
   (was \ were)

5. Half of the glasses _____ empty,
   (is \ are)

   and half of the glasses _____ full.
   (is \ are)

6. Half of the glass

   _____ empty.
   (is \ are)

IT'S HALF EMPTY.    IT'S HALF FULL.

Pessimist          Optimist

7. A lot of those words _____ new to me.
   (is \ are)

8. A lot of that vocabulary _____ new to me.
   (is \ are)

9. Almost all of the air in the city _____ polluted.
   (is \ are)

10. Almost all of the oceans in the world _____ polluted.
    (is \ are)

11. Most of the students _____ on time.
    (arrives \ arrive)

12. Most of our mail _____ in the morning.
    (arrives \ arrive)

## 8-5 EXPRESSIONS OF QUANTITY: ONE OF, NONE OF

| | |
|---|---|
| ONE OF + PLURAL NOUN<br>(a) Sam is **one** of my **friends**.<br><br>(b) INCORRECT: *Sam is one of my friend.* | **One of** is followed by a specific **plural noun**, as in (a).<br>It is INCORRECT to follow **one of** with a singular noun, as in (b). |
| ONE OF + PL. NOUN + SING. VERB<br>(c) **One** of my **friends** **is** here.<br>(d) INCORRECT: *One of my friends are here.* | When **one of** + *a plural noun* is the subject of a sentence, it is followed by a **singular verb**, as in (c): ONE OF + PLURAL NOUN + SINGULAR VERB. |
| (e) **None of** the students **was** late.<br>(f) **None of** the students **were** late. | In (e): Not one of the students was late.<br>    **none of** = **not one of**<br>The verb following **none of** + *a plural noun* can be singular, as in (e), or plural, as in (f). Both are correct.\* |

\*In very formal English, a singular verb is used after **none of** + *a plural noun: None of the students* **was** *late*. In everyday English, both singular and plural verbs are used.

■ **EXERCISE 14:** Make sentences from the given words and phrases.

1. One of my \ teacher \ be \ *(name of a teacher)*

   *One of my teachers is Ms. Lopez.* _____

2. *(name of a student)* \ be \ one of my \ classmate

   _____

3. one of my \ book \ be \ red

_____

4. one of my \ book \ have \ a green cover

_____

5. *(name of a place)* \ be \ one of my favorite \ place \ in the world

_____

6. one of the \ student \ in my class \ always come \ late

_____

7. *(name of a person)* \ be \ one of my best \ friend

_____

8. one of my \ friend \ live \ in *(name of a place)*

_____

9. *(title of a TV program)* \ be \ one of the best \ program \ on TV

_____

10. *(name of a person)* \ be \ one of the most famous \ people★ \ in the world

_____

11. one of my biggest \ problem \ be \ my inability to understand spoken English

_____

12. *(name of a newspaper)* \ be \ one of the \ leading newspaper \ in *(name of a city)*

_____

13. none of the \ student \ in my class \ speak \ *(name of a language)*

_____

14. none of the \ furniture \ in this room \ be \ soft and comfortable

_____

_____

★*People* is a plural noun even though it does not have a final **-s**.

■ **EXERCISE 15:** Complete the sentences with your own words.

1. One of my favorite _____ is _____.

2. _____ is one of the most interesting _____ in the world.

3. One of the _____ in my _____ is _____.

4. _____ is one of my best _____.

5. One of _____.

6. None of _____.

■ **EXERCISE 16:** Choose the correct VERB.

1. My grammar book _____*is*_____ red.
   (is \ are)

2. Some of my books _____ on my desk.
   (is \ are)

3. One of my books _____ blue and green.
   (is \ are)

4. My favorite colors _____ red and yellow.
   (is \ are)

5. Sue's favorite color _____ green.
   (is \ are)

6. One of my favorite colors _____ red.
   (is \ are)

BRAZIL

7. My best friends _____ in Brazil.
   (lives \ live)

8. One of my best friends _____ in Australia.
   (lives \ live)

9. Some of the students in my class _____ lap-top computers.
   (has \ have)

10. One of the students in Pablo's class _____ a mustache.
    (has \ have)

11. None of these letters _____ for you.
    (is \ are)

12. None of this mail _____ for you.
    (is \ are)

■ **EXERCISE 17:** Complete the sentences with *is* or *are*.

1. Some of the children's toys _____*are*_____ broken.

2. Most of my classmates _____ always on time for class.

3. One of my classmates _____ always late.

4. All of my friends _____ kind people.

5. One of my friends _____ Sam Brown.

6. Most of the rivers in the world _____ polluted.

7. Some of the Pacific Ocean _____ badly polluted.

8. Most of this page _____ white.

9. Most of the pages in this book _____ full of grammar exercises.

10. One of the pages in this book _____ the title page.

■ **EXERCISE 18—ORAL (BOOKS CLOSED):** Answer the questions in complete sentences. Use any expression of quantity (*all of, most of, some of, a lot of, one of, three of, etc.*).

*Example:* How many of the people in this room are wearing shoes?
*Response:* All of the people in this room are wearing shoes.

*Example:* How many of us are wearing blue jeans?
*Response:* Some of us are wearing blue jeans.

1. How many people in this room have (short) hair?
2. How many of the students in this class have red grammar books?
3. How many of us are sitting down?
4. How many of your classmates are from (*name of a country*)?
5. How many of the people in this room can speak (English)?
6. How many of the women in this room are wearing earrings? How many of the men?
7. What is one of your favorite TV programs?
8. How many of the people in this city are friendly?
9. Who is one of the most famous people in the world?
10. How many of the married women in your country work outside the home?

## 8-6 USING EVERY

| | |
|---|---|
| (a) **Every student** **has** a book. <br> (b) *All of the students* have books. | (a) and (b) have essentially the same meaning. <br> In (a): *every* + **singular** noun + **singular** verb. |
| (c) INCORRECT: *Every of the students has a book.* <br> (d) INCORRECT: *Every students have books.* | *Every* is not immediately followed by *of*. <br> *Every* is immediately followed by a **singular** noun, NOT a plural noun. |
| (e) **Everyone** **has** a book. <br> (f) **Everybody** **has** a book. | (e) and (f) have the same meaning. <br> *Everyone* and *everybody* are followed by a **singular** verb. |
| (g) I looked at **everything** in the museum. | In (g): *everything* = each thing. |
| (h) **Everything** **is** okay. | In (h): *everything* is followed by a **singular** verb. |

■ **EXERCISE 19:** Choose the correct completion.

1. All of the _____*books*_____ on this desk _____*are*_____ mine.
   <br>              (book \ books)              (is \ are)

2. Every _____ on this desk _____ mine.
   <br>           (book \ books)           (is \ are)

3. All of the _____ _____ here today.
   <br>         (student \ students)     (is \ are)

4. Every _____ _____ here today.
   <br>       (student \ students)     (is \ are)

5. Every _____ at my college _____ tests regularly.
   <br>       (teacher \ teachers)       (gives \ give)

6. All of the _____ at my college _____ a lot of tests.
   <br>       (teacher \ teachers)       (gives \ give)

7. Every _____ in my country _____ bedtime stories.
   <br>       (child \ children)       (likes \ like)

8. All of the _____ in my country _____ that story.
   <br>       (child \ children)       (knows \ know)

9. All of the _____ in this class _____ studying English.
   <br>       (person \ people)       (is \ are)

10. Everyone in this class _____ to learn English.
    <br>       (wants \ want)

11. _____ all of the _____ in this class speak English well?
      (Does \ Do)              (student \ students)

12. _____ every _____ in the world like to listen to music?
      (Does \ Do)          (person \ people)

13. _____ all of the _____ in the world enjoy dancing?
      (Does \ Do)              (person \ people)

14. _____ everybody in the world have enough to eat?
      (Does \ Do)

15. Every _____ in Sweden _____ a good transportation system.
        (city \ cities)            (has \ have)

■ **EXERCISE 20—ERROR ANALYSIS:** Find and correct the errors.

1. I work hard every days.

2. I live in an apartment with one of my friend.

3. We saw a pretty flowers garden in the park.

4. Almost of the students are in class today.

5. Every people in my class are studying English.

6. All of the cities in North America has traffic problems.

7. One of my books are green.

8. Nadia drives a blue small car.

9. Istanbul is one of my favorite city in the world.

10. Every of students in the class have a grammar book.

11. The work will take a long time. We can't finish every things today.

12. Everybody in the world want peace.

## 8-7 POSSESSIVE NOUNS

| | | SINGULAR NOUN | POSSESSIVE NOUN | To show that a person possesses something, add an apostrophe (') and **-s** to a singular noun. |
|---|---|---|---|---|
| (a) | My *friend* has a car.<br>My ***friend's*** car is blue. | **friend** | **friend's** | POSSESSIVE NOUN, SINGULAR<br>noun + apostrophe (') + **-s** |
| (b) | The *student* has a book.<br>The ***student's*** book is red. | **student** | **student's** | |

| | | PLURAL NOUN | POSSESSIVE FORM | Add an apostrophe (') at the end of a plural noun (after the **-s**). |
|---|---|---|---|---|
| (c) | The *students* have books.<br>The ***students'*** books are red. | **students** | **students'** | POSSESSIVE NOUN, PLURAL<br>noun + **-s** + apostrophe (') |
| (d) | My *friends* have a car.<br>My ***friends'*** car is blue. | **friends** | **friends'** | |

■ **EXERCISE 21:** Add APOSTROPHES to the POSSESSIVE NOUNS.

*Jim's*
1. Jims ∧ last name is Smith.

2. Bobs cat likes to sleep on the sofa.

3. My teachers names are Ms. Rice and Mr. Molina.

4. My mothers first name is Marika.

5. My parents telephone number is 555-9876.

6. My Uncle George is my fathers brother.

7. Nicole is a girls name.

8. Erica and Heidi are girls names.

9. Do you like Toms shirt?

10. Do you know Anitas brother?

11. The teacher collected the students test papers at the end of the period.

12. Alexs friends visited him last night.

13. How long is an elephants trunk?

14. A monkeys hand looks like a human hand.

15. Monkeys hands have thumbs.

■ **EXERCISE 22:** Complete the sentences. Use your classmates' names.

1. _____ hair is short and straight.

2. _____ grammar book is on her desk.

3. _____ last name is _____.

4. I don't know _____ address.

5. _____ eyes are gray.

6. _____ shirt is blue.

7. _____ briefcase is on the floor.

8. I need to borrow _____ dictionary.

9. Do you like _____ mustache?

10. Do you know _____ wife?

■ **EXERCISE 23—WRITTEN:**  Write sentences about things your classmates possess.

    *Example:*  Kim's book is on his desk.  Anna's purse is brown.  Pablo's shirt is green.

■ **EXERCISE 24:**  Complete the sentences.

1. My husband's _____*brother*_____ is my brother-in-law.

2. My father's _____ is my uncle.

3. My mother's _____ is my grandmother.

4. My sister's _____ are my nieces and nephews.

5. My aunt's _____ is my mother.

6. My wife's _____ is my mother-in-law.

7. My brother's _____ is my sister-in-law.

8. My father's _____ and _____ are my grandparents.

9. My niece is my brother's _____.

10. My nephew is my sister's _____.

---

## 8-8  POSSESSIVE: IRREGULAR PLURAL NOUNS

| | |
|---|---|
| (a)  The **children's** *toys* are on the floor. | Irregular plural nouns *(children, men, women, people)* have an irregular plural possessive form.  The apostrophe (') comes <u>before</u> the final **-s**. |
| (b)  The store sells **men's** *clothing*. | |
| (c)  That store sells **women's** *clothing*. | REGULAR PLURAL POSSESSIVE NOUN:<br>    the **students'** *books* |
| (d)  I like to know about other **people's** *lives*. | IRREGULAR PLURAL POSSESSIVE NOUN:<br>    the **women's** *books* |

---

■ **EXERCISE 25:**  Complete the sentences with the correct possessive form of the NOUNS in *italics*.

1. *children*       That store sells _____*children's*_____ books.

2. *girl*       Mary is a _____ name.

3. *girls*       Mary and Sue are _____ names.

4. *women*       Mary and Sue are _____ names.

5. *uncle*        Robert is living at his _____ house.

6. *person*       A biography is the story of a _____ life.

7. *people*       Biographies are the stories of _____ lives.

8. *students*     _____ lives are busy.

9. *brother*      Do you know my _____ wife?

10. *brothers*    Do you know my _____ wives?

11. *wife*         My _____ parents live in California.

12. *dog*          My _____ name is Fido.

13. *dogs*        My _____ names are Fido and Rover.

14. *men*         Are Jim and Tom _____ names?

15. *man, woman*   Chris can be a _____ nickname or a

                                  _____ nickname.

16. *children*    Our _____ school is near our house.

■ **EXERCISE 26:**   Add appostrophes and final **-s** as necessary to make possessive nouns.

                         *Paul's*

1. Someone stole Paul ∧ bicycle.

2. Do you know Yuko roommate?

3. Does that store sell women clothes?

4. My roommate desk is always a mess.

5. What is your parent new address?

6. I have my father nose.*

7. Where is Rosa apartment?

8. I can't remember all of my classmate names.

---

*\*I have my father's nose* = My nose looks like my father's nose; I inherited the shape of my nose from my father.

9. It's important to respect other people opinions.

10. My husband sister is visiting us this week.

11. Excuse me. Where is the men room?

12. That store sells children toys.

## 8-9 POSSESSIVE PRONOUNS: *MINE, YOURS, HIS, HERS, OURS, THEIRS*

| | | | |
|---|---|---|---|
| (a) This book belongs to me.<br>It is *my* book.<br>It is *mine*.<br>(b) That book belongs to you.<br>It is *your* book.<br>It is *yours*. | POSSESSIVE<br>ADJECTIVE<br><br>*my*<br>*your*<br>*her*<br>*his*<br>*our*<br>*their* | POSSESSIVE<br>PRONOUN<br><br>*mine*<br>*yours*<br>*hers*<br>*his*<br>*ours*<br>*theirs* | A possessive adjective is used in front of a noun: *my* book.<br><br>A possessive pronoun is used alone, without a noun following it:<br>    *That book is **mine**.*<br><br>INCORRECT: *That is mine book.* |

■ **EXERCISE 27:** Complete the sentences. Use OBJECT PRONOUNS, POSSESSIVE ADJECTIVES, and POSSESSIVE PRONOUNS.

1. *I* own this book.

   This book belongs to ____me____.

   This is ____my____ book.

   This book is ____mine____.

2. *They* own these books.

   These books belong to _____.

   These are _____ books.

   These books are _____.

3. *You* own that book.

   That book belongs to _____.

   That is _____ book.

   That book is _____.

4. *She* owns this pen.

   This pen belongs to _____.

   This is _____ pen.

   This pen is _____.

5. *He* owns that pen.

   That pen belongs to _____.

   That is _____ pen.

   That pen is _____.

6. *We* own those books.

   Those books belong to _____.

   Those are _____ books.

   Those books are _____.

■ **EXERCISE 28:** Complete the sentences. Use the correct possessive form of the words in *italics*.

1. *I*       a. This bookbag is _____*mine*_____.

   *Sue*     b. That bookbag is _____*Sue's*_____.

   *I*       c. _____*My*_____ bookbag is red.

   *she*     d. _____*Hers*_____ is green.


2. *we*      a. These books are _____.

   *they*    b. Those books are _____.

   *we*      c. _____ books are on the table.

   *they*    d. _____ are on the desk.


3. *Tom*     a. This raincoat is _____.

   *Mary*    b. That raincoat is _____.

   *he*      c. _____ is light brown.

   *she*     d. _____ is light blue.


4. *I*       a. This notebook is _____.

   *you*     b. That one is _____.

   *I*       c. _____ has _____ name on it.

   *you*     d. _____ has _____ name on it.


5. *Jim*     a. _____ apartment is on Pine Street.

   *we*      b. _____ is on Main Street.

   *he*      c. _____ apartment has three rooms.

   *we*      d. _____ has four rooms.


6. *I*       a. This is _____ pen.

   *you*     b. That one is _____.

   *I*       c. _____ is in _____ pocket.

   *you*     d. _____ is on _____ desk.

7. *we*    a. _____ car is a Chevrolet.

   *they*    b. _____ is a Volkswagen.

   *we*    c. _____ gets 17 miles to the gallon.

   *they*    d. _____ car gets 30 miles to the gallon.

8. *Ann*    a. These books are _____ .

   *Paul*    b. Those are _____ .

   *she*    c. _____ are on _____ desk.

   *he*    d. _____ are on _____ desk.

■ **EXERCISE 29:** Choose the correct completion.

1. Is this _____*your*_____ pen?
   (your \ yours)

2. Please give this dictionary to Olga. It's _____.
   (her \ hers)

3. A: Don't forget _____ hat. Here.
   (your \ yours)

   B: No, that's not _____ hat. _____ is green.
   (my \ mine)      (My \ Mine)

4. A: Please take this wood carving as a gift from me. Here. It's _____.
   (your \ yours)

   B: Thank you. You're very thoughtful.

5. A: Isn't that the Smiths' car? That one over there. The blue one.

   B: No, that's not _____. _____ car is dark blue.
   (their \ theirs)      (Their \ Theirs)

6. A: Jim and I really like _____ new apartment. It has lots of
   (our \ ours)

   space. How do you like _____?
   (your \ yours)

   B: _____ is small, but it's comfortable.
   (Our \ Ours)

7. A: Excuse me. Is this _____ umbrella?
   (your \ yours)

   B: I don't have an umbrella. Ask Ken. Perhaps it is _____.
   (him \ his)

8. A: When do _____ classes begin?
      (your \ yours)

   B: September second. How about _____? When do
                                   (your \ yours)

      _____ begin?
      (your \ yours)

   A: _____ begin August twenty-ninth.
      (My \ Mine)

9. A: Maria, _____ spaghetti sauce is delicious!
            (your\ yours)

   B: Thank you, but it's not as good as _____.
                                          (your \ yours)

   A: Oh, no. _____ is much better! It tastes just as good as Anna's.
               (Your \ Yours)

   B: Do you like Anna's spaghetti sauce? I think _____ is too salty.
                                                   (her\ hers)

   A: Maybe. _____ husband makes good spaghetti sauce too.
              (My\ Mine)

      _____ is thick and rich.
      (His \ He)

   B: In truth, making spaghetti sauce is easy, but everyone's sauce is just a little different.

| | |
|---|---|
| (a) **Whose book** is this? → Mine.<br>→ It's mine.<br>→ It's my book.<br>(b) **Whose books** are these? → Rita's.<br>→ They're Rita's.<br>→ They're Rita's books. | **Whose** asks about possession.<br><br>**Whose** is often used with a noun (e.g., *whose book*), as in (a) and (b). |
| (c) **Whose** is this? *(The speaker is pointing to a book.)*<br>(d) **Whose** are these? *(The speaker is pointing to some books.)* | **Whose** can be used without a noun if the meaning is clear, as in (c) and (d). |

WHOSE IS THIS? THERE'S NO NAME ON IT. WHO'S THE ARTIST?

■ **EXERCISE 30:** Choose the correct completion.

1. Whose watch _____*is*_____ _____*this*_____?
   (is \ are)        (this \ these)

2. Whose glasses _____ _____?
   (is \ are)        (that \ those)

3. Whose keys _____ _____?
   (is \ are)        (this \ these)

4. Whose hat _____ _____?
   (is \ are)        (that \ those)

5. Whose shoes _____ _____?
   (is \ are)        (that \ those)

6. Whose handbag _____ _____?
   (is \ are)        (this \ these)

■ **EXERCISE 31:** Point to or touch something in the classroom that belongs to someone and ask a question with **whose**.

*Example:* (Student A points to or touches a grammar book.)
STUDENT A: Whose book is this?
STUDENT B: It's mine. / Mine. / It's my book.
STUDENT A: Whose book is that?
STUDENT B: It's Po's. / Po's. / It's Po's book.

## 8-11  SUMMARY: USES OF THE APOSTROPHE

| | |
|---|---|
| (a) **I'm** happy. (INCORRECT: *I'am happy.*) <br> **She's** happy. <br> **We're** happy. <br><br> (b) **Tom's** happy. <br><br> (c) **That's** my notebook. <br><br> (d) **There's** a book on the table. <br> **There're** some books on the table. <br><br> (e) **What's** this? <br> **Where's** Anna? <br><br> (f) **Who's** that?  →  It's *Mike.* <br> **Whose** is that?  →  It's *Mike's.* | USES OF THE APOSTROPHE <br> • With contractions of pronouns and **am, is,** and **are.** See Chart 1-4. <br><br> • With contractions of nouns and **is.** In (b), **Tom's** = *Tom is.*\* <br> • With the contraction of **that** and **is.** <br> • With the contractions of **there** and **is/are.** <br><br> • With contractions of some question words and **is.** <br><br> COMPARE <br> In (f): **Who's** = *who is.* <br> In (g): **Whose** = a question word that asks about possession. It has NO apostrophe. |
| (h)  Tina **isn't** here. | • With negative contractions: **isn't, aren't, wasn't, weren't, doesn't, don't, won't, can't.** |
| (i) **Tom's** hair is brown. <br> (j) My **parents'** house is white. <br> (k) This pen belongs to Ann. It is **hers.** <br> (l) INCORRECT: *It is her's.* | • With possessive nouns, as in (i) and (j). See Charts 8-7 and 8-8. <br> Apostrophes are NOT used with possessive pronouns. In (l): *hers* with an apostrophe (*her's*) is NEVER correct. |
| (m) **It's** sunny today. <br> (n) I'm studying about India. I'm interested in **its** history. <br> (o) INCORRECT: *I'm interested in it's history.* | COMPARE: In (m): **it's** = *it is.* <br> In (n): **its** = a possessive adjective: **its** *history* = **India's** *history.* A possessive adjective has NO apostrophe. |

\*Nouns are regularly contracted with **is** in spoken English. In written English, contractions of a noun and **is** (e.g., *Tom's happy*) are found in informal English (for example, in a letter to a friend), but not in formal English (for example, an academic paper). In general, verb contractions (*I'm, you're, isn't, there's,* etc.) are found in informal English, but are not used in very formal English.

■ **EXERCISE 32:** Add apostrophes where necessary.

1. Thats Anns book. → *That's Ann's book.*

2. That book is hers. → *(no change)*

3. Jims car is small.

4. Jims in New York this week.

5. Hes visiting his brother.

6. Im a little hungry this morning.

7. Tonys my neighbor.

8. Tonys apartment is next to mine.

9. Whos that woman?

10. Shes Bobs wife.

11. Whose book is that?

12. Is it yours?

13. Its Ginas book.

14. Wheres your dictionary?

15. Amy wont go to the movie with us.   She doesnt have enough money.

16. Paris is a popular tourist destination.  Its most famous attraction is the Eiffel Tower.

    Its most famous building is the Louvre Museum.  Its also famous for its night life.

■ **EXERCISE 33:** Add apostrophes where necessary.

*Yoko's*
1. Yokos ∧ last name is Yakamoto.

2. Yokos a student in my English class.

3. Pablo is a student.  Hes in my class.  His last name is Alvarez.

4. Pablos full name is Pablo Alvarez.

5. Youre a student.  Your name is Ali.

6. Im a student.  I am in Mr. Lees English class.

7. Mary and Anita have purses.  Marys purse is black.  Anitas purse is brown.

8. Marys in class today.  Anitas at home.

9. Whose books are these?  This book is mine.  Thats yours.

10. Whats wrong?  Whats happening?  Whos that man?  Wheres he going?

11. Im looking at a book.  Its a grammar book.  Its cover is red.  Its on my desk.  Its open.  Its title is *Basic English Grammar.*

12. Theres a bird in the tree.  Its black and red.  Its chest is red.  Its wings, tail, and back are black.  Its sitting on a branch.

13. People admire the tiger for its beauty and strength.  Its a magnificent animal. Unfortunately, its survival as a species is in doubt.  Its an endangered species. Therere very few tigers in the world today.

## 8-12 SUMMARY: USES OF NOUNS

| | NOUNS ARE USED AS: |
|---|---|
| (a) **NOUN** **Birds** \| fly. <br> subject   verb | • subjects of a sentence, as in (a). |
| (b) **NOUN** Ken \| opened \| *the **door.*** <br> subject   verb   object | • objects of a verb, as in (b). |
| (c) **NOUN** Birds \| fly \| in \| *the **sky.*** <br> subject   verb   prep. object of prep. | • objects of a preposition, as in (c). |
| (d) **NOUN** Yoko \| is \| *a **student.*** <br> subject   *be*   noun complement | • noun complements* after **be**, as in (d). |
| (e) **NOUN  +  NOUN** I don't like **winter**   weather. | • modifiers of other nouns, as in (e). |
| (f) **NOUN  +  NOUN** I like **Jim's**   hat. | • possessives, as in (f). |

*A *complement* is a word that <u>completes</u> a sentence or a thought.

■ **EXERCISE 34:** Write the sentences that fit the grammatical descriptions. Circle the NOUNS.

   a. A kangaroo is an animal.
   b. My wallet is in my pocket.

1.

2.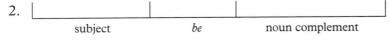

   c. Jason works in an office.
   d. Karen held the baby in her arms.
   e. Restaurants serve food.

3.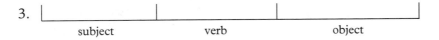

4.

5.

f.  Korea is in Asia.
g.  Korea is a peninsula.

6. ⌐——————————|——————————|——————————————⌐
       subject           *be*          prep.         object of prep.

7. ⌐——————————|——————————|——————————————⌐
       subject           *be*          noun complement

h.  Children play with toys.
i.  Monkeys eat fruit.
j.  Jack tied a string around the package.

8. ⌐——————————|——————————|——————————————⌐
       subject           verb           object

9. ⌐——————————|——————————|——————————|——————⌐
       subject           verb           prep.         object of prep.

10. ⌐——————————|——————————|——————————|——————⌐
        subject           verb           object       prep.   object of prep.

## 8-13 CONNECTED NOUNS: NOUN + *AND/OR* + NOUN

| | |
|---|---|
| **NOUN + *and* + NOUN**<br><br>(a) \|***Birds*** and ***airplanes*** \| fly. \|<br>　　　　subject　　　　　　　verb<br><br>　　　　　　　　NOUN + *and* + NOUN<br>(b) \| Ken \| opened \| *the* ***door*** and *the* ***window.*** \|<br>　subject　verb　　　　　　　object<br><br>　　　　　NOUN + NOUN + *and* + NOUN<br>(c) \| I \| have \|*a* ***book***, *a* ***pen***, and *a* ***pencil.*** \|<br>　subject　verb　　　　　object | ***And*** can connect two or more nouns.<br>In (a): the subject = two nouns.<br>In (b): the object = two nouns.<br>In (c): the object = three nouns.<br>Three (or more) nouns are separated by commas, as in (c). Two nouns, as in (a) and (b), are NOT separated by commas. |
| **NOUN + *or* + NOUN**<br>(d)　I'd like *some coffee* **or** *some tea.* | ***Or*** can also connect two nouns, as in (d). |

■ **EXERCISE 35:** Find the CONNECTED NOUNS and discuss how they are used.

1. You bought apples and bananas.
   → *apples and bananas* = *connected nouns, used as the object of the verb "bought"*

2. I bought apples, bananas, and oranges.

3. Jack and Olga bought bananas.

4. Julia wants apples or bananas.

5. Julia is at the market with Jack and Olga.

6. Tennis and golf are popular sports.

7. Tokyo has excellent museums and libraries.

8. A tree has a trunk, branches, leaves, and roots.

9. Automobiles, trains, and trucks are kinds of vehicles.

10. I'll have some soup or a sandwich for lunch.

■ **EXERCISE 36:** Add commas where necessary.

1. Ants bees and mosquitoes are insects.
   → *Ants, bees, and mosquitoes are insects.*★

2. Ants and bees are insects. *(no change)*

3. Bears tigers and elephants are animals.

4. Bears and tigers are animals.

5. I bought some rice fruit and vegetables at the market.

6. I bought some rice and fruit at the market.

7. The three countries in North America are Canada the United States and Mexico.

8. I read a lot of newspapers and magazines.

9. I had some soup and a sandwich for lunch.

10. Shelley had some soup a salad and a sandwich for lunch.

11. My favorite things in life are sunny days music good friends and books.

12. What do birds butterflies and airplanes have in common?

■ **EXERCISE 37:** Find the NOUNS. Discuss how they are used.

1. A turtle is a reptile.
   → *turtle = a noun, used as the subject of the sentence.*
   → *reptile = a noun, used as a complement after "be."*

2. A turtle has a hard shell.

3. A turtle pulls its head, legs, and tail into its shell.

4. Some turtles spend almost all of their lives in water.

5. Some turtles live on land for their entire lives.

6. Turtles don't have teeth, but they have powerful jaws.

---

★In a series of connected nouns, the comma immediately before **and** is optional.
ALSO CORRECT: *Ants, bees and mosquitoes are insects.*

7. Turtles bury their eggs in sand or mud.

8. Baby turtles face many dangers.

9. Birds and fish eat baby turtles.

10. Some green sea turtles live for 100 years.

11. Turtles face many dangers from people.

12. People destroy turtles' natural homes.

13. People replace beaches, forests, and other natural areas with towns and farms.

14. People poison natural areas with pollution.

15. Many species of turtles face extinction.

## 8-14 SUMMARY: USES OF ADJECTIVES

| | | |
|---|---|---|
| (a) I bought some **beautiful** **flowers**.<br><br>ADJECTIVE + NOUN | | Adjectives describe nouns; they give information about nouns. See Chart 4-2 for a list of common adjectives.<br>Adjectives can come in front of nouns, as in (a). |
| (b) The flowers **were** **beautiful**.<br><br>BE + ADJECTIVE | | Adjectives can follow **be**, as in (b). The adjective describes the subject of the sentence. See Chart 1-6. |
| (c) The flowers **looked** **beautiful**.<br>(d) The flowers **smelled** **good**.<br>(e) I **feel** **good**.<br>(f) Candy **tastes** **sweet**.<br>(g) That book **sounds** **interesting**.<br><br>LINKING VERB + ADJECTIVE | | Adjectives can follow a few other verbs. These verbs are called "linking verbs." The adjective describes the subject of the sentence.<br>Common linking verbs are:<br>  *look, smell, feel, taste,* and *sound*. |

■ **EXERCISE 38:** Find the ADJECTIVES and discuss ways adjectives are used.

1. The sun is bright today.
   → *bright = an adjective. It follows "be" and describes the subject of the sentence, "sun."*

2. I drank some cold water.

3. My dog's nose is cold.

4. Ice feels cold.

5. This exercise looks easy.

6. Our teacher gives easy tests.

7. English grammar is easy.

8. Lemons taste sour.

9. What's the matter? You look unhappy.

10. I'm sad.

11. Who is your favorite author?

12. What's the matter? You sound angry.

13. Ummm. These flowers smell wonderful!

14. That chair looks soft and comfortable.

15. Mr. White is a good history teacher.

■ **EXERCISE 39—ORAL:** Practice using linking verbs.

*PART I:*  Do any of the following ADJECTIVES describe how you feel today?

| | | |
|---|---|---|
| 1. good | 5. sleepy | 9. happy |
| 2. fine | 6. tired | 10. calm |
| 3. terrible | 7. lazy | 11. sick |
| 4. terrific | 8. nervous | 12. old |

*PART II:*  Name things that . . .

| | |
|---|---|
| 13. taste good | 17. taste sour |
| 14. taste terrible | 18. smell good |
| 15. taste delicious | 19. smell bad |
| 16. taste sweet | 20. smell wonderful |

*PART III:* Name something in this room that looks . . .

| | |
|---|---|
| 21. clean | 25. expensive |
| 22. dirty | 26. comfortable |
| 23. new | 27. messy |
| 24. old | 28. familiar |

■ **EXERCISE 40—ORAL:**  Describe how your classmates look.

STUDENT A: Choose one of the emotions listed below.  Show that emotion through expressions on your face and through your actions.  Don't tell anyone which emotion you're trying to show.

STUDENT B: Describe how Student A looks.  Use the linking verb *look* and an adjective.

| | |
|---|---|
| 1. angry | 5. busy |
| 2. sad / unhappy | 6. comfortable |
| 3. happy | 7. surprised |
| 4. tired / sleepy | 8. nervous |

■ **EXERCISE 41:**  Use any possible completions for the following sentences.  Use the words in the list or your own words.

| | | |
|---|---|---|
| *easy* | *good / terrific / wonderful / great* | *interesting* |
| *hard / difficult* | *terrible / awful* | *tired / sleepy* |

1. Rosa told me about a new book.  I want to read it.  It sounds ___*interesting / good / terrific*___.

2. Karen learned how to make paper flowers.  She told me how to do it.  It sounds

_____.

3. There's a new play at the community theater. I read a review of it in the newspaper. I'd like to see it. It sounds _____.

4. Professor Wilson is going to lecture on the problems of overpopulation tomorrow evening. I think I'll go. It sounds _____.

5. Chris explained how to fix a flat tire. I think I can do it. It sounds

_____.

6. Shelley didn't finish her dinner because it didn't taste _____.

7. What's for dinner? Something smells _____. Ummm! What is it?

8. Amy didn't get any sleep last night because she studied all night for a test. Today she looks _____.

9. Ymmmm! This dessert tastes _____. What is it?

10. A: What's the matter? Do you feel okay?

    B: No. I feel _____. I think I'm getting a cold.

11. A: Do you like my new dress, darling?

    B: You look _____, honey.

12. A: Pyew!* Something smells _____! Do you smell it too?
    B: I sure do. It's the garbage in the alley.

■ **EXERCISE 42:** Work in pairs or small groups. In a given time limit (e.g., fifteen seconds, thirty seconds, a minute), think of as many ADJECTIVES or NOUNS USED AS ADJECTIVES as you can that can be used to describe the nouns. Make a list.

*Example:* car
*Response:* big, little, fast, slow, comfortable, small, large, old, new, used, noisy, quiet, foreign, electric, antique, police, etc.

1. weather          5. country
2. animal           6. person
3. food             7. river
4. movie            8. student

---

*Pyew is sometimes said "p.u." Both Pyew and p.u. mean that something smells very bad.

## 8-15 SUMMARY: PERSONAL PRONOUNS

| | SUBJECT PRONOUNS | OBJECT PRONOUNS | POSSESSIVE PRONOUNS | POSSESSIVE ADJECTIVES |
|---|---|---|---|---|
| SINGULAR | *I* | *me* | *mine* | *my* name(s) |
| | *you* | *you* | *yours* | *your* name(s) |
| | *she* | *her* | *hers* | *her* name(s) |
| | *he* | *him* | *his* | *his* name(s) |
| | *it* | *it* | | *its* name(s) |
| PLURAL | *we* | *us* | *ours* | *our* name(s) |
| | *you* | *you* | *yours* | *your* name(s) |
| | *they* | *them* | *theirs* | *their* name(s) |

| | |
|---|---|
| (a) *We* saw an accident. <br> (b) Anna saw *it* too. <br> (c) I have my pen. Sue has *hers*. <br> (d) *Her* pen is blue. | Personal pronouns are used as: <br> • subjects, as in (a); <br> • objects, as in (b); <br> • OR to show possession, as in (c) and (d). |
| (e) I have a book. *It* is on my desk. <br><br> (f) I have some books. *They* are on my desk. | Use a singular pronoun to refer to a singular noun. In (e): *book* and *it* are both singular. <br><br> Use a plural pronoun to refer to a plural noun. In (f): *books* and *they* are both plural. |

■ **EXERCISE 43:** PRONOUN review. Find and correct the errors in pronoun usage.

Dear Heidi,

(1) Everything is going fine. I like ~~mine~~ *my* new apartment very much. Its large and

(2) comfortable. I like me roommate too. Him name is Alberto. You will meet them

(3) when your visit I next month. His from Colombia. His studying English too. Were

(4) classmates. We were classmates last semester too.

(5) We share the rent and the utility bills, but us don't share the telephone bill.

(6) He pays for his's calls and my pay for my. He's telephone bill is very high because

(7) he has a girlfriend in Colombia. He calls she often. Sometimes her calls he. Them

(8) talk on the phone a lot.

(9) Ours neighbors are Mr. and Mrs. Black. Their very nice. We talk to it often.

(10) Ours apartment is next to their. Theirs have a three-year-old* daughter. Shes

(11) really cute. Hers name is Joy. Them also have a cat. Its black and white. Its eyes

---

*NOTE: When a person's age is used as an adjective in front of a noun, the word *year* is singular (NOT plural) and hyphens (-) are used: *a three-year-old daughter*.
> INCORRECT: *They have a three years old daughter.*
> CORRECT: *They have a three-year-old daughter.* OR: *Their daughter is three years old.*

(12)    are yellow.  Its name is Whiskers.  Its a friendly cat.  Sometimes they're cat leaves a

(13)    dead mouse outside ours door.

(14)        I'am looking forward to you're visit.

Love,  Carl

## 8-16   INDIRECT OBJECTS

| | |
|---|---|
| (a)   I wrote │ *a letter* │ **to Alex.** │<br>             direct object  INDIRECT object<br><br>(a)   I wrote │ ***Alex*** │ │ a letter. │<br>       INDIRECT object   direct object<br><br>(c)   INCORRECT: *I wrote to Alex a letter.* | Some verbs are followed by two objects:  a direct object and an indirect object.<br><br>(a) and (b) have the same meaning.<br><br>The preposition **to** is NOT used when the indirect object is first and the direct object is second. |
| (d)   DIRECT OBJECT<br>      What did you write?  →  A letter. | A direct object answers the question *What?* |
| (e)   INDIRECT OBJECT<br>      Who(m) did you write a letter to?  →  Alex.<br><br>(f)   —Did you write these letters to Alex?<br>      —Yes, I did.  I wrote **them to him**.<br><br>(g)   INCORRECT: *I wrote him them.* | An indirect object answers the question *Who(m)?*<br><br>When the direct object is a pronoun (e.g., *them*), it must precede the indirect object, as in (f). |

| |
|---|
| VERBS FOLLOWED BY INDIRECT OBJECTS INTRODUCED BY **TO**<br>   *give*      *send*<br>   *hand*    *show*<br>   *lend*     *tell*<br>   *pass*     *write* |

■ **EXERCISE 44:**   Use the given words to complete the grammar descriptions.

      1.   my pen \ Heidi \ I gave

          a. │     *I gave*     │   *my pen*   │  *to Heidi.*  │
                 subject and verb      direct object     INDIRECT object

          b. │     *I gave*     │    *Heidi*   │  *my pen.*  │
                 subject and verb    INDIRECT object    direct object

     2.   I wrote \ Kim \ a letter

          a. │               │           │           │
                 subject and verb      direct object     INDIRECT object

          b. │               │           │           │
                 subject and verb    INDIRECT object    direct object

3. Jack handed \ a book \ Hiroki

a.
| subject and verb | direct object | INDIRECT object |

b.
| subject and verb | INDIRECT object | direct object |

4. Stacy \ I passed \ the salt

a.
| subject and verb | direct object | INDIRECT object |

b.
| subject and verb | INDIRECT object | direct object |

5. I lent \ my car \ Tom

a.
| subject and verb | direct object | INDIRECT object |

b.
| subject and verb | INDIRECT object | direct object |

6. Alice \ a postcard \ I sent

a.
| subject and verb | direct object | INDIRECT object |

b.
| subject and verb | INDIRECT object | direct object |

7. Ann told \ a story \ us

a.
| subject and verb | direct object | INDIRECT object |

b.
| subject and verb | INDIRECT object | direct object |

8. us \ a picture \ Jack showed

a.
| subject and verb | direct object | INDIRECT object |

b.
| subject and verb | INDIRECT object | direct object |

■ **EXERCISE 45—ORAL:** Change the position of the INDIRECT OBJECT in the following sentences. Be sure to omit *to*.

1. I gave my pen to Alex.
   → *I gave Alex my pen.*
2. Please hand that book to me.
3. Rosa wrote a letter to her brother.
4. I gave a birthday present to Ahmed.
5. Please tell a story to us.
6. Did you send a package to your parents?
7. Mr. Hong showed a photograph of his wife to me.
8. Would you lend your camera to me?

■ **EXERCISE 46—ORAL (BOOKS CLOSED):** Change the position of the INDIRECT OBJECT.

*Example:* You gave your book to ( . . . ). What did you do?
*Response:* I gave ( . . . ) my book.

1. You gave your pen to ( . . . ).
2. You wrote a letter to ( . . . ).
3. You sent a package to ( . . . ).
4. You told a funny story to ( . . . ).
5. You showed a photograph to ( . . . ).
6. You sent a check to the telephone company.
7. You passed your dictionary to ( . . . ).
8. You handed your notebook to ( . . . ).
9. You lent *(an amount of money)* to ( . . . ).

■ **EXERCISE 47—ORAL:** Complete the sentences using the words in *italics*.

1. *a letter, my sister*  I wrote . . . yesterday.
   → *I wrote a letter to my sister yesterday.*
   → *I wrote my sister a letter yesterday.*

2. *my parents, a telegram*  I sent . . . two days ago.
3. *some candy, her children*  Mrs. Kelly gave . . . after dinner.
4. *her car, me*  Sue is going to lend . . . tomorrow.
5. *the class, a joke*  Sam told . . . yesterday.
6. *a letter, the newspaper*  I'm going to write . . . .
7. *the scissors, John*  Did you hand . . . ?
8. *me, the soy sauce*  Could you please pass . . . ?
9. *Liz, a picture*  Mr. Schwartz showed . . . of his baby daughter.
10. *the students, some good advice*  Yesterday the teacher gave . . . .

■ **EXERCISE 48—ORAL (BOOKS CLOSED):**  Perform the action.  Answer the question.

*Example:*  Give your book to ( . . . ).  What did you do?
*Response:*  I gave my book to ( . . . ).  OR:  I gave ( . . . ) my book.

1. Pass your dictionary to ( . . . ).
2. Please hand me your pen/pencil.
3. Lend ( . . . ) some money.
4. Tell ( . . . ) your name.
5. Please pass my pen to ( . . . ).
6. Give ( . . . ) some good advice.
7. Show ( . . . ) a picture.
8. Write ( . . . ) a note and pass it to him/her.
9. Give ( . . . ) a gift.
10. Please hand that piece of chalk to me.

## 8-17   INDIRECT OBJECTS:  USING *FOR*

| | |
|---|---|
| (a)  Bob opened &#124; *the door*  &#124; ***for Mary***. &#124;<br>                   direct obj.   INDIRECT obj.<br>(b)  Sue answered &#124; *a question*  &#124; ***for me***. &#124;<br>                    direct obj .   INDIRECT obj.<br>(c)  INCORRECT: *Sue answered me a question.*<br>(d)  INCORRECT: *Ken opened Anita the door.* | With some verbs, ***for*** is used with the indirect object.  With these verbs, the indirect object follows the direct object.  ***For*** is not omitted.  The position of the indirect object is not changed. |
| VERBS FOLLOWED BY INDIRECT OBJECTS WITH ***FOR***<br><br>*answer*      He *answered* a question ***for me***.<br>*cash*         The teller *cashed* a check ***for me***.<br>*fix*           Can you *fix* my car ***for me***?<br>*open*        Mr. Smith *opened* the door ***for his wife***.<br>*pronounce*  I *pronounced* the word ***for the students***.<br>*translate*   I *translated* a letter ***for my brother***. | Notice in the examples:  All of the sentences give the idea that someone is helping another person. |

NOUNS, ADJECTIVES, AND PRONOUNS  ■  **367**

■ **EXERCISE 49:** Complete the sentences by adding *for* or *to*.

1. The teacher answered a question _____ me.

2. I opened the door _____ my mother.

3. My roommate translated a newspaper story _____ me.

4. Fred gave some candy _____ his girlfriend.

5. The teller cashed a check _____ me.

6. The mechanic fixed my car _____ me.

7. Mrs. Baker handed the baby _____ her husband.

8. The teacher pronounced "bat" and "but" _____ the students.

9. Our landlord fixed the air conditioner _____ us.

10. Could you please answer a question _____ me?

11. My hands are wet. Could you please open this jar of pickles _____ me?

■ **EXERCISE 50—ORAL (BOOKS CLOSED):** Ask and answer questions.
STUDENT A: Use *"Could you please . . . for me?"*
STUDENT B: Answer the question.

*Example:* open the window
STUDENT A: Could you please open the window for me?
STUDENT B: Certainly. / I'd be happy to. / Sure.

1. answer a question
2. translate a word
3. pronounce a word
4. cash a check
5. fix *(name of something)*
6. open the door

■ **EXERCISE 51—ORAL (BOOKS CLOSED):**   Ask and answer questions.

STUDENT A:   Ask a question using *"Could you please . . . ?"* Use *me, to me,* or *for me* in your question.
STUDENT B:   Answer the question.

*Example:*      pass the butter
STUDENT A:   Could you please pass me the butter/pass the butter to me?
STUDENT B:   Certainly. / I'd be happy to. / Sure.

1. pass the salt
2. hand a napkin
3. pass the salt and pepper
4. answer a question
5. translate this paragraph

6. pronounce this word
7. open the door
8. lend your dictionary
9. give *(name of something in the classroom)*
10. fix *(name of something)*

---

## 8-18   INDIRECT OBJECTS WITH *BUY, GET, MAKE*

| | |
|---|---|
| (a)   Tina **bought** a gift **for us**.<br>(b)   Tina **bought us** a gift.<br>(c)   I **got** a new toy **for my son**.<br>(d)   I **got my son** a new toy.<br>(e)   Tom **made** lunch **for his wife**.<br>(f)   Tom **made his wife** lunch. | With the verbs **buy**, **get**, and **make**, two patterns are possible:<br>• **for** introduces the indirect object,  OR<br>• the indirect object precedes the direct object. |

---

■ **EXERCISE 52—ORAL:**   Complete the sentences.  Use the words in parentheses.

1. I bought . . . *(Jim, a new hat)*
   → *I bought a new hat for Jim.*
   → *I bought Jim a new hat.*

2. Jack got . . . *(a stuffed animal, his daughter)*

3. I bought . . . *(some gloves, Robert)*

4. I made . . . *(Mike,  a cake)*

5. Carmen got . . . *(a new television set, her parents)*

6. Eric bought . . . *(a necklace, his mother)*

7. Oscar made . . . *(his guests, dinner)*

8. Heidi bought . . . *(a nice birthday gift, her brother)*

9. Could you please get . . . *(a glass of water, me)*

## 8-19 INDIRECT OBJECTS WITH *EXPLAIN* AND *INTRODUCE*

| | |
|---|---|
| (a) The teacher **explained** the grammar **to us**.<br>(b) Anna **introduced** her sister **to me**.<br>(c) INCORRECT: *She explained us the grammar.*<br>(d) INCORRECT: *Anna introduced me her sister.* | With the verbs **explain** and **introduce**:<br>• **to** is used with the indirect object, and<br>• the indirect object always follows the direct object. |

■ **EXERCISE 53—ORAL:**   Complete the sentences.  Use the words in parentheses.

1. Elizabeth explained . . . *(me, the problem)*
    → *Elizabeth explained the problem to me.*
2. The professor explained . . . *(the students, the chemistry formula)*
3. Tina introduced . . . *(her son, me)*
4. Mr. Schwartz explained . . . *(the doctor, his problem)*
5. Could you please translate . . . *(me, this sentence)*
6. Could you please explain . . . *(me, this sentence)*
7. Fred told . . . *(me, his ideas)*
8. I explained . . . *(my husband, Fred's ideas)*

■ **EXERCISE 54:**   Add the word(s) in parentheses.  If necessary, add **to** or **for**.

1. *(Bob)* I wrote a letter.
    → *I wrote Bob a letter.*   OR:   *I wrote a letter to Bob.* ★
2. *(my cousin)* I sent a postcard.

3. *(me)* The teacher answered a question.

4. *(his girlfriend)* Jim opened the car door.

5. *(the bride and groom)* Ann Miller gave a nice wedding present.

6. *(the class)* The teacher pronounced the new vocabulary words.

7. *(us)* The teacher explained the meaning of the word.

8. *(my roommate)* I translated the title of a book.

9. *(me)* My friend answered the phone because my hands were full.

10. *(the University of Texas)* I sent an application.

---

★*I wrote a letter for Bob* is possible, but it has a special meaning: It gives the idea that I helped Bob.  (For example: Bob broke his hand.  He can't write.  He wanted to write a letter.  I helped him by writing the letter.)

11. *(his wife)* Ron fixed the sewing machine.

12. *(us)* Don told a funny joke at the party.

13. *(me)* Jane explained her problems.

14. *(me)* My father wrote a letter.

15. *(the teacher)* Samir showed a picture of his family.

16. *(my friend)* I bought a gift.

■ **EXERCISE 55—ORAL (BOOKS CLOSED):** Answer the questions in complete sentences.

*Example:*     It's ( . . . )'s birthday next week. What are you going to give her/him?
            [Followup: What is (Student A) going to do?]
STUDENT A:    A box of candy.
TEACHER:      What is (Student A) going to do?
STUDENT B:    She/He's going to give ( . . . ) a box of candy for her/his birthday. OR
              She/He's going to give a box of candy to ( . . . ) for her/his birthday.

1. ( . . . ) is getting married next month. What are you going to give her/him?
[Followup: What is (Student A) going to do?]

2. Take something out of your pocket or purse and hand it to ( . . . ).
[What did (Student A) do?]

3. Please explain the location of your country to ( . . . ).
[What did (Student A) explain?]

4. ( . . . ), ask ( . . . ) a question. ( . . . ), answer the question for her/him.
[What did (Student A) do and (Student B) do?]

5. ( . . . ) needs some money desperately to pay her/his rent so s/he won't get kicked out
of her/his apartment. How much money will you lend her/him?
[What is (Student A) going to do?]

6. Hide a small item in your hand. Show it to ( . . . ), but don't show it to ( . . . ).
[What did (Student A) do?]

7. Say a word in your native language and then translate it into English for ( . . . ).
[What did (Student A) do?]

8. Teach ( . . . ) how to say a word in your native language. Pronounce it for ( . . . )
several times. [What did (Student A) do?]

9. Get a piece of chalk for ( . . . ). [What did (Student A) do?]

10. Make a paper airplane for ( . . . ). [What did (Student A) do?]

■ **EXERCISE 56—WRITTEN:**  Write complete sentences by adding DIRECT OBJECTS and INDIRECT OBJECTS.

1. I wrote _____ _____ yesterday.

2. I sent _____ _____ last week.

3. Please pass _____ _____.

4. The taxi driver opened _____ _____.

5. ( . . . ) gave _____ _____.

6. Could you please pronounce _____ _____?

7. Could you please lend _____ _____?

8. ( . . . ) translated _____ _____.

9. Could you please answer _____ _____?

10. My friend explained _____ _____.

11. I bought _____ _____.

12. Could you please get _____ _____?

■ **EXERCISE 57—REVIEW:**  Choose the correct completion.

1. This newspaper is yours.  That newspaper is _____.
   A. our          B. ours          C. our's          D. ours'

2. The teacher gave a test paper to every _____ in the class.
   A. student       B. students       C. of student       D. of students

3. Rosa is a _____ woman.
   A. beautiful Mexican young          C. Mexican beautiful young
   B. beautiful young Mexican          D. young beautiful Mexican

4. _____ the students in our class have dark hair.
   A. All most of          C. Almost
   B. Almost of           D. Almost all of

5. I handed _____.
   A. to the teacher my book          C. my book the teacher
   B. my book to the teacher          D. my book for the teacher

6. I had some _____ soup for lunch.
   A. vegetable good          C. vegetables good
   B. good vegetables         D. good vegetable

7. Jack introduced me to one _____.
        A. friends         B. of his friend      C. of his friends    D. his friends

8. My _____ name is Ernesto.
        A. father          B. fathers        C. fathers'        D. father's

9. Ahmed pronounced _____.
        A. for me his name            C. his name to me
        B. me his name                D. his name for me

10. _____ books are these?
         A. Who's         B. Whose        C. Who         D. Who are

■ **EXERCISE 58—ERROR ANALYSIS:**   Find and correct the mistakes.

1. I bought an airplane's ticket. Was expensive.

2. Some of those book's is mine.

3. Hiroki is a japanese businessman.

4. Theres an old big tree in our backyard.

5. Did you give to Jim my message?

6. The cat licked it's paw.

7. Everybody want to be happy.

8. One of the building on Main Street is the post office.

9. Whose that woman?

10. What are those peoples names?

11. Is the bedroom's window open?

12. Mr. and Mrs. Swan like their's apartment. Its large and comfortable.

13. I walk in the park every days.

14. Who's book is this?

15. I'am studying English.

16. Tina her last name Miller.

17. Please explain me this sentence.

18. My roommate desks are always messy.

19. Could you pronounce me this word?

20. I know the name's of almost of the students' in my class.

■ **EXERCISE 59—REVIEW:** Play this game in small groups. Think of a NOUN. Describe this noun to your group by giving clues. Don't mention the noun. The group will guess the noun you're thinking of.

*Examples:*

STUDENT A: I'm thinking of a kind of plant. It's small and colorful. It smells good.
GROUP:      A flower!

STUDENT B: I'm thinking of a person. She has short black hair. She's wearing a blue sweater and a black skirt today.
GROUP:      That's too easy! Yoko!

STUDENT C: I'm thinking of a very big cat. It's a wild animal.
GROUP:      A lion!
STUDENT C: No. It's orange and black. It lives in Asia. It has stripes.
GROUP:      A tiger!

■ **EXERCISE 60—REVIEW:** Bring to class an object from your country. In a small group, describe your object and tell your classmates about it: What is it? How is it used? Why is it special? Answer questions from the group.

When all of the groups finish discussing the objects, all of the objects should be brought to the center of the room.

STUDENT A: Choose one of the objects. Ask questions about it. Find out who it belongs to and what it is. (The owner of the object should NOT speak. People from the owner's group will give Student A the necessary information.)
STUDENT B: Choose another one of the objects and ask questions.
STUDENT C: Etc.

After all of the objects have been discussed, choose five of them to write about. Write a short paragraph on each object. What is it? What does it look like? Whose is it? What's it for? Why is it special? Why is it interesting to you? Etc.

## 8-20 MORE IRREGULAR VERBS

| | |
|---|---|
| *become – became* | *feed – fed* |
| *bend – bent* | *fight – fought* |
| *bite – bit* | *hide – hid* |
| *build – built* | *hold – held* |
| *shake – shook* | |

■ **EXERCISE 61—ORAL (BOOKS CLOSED):**  Practice using the IRREGULAR VERBS in the above list.

1. *become - became*    When strangers meet, they can become friends.  I met ( . . . ) *(a length of time)* ago.  We became friends.  What happened between ( . . . ) and me?

2. *bend - bent*    When I drop something, I bend over to pick it up.  I just dropped my pen, and then I bent over to pick it up.  What did I do?

3. *bite - bit*    Sometimes dogs bite people.  Yesterday my friend's dog bit my hand while we were playing.  What happened to my hand?

4. *build - built*    I have some friends who know how to build houses.  They built their own house next to the river.  What did my friends do?

5. *feed - fed*    I have a *(dog, cat, parrot, etc.)*.  I have to feed it every day. Yesterday I fed it once in the morning and once in the evening. What did I do yesterday?

6. *fight - fought*    People fight in wars.  People fight diseases.  They fight for freedom and equality.  My country fought a war *(against another country in a time period)*.  What happened *(in that time period)*?

7. *hide - hid*    I have a coin in my hand.  Close your eyes while I hide it.  Okay, open your eyes.  I hid the coin.  Where's the coin?  Why don't you know?

8. *hold - held*    When it rains, I hold my umbrella.  Yesterday it rained.  I held my umbrella.  What did I do yesterday?

9. *shake - shook*    People sometimes shake their finger or their head.  Sometimes they shake when they're cold.  Right now I'm shaking my finger/my head.  What did I just do?

■ **EXERCISE 62:**  Complete the sentences.  Use the words in parentheses.

1. I *(hide)* _____ my husband's birthday present in the closet yesterday.

2. A:  Ow!
   B:  What's the matter?

   A:  I *(bite)* _____ my tongue.

3. When I asked Dennis a question, he *(shake)* _____ his head no.

4. A: I've lost touch with some of our childhood friends. What happened to Greg Jones?

   B: He *(become)* _____ a doctor.
   A: What happened to Sandy Peterson?

   B: She *(become)* _____ a lawyer.

5. I offered the child a red lollipop or a green lollipop. He *(choose)* _____ the red one.

6. Doug is a new father. He felt very happy when he *(hold)* _____ his baby for the first time.

7. Nancy and Tom saved money. They didn't buy a bookcase for their new apartment.

   They *(build)* _____ one.

8. We saw a strong man at the circus. He *(bend)* _____ an iron bar.

9. A: Why did the children fight?

   B: They *(fight)* _____ because both of them wanted the same toy.

10. Diane is a computer programmer.

    Yesterday she *(feed)* _____ information into the computer.

■ **EXERCISE 63:** Complete the sentences with the correct form of the verbs from the given list.

| | | |
|---|---|---|
| *become* | *build* | *hide* |
| *bend* | *feed* | *hold* |
| *bite* | *fight* | ✔ *shake* |

1. When my dog got out of the lake, it _____*shook*_____ itself. Dogs always

   _____*shake*_____ themselves when they're wet.

2. Many countries in the world _____ in World War II.

3. Sometimes snakes _____ people. My cousin Jake died after a

   poisonous snake _____ him.

4. My daughter _____ a table in her woodworking class in high school.

5. When Kathy dropped her pen, Sam _____ over and picked it up for her.

6. The baby is sleeping peacefully. She's not hungry. Her mother _____ her before she put her in bed.

7. Mike stole a spoon from the restaurant. He _____ it in his pocket before he walked out of the restaurant.

8. David is a Canadian citizen. Maria was born in Puerto Rico, but when she married

    David, she _____ a Canadian citizen too.

■ **EXERCISE 64—ORAL (BOOKS CLOSED):** In order to practice IRREGULAR VERBS, answer *yes*.

*Example:* Did you write a letter yesterday?
*Response:* Yes, I did. I wrote a letter yesterday.

1. Did you fly to *(this city)*?
2. Did you drink a cup of tea this morning?
3. Did you come to class yesterday?
4. Did you go downtown yesterday?
5. Did you eat breakfast this morning?
6. Did you lend some money to ( . . . )?
7. Did you lose your pen yesterday? Did you find it?
8. Did you give your dictionary to ( . . . )?
9. Did you throw your book to ( . . . )? ( . . . ), did you catch it?
10. Did someone steal your wallet? Did you get it back?
11. Did you wake up at seven this morning?
12. Did you get up at seven this morning?
13. Did the wind blow yesterday?
14. Did you shut the door?
15. Did class begin at ( . . . )?
16. Did you say hello to ( . . . )?
17. Did you tell ( . . . ) to sit down? ( . . . ), did you sit down?
18. Did you hear my last question?
19. Did you teach your daughter/son to count to ten?
20. Did you bring your books to class today?
21. Did you forget your books?
22. Did you see ( . . . ) yesterday?
23. Did you meet ( . . . )'s wife?
24. Did you leave your sunglasses at the restaurant?
25. Did you read the newspaper this morning?
26. Did you go shopping yesterday?
27. Did you drive your car to school today?
28. Did you ride a horse to school today?

29. Did a barber cut your hair?
30. Did you run to class this morning?
31. Did your pen cost *(an amount of money)*?
32. Did you understand my question?
33. Did you come to class yesterday?
34. Did you make a mistake?
35. Did you take the bus to school today?
36. Did you write a letter yesterday?  Did you send it?
37. Did the telephone ring?
38. Did you break your arm?
39. Did you shake your head?
40. Did you draw a picture?
41. Did you bend your elbow?
42. Did you win a million dollars?
43. Did you feel good yesterday?
44. Did you feed the birds at the park?
45. Did you bite your finger?
46. Did you hurt your finger?
47. Did you hold ( . . . )'s hand?
48. Did you build a bookcase?
49. Did you stand at the bus stop?
50. Did you sing in the shower this morning?
51. Did you grow up in *(country)*?
52. Did you become an adult?
53. Did *(name of a sports team)* win yesterday?
54. Did you fall down yesterday?
55. Did you think about me yesterday?
56. Did you fight yesterday?
57. Which pen do you want?  Did you choose this one?
58. Did you hide your money under your mattress?
59. Did your car hit a telephone pole yesterday?
60. Did you put your books under your desk?

CHAPTER **9**

# Making Comparisons

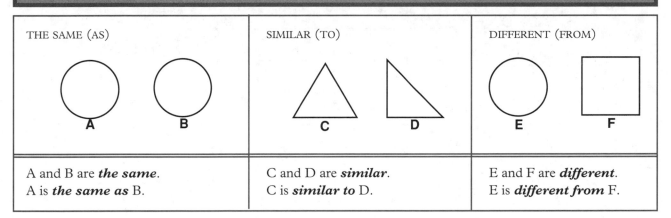

| THE SAME (AS) | SIMILAR (TO) | DIFFERENT (FROM) |
|---|---|---|
| A and B are **the same**. | C and D are **similar**. | E and F are **different**. |
| A is **the same as** B. | C is **similar to** D. | E is **different from** F. |

■ **EXERCISE 1—ORAL:**  Which of the pictures are the same, similar, or different?

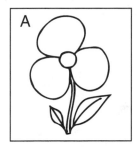 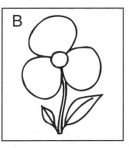 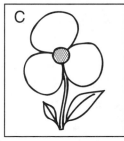 

1. Are Pictures A and B the same?

2. Are Pictures A and C the same?

3. Are Pictures A and C similar?

4. Are Pictures A and C different?

5. Are Pictures C and D similar?

6. Are Pictures C and D different?

■ **EXERCISE 2:** Complete the sentences. Use *the same (as)*, *similar (to)*, and *different (from)* in your completions.

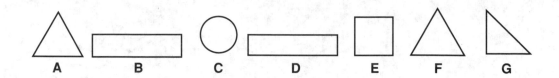

A       B       C       D       E       F       G

1. A _____*is the same as*_____ F.

2. D and E _____*are similar* OR*: are different**_____ .

3. C _____ D.

4. B _____ D.

5. B and D _____.

6. C and D _____.

7. A and F _____.

8. F and G _____.

9. F _____ G.

10. G _____ A and F, but

_____ C.

■ **EXERCISE 3—ERROR ANALYSIS:** Find and correct the mistakes.

1. A rectangle is similar a square.

2. Pablo and Rita come from same country.

3. Girls and boys are differents. Girls are different to boys.

4. My cousin is the same age with my brother.

5. Dogs are similar with wolves.

6. Jim and I started to speak at same time.

_____

*Similar* gives the idea that two things are the same in some ways (e.g., both D and E have four edges) but different in other ways (e.g., D is a rectangle and E is a square).

■ **EXERCISE 4:** Answer the questions.

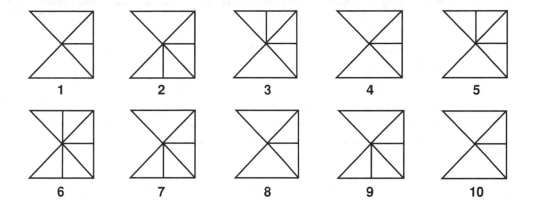

1. Which of the figures are the same?

2. Is there at least one figure that is different from all the rest?

3. How many triangles are there in figure 1? *(answer: Seven.)*

4. How many triangles are there in figure 2?

5. How many triangles are there in figure 6?

■ **EXERCISE 5—ORAL (BOOKS CLOSED):** Practice using *the same (as)*, *similar (to)*, and *different (from)*.

*Example:* Look at ( . . . )'s clothes and ( . . . )'s clothes. What is different about the clothes they are wearing today?

*Response:* Their shoes are different. Mr. Lopez is wearing running shoes, and Mr. Gow is wearing sandals.

1. Look around the room. Name things that are the same.
2. Look around the room. Name things that are similar but not the same.
3. Find two pens that are the same length. Find two pieces of paper that are the same size. Find two notebooks that are different sizes.
4. Find two people in the class who are wearing (earrings). Are their (earrings) the same, similar, or different?
5. Who in the class has a (notebook, briefcase, bookbag) that is similar to yours? Does anyone have a (notebook, briefcase, bookbag) that is the same as yours?
6. Do any of the people in this room have the same hairstyle? Name two people who have similar hairstyles.
7. Whose shirt is the same color as yours today? Name some things in this room that are the same color. Name things that are similar colors.
8. Do any of the people in this room come from the same country? Who? Name two people who come from different countries.
9. Name an animal that is similar to a tiger. Name a bird that is similar to a duck.
10. Are Egypt and Italy on the same continent? Egypt and Algeria? Thailand and Korea? Mexico and Brazil?

## 9-2 COMPARISONS: USING *LIKE* AND *ALIKE*

| | |
|---|---|
| You have a ballpoint pen with blue ink. I have a ballpoint pen with blue ink. | *like* = *similar to* <br> *alike* = *similar* <br> *Like* and *alike* have the same meaning, but the sentence patterns are different: |
| (a) Your pen *is like* my pen. <br> (b) Your pen and my pen *are alike*. <br> (c) Our pens *are alike*. | This + *be* + *like* + that. <br> This and that + *be* + *alike*. |

■ **EXERCISE 6:** Complete the sentences with *like* and *alike*.

1. You and I have similar books. In other words, your book is ____*like*____ mine. Our books are ____*alike*____.

2. Mr. Chang and I have similar coats. In other words, Mr. Chang's coat is _____ mine. Our coats are _____.

3. Ken and Sue have similar cars. In other words, their cars are _____.

4. You and I have similar hats. In other words, your hat is _____ mine.

5. A town is _____ a city in some ways.

6. A foot and a hand are _____ in some ways, but different in other ways.

7. A dormitory and an apartment building are _____ in many ways.

8. A motorcyle is _____ a bicycle in some ways.

■ **EXERCISE 7—ORAL:** Make sentences with *like*. Compare the things in Column A with the things in Column B. Discuss how the two things you are comparing are similar.

*Example:* A pencil is like a pen in some ways. They are both writing instruments.

| COLUMN A | COLUMN B |
|---|---|
| an alley | a glass |
| a bus | a human hand |
| a bush | a lemon |
| a cup | a chair |
| a hill | a mountain |
| honey | an ocean |
| a monkey's hand | ✔ a pen |
| an orange | a street |
| ✔ a pencil | sugar |
| a sea | a suit coat |
| a sofa | a taxi |
| a sports jacket | a tree |

## 9-3 THE COMPARATIVE: USING -ER AND MORE

| | |
|---|---|
| Mary is 25 years old.<br>John is 20 years old.<br>(a) Mary is **older than** John.<br><br>(b) Health is **more important than** money.<br><br>(c) INCORRECT: *Mary is more old than John.*<br>(d) INCORRECT: *Health is importanter than money.* | When we use adjectives (e.g., *old, important*) to compare two people or two things, the adjectives have special forms:<br>In (a): we add **-er** to an adjective, OR<br>In (b): we use **more** in front of an adjective.<br>The use of **-er** or **more** is called the COMPARATIVE FORM. |
| | Notice in the examples: **than** follows the comparative form: *older* **than**, *more important* **than**. |

| | ADJECTIVE | COMPARATIVE | |
|---|---|---|---|
| ADJECTIVES WITH ONE SYLLABLE | **old**<br>**cheap**<br>**big** | **older**<br>**cheaper**<br>**bigger** | Add **-er** to one-syllable adjectives.<br><br>Spelling note: if an adjective ends in one vowel and one consonant, double the consonant: *big–bigger, fat–fatter, thin–thinner, hot–hotter.* |
| ADJECTIVES THAT END IN -Y | **pretty**<br>**funny** | **prettier**<br>**funnier** | If an adjective ends in **-y**, change the **-y** to **i** and add **-er**. |
| ADJECTIVES WITH TWO OR MORE SYLLABLES | **famous**<br>**important**<br>**interesting** | **more famous**<br>**more important**<br>**more interesting** | Use **more** in front of adjectives that have two or more syllables (except adjectives that end in **-y**). |
| IRREGULAR COMPARATIVE FORMS | **good**<br>**bad**<br>**far** | **better**<br>**worse**<br>**farther/further** | The comparative forms of **good, bad**, and **far** are irregular. |

■ **EXERCISE 8:** Write the comparative forms for the following ADJECTIVES.

1. old ___*older than*___

2. small _____

3. big _____

4. important _____

5. easy _____

6. difficult _____

7. long _____

8. heavy _____

9. sweet _____

10. expensive _____

11. hot _____

12. cheap _____

13. good _____

14. bad _____

15. far _____

16. lazy _____

■ **EXERCISE 9:** Complete the sentences. Use the COMPARATIVE form of the words in *italics*.

1. *comfortable*  This chair is _____*more comfortable than*_____ that chair.

2. *large*  Your apartment is _____ mine.

3. *warm*  It's _____ today _____ yesterday.

4. *dark*  Tom's mustache is _____ Don's.

5. *important*  Love is _____ money.

6. *lazy*  I'm _____ my roommate.

7. *tall*  My brother is _____ I am.*

8. *heavy*  Iron is _____ wood.

9. *difficult*  My physics course is _____ my math course.

10. *good*  Nadia's English is _____ her husband's.

11. *long*  The Nile River is _____ the Mississippi.

12. *intelligent*  A dog is _____ a chicken.

13. *good*  My wife's cooking is _____ mine.

14. *bad*  My cooking is _____ my wife's.

15. *short*  My little finger is _____ my middle finger.

16. *pretty*  This dress is _____ that one.

17. *far*  Your apartment is _____ from school

_____ mine.

18. *strong*  A horse is _____ a person.

19. *curly*  Ken's hair is _____ mine.

20. *beautiful*  A rose is _____ a weed.

_____

*Formal written English: *My brother is taller than I (am).*
Informal spoken English: *My brother is taller than me.*

■ **EXERCISE 10:** Complete the sentences. Use the COMPARATIVE form of the words in *italics*.

1. *good*        The weather today is _____ it was yesterday.

2. *bad*         The weather yesterday was _____ it is today.

3. *funny*       This story is _____ that story.

4. *interesting* This book is _____ that book.

5. *smart*       Joe is _____ his brother.

6. *famous*      A movie star is _____ I am.

7. *wide*        A highway is _____ an alley.

8. *deep*        The Pacific Ocean is _____ the Mediterranean Sea.

9. *confusing*   This story is _____ that story.

10. *hot*        Thailand is _____ Korea.

11. *thin*       A giraffe's neck is _____ an elephant's neck.

12. *far*        My house is _____ from downtown

                 _____ your house is.

13. *good*       Reading a good book is _____ watching television.

14. *easy*       My English class is _____ my history class.

15. *nervous*    The groom was _____

                 at the wedding _____ the bride.

■ **EXERCISE 11—ORAL:** Compare the following. Use the ADJECTIVE in parentheses. Use *more* or *-er*.

*Example:* A mouse is smaller than an elephant.

1. a mouse
   an elephant
   *(small)*

2. my old shoes
   my new shoes
   *(comfortable)*

3. your hair
   my hair
   *(dark)*

4. my arm
   your arm
   *(long)*

5. biology
   chemistry
   *(interesting)*

6. I
   my brother
   *(thin)*

7. my hair
   her hair
   *(curly)*

8. her hair
   his hair
   *(straight)*

9. this book
   that one
   *(good)*

10. the weather here
    the weather in my hometown
    *(bad)*

11. this chapter
    Chapter 8
    *(easy)*

12. Japanese grammar
    English grammar
    *(difficult)*

■ **EXERCISE 12—ORAL (BOOKS CLOSED):** Practice comparative forms.

A. Put several different books in a central place. Compare one to another, using the given adjectives.

*Example:* big
*Response:* This book is bigger than that book/that one.

1. large
2. interesting
3. small
4. heavy

5. difficult
6. easy
7. good
8. bad

9. expensive
10. cheap
11. thick
12. important

B. The following adjectives describe a man named Bob. A man named Jack does not have the same qualities. Draw pictures of Bob and Jack on the board. Compare Bob to Jack.

*Example:* tall
*Response:* Bob is taller than Jack.

1. tall
2. strong
3. lazy
4. intelligent

5. young
6. happy
7. kind
8. generous

9. friendly★
10. responsible
11. famous
12. busy

---

★The comparative of *friendly* has two possible forms: *friendlier than* or *more friendly than*.

■ **EXERCISE 13:** Complete the sentences. Use the COMPARATIVE form of the words in the list (or your own words).

| | | |
|---|---|---|
| *big* | *easy* | *important* |
| *bright* | *expensive* | *intelligent* |
| *cheap* | *fast* | *large* |
| *cold* | *high* | *small* |
| *comfortable* | *hot* | *sweet* |

1. An elephant is _____*bigger than / larger than*_____ a mouse.

2. A lemon is sour. An orange is _____ a lemon.

3. The weather today is _____ it was yesterday.

4. A diamond costs a lot of money. A diamond is _____ a ruby.

5. I can afford a radio, but not a TV set. A radio is _____ a TV set.

6. An airplane moves quickly. An airplane is _____ an automobile.

7. A lake is _____ an ocean.

8. A person can think logically. A person is _____ an animal.

9. Hills are low. Mountains are _____ hills.

10. The sun gives off a lot of light. The sun is _____ the moon.

11. Texas is a large state, but Alaska is

    _____ Texas.

12. Sometimes my feet hurt when I wear high heels. Bedroom slippers are

    _____

    shoes with high heels.

13. Arithmetic isn't difficult. Arithmetic is

    _____ algebra.

14. Good health is _____ money.

■ **EXERCISE 14—ORAL (BOOKS CLOSED):**   Compare the following.

*Example:*  an elephant to a mouse
*Response:*  An elephant is bigger than a mouse / more intelligent than a mouse, etc.

1. an orange to a lemon
2. a lake to an ocean
3. good health to money
4. a radio to a TV set
5. an airplane to an automobile
6. (Alaska) to (Texas)
7. a person to an animal
8. the sun to the moon
9. a mountain to a hill
10. arithmetic to algebra
11. a diamond to a ruby
12. bedroom slippers to high heels
13. a child to an adult
14. a horse to a person
15. the Nile River to the Mississippi River
16. your little finger to your ring finger
17. love to money
18. your hair to ( . . . )'s hair
19. food in *(your country)* to food in *(another country)*
20. the weather today to the weather yesterday

■ **EXERCISE 15—ORAL (BOOKS CLOSED):**   Make sentences by using *-er/more* with these ADJECTIVES.

*Example:*  large
*Response:*  Canada is larger than Mexico. / My feet are larger than yours. / etc.

1. tall
2. important
3. cold
4. curly
5. expensive
6. long
7. easy
8. comfortable
9. old
10. strong
11. small
12. intelligent
13. big
14. heavy
15. cheap
16. sweet
17. high
18. interesting
19. good
20. bad

■ **EXERCISE 16:**   Write a sentence by using *-er/more* with an ADJECTIVE in the list in Exercise 15 above.  Tear the sentence into pieces, with one word or phrase on each piece.  Give the pieces to a classmate who will reassemble your sentence.  Repeat this exercise several times, using a different adjective for each new sentence you write.

## 9-4 USING *AS . . . AS*; USING *LESS*

| | |
|---|---|
| John is 21 years old.<br>Mary is 21 years old.<br>(a) John **is as old as** Mary. | Notice the pattern: **as** + *adjective* + **as**<br><br>In (a): Their ages are the same. |
| (b) This watch **is as expensive as** that watch. | In (b): The price of the watches is the same. |
| Fred is 20 years old.<br>Jean is 21 years old.<br>(c) Fred **isn't as old as** Jean.<br>(d) Fred **is younger than** Jean. | (c) and (d) have the same meaning. |
| (e) This book **isn't as expensive as** that book.<br>(f) This book **is cheaper than** that book. | (e) and (f) have the same meaning. |
| (g) This book **isn't as expensive as** that book.<br>(h) This book **is less expensive than** that book. | (g) and (h) have the same meaning. **Less** is the opposite of **more**. **Less** is used with adjectives that have two or more syllables (except most adjectives that end in **-y**). **Less** is usually not used with one-syllable adjectives or adjectives that end in **-y**.<br>INCORRECT: *Fred is less old than Jean.*<br>CORRECT: *Fred isn't as old as Jean.*<br>*Fred is younger than Jean.* |

■ **EXERCISE 17:** Complete the following sentences by using **as . . . as** and the ADJECTIVE in *italics*.

1. *tall*      Mary is ____*as tall as*____ her brother.

2. *sweet*     A lemon isn't _____ an orange.

3. *big*       A donkey isn't _____ a horse.

4. *friendly*  People in this city are _____ the people in my hometown.

5. *dark*      Paul's hair isn't _____ his brother's.

6. *cold*      The weather isn't _____ today

_____ yesterday.

7. *pretty*    This dress is _____ that one.

8. *expensive* A pencil isn't _____ a pen.

■ **EXERCISE 18:** Make sentences with the same meaning by using *less*, if possible.

1. This book isn't as expensive as that book.
   → *This book is less expensive than that book.*

2. Bob isn't as old as Jim. → *(no change)*

3. Arithmetic isn't as difficult as algebra.

4. Arithmetic isn't as hard as algebra.

5. This chair isn't as comfortable as that chair.

6. This box isn't as heavy as that box.

7. A hill isn't as high as a mountain.

8. Swimming isn't as dangerous as boxing.

9. I'm not as tall as my brother.

10. This letter isn't as important as that letter.

■ **EXERCISE 19:** Make sentences with the same meaning by using *as . . . as* with the ADJECTIVE in parentheses.

1. Bob is younger than Sally. *(old)*
   → *Bob isn't as old as Sally.*

2. This book is less expensive than that one. *(expensive)*
   → *This book isn't as expensive as that one.*

3. I'm shorter than my sister. *(tall)*

4. This exercise is more difficult than the last one. *(easy)*

5. My new shoes are less comfortable than my old shoes. *(comfortable)*

6. My little finger is shorter than my index finger. *(long)*

7. A radio is less expensive than a TV set. *(expensive)*

8. This book is worse than that book. *(good)*

9. My apartment is smaller than yours. *(big)*

10. In my opinion, chemistry is less interesting than psychology. *(interesting)*

■ **EXERCISE 20:** Make sentences with the same meaning by using *as . . . as*.

1. This room is smaller than that room.
   → *This room isn't as big as that room.*

2. An animal is less intelligent than a human being.

3. Soda pop is less expensive than fruit juice.

4. The Mississippi River is shorter than the Nile River.

5. Tom's pronunciation is worse than Sue's.

6. Algebra is more difficult than arithmetic.

7. Money is less important than good health.

8. American coffee is weaker than Turkish coffee.

9. A wooden chair is less comfortable than a sofa.

10. A van is smaller than a bus.

■ **EXERCISE 21—ORAL (BOOKS CLOSED):**   Work in pairs.   Practice making comparisons.

STUDENT A: Your book is open.
STUDENT B: Your book is closed.  Respond in complete sentences.

*Example:*   Name something that is sweeter than an apple.
STUDENT A: What's sweeter than an apple? / Can you name something that is sweeter than an apple? / Name something that is sweeter than an apple.
STUDENT B: Candy is sweeter than an apple.

1. Name a country that is larger than Mexico.
2. Name a planet that is closer to or farther away from the sun than the earth.
3. Name someone in the class who isn't as old as (I am, you are).
4. Name an animal that is more dangerous than a zebra.
5. Name an animal that is as dangerous as a wild tiger.
6. Name a bird that is larger than a chicken.
7. Name something that is more expensive than a diamond ring.
8. Name something that is less expensive than *(an object in this room)*.
9. Name someone who is more famous than *(name of a famous person)*.

*Switch roles.*

10. Name something that is more interesting than *(name of a field of study)*.
11. Name something that is less important than good health.
12. Name a place that is as far away from here as *(name of a place)*.
13. Name an ocean that is smaller than the Pacific Ocean.
14. Name an animal that is stronger than a horse.
15. Name an animal that isn't as strong as a horse.
16. Name a game that is, in your opinion, more exciting than *(name of a sport)*.
17. Name a sport that is less popular internationally than *(name of a sport)*.
18. Name a place that is more beautiful than this city.

■ **EXERCISE 22:**   Complete the following with your own words.

1. I'm taller _____

2. I'm not as old _____

3. A monkey isn't as big _____

4. American food isn't as good _____

5. An ocean is deeper and wider _____

6. An apple is less expensive _____

7. It's warmer / colder today _____

8. _____'s  hair isn't as curly _____

9. A hill isn't as high _____

10. A dog is less intelligent _____ but more intelligent

_____

11. _____'s hair is darker _____

12. A hotel room is less comfortable _____

13. Moonlight isn't as bright _____

14. Money is less important _____

15. English grammar isn't as difficult _____

16. Earth is closer to the sun _____

17. Venezuela isn't as far south _____

18. Tokyo isn't as far north _____

19. People in _____ are friendlier _____

20. Children are less powerful _____

## 9-5 USING *BUT*

| | |
|---|---|
| (a)  John is rich, ***but*** Mary is poor. | ***But*** gives the idea that "This is the opposite of that." |
| (b)  The weather was cold, ***but*** we were warm inside our house. | A comma usually precedes ***but***. |

■ **EXERCISE 23:**  Complete the following sentences by using ADJECTIVES.

1. An orange is sweet, but a lemon is _____ _sour._____

2. The weather is hot today, but it was _____ yesterday.

3. These dishes are clean, but those dishes are _____

4. This suitcase is heavy, but that suitcase is _____

5. My hair is light, but my brother's hair is _____

6. These shoes are uncomfortable, but those shoes are _____

7. Linda is tall, but her sister is _____

8. This street is narrow, but that street is _____

9. This exercise is easy, but that exercise is _____

10. My old apartment is big, but my new apartment is _____

11. This food is good, but that food is _____

12. A chicken is stupid, but a human being is _____

13. Smoke is visible, but clean air is _____

14. This answer is right, but that answer is _____

15. This towel is dry, but that towel is _____

16. This cup is full, but that cup is _____

17. This street is noisy, but that street is _____

18. This picture is ugly, but that picture is _____

19. This sentence is confusing, but that sentence is _____

20. This car is safe, but that car is _____

21. A kitten is weak, but a horse is _____

22. This watch is expensive, but that watch is _____

23. Tom is hard-working, but his brother is _____

24. My apartment is messy, but Bob's apartment is always _____

25. A pillow is soft, but a rock is _____

## 9-6 USING VERBS AFTER *BUT*

| | AFFIRMATIVE VERB | + | *but* | + | NEGATIVE VERB | Often the verb phrase following *but* is shortened, as in the examples. |
|---|---|---|---|---|---|---|
| (a) | John *is* rich, | | *but* | | Mary *isn't*. | |
| (b) | Balls *are* round, | | *but* | | boxes *aren't*. | |
| (c) | I *was* in class, | | *but* | | Po *wasn't*. | |
| (d) | Sue *studies* hard, | | *but* | | Sam *doesn't*. | |
| (e) | We *like* movies, | | *but* | | they *don't*. | |
| (f) | Alex *came*, | | *but* | | Maria *didn't*. | |
| (g) | People *can* talk, | | *but* | | animals *can't*. | |
| (h) | Olga *will* be there, | | *but* | | Ivan *won't*. | |
| | NEGATIVE VERB | + | *but* | + | AFFIRMATIVE VERB | |
| (i) | Mary *isn't* rich, | | *but* | | John *is*. | |
| (j) | Boxes *aren't* round, | | *but* | | balls *are*. | |
| (k) | Po *wasn't* in class, | | *but* | | I *was*. | |
| (l) | Sam *doesn't* study, | | *but* | | Sue *does*. | |
| (m) | They *don't like* cats, | | *but* | | we *do*. | |
| (n) | Maria *didn't come*, | | *but* | | Alex *did*. | |
| (o) | Animals *can't* talk, | | *but* | | people *can*. | |
| (p) | Ivan *won't* be there, | | *but* | | Olga *will*. | |

■ **EXERCISE 24:** Complete each sentence with an appropriate VERB, affirmative or negative.

1. Sara is at home, but her husband _____*isn't*_____.

2. Hiroki isn't at home, but his wife _____.

3. Beds are comfortable, but park benches _____.

4. I wasn't at home last night, but my roommate _____.

5. Kim was in class yesterday, but Anna and Linda _____.

6. Jack wants to go to the zoo, but Barbara _____.

7. I don't want to go to the movie, but my friends _____.

8. Pablo went to the party, but Steve _____.

9. Ahmed can speak French, but I _____.

10. Amanda will be at the meeting, but Helen _____.

11. I was at home yesterday, but my roommate _____.

12. This shirt is clean, but that one _____.

13. These shoes aren't comfortable, but those shoes _____.

14. I like strong coffee, but Karen _____.

15. Mike doesn't write clearly, but Ted _____.

16. I ate breakfast this morning, but my roommate _____.

17. Carol has a car, but Jerry _____.

18. Jerry doesn't have a car, but Carol _____.

19. Ron was at the party, but his wife _____.

20. Ron went to the party, but his wife _____.

21. Ellen can speak Spanish, but her husband _____.

22. Boris can't speak Spanish, but his wife _____.

23. I won't be at home tonight, but Sue _____.

24. Ken will be in class tomorrow, but Chris _____.

25. Amy won't be here tomorrow, but Alice _____.

■ **EXERCISE 25—ORAL (BOOKS CLOSED):** Practice using *but* . . . .

*Example:*      Who in the class was at home last night?  Who wasn't at home last night?
TEACHER:      Who was at home last night?
STUDENT A:   I was.
TEACHER:      Who wasn't at home last night?
STUDENT B:   I wasn't at home last night.
TEACHER:      Summarize, using *but*.
STUDENT C:   (Ali) was at home last night, but (Kim) wasn't.

1. Who wears glasses?  Who doesn't wear glasses?
2. Who is married?  Who isn't married?
3. Who didn't watch TV last night?  Who watched TV last night?
4. Who will be in class tomorrow?  Who won't be in class tomorrow?
5. Who has a car?  Who doesn't have a car?
6. Who studied last night?  Who didn't study last night?
7. Who can play *(a musical instrument)*?  Who can't play *(that musical instrument)*?
8. Who is hungry right now?  Who isn't hungry right now?
9. Who lives in an apartment?  Who lives in a house or in a dorm?
10. Who doesn't drink coffee?  Who drinks coffee?
11. Who won't be at home tonight?  Who will be at home tonight?
12. Who was in class yesterday?  Who wasn't in class yesterday?
13. Who can't speak *(a language)*?  Who can speak *(a language)*?
14. Who didn't stay home last night?  Who stayed home last night?
15. Who has *(a mustache)*?  Who doesn't have *(a mustache)*?

■ **EXERCISE 26:**   Picture A and Picture B are not the same.  There are many differences between A and B.  Can you find all of the differences?
*Example:*   There's a wooden chair in Picture A, but there isn't a chair in B.

■ **EXERCISE 27—ERROR ANALYSIS:**   Find and correct the mistakes.

1.  My cousin is the same tall as my brother.

2.  A blue whale is more large from an elephant.

3.  A dog is less small as a wolf.

4.  Your handwriting is more better than mine.

5.  Robert and Maria aren't same age.  Robert is more young than Maria.

6.  A lake isn't as deep than an ocean.

■ **EXERCISE 28—WRITTEN:** Write about one or more of the following topics.

1. Write about this city. Compare it to your hometown.
2. Write about your present residence. Compare it to a past residence. For example, compare your new apartment to your old apartment.
3. Write about two members of your family. Compare them.
4. Write about two animals. Compare them.
5. Write about two countries. Compare them.

| CHECKLIST OF WORDS USED IN COMPARISONS | | |
|---|---|---|
| *the same (as)* | *like* | *-er/more* |
| *similar (to)* | *alike* | *less* |
| *different (from)* | | *as . . . as* |
| | | *but* |

## 9-7 THE SUPERLATIVE: USING *-EST* AND *MOST*

| | |
|---|---|
| (a) COMPARATIVE:<br>My thumb is **shorter than** my index finger.<br><br>(b) SUPERLATIVE:<br>My hand has five fingers. My thumb is **the shortest** (finger) of all. | The comparative **(-er/more)** compares two things or people.<br><br>The superlative **(-er/most)** compares three or more things or people. |

| | ADJECTIVE | COMPARATIVE | SUPERLATIVE |
|---|---|---|---|
| ADJECTIVES WITH ONE SYLLABLE | **old**<br>**big** | **older** (than)<br>**bigger** (than) | **the oldest** (of all)<br>**the biggest** (of all) |
| ADJECTIVES THAT END IN *-Y* | **pretty**<br>**easy** | **prettier** (than)<br>**easier** (than) | **the prettiest** (of all)<br>**the easiest** (of all) |
| ADJECTIVES WITH TWO OR MORE SYLLABLES | **expensive**<br>**important** | **more expensive** (than)<br>**more important** (than) | **the most expensive** (of all)<br>**the most important** (of all) |
| IRREGULAR FORMS | **good**<br>**bad**<br>**far** | **better** (than)<br>**worse** (than)<br>**farther/further** (than) | **the best** (of all)<br>**the worst** (of all)<br>**the farthest/furthest** (of all) |

■ **EXERCISE 29:** Write the comparative and superlative forms of the following ADJECTIVES.

|     |             | COMPARATIVE | SUPERLATIVE |
|-----|-------------|-------------|-------------|
| 1.  | long        | _longer (than)_ | _the longest (of all)_ |
| 2.  | small       |             |             |
| 3.  | heavy       |             |             |
| 4.  | comfortable |             |             |
| 5.  | hard        |             |             |
| 6.  | difficult   |             |             |
| 7.  | easy        |             |             |
| 8.  | hot*        |             |             |
| 9.  | cheap       |             |             |
| 10. | interesting |             |             |
| 11. | pretty      |             |             |
| 12. | strong      |             |             |
| 13. | good        |             |             |
| 14. | bad         |             |             |
| 15. | far         |             |             |

■ **EXERCISE 30:** Complete the sentences. Use the correct form of the ADJECTIVES in *italics*.

1. *large*        _The largest_ _____ city in Canada is Toronto.

2. *long*        The Nile is _____ river in the world.

3. *interesting*        I'm taking four classes. My history class is _____

     _____ of all.

4. *high*        Mt. McKinley in Alaska is _____
     mountain in North America.

5. *tall*        The Sears Tower is _____ building in
     Chicago.

---

*Spelling note:  If an adjective ends in one vowel and one consonant, double the consonant to form the
superlative: *big-biggest, fat-fattest, thin-thinnest, hot-hottest.*

6. *big*         Lake Superior is _____ lake in North America.

7. *short*     February is _____ month of the year.

8. *far*         Pluto is _____ planet from the sun.

9. *beautiful*     In my opinion, Seattle is _____ city in the United States.

10. *bad*       In my opinion, Harry's Steak House is _____ restaurant in the city.

11. *good*     In my opinion, the Doghouse Cafe has _____ food in the city.

12. *comfortable*     Ken is sitting in _____ chair in the room.

13. *fast*     _____ way to travel is by airplane.

14. *good*     When you feel depressed, laughter is _____ medicine.

15. *large*     Asia is _____ continent in the world.

16. *small*     Australia is _____ continent in the  world.

17. *expensive*     Sally ordered _____ food on the menu for dinner last night.

18. *easy*     Taking a taxi is _____ way to get to the airport.

19. *important*     I think good health is _____ thing in life.

20. *famous*     The Gateway Arch is _____ landmark in St. Louis, Missouri.

■ **EXERCISE 31:**   Make at least four statements of COMPARISON about each group of pictures.

### A.  COMPARE THE SIZES OF THE THREE BALLS.

1. The golf ball is _____*smaller than*_____ the baseball.

2. The soccer ball is _____ the baseball.

3. The soccer ball is _____ of all.

4. The baseball isn't _____ as the soccer ball.

### B.  COMPARE THE AGES OF THE CHILDREN.

TOMMY        HELEN         ANN
(3 years old)  (6 years old)  (8 years old)

5. Ann is _____ Helen.

6. Tommy is _____ Helen and Ann.

7. Ann is _____ of all.

8. Helen isn't _____ as Ann.

## C. COMPARE THE HEIGHTS OF THE THREE WOMEN.

LINDA      KAREN      ALICE

9. _____ is the tallest

10. _____ is the shortest.

11. _____ is taller than _____ but

shorter than _____.

12. _____ isn't as tall as _____.

## D. COMPARE THE STRENGTH OF THE THREE MEN.

MIKE      JOE      DON

13. _____

14. _____

15. _____

16. _____

## E. COMPARE THE PRICES OF THE THREE VEHICLES.

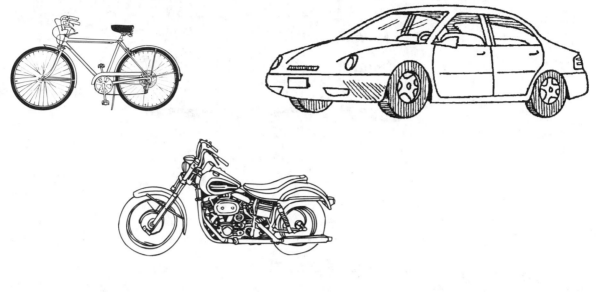

17. _____

18. _____

19. _____

20. _____

## F. COMPARE HOW GOOD THE THREE TEST PAPERS ARE.

21. _____

22. _____

23. _____

24. _____

**G. COMPARE HOW INTERESTING (TO YOU) THE THREE BOOKS LOOK.**

25. _____

26. _____

27. _____

28. _____

■ **EXERCISE 32:** Complete the sentences. Use the correct form (comparative or superlative) of the ADJECTIVES in *italics*.

1. *long*        The Yangtze River is _____ the Mississippi River.

2. *long*        The Nile is _____ river in the world.

3. *large*      The Caribbean Sea is _____ the Mediterranean Sea.

4. *large*      The Caribbean Sea is _____ sea in the world.

5. *high*       Mt. Everest is _____ mountain in the world.

6. *high*       Mt. Everest is _____ Mt. McKinley.

7. *big*         Africa is _____ North America.

8. *small*     Europe is _____ South America.

9. *large*      Asia is _____ continent in the world.

10. *big*        Canada is _____ the United States in area.

11. *large*      Indonesia is _____ Japan in population.

12. *good*       Fruit is _____ for your health

_____ candy.

13. *good*       The student cafeteria has _____ roast
beef sandwiches in the city.

14. *comfortable*   I have a pair of boots, a pair of sandals, and a pair of running

shoes.  The sandals are _____

the boots, but the running shoes are _____

_____ of all.

15. *easy*       This exercise is _____ that one.  This is

one of _____ exercises in the book.

16. *bad*        There are over 800 million people in the world who don't get to

eat.  With few exceptions, poverty and hunger are _____
in rural areas than in cities and towns.

## 9-8   USING *ONE OF* + SUPERLATIVE + PLURAL NOUN

| | |
|---|---|
| (a)  The Amazon is *one of the longest rivers* in the world. | The superlative often follows *one of*. Notice the pattern: |
| (b)  A Rolls Royce is *one of the most expensive cars* in the world. | *one of* + *superlative* + *plural noun* |
| (c)  Alice is *one of the most intelligent people* in our class. | See Chart 8-5 for more information about *one of*. |

■ **EXERCISE 33:**  Make sentences about the following.  Use *one of* + *superlative* + *plural noun*.

1. a high mountain in the world
   → *Mt. McKinley is one of the highest mountains in the world.*

2. a pretty park in *(this city)*
   → *Forest Park is one of the prettiest parks in St. Louis.*

3. a tall person in our class
   → *Talal is one of the tallest people\* in our class.*

4. a big city in the world

5. a beautiful place in the world

6. a nice person in our class

7. a long river in the world

_____
\**People* is usually used instead of *persons* in the plural.

8. a good restaurant in *(this city)*

9. a famous landmark in the world

10. an important event in the history of the world

■ **EXERCISE 34—WRITTEN:**   Make sentences using *one of* + *superlative* + *plural noun.*

> *Example:*   a big city in Canada
> *Written:*   Montreal is one of the biggest cities in Canada.

1. a big city in Asia

2. a large state in the U.S.

3. a beautiful city in the world

4. a friendly person in our class

5. a good place to visit in the world

6. a famous person in the world

7. an important thing in life

8. a bad restaurant in *(this city)*

9. a famous landmark in *(name of a country)*

10. a tall building in *(this city)*

11. a dangerous sport in the world

12. a serious problem in the world

■ **EXERCISE 35—ORAL:**   Discuss the questions.

1. How many brothers and sisters do you have?  Are you the oldest?
2. Who is one of the most famous movie stars in the world?
3. In your opinion, what is the most exciting sport?
4. What is one of the most interesting experiences in your life?
5. In your opinion, what is the most beautiful place in the world?
6. What is one of the most important inventions in the modern world?
7. What is one of the worst experiences of your life?
8. What are the best things in life?
9. What was the happiest day of your life — or one of the happiest days of your life?
10. Who are the most important people in your life today?

■ **EXERCISE 36:** Take this quiz. If you don't know an answer, guess. After you take the quiz, form small groups to discuss the answers. You can figure out the correct answers by looking at the Table of Statistics on page 410.

*PART I*

1. What is the longest river in the world?
   A. the Yangtze
   B. the Amazon
   C. the Nile
   D. the Mississippi

2. Is the Amazon River longer than the Mississippi River?
   A. yes
   B. no

3. Is the Yangtze River longer than the Mississippi River?
   A. yes
   B. no

4. Is the Yangtze River as long as the Nile River?
   A. yes
   B. no

5. Which two rivers are almost the same length?
   A. the Nile and the Amazon
   B. the Amazon and the Yangtze
   C. the Nile and the Mississippi
   D. the Mississippi and the Amazon

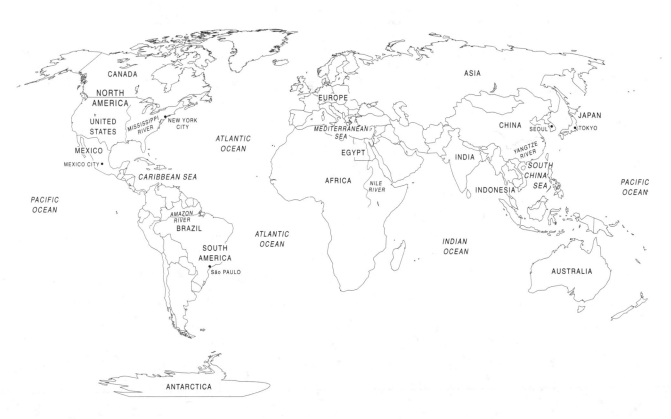

*PART II*

6. What is the largest sea in the world?
   A. the Mediterranean Sea
   B. the South China Sea
   C. the Caribbean Sea

7. Is the South China Sea the smallest of the three seas listed above?
   A. yes
   B. no

*PART III*

8. What is the deepest ocean in the world?
   A. the Atlantic Ocean
   B. the Indian Ocean
   C. the Pacific Ocean

9. Is the Indian Ocean larger than the Atlantic Ocean?
   A. yes
   B. no

*PART IV*

10. Below is a list of the continents in the world.  List them in order according to size, from the largest to the smallest.

    | | |
    |---|---|
    | *Africa* | *Europe* |
    | ✔ *Antarctica* | *North America* |
    | *Asia* | *South America* |
    | *Australia* | |

    (1) _____ (the largest)

    (2) _____

    (3) _____

    (4) _____

    (5) ____*Antarctica*_____

    (6) _____

    (7) _____ (the smallest)

*PART V*

11. Which of the following cities is the largest in population in the world?
    A. New York City, U.S.A.
    B. Seoul, Korea
    C. Mexico City, Mexico
    D. Tokyo, Japan

12. Is the population of Sao Paulo, Brazil, larger than the population of New York City, U.S.A.?
    A. yes
    B. no

13. Is the population of Sao Paulo, Brazil, larger than the population of Seoul, Korea?
    A. yes
    B. no

14. What is the largest city in North America?
    A. Mexico City
    B. New York City

*PART VI*

15. Which of the following countries is the largest in area in the world?
    A. Canada
    B. China
    C. the United States
    D. Brazil

16. Which of the following two countries is larger in area?
    A. Canada
    B. Brazil

17. Which of the following countries is the largest in population in the world?
    A. India
    B. China
    C. the United States
    D. Indonesia

18. Which of the following two countries is larger in population?
    A. India
    B. Indonesia

19. Which of the following two countries is larger in population?
    A. the United States
    B. Brazil

20. Which of the following two countries is smaller in population?
    A. Egypt
    B. Japan

# TABLE OF STATISTICS

*PART I*

| RIVER | LENGTH |
|---|---|
| the Amazon River | 3,915 miles |
| the Mississippi River | 2,348 miles |
| the Nile River | 4,145 miles |
| the Yangtze River | 3,900 miles |

*PART II*

| SEA | SIZE |
|---|---|
| the Caribbean Sea | 970,000 square miles |
| the Mediterranean Sea | 969,000 square miles |
| the South China Sea | 895,000 square miles |

*PART III*

| OCEAN | SIZE | AVERAGE DEPTH |
|---|---|---|
| Atlantic Ocean | 33,420,000 square feet | 11,730 feet |
| Indian Ocean | 28,350,500 square feet | 12,598 feet |
| Pacific Ocean | 64,186,300 square feet | 12,925 feet |

*PART IV*

| CONTINENT | SIZE |
|---|---|
| Africa | 11,707,000 square miles |
| Antarctica | 5,500,000 square miles |
| Asia | 17,129,000 square miles |
| Australia | 2,942,000 square miles |
| Europe | 4,057,000 square miles |
| North America | 9,363,000 square miles |
| South America | 6,886,000 square miles |

*PART V*

| CITY | POPULATION* |
|---|---|
| Mexico City, Mexico | 28 million |
| New York, U.S.A. | 15 million |
| Sao Paulo, Brazil | 25 million |
| Seoul, Korea | 22 million |
| Tokyo, Japan | 30 million |

*PART VI*

| COUNTRY | AREA | POPULATION* |
|---|---|---|
| Brazil | 3,286,470 sq mi | 180 million |
| Canada | 3,851,809 sq mi | 29 million |
| China | 3,691,000 sq mi | 1,250 million ** |
| Egypt | 386,650 sq mi | 65 million |
| India | 1,269,339 sq mi | 960 million |
| Indonesia | 788,430 sq mi | 205 million |
| Japan | 145,740 sq mi | 128 million |
| the United States | 3,615,123 sq mi | 268 million |

\* Approximate population in the year 2000.

\*\* *1,250 million* is said as "one billion, two hundred fifty million." (It can also be said as "one thousand, two hundred and fifty million" in old-fashioned British English.)

## 9-9   ADJECTIVES AND ADVERBS

| | ADJECTIVE | ADVERB | |
|---|---|---|---|
| (A)  Ann is a  *careful*  driver.<br>*adjective* | *careful*<br>*slow*<br>*quick*<br><br>*easy* | *carefully*<br>*slowly*<br>*quickly*<br><br>*easily* | An adjective describes a noun.  In (a): *careful* describes *driver*.<br>An adverb describes the action of a verb.  In (b): *carefully* describes *drives*.<br>Most adverbs are formed by adding *-ly* to an adjective. |
| (b)  Ann drives  *carefully*.<br>*adverb* | | | |
| (c)  John is a  *fast*  driver.<br>*adjective* | *fast*<br>*hard*<br>*early*<br>*late* | *fast*<br>*hard*<br>*early*<br>*late* | The adjective form and the adverb form are the same for *fast*, *hard*, *early*, *late*. |
| (d)  John drives  *fast*.<br>*adverb* | | | |
| (e)  Linda is a  *good*  writer.<br>*adjective* | *good* | *well* | *Well* is the adverb form of *good*.★ |
| (f)  Linda writes  *well*.<br>*adverb* | | | |

*★Well* can also be used as an adjective to mean "not sick."  *Paul was sick last week, but now he's well.*

■ **EXERCISE 37:**  Complete the sentences by using the ADJECTIVE or ADVERB in *italics*.

1. *quiet, quietly*      My hometown is small and ____quiet____.

2. *quiet, quietly*      Mr. Wilson whispered.  He spoke ____quietly____.

3. *clear, clearly*      Anna pronounces every word _____.

4. *clear, clearly*      We like to go boating in _____ weather.

5. *careless, carelessly*   Boris makes a lot of mistakes when he writes.  He's a

    _____ writer.

6. *careless, carelessly*   Boris writes _____.

7. *easy, easily*       The teacher asked an _____ question.

8. *easy, easily*       I answered the teacher's question _____.

9. *good, well*       You speak English very _____.

10. *good, well*      Your English is very _____.

■ **EXERCISE 38:** Complete the sentences by using the correct form (ADJECTIVE or ADVERB) of the word in *italics*.

1. *careful*     Do you drive _____?

2. *correct*     Carmen gave the _____ answer to the question.

3. *correct*     She answered the question _____.

4. *fast*     Mike is a _____ reader.

5. *quick*     Mike reads _____.

6. *fast*     Mike reads _____.

7. *neat*     Barbara has _____ handwriting. It is easy to read what she writes.

8. *neat*     Barbara writes _____.

9. *hard*     I study _____.

10. *hard*     The students took a _____ test.

11. *honest*     Roberto answered the question _____.

12. *slow*     Karen and Fumiko walked through the park _____.

13. *careless*     I made some _____ mistakes in my last composition.

14. *quick*     We were in a hurry, so we ate lunch _____.

15. *early*     Last night we had dinner _____ because we had to leave for the theater at 6:00.

16. *early*     We had an _____ dinner last night.

17. *good*     Jake has poor eyesight. He can't see

_____ without his glasses.

18. *good*     David is kind, generous, and thoughtful. He is a

_____ person.

19. *loud*      I speak _____ when I talk to my grandfather because he has trouble hearing.

20. *slow, clear*   Kim speaks English _____ and _____.


■ **EXERCISE 39:** Complete the sentences by using the correct form (ADJECTIVE or ADVERB) of the word in *italics*.

1. *good*      Did you sleep _____ last night?

2. *fast*      Anita is a _____ learner.

3. *quick*     She learns everything _____.

4. *fast*      Ahmed walks too _____. I can't keep up with him.

5. *soft*      Please speak _____. The children are asleep.

6. *easy*      This is an _____ exercise.

7. *hard*      It rained _____ yesterday.

8. *clear*     Our teacher explains everything _____.

9. *late*      Spiro came to class _____ yesterday.

10. *safe*     The plane arrived at the airport _____.

11. *hard*     Ms. Chan is a _____ worker.

12. *hard*     She works _____.

13. *late*     I paid my telephone bill _____.

14. *easy*     Ron lifted the heavy box _____. He's very strong.

15. *quiet*    Olga entered the classroom _____ because she was late for class.

16. *fast*     Mike talks too _____. I can't understand him.

17. *honest*   Shelley is an _____ person. I trust her completely.

18. *honest*   She speaks _____.

19. *good*     I didn't understand the teacher's explanation very _____.

20. *good*     We had a _____ time at the party last night.

21. *good*       Linda speaks _____, but she doesn't write

_____.

22. *fluent*     Nadia speaks French _____.

---

## 9-10   MAKING COMPARISONS WITH ADVERBS

| | | COMPARATIVE | SUPERLATIVE | Use *more* and *most* with adverbs that end in *-ly*.* |
|---|---|---|---|---|
| (a) | Kim speaks *more fluently than* Ali (does). | *more fluently* *more slowly* *more quickly* | *the most fluently* *the most slowly* *the most quickly* | |
| (b) | Anna speaks *the most fluently of all*. | | | |
| (c) | Mike worked *harder than* Sam (did). | *harder* *faster* *earlier* *later* | *the hardest* *the fastest* *the earliest* *the latest* | Use *-er* and *-est* with irregular adverbs: *hard, fast, early, late*. |
| (d) | Sue worked *the hardest of all*. | | | |
| (e) | Rosa writes *better than* I do. | *better* | *the best* | *Better* and *best* are forms of the adverb *well*. |
| (f) | Kim writes *the best of all*. | | | |

*Exception: *early–earlier–earliest*.

---

■ **EXERCISE 40:**   Complete the sentences by using the correct form (COMPARATIVE or SUPERLATIVE) of the ADVERBS in *italics*.

1. *late*            Karen got home ____*later than*____ Alice (did).

2. *quickly*         I finished my work _____ Tom (did).

3. *beautifully*     Gina sings _____ Susan (does).

4. *beautifully*     Ann sings _____ of all.

5. *hard*            My sister works _____ I (do).

6. *hard*            My brother works _____ of all.

7. *carefully*       My husband drives _____ I (do).

8. *early*           We arrived at the party _____ the Smiths (did).

9. *early*           The Wilsons arrived at the party _____ of all.

10. *well*      You can write _____ I (can).

11. *well*      Ken can write _____ of all.

12. *clearly*   Anita pronounces her words _____ Tina (does).

13. *fast*      I work _____ Jim (does).

14. *fast*      Toshi finished his work _____ of all.

15. *loudly*    Ali speaks _____ Yoko (does.)

16. *fluently*  Sue speaks Spanish _____ I (do).

17. *fluently*  Ted speaks Spanish _____ of all.

18. *slowly*    A snail moves _____ a crab (does).

■ **EXERCISE 41:**   Use the correct form (ADJECTIVE or ADVERB, COMPARATIVE or SUPERLATIVE) of the words in *italics*.

1. *careful*    Karen drives _____ *more carefully than* _____ her brother does.

2. *beautiful*  A tiger is _____ a goat.

3. *neat*       Paul's apartment is _____ mine.

4. *neat*       Peter's apartment is _____ of all.

5. *neat*       You write _____ I do.

6. *neat*       Ann writes _____ of all.

7. *heavy*      This suitcase is _____ that one.

8. *clear*      This author explains her ideas _____ that author.

9. *good*  I like rock music _____ classical music.

10. *good*  My husband can sing _____ I can.

11. *good*  My daughter can sing _____ of all.

12. *hard*  Sue studies _____ Fred.

13. *hard*  Jean studies _____ of all.

14. *long*  Almost universally, wives work _____
hours than their husbands because women take primary responsibility
for household chores and child-rearing.

15. *late*  Robert usually goes to bed _____
his roommate.

16. *clear*  Anna pronounces her words _____
of all the students in the class.

17. *sharp*  A razor is usually _____ a kitchen knife.

18. *artistic*  My son is _____ my daughter.

19. *slow*  I eat _____ my husband does.

20. *dangerous*  A motorcycle is _____ a bicycle.

## 9-11 USING *AS . . . AS* WITH ADVERBS

| | |
|---|---|
| (a) Bob doesn't study **as hard as** his brother (does). <br> (b) I didn't finish my work **as quickly as** Sue (did). <br> (c) Yoko can speak English **as well as** Tony (can). | Notice the pattern in the examples: <br> **as** + *adverb* + **as** |
| (d) I'm working **as fast as I can**. <br> (e) I'm working **as fast as possible**. <br> (f) Alex came **as quickly as he could**. <br> (g) Alex came **as quickly as possible**. | Notice the patterns in the examples: <br> **as** + *adverb* + **as** is frequently followed by <br> *subject* + **can/could** or by **possible**. |

■ **EXERCISE 42:**  Complete the sentences.  Compare John to your classmates or yourself.

1. John is lazy.  He doesn't work as hard _____*as Yoko (does). / as I (do).*_____

2. John is a reckless driver.  He doesn't drive as carefully _____

3. I can't read John's handwriting.  He doesn't write as neatly _____

4. John goes to bed late.  He doesn't go to bed as early _____

5. John was the last person to finish the test. He didn't finish it as quickly

   _____

6. John speaks softly. He doesn't speak as loudly _____

7. John is never in a hurry. He takes his time. He doesn't walk as fast _____

8. John is an insomniac. He doesn't sleep as well _____

9. John rarely studies. He doesn't study as hard _____

■ **EXERCISE 43—ORAL:**  Change the sentences by using *as . . . as + possible* or *can/could*.

   *Example:*  Please come early.
   *Response:*  Please come as early as possible. / Please come as early as you can.

   *Example:*  ( . . . ) walked fast.
   *Response:*  Surasuk walked as fast as possible. / Surasuk walked as fast as he could.

   1. Please come quickly.
   2. ( . . . ) came quickly.
   3. Please write neatly.
   4. I opened the door quietly.
   5. Please come soon.
   6. ( . . . ) came soon.
   7. Pronounce each word clearly.
   8. Do you study hard?
   9. When ( . . . ) saw a mean dog, he/she ran home fast.
   10. I write to my parents often.
   11. ( . . . ) is working fast.
   12. Please give me your homework soon.
   13. I'll get home early.
   14. ( . . . ) answered the question well.
   15. I'll call you soon.
   16. ( . . . ) goes swimming often.
   17. Please finish the test soon.
   18. I'll pay my telephone bill soon.

■ **EXERCISE 44—REVIEW:**  Choose the correct completion.

   1. A lion is _____ a tiger.
        A. similar        B. similar with        C.  similar from        D.  similar to

   2. Lions and tigers are _____.
        A. the same       B.  similar            C.  similar to          D.  the same as

   3. Good health is one of _____ in a person's life.
        A.  best thing                           C.  the best things
        B.  the best thing                       D.  best things

   4. There were many chairs in the room. I sat in _____ chair.
        A.  the comfortablest                    C.  most comfortable
        B.  the most comfortable                 D.  more comfortable

5. Jane's story was _____ Jack's story.
    A. funnier than                                  C. more funnier than
    B. funny than                                     D. more funny

6. My last name is _____ my cousin's.
    A. same         B. same from         C. same as         D. the same as

7. I live _____ away from school than you do.
    A. far         B. farther         C. more far         D. farthest

8. Ali speaks _____ than Hamid.
    A. more clearly                               C. more clear
    B. clearlier                                  D. more clearer

9. The weather in Canada _____ the weather in Mexico.
    A. is less hot than                           C. is hotter
    B. isn't as hot as                           D. isn't hot

10. Robert works hard every day, but his brother _____.
    A. is         B. isn't         C. does         D. doesn't

## ■ EXERCISE 45—ERROR ANALYSIS: Find and correct the mistakes in the following sentences.

1. Your pen is alike mine.

2. Kim's coat is similar with mine.

3. Jack's coat is same mine.

4. Soccer balls are different with basketballs.

5. Soccer is one of most popular sports in the world.

6. Green sea turtles live more long from elephants.

7. My grade on the test was worst from yours. You got a more better grade.

8. A monkey is intelligenter than a turtle.

9. Africa isn't as large than Asia.

10. Pedro speaks English more fluent than Ernesto.

11. The exploding human population is the most great threat to all forms of life on earth.

12. The Mongol Empire was the bigger land empire in the entire history of the world.

■ **EXERCISE 46—ORAL REVIEW (BOOKS CLOSED):**  Pair up with a classmate.

> STUDENT A:  Your book is open.
> STUDENT B:  Your book is closed.  Respond in complete sentences.

1. What's the longest river in the world?
2. What's the biggest continent?  What's the second biggest continent?
3. What country has the largest population?
4. Is a square the same as a rectangle?
5. Name a country that is farther south than Mexico.
6. Name an animal that is similar to a horse.
7. Name a place that is noisier than a library.
8. Is a dormitory like an apartment building?  How are they different?  How are they similar?
9. Is ( . . . )'s grammar book different from yours?
10. What is one of the most famous landmarks in the world?

*Switch roles.*

11. Is the population of Seoul, Korea, larger or smaller than the population of Sao Paulo, Brazil?
12. Is the Atlantic Ocean deeper than the Indian Ocean?
13. What's the smallest continent in the world?
14. Name two students in this class who speak the same native language.  Do they come from the same country?
15. Look at ( . . . ) and ( . . . ).  How are they different?
16. Is a lake like a river?  How are they different?  How are they similar?
17. Name an insect that is smaller than a bee.
18. Name a city that is farther north than Rome, Italy.
19. What is the most popular sport in your country?
20. What is one of the most important inventions in the modern world?  Why is it more important than *(name of another invention).*


■ **EXERCISE 47—REVIEW:**  Write about or talk about things and people in this room.  Orally or in writing, compare things and people you see in the classroom right now.  Look at this thing and that thing, and then compare them.  Look at this person and that person, and then compare them.


■ **EXERCISE 48—REVIEW:**  Write about one or more of the following topics.

1. Write about your family.  Compare the members of your family.  Include yourself in the comparisons.  (Who is younger than you?  Who is the youngest of all? Etc.)
2. Write about your childhood friends when you were ten years old.  Compare them.  Include yourself in the comparisons.  (Who could run faster than you?  Who could run the fastest of all? Etc.)
3. What are your three favorite places in the world?  Why?  Compare them.
4. What are the roles of health, money, and love in your life?  Compare them.

**CHAPTER 10**

# Expressing Ideas with Verbs

| | |
|---|---|
| (a) My clothes are dirty.  I *should wash* them. <br> (b) Tom is sleepy.  He *should go* to bed. <br> (c) You're sick.  You *should see* a doctor. | *Should* means "This is a good idea.  This is good advice." |
| (d) $\left.\begin{array}{l} I \\ You \\ She \\ He \\ It \\ We \\ They \end{array}\right\}$ *should go*. | *Should* is followed by the simple form of a verb. <br><br> INCORRECT:  *He should goes.* <br> INCORRECT:  *He should to go.* |
| (e) You *should not leave* your grammar book at home.  You need it in class. <br> (f) You *shouldn't leave* your grammar book at home. | NEGATIVE:  *should not* <br><br> CONTRACTION:  *should + not = shouldn't* |

■ **EXERCISE 1:**  Complete the sentences.  Begin the sentences with "**You should . . . .**" Use the expressions in the list or your own words.

| | |
|---|---|
| *buy a new pair of shoes* <br> *call the landlady* <br> *go to the bank* <br> *go to the immigration office* | ✔ *go to the post office* <br> *go to bed and take a nap* <br> *see a dentist* <br> *study harder* |

1. A:  I want to mail a package.

   B:  _____ *You should go to the post office.* _____

2. A: I'm sleepy.

   B: _____

3. A: I need to cash a check.

   B: _____

4. A: I have a toothache.

   B: _____

5. A: I'm flunking all of my courses at school.

   B: _____

6. A: The plumbing in my apartment doesn't work.

   B: _____

7. A: I need to renew my visa.

   B: _____

8. A: My shoes have holes in the bottom.

   B: _____

■ **EXERCISE 2:** Complete the sentences.  Use **should** or **shouldn't**.

1. Students _____*should*_____ come to class every day.

2. Students _____*shouldn't*_____ cut class.

3. We _____ waste our money on things we don't need.

4. It's raining.  You _____ take your umbrella when you leave.

5. Jimmy, you _____ pull the cat's tail!

6. People _____ be cruel to animals.

7. Your plane leaves at 8:00.  You _____ get to the airport by 7:00.

8. Life is short. We _____ waste it.

9. You _____ smoke in a public place because the smoke bothers other people.

10. We _____ cross a street at an intersection. We

_____ jaywalk.

11. When you go to New York City, you _____ see a play on Broadway.

12. You _____ walk alone on city streets after midnight. It's dangerous.

13. When you go to Bangkok, you _____ visit the Floating Market.

14. When you go to a football game, you _____ throw things on the field.

■ **EXERCISE 3—ORAL:** In groups of four, give advice using *should* and *shouldn't*. Student A should request advice first, then Student B, etc.

1. STUDENT A: English is not my native language. What advice can you give me about good ways to learn English?
2. STUDENT B: I am a teenager. What advice can you give me about being a good person and living a happy life?
3. STUDENT C: I am a newcomer. What advice can you give me about going to this school and living in this city?
4. STUDENT D: I have a job interview tomorrow. What advice can you give me about going to a job interview?

■ **EXERCISE 4—WRITTEN:** Write about your hometown. Use a separate piece of paper.

I'm a tourist. I'm going to visit your hometown. Is your hometown a good place for a tourist to visit? Why? What should I do when I'm there? Where should I go? What should I see? What shouldn't I do? Are there places I shouldn't visit? Will I enjoy my visit? Write a composition in which you tell me (a tourist) about your hometown.

## 10-2 USING *LET'S*

| | |
|---|---|
| (a) Bob: What should we do tonight?<br>    Ann: **Let's go to a movie.**<br>    Bob: Okay.<br>(b) Sue: I'm tired.<br>    Don: I'm tired, too. **Let's take a break.**<br>    Sue: That's a good idea! | *Let's (do something) = I have a suggestion for you and me. (let's = let us)*<br><br>In (a): *Let's go to a movie = I think we should go to a movie. Do you want to go to a movie?* |

■ **EXERCISE 5:** Complete the dialogues. Use *let's*. Use the expressions in the list or your own words.

| | |
|---|---|
| eat<br>get a cup of coffee<br>go dancing<br>go to Florida<br>go to a movie | go to a seafood restaurant<br>go to the zoo<br>✔ leave at six-thirty<br>walk |

1. A: What time should we leave for the airport?

   B:        *Let's leave at six-thirty.*
   A: Okay.

2. A: Where should we go for our vacation?

   B: _____
   A: That's a good idea.

3. A: Where do you want to go for dinner tonight?

   B: _____

4. A: The weather is beautiful today. _____
   B: Okay. Great!

5. A: I'm bored. _____
   B: I can't. I have to study.

6. A: Should we take the bus downtown or walk downtown?

   B: It's a nice day. _____

7. A: Dinner's ready! The food's on the table!

   B: Great! _____ I'm starving!

8. A: Where should we go Saturday night?

    B: _____

    A: Good idea!

9. A: We have an hour between classes. _____

    B: Okay. That sounds like a good idea.

■ **EXERCISE 6—ORAL:** Pair up with a classmate. Practice using **let's**.

    STUDENT A: Your book is open. Say the words in the book.

    STUDENT B: Your book is closed. Use **let's** in your response.

    STUDENT A: Respond to Student B's suggestion.

    *Example:*    It's a beautiful day today. What should we do?

    STUDENT A: It's a beautiful day today. What should we do?

    STUDENT B: Let's go to Woodland Park Zoo.

    STUDENT A: Great! What a good idea! Let's go!

1. What time should we go out to dinner tonight?
2. When should we go to *(name of a place)?*
3. What should we do this evening?
4. I want to do something fun tomorrow.

*Switch roles.*

5. What should we do tomorrow? It's a holiday, and we don't have to go to class.
6. I'm bored. Think of something we can do.
7. My plane leaves at six. What time should we leave for the airport?
8. It's *(name of a classmate)*'s birthday tomorrow. Should we do something special for him/her?

## 10-3 USING *HAVE* + INFINITIVE *(HAS TO / HAVE TO)*

| | |
|---|---|
| (a) People **need to eat** food.<br>(b) People **have to eat** food.<br>(c) Jack **needs to study** for his test.<br>(d) Jack **has to study** for his test. | (a) and (b) have basically the same meaning.<br>(c) and (d) have basically the same meaning.<br>**Have** + *infinitive* has a special meaning: it expresses the same idea as **need**. |
| (e) I **had to study** last night. | PAST FORM: **had** + *infinitive*. |
| (f) **Do** you **have to** leave now?<br>(g) What time **does** Jim **have to** leave?<br>(h) Why **did** they **have to** leave yesterday? | QUESTION FORM: **do**, **does**, or **did** is used in questions with **have to**. |
| (i) I **don't have to** study tonight.<br>(j) The concert was free. We **didn't have to** buy tickets. | NEGATIVE FORM: **do**, **does**, or **did** is used with **have to** in the negative. |

■ **EXERCISE 7—ORAL:** Answer the questions.

1. What do you want to do today?
2. What do you have to do today?
3. What do you want to do tomorrow?
4. What do you have to do tomorrow?
5. What does a student need to do or have to do?
6. Who has to go shopping? Why?
7. Who has to go to the post office? Why?
8. Who has to go to the bank? Why?
9. Where do you have to go today? Why?
10. Where do you want to go tomorrow? Why?
11. What did you have to do yesterday? Why?
12. Did you have responsibilities at home when you were a child? What did you have to do?
11. If you're driving a car and the traffic light turns red, what do you have to do?
12. What do you have to do before you cross a busy street?
13. Do you have to learn English? Why?
14. Who has a job? What are some of the things you have to do when you're at work?
15. What kind of job did you have in the past? What did you have to do when you had that job?

■ **EXERCISE 8—ORAL (BOOKS CLOSED):** Use *have to/has to*. Use *because*.

*Example:*     go downtown / buy some new shoes
STUDENT A: I have to go downtown because I have to buy some new shoes.
TEACHER:     Why does (Student A) have to go downtown?
STUDENT B: (Student A) has to go downtown because he/she has to buy some new shoes.

1. go to the drugstore / buy some toothpaste
2. go to the grocery store / get some milk
3. go shopping / get a new coat
4. go to the post office / mail a package
5. stay home tonight / study grammar
6. go to the hospital / visit a friend
7. go to the bank / cash a check
8. go downtown / go to the immigration office
9. go to the bookstore / buy a notebook
10. go to *(name of a store in the city)* / buy *(a particular thing at that store)*

■ **EXERCISE 9:** Complete the sentences. Use the words in parentheses. Use a form of
*has/have* + *infinitive* in all the completions.

1. A: Jack can't join us for dinner tonight.
   B: Why not?

   A: *(he, work)* ___He has to work___.

   B: *(he, work)* ___Does he have to work___ tomorrow night too? If he doesn't,
   maybe we should postpone the dinner until then.

2. A: Why *(you, go)* _____ to the library later tonight?

   B: *(I, find)* _____ some information for my research
   paper.

3. A: It's almost four-thirty. What time *(Sue, leave for)* _____
   the airport?

   B: Around five. *(she, be)* _____ at the airport at six-fifteen.

4. A: Why did you go to the bookstore after class yesterday?

   B: *(I, buy)* _____ some colored pencils.

   A: Oh? Why *(you, buy)* _____ colored pencils?
   B: I need them for some drawings I plan to do for my botany class.

5. A: *(I, go)* _____ to the store.
   B: Why?

   A: Because *(I, get)* _____ some rice and fresh fruit.

6. A: Kate didn't come to the movie with us last night.
   B: Why?

   A: Because *(she, study)* _____ for a test.

7. A: What time *(you, be)* _____ at the dentist's office?
   B: Three. I have a three o'clock appointment.

8. A: *(Tom, find)* _____ a new apartment?
   B: Yes, he does. He can't stay in his present apartment.

9. A: *(Yoko, not, take)* _____ another
   English course. Her English is very good.

   B: *(you, take)* _____ another English course?
   A: Yes, I do. I need to study more English.

10. A: Was Steve at home yesterday evening?

     B: No. *(he, stay)* _____ late at the office.

     B: Why?

     A: *(he, finish)* _____ a report for his boss.

## 10-4 USING *MUST*

| | |
|---|---|
| (a) People need food. People ***have to eat*** food.<br>(b) People need food. People ***must eat*** food. | (a) and (b) have the same meaning:<br>   *must eat = have to eat* |
| (c)   *I*<br>     *You*<br>     *She*<br>     *He*    } ***must work***.<br>     *It*<br>     *We*<br>     *They* | ***Must*** is followed by the simple form of a verb.<br><br>INCORRECT: *He must works.*<br>INCORRECT: *He must to work.* |
| (d) You ***must not be*** late for work if you want to keep your job. | ***must not*** = Don't do this! You don't have a choice. |
| (e) You ***don't have to go*** to the movie with us if you don't want to. | ***don't have to*** = It's not necessary, but you have a choice. |

Compare the following examples. Notice the difference between ***should*** and ***must***.

| MUST | SHOULD |
|---|---|
| SOMETHING IS VERY IMPORTANT.<br>SOMETHING IS NECESSARY. YOU DO NOT HAVE A CHOICE. | SOMETHING IS A GOOD IDEA, BUT YOU HAVE A CHOICE. |
| (f) I ***must study*** tonight. I'm going to take a very important test tomorrow. | (g) I ***should study*** tonight. I have some homework to do, but I'm tired. I'll study tomorrow night. I'm going to go to bed now. |
| (h) You ***must take*** an English course. You cannot graduate without it. | (i) You ***should take*** an English course. It will help you. |
| (j) Johnny, this is your mother speaking. You ***must eat*** your vegetables. You can't leave the table until you eat your vegetables. | (k) Johnny, you ***should eat*** your vegetables. They're good for you. You'll grow up to be strong and healthy. |

■ **EXERCISE 10:** Complete the sentences. Use ***must***. Use the expressions in the list.

> close the door behind you                     pay an income tax
> go to medical school                          read English newspapers and magazines
> ✔ have a driver's license                     speak English outside of class every day
> have a library card                           stop
> have a passport                               study harder
> listen to English on the radio and TV         talk to myself in English
> make new friends who speak English            take one pill every six hours

1. According to the law,* a driver     <u>*must have a driver's license.*</u>

2. If a traffic light is red, a car _____

3. If you want to check a book out of the library, you _____

   _____

4. Nancy has a job in Chicago. She earns a good salary. According to the law, she

   _____

5. I failed the last two tests in my biology class. According to my professor, I

   _____

6. I want to travel abroad. According to the law, I _____

   _____

7. If you want to become a doctor, you _____

8. John's doctor gave him a prescription. According to

   the directions on the bottle, John _____

   _____

9. Jimmy ! It's cold outside. When you come inside, you

   _____

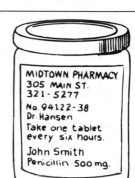

MIDTOWN PHARMACY
305 MAIN ST.
321-5277
No. 94122-38
Dr. Hansen
Take one tablet
every six hours.
John Smith
Penicillin 500 mg.

10. I want to improve my English. According to my teacher, I _____

   _____

_____
*according to the law = the law says.

■ **EXERCISE 11—ORAL:**   Answer the questions.

1. When must you have a passport?
2. If you live in an apartment, what is one thing you must do and one thing you must not do?
3. Name one thing a driver must do and one thing a driver must not do.
4. If you are on an airplane, what is one thing you must do and one thing you must not do?
5. Name something you must have a ticket for.  Name something you don't have to have a ticket for.

■ **EXERCISE 12:**   Choose the correct completion.

1. If you want to keep your job, you _____ be late for work.  It is necessary for you to be on time.
    A.  must not          B.  don't have to          C.  doesn't have to

2. My office is close enough to my apartment for me to walk to work.  I _____ take a bus.  I only take a bus in bad weather.
    A.  must not          B.  don't have to          C.  doesn't have to

3. Some schools require schoolchildren to wear uniforms to school, but my children's

    school doesn't require uniforms.  My children _____ wear uniforms to school.
    A.  must not          B.  don't have to          C.  doesn't have to

4. Jimmy, it is very important to be careful with matches!  You _____ play with matches.
    A.  must not          B.  don't have to          C.  doesn't have to

5. Jack is twenty-four, but he still lives with his parents.  That saves him a lot of money.

For example, he _____ pay rent or buy his own food.
    A.  must not             B.  don't have to           C.  doesn't have to

6. The water in that river is badly polluted.  You _____ drink it.
    A.  must not             B.  don't have to           C.  doesn't have to _____

7. If you have a credit card, you _____ pay for a purchase in cash.  You can charge it.
    A.  must not             B.  don't have to           C.  doesn't have to

8. When an airplane is taking off, you have to be in your seat with your seat belt on.

You _____ stand up and walk around when an airplane is taking off.
    A.  must not             B.  don't have to           C.  doesn't have to

## 10-5  MODAL AUXILIARIES

| | | |
|---|---|---|
| (a)  Anita | *can*<br>*couldn't*<br>*may*<br>*might*<br>*must*<br>*should*<br>*will* } go to class. | An auxiliary is a helping verb.  It comes in front of the simple form of a main verb.<br>The following helping verbs are called "modal auxiliaries": *can*, *could*, *may*, *might*, *must*, *should*, *will*, *would*.<br>They are followed by the simple form of a verb (without *to*). |
| (b)  Anita | *is able to*<br>*is going to*<br>*has to* } go to class. | Expressions that are similar to modal auxiliaries are: *be able to*, *be going to*, *have to*. |

■ **EXERCISE 13:**  Add *to* where necessary.  If *to* is not necessary, write "X."

1. My sister can _____X_____ play the guitar very well.

2. We have _____to_____ pay our rent on the first of the month.

3. Could you please _____ open the window?  Thanks.

4. I wasn't able _____ visit my friends yesterday because I was busy.

5. You shouldn't _____ drink twenty cups of coffee a day.

6. Will you _____ be at the meeting tomorrow?

7. Does everyone have _____ be at the meeting?

8. You must not _____ miss the meeting.  It's important.

9. Jennifer might not _____ be there tomorrow.

10. May I _____ use your telephone?

11. We couldn't _____ go to the concert last night because we didn't have tickets.

12. Can you _____ play a musical instrument?

13. What time are you going _____ arrive?

14. It may _____ be too cold for us to go swimming tomorrow.

## 10-6 SUMMARY CHART: MODAL AUXILIARIES AND SIMILAR EXPRESSIONS

| | AUXILIARY* | MEANING | EXAMPLE |
|---|---|---|---|
| (a) | *can* | ability | I *can* sing. |
| | | polite question | *Can* you please help me? |
| (b) | *could* | past ability | I *couldn't* go to class yesterday. |
| | | polite question | *Could* you please help me? |
| (c) | *may* | possibility | It *may* rain tomorrow. |
| | | polite question | *May* I help you? |
| (d) | *might* | possibility | It *might* rain tomorrow. |
| (e) | *must* | necessity | You *must* have a passport. |
| (f) | *should* | advisability | You *should* see a doctor. |
| (g) | *will* | future happening | My sister *will* meet us at the airport. |
| (h) | *would* | polite question | *Would* you please open the door? |
| (i) | *be able to* | ability | I *wasn't able to* attend the meeting. |
| (j) | *be going to* | future happening | Tina *is going to* meet us at the airport. |
| (k) | *has / have to* | necessity | I *have to* study tonight. |
| (l) | *had to* | past necessity | I *had to* study last night too. |

*See the following charts for more information: *can*, Charts 7-1 and 7-2; *could*, Chart 7-4; *may* and *might*, Chart 6-10; *must*, Chart 10-4; *should*, Chart 10-1; *will*, Charts 6-5, 6-6, and 6-10; *would*, Chart 7-14; *be able to*, Chart 7-12; *be going to*, Chart 6-1; *has/have/had to*, Chart 10-3.

■ **EXERCISE 14—ORAL:** In small groups, give responses to the following. Each person in the group should give a different response.

*Example:*      Name something you *had to* do yesterday.
STUDENT A:  I had to go to class.
STUDENT B:  I had to go to the post office to buy some stamps.
STUDENT C:  I had to study for a test.
STUDENT D:  Etc.

1.  Name something you *can* do.
2.  Name something you *couldn't* do yesterday.
3.  Name something you *may* do tomorrow,
4.  Name something you *might* do tomorrow.
5.  Name something you *must* do this week.
6.  Name something you *have to* do today.
7.  Name something you *don't have to* do today.
8.  Name something you *should* do this evening.
9.  Name something you *will* do this evening.
10. Name something you *are going to* do this week.
11. Name something you *weren't able to* do when you were a child.
12. Name something you *had to* do when you were a child.
13. You want to borrow something from a classmate. Ask a polite question with **could**.
14. You want a classmate to do something for you. Ask a polite question with **would**.
15. A classmate has something that you want. Ask a polite question with **may**.
16. Name something that *may* happen in the world in the next ten years.
17. Name something that (probably) *won't* happen in the world in the next ten years.
18. Name some things that this school *should* do or *shouldn't* do to make the school a better place for students.

■ **EXERCISE 15—ERROR ANALYSIS:** Find and correct the mistakes in the following.

1.  Would you please to help me?

2.  I will can go to the meeting tomorrow.

3.  Ken should writes us a letter.

4.  I have to went to the store yesterday.

5.  Susie! You must not to play with matches!

6.  May you please hand me that book?

7. Ann couldn't answered my question.

8. Shelley can't goes to the concert tomorrow.

9. Let's to go to a movie tonight.

■ **EXERCISE 16—REVIEW OF VERBS:** Choose the correct completion.

1. Tom _____ every day.
   A. shaves          B. is shaving          C. has to shaves

2. _____ go to class every day?
   A. Are you          B. Do you have          C. Do you

3. Yoko _____ to be here tomorrow.
   A. will          B. may          C. is going

4. Jack _____ be in class yesterday.
   A. didn't          B. can't          C. couldn't

5. Fatima _____ to her sister on the phone yesterday.
   A. spoke          B. can speak          C. speaks

6. I _____ my rent last month.
   A. might pay          B. will pay          C. paid

7. Shh. Ken _____ on the phone right now.
   A. talks          B. can talk          C. is talking

8. I want to go to a movie tonight, but I _____ home and study.
   A. should stay          B. stayed          C. stay

9. We _____ to the zoo tomorrow.
   A. will going          B. might go          C. will can go

10. I _____ in class right now.
    A. sit          B. am sitting          C. sitting

| | |
|---|---|
| **PRESENT PROGRESSIVE** (right now)<br><br>(a)   It's 10:00 now.  Boris ***is sitting*** in class. | The present progressive describes an activity in progress right now, at the moment of speaking.  See Chart 3-1.<br>In (a):  Right now it is 10:00.  Boris began to sit before 10:00.  Sitting is in progress at 10:00. |
| **PAST PROGRESSIVE** (in progress yesterday)<br><br>(b)   It was 10:00.  Boris ***was sitting*** in class. | The past progressive describes an activity in progress at a particular time in the past.<br>In (b):  Boris began to sit in class before 10:00 yesterday.  At 10:00 yesterday, sitting in class was in progress. |
| **PRESENT PROGRESSIVE FORM:**  *AM, IS, ARE* + *-ING*<br>(c)   It's 10:00.      I      ***am sitting***     in class.<br>                   Boris  ***is sitting***      in class.<br>                   We    ***are sitting***    in class. | The forms of the present progressive and the past progressive consist of ***be*** + ***-ing***.<br>The present progressive uses the present forms of ***be***: ***am***, ***is***, and ***are*** + ***-ing***. |
| **PAST PROGRESSIVE FORM:**  *WAS, WERE* + *-ING*<br>(d)   It was 10:00.  Boris  ***was sitting***     in class.<br>                   We    ***were sitting***    in class. | The past progressive uses the past forms of ***be***: ***was*** and ***were*** + ***-ing***. |

Boris ***is sitting*** in class right now at ten o'clock.

Boris ***was sitting*** in class yesterday at ten o'clock.

■ **EXERCISE 17:** Complete the sentences. Use a form of **be** + **sit**.

1.  I ____*am sitting*____ in class right now.

2.  I ____*was sitting*____ in class yesterday too.

3.  You _____ in class right now.

4.  You _____ in class yesterday too.

5.  Tony _____ in class right now.

6.  He _____ in class yesterday too.

7.  We _____ in class today.

8.  We _____ in class yesterday too.

9.  Rita _____ in class now.

10.  She _____ in class yesterday too.

11.  Rita and Tony _____ in class today.

12.  They _____ in class yesterday too.

■ **EXERCISE 18:** Use the words in parentheses to complete the sentences. Discuss the meaning of the phrase "in progress."

1.  Paul started to eat dinner at 7:00. At 7:05, Mary came. Paul *(eat)* _____

    _____ when Mary *(come)* _____ at 7:05.

2. Bobby was at home yesterday evening. His favorite program was on television last night. It started at 8:00. It ended at 9:00. At 8:30, his friend Kristin called. When Kristin *(call)* _____ at 8:30, Bobby *(watch)* _____ _____ TV.

3. Rosa played her guitar for an hour yesterday morning. She started to play her guitar at 9:30. She stopped at 10:30. Mike arrived at her apartment at 10:00. At 10:00, Rosa *(play)* _____ her guitar.

■ **EXERCISE 19—ORAL:** Look at the pictures. Use the PAST PROGRESSIVE to describe the activities that were in progress.

Mr. and Mrs. Gold invited several friends to their house for the weekend. A thief stole Mrs. Gold's jewelry at midnight on Saturday. What were the guests doing at midnight?

## 10-8 USING *WHILE* WITH THE PAST PROGRESSIVE

| | |
|---|---|
| (a) The phone rang **while** *I was sleeping*. OR:<br>(b) **While** *I was sleeping*, the phone rang. | **while** + *subject* + *verb* = *a time clause*<br>*While I was sleeping* is a time clause.<br>A *while*-clause describes an activity that was in progress at the time another activity happened.<br>The verb in a *while*-clause is often past progressive (e.g., *was sleeping*). |

■ **EXERCISE 20—ORAL:** Combine the sentences. Use **while**.

1. I was studying last night.
   Rita called.
   → *While I was studying last night, Rita called.*
   → *Rita called while I was studying last night.*

2. Someone knocked on my apartment door.
   I was eating breakfast yesterday morning.

3. I was cooking dinner yesterday evening.
   I burned my hand.

4. I was studying last night.
   A mouse suddenly appeared
   on my desk.

5. Yoko raised her hand.
   The teacher was talking.

6. A tree fell on my car.
   I was driving home yesterday.

## 10-9 *WHILE* vs. *WHEN* IN PAST TIME CLAUSES

| | |
|---|---|
| (a) The mouse appeared *while* **I was studying**. OR:<br>(b) *While* **I was studying**, the mouse appeared.<br>(c) *When the mouse* **appeared**, I was studying. OR:<br>(d) I was studying *when the mouse* **appeared**. | The verb in a *while*-clause is often past progressive, as in (a) and (b).<br>The verb in a *when*-clause is often simple past, as in (c) and (d). |

■ **EXERCISE 21:** Complete the sentences. Use the PAST PROGRESSIVE in the **while**-clauses. Use the SIMPLE PAST in the **when**-clauses.

1. While I *(wash)* _____*was washing*_____ dishes last night, I *(get)*

   _____*got*_____ a phone call from my best friend.

2. When my best friend *(call)* _____ last night, I *(wash)*

   _____ dishes.

3. My friend Jessica *(come)* _____ while I *(eat)*

   _____ dinner last night.

4. I *(eat)* _____ dinner when my friend Jessica *(come)*

   _____ last night.

5. Jason *(wear)* _____ a suit and tie when I *(see)*

   _____ him yesterday.

6. My roommate came home late last night. I *(sleep)* _____

   when she *(get)* _____ home.

7. When Gina *(call)* _____ last night, I *(take)*

   _____ a bubble bath.

8. While I *(watch)* _____ TV last night and *(relax)*

   _____ after a long day, my new puppy *(take)*

   _____ my wallet from my bedside table.

■ **EXERCISE 22—ORAL:** Perform and describe actions using *while*-clauses or *when*-clauses.

> STUDENT A: Perform your action. Use the PRESENT PROGRESSIVE to describe what you are doing. Continue to perform the action.
> STUDENT B: Perform your action, then stop.
> STUDENT A: After Student B stops, you stop too.

> *Example:*   A: erase the board
> B: open the door
> TEACHER: (Student A), what are you doing?
> STUDENT A: I'm erasing the board right now.
> TEACHER: (Student B), would you please open the door?
> STUDENT B: *(Student B opens the door.)*
> TEACHER: Thank you. You may both sit down again. (Student C), will you please describe the two actions we saw?
> STUDENT C: While (Student A) was erasing the board, (Student B) opened the door. OR: (Student A) was erasing the board when (Student B) opened the door.

1. A: Write on the board.
   B: Drop a book on the floor.
2. A: Walk around the room.
   B: Say hello to (Student A).
3. A: Look out the window.
   B: Take (Student A)'s grammar book.
4. A: Draw a picture on the board.
   B: Ask (Student A) a question.

## 10-10   SIMPLE PAST vs. PAST PROGRESSIVE

| | |
|---|---|
| (a) Jane **called** me yesterday. <br> (b) I **talked** to Jane for an hour last night. <br> (c) We **went** to Jack's house last Friday. <br> (d) What time **did** you **get up** this morning? | The **simple past** describes activities or situations that began and ended at a particular time in the past (e.g., *yesterday, last night*). |
| (e) I **was studying** when Jane called me yesterday. <br> (f) While I **was studying** last night, Jane called. | The **past progressive** describes an activity that was in progress (was happening) at the time another action happened. In (e) and (f): The studying was in progress when Jane called. |
| (g) I **opened** my umbrella when it **began** to rain. | If both the *when*-clause and the main clause in a sentence are simple past, it means that the action in the *when*-clause happened first and the action in the main clause happened second. In (g): First, it began to rain; second, I opened my umbrella. |
| COMPARE <br> (h) When the phone **rang**, I **answered** it. <br> (i) When the phone **rang**, I **was studying**. | In (h): First, the phone rang; second, I answered it. <br> In (i): First, the studying was in progress; second, the phone rang. |

■ **EXERCISE 23:** Complete the sentences. Use the SIMPLE PAST or the PAST PROGRESSIVE.

1. I *(have)* _____ a busy day yesterday. I *(go)* _____ to

   class in the morning. I *(eat)* _____ lunch with my brother after class.

   In the afternoon, I *(drive)* _____ to the airport to pick up my cousin. I

   *(take)* _____ her to a restaurant for dinner. After dinner, we *(go)*

   _____ back to my apartment and *(watch)* _____ a

   movie on TV. After the movie, we *(talk)* _____ for a couple of

   hours before we *(go)* _____ to bed.

2. While I *(walk)* _____ to class yesterday morning, I *(see)*

   _____ Abdullah. We *(say)* _____ hello and *(walk)*

   _____ the rest of the way to school together.

3. I *(eat)* _____ lunch with my brother when I suddenly

   *(remember)* _____ my promise to pick my cousin up at
   the airport.

4. While I *(drive)* _____ to the airport, I *(see)* _____
   an accident.

5. While my cousin and I *(have)* _____ dinner at the

   restaurant last night, we *(see)* _____ a friend of mine. I *(introduce)*

   _____ her to my cousin.

6. When I *(hear)* _____ a knock at the door last night, I *(walk)*

   _____ to the door and *(open)* _____ it.

7. When I *(open)* _____ the door, I *(see)* _____ my brother. I

   *(greet)* _____ him and *(ask)* _____ him to come in.

8. My cousin and I *(watch)* _____ a movie on TV

   last night when my brother *(come)* _____. He *(watch)*

   _____ the end of the movie with us.

■ **EXERCISE 24:** Complete the sentences. Use the SIMPLE PAST or the PAST PROGRESSIVE.

1. Mrs. Reed *(turn)* _____ on the radio in her car while she *(drive)*

   _____ home yesterday. She *(listen)* _____

   to some music when she suddenly *(hear)* _____ a siren.

   When she *(look)* _____ in her rearview mirror, she *(see)* _____

   an ambulance behind her. She immediately *(pull)* _____ her car

   to the side of the road and *(wait)* _____ for the ambulance to pass.

2. I *(have)* _____ a strange experience yesterday. I *(read)*

   _____ my book on the bus when a man *(sit)*

   _____ down next to me and *(hand)* _____ me some

   money. I *(want, not)* _____ his money. I *(be)*

   _____ very confused. I *(stand)* _____ up and

   *(walk)* _____ toward the door of the bus. While I *(wait)*

   _____ for the door to open, the man *(offer)*

   _____ me some money again. When the door *(open)*

   _____, I *(get)* _____ off the bus quickly. I still don't

   know why he was trying to give me money.

3. A: I (be) _____ at my friends' house last night. While we (eat)

_____ dinner, their cat (jump) _____

on the table. My friends (seem, not) _____

_____ to care, but I lost my appetite.

B: What (you, say) _____?
A: Nothing.

B: Why (you, ask, not) _____ your friends to get
their cat off the table?

A: I (want, not) _____ to be impolite.
B: I think your friends were impolite to let their cat sit on the table during dinner.

■ **EXERCISE 25—REVIEW:** Choose the best completion.

1. I was watching TV. I heard a knock on the door. When I heard the knock on the

door, I _____ it.
   A. open                    C. opened
   B. am opening              D. was opening

2. "When _____ you talk to Jane?"
"Yesterday."
   A. do          B. should          C. did          D. were

3. I _____ TV when Gina called last night. We talked for an hour.
   A. watch                   C. was watching
   B. watched                 D. am watching

4. Mike is in his bedroom right now. He _____, so we need to be quiet.
     A. is sleeping                   C. slept
     B. sleeps                      D. was sleeping

5. Kate _____ tell us the truth yesterday. She lied to us.
     A. don't         B. doesn't         C. didn't         D. wasn't

6. I saw a fish while I _____ in the ocean yesterday.
     A. swim                    C. were swimming
     B. was swimming            D. was swimming

7. When I heard the phone ring, I _____ it.
     A. answer                  C. answered
     B. am answering           D. was answering

8. "_____ you go to concerts often?"
   "Yes. I go at least once a month."
     A. Do         B. Did         C. Was         D. Were

9. While I _____ dinner last night, I burned my finger.
     A. cooking       B. cook         C. was cooking     D. was cook

10. "Where _____ after work yesterday?"
     A. you went      B. you did go     C. did you went     D. did you go

## 10-11    USING *HAVE BEEN* (THE PRESENT PERFECT)

| | |
|---|---|
| SITUATION: I came to this city on February 1st. It is now April 1st. I am still in this city.<br>(a) I **have been** here **since** *February 1st*.<br>(b) I **have been** here **for** *two months*.<br><br>SITUATION: Kim came to this city on January 1st. It is now April 1st. Kim is still in this city.<br>(c) Kim **has been** here **since** *January*.<br>(d) Kim **has been** here **for** *three months*. | **Have been** expresses the idea that a situation began in the past and still exists at present. **Have been** is used with **since** or **for** to tell how long the situation has existed. (a) and (b) have the same meaning.<br><br>Third person singular = **has been**, as in (c) and (d). |
| SITUATION: I came to the classroom at nine o'clock. I am in the classroom now. It's nine-thirty now.<br>(e) I *have been* here **since nine o'clock**.<br>(f) I *have been* here **for 30 minutes**.<br><br>SITUATION: Ann lives in another city. She came to visit me Monday morning. Now it is Friday morning. She is still here.<br>(g) Ann *has been* here **since Monday**.<br>(h) Ann *has been* here **for four days**. | **Since** is followed by *a specific time*:<br>    *since February* (specific month)<br>    *since nine o'clock* (specific clock time)<br>    *since 1995* (specific year)<br><br>**For** is followed by *a length of time*:<br>    *for two months* (number of months)<br>    *for 30 minutes* (length of clock time)<br>    *for four days* (number of days)<br>    *for three years* (number of years) |

■ **EXERCISE 26:**  Complete the sentences with *since* or *for*.

1. I came to this city six months ago.  I am still here.  I have been in this city

   _____*for*_____ six months.

2. Kim has been in this city _____*since*_____ January.

3. It's now two o'clock.  Carmen has been in class _____ one o'clock.

4. Carmen has been in class _____ an hour.

5. Erica has been a teacher _____ 1994.

6. Mr. Gow has been a plumber _____ 20 years.

7. My parents are visiting me this week.  They have been here _____ five days.

8. They have been here _____ last Saturday.

9. India has been an independent nation _____ 1947.

10. I have been awake _____ six o'clock this morning.

11. My friend is very ill.  She has been in the hospital _____ four days.

12. I hope the weather gets warmer soon.  It's been cold and rainy _____ two weeks.

■ **EXERCISE 27:**  Complete the following with your own words.

*Example:*

a. Today is _____*Monday, March 4*_____.

b. I came to this city _____*in January* OR: *two months ago*_____.

c. I have been in this city since _____*January*_____.

d. I have been in this city for _____*two months*_____.

*Example:*

a. Today is _____*Monday, March 4*_____.

b. I came to this city _____*on Friday, March 1* OR: *three days ago*_____.

c. I have been in this city since _____*Friday* OR: *March 1*_____.

d. I have been in this city for _____*three days*_____.

1. a. Today is _____.

   b. I came to this city _____.

   c. I have been in this city since _____.

   d. I have been in this city for _____.

2. a. Today is _____.

   b. _____* came to this city _____.

   c. _____ has been in this city since _____.

   d. _____ has been in this city for _____.

3. a. I am in the classroom. The time right now is _____.

   b. The time I entered the classroom today was _____.

   c. I have been in this room since _____.

   d. I have been in this room for _____.

4. a. Our teacher taught her/his first class in her/his life _____.

   b. She/He has been a teacher since _____.

   c. She/He has been a teacher for _____.

5. a. I started to go to school in *(year)* _____. I am still a student.

   b. I have been a student since _____.

   c. I have been a student for _____.

## 10-12   USING *SINCE*-CLAUSES

|     |     |     |     |
| --- | --- | --- | --- |
| (a) | I've been afraid of dogs<br>main clause | S  V<br>**since** *I was a child.*<br>*since*-clause | **Since** can be followed by a subject and verb. In (a): *since I was child* = a *since*-clause.* |
| (b) | Mr. Lo has been a teacher **since** *he graduated from college.* | | Notice in the examples: The verb in the main clause is **present perfect**. The verb in the *since*-clause is **simple past**. |
| (c) | Sue and I have been friends **since** *we were children.* | | |

*A *since*-clause is a time clause. See Charts 5-18 and 5-19 for more information about time clauses.

_____

*Use the name of a classmate.

■ **EXERCISE 28:** Complete the sentences with the words in parentheses. Use the PRESENT
PERFECT or the SIMPLE PAST.

1. Maria got some bad news last week. She *(be)* _____*has been*_____ sad since

   she *(get)* _____*got*_____ the bad news.

2. I started school when I was five years old. I *(be)* _____ in

   school since I *(be)* _____ five years old.

3. Ann's brother arrived a few days ago to visit her. She loves her brother and is happy

   to be with him. She *(be)* _____ happy since her brother

   *(come)* _____.

4. Jack moved to Hong Kong after he graduated from the university. Jim *(be)*

   _____ in Hong Kong since he *(graduate)*

   _____ from the university.

5. The weather was hot and dry for many weeks. Two days ago it rained. The weather

   *(be)* _____ cool and wet since it *(rain)* _____.

   two days ago.

6. Jack broke his leg five days ago. He's in the hospital. He *(be)* _____

   in the hospital since he *(break)* _____ his leg.

| SIMPLE FORM | SIMPLE PAST | PAST PARTICIPLE | Form of the present perfect: **have/has** + past participle |
|---|---|---|---|
| be | was, were | **been** | |
| know | knew | **known** | Irregular verbs have irregular past participles. (See Chart 10-18 and Appendix 5 for additional lists of irregular verbs.) |
| have | had | **had** | |
| see | saw | **seen** | |
| teach | taught | **taught** | The past participle of regular verbs is the same form as the simple past: |
| live | lived | **lived** | |
| own | owned | **owned** | verb + **-ed** |
| work | worked | **worked** | |
| touch | touched | **touched** | |

| | |
|---|---|
| (a) I **have known** Tom for five years. | Notice in the examples: |
| (b) Sue **has had** a bad cold for three days. | The present perfect is formed by |
| (c) They **have lived** here since 1994. | **have / has** + past participle. |
| (d) We **have owned** our own home since 1989. | |

| | |
|---|---|
| (e) *I've*<br>*We've*<br>*You've*<br>*They've* } been here for two months.<br>*She's*<br>*He's*<br>*It's* | **Have** and **has** are contracted with *subject pronouns* as shown in the examples. |

| | |
|---|---|
| COMPARE<br>(f) **She's** been here for two months. | In (f): *she's = she has*<br>In (g): *she's = she is* |

■ **EXERCISE 29:** Complete the sentences with the given verbs. Use the PRESENT PERFECT.

1. *teach*    Mr. Jackson is a teacher. He <u>'s taught</u> biology for twenty years.

2. *know*    I _____ Mary Adams since I was a child.

3. *be*    She _____ a good friend for a long time.

4. *live*    My parents live in a suburb of Mexico City. They _____
_____ in the same apartment for twenty-five years.

5. *have*    Janet and Sam _____ their dog Fido for three years.

6. *work*    My uncle _____ at the automobile factory for
seventeen years.

7. *be*    We _____ in class since nine o'clock this morning.

8. *own*     Ken is a businessman. He sells car parts. He _____

              his own business since 1994.

9. *have*    Mr. Cook's hair started to turn gray when he was forty. He _____

              _____ gray hair since he was forty years old.

10. *see*    I _____ several movies since I came to this city.

■ **EXERCISE 30—ORAL:** Complete the sentences with the given verbs and your own words. Use the PRESENT PERFECT.

    *Example:*   know     I . . . *(name of a person)* for . . . .
           →  *I've known Li Ming for three months.*
           →  *My best friend is Maria Alvarez. I've known her for fifteen years.*

1. *be*      I . . . in this classroom today since . . . .
2. *live*    Right now I am living *(in an apartment, a dorm, etc.)*. I . . . there since . . . .
3. *have*    I have *(name of something you own)*. I . . . it/them for . . . .
4. *be*      I . . . in *(name of a place)* since . . . .
5. *know*    I . . . *(name of a classmate)* since . . . .
6. *work*    *(name of someone you know)* works at *(name of a place)*. He/She . . . there for . . . .
7. *be*      I . . . awake since . . . .
8. *teach*   Our teacher . . . English since . . . .
9. *live*    My *(name of a family member)* . . . *(name of a place)* for . . . .
10. *be*     I . . . afraid of . . . since . . . .

## 10-14   USING *NEVER* WITH THE PRESENT PERFECT

| | |
|---|---|
| (a) *I've **never** touched* an elephant. <br> (b) Anna *has **never** seen* the Pacific Ocean. | ***Never*** is frequently used with the *present perfect*. <br><br> In (a): the speaker is saying, "From the beginning of my life to the present moment, I have never touched an elephant. In my entire lifetime, since I was born, I have never touched an elephant." |

■ **EXERCISE 31—ORAL:** Use ***never*** with the PRESENT PERFECT.

    *Example:*    Name some places you have never lived.
    STUDENT A: I've never lived in a small town.
    STUDENT B: I've never lived in a dormitory.
    STUDENT C: I've never lived in South America.
    STUDENT D: Etc.

1. countries you've never been in
2. cities you've never lived in
3. pets you've never had
4. animals you've never touched
5. things you've never seen
6. things you've never owned

## 10-15 PRESENT PERFECT: QUESTIONS AND NEGATIVES

| | |
|---|---|
| (a) **Have** *you* **lived** here for a long time?<br>(b) **Has** *Ken* **been** in this class since the beginning of the term? | Question form of the present perfect:<br>**have/has** + *subject* + *past participle* |
| (c) I **have not (haven't) lived** here for a long time.<br>(d) Ken **has not (hasn't) been** in the class since the beginning of the term. | Negative form of the present perfect:<br>**have/has** + **not** + *past participle*<br>Negative contractions:<br>   *have not = haven't*<br>   *has not = hasn't* |

■ **EXERCISE 32:** Complete the sentences with the PRESENT PERFECT.

1. (Mr. Jackson, teach) _____*Has Mr. Jackson taught*_____ biology for a long time?

2. Ms. Smith is a new teacher. She (teach, not) _____*hasn't taught*_____ biology for a long time.

3. (you, know) _____ Mary Adams since you were a child?

4. I met Mary Adams only two months ago. I (know, not) _____

   _____ her for a long time. I've known her for only a short time.

5. (she, be) _____ a good friend of yours for a long time?

6. She (be, not) _____ a friend of mine for a long time.

7. (your parents, live) _____ near Mexico City for a long time?

8. I came here only a couple of months ago. I (live, not) _____ here for a long time.

9. (Janet and Sam, have) _____ their dog Fido for a long time?

10. Pedro got his new bicycle a few months ago. He (have, not) _____

    _____ his bicycle for a long time.

11. (your uncle, work) _____ at the automobile factory for a long time?

12. My aunt has a new job at a candy factory. She (work, not) _____ there for a long time.

| | |
|---|---|
| (a)  *Have* you **ever** *been* in Hawaii? <br> (b)  *Has* Pedro **ever** *had* a job (in his lifetime)? | In (a): **ever** means "in your lifetime, from the time you were born to the present moment." <br> Questions with **ever** frequently use the present perfect. |
| (c)  A:  Have you ever been in London? <br>    B:  Yes, I **have**.  (I have been in London.) <br> (d)  A:  Has Tom ever lived in Chicago? <br>    B:  Yes, he **has**.  (He has lived in Chicago.) <br> (e)  A:  Have you ever been in Korea? <br>    B:  No, I **haven't**.  (I haven't ever been in Korea.) <br> (f)  A:  Has Sue ever lived in Paris? <br>    B:  No, she **hasn't**.  (She hasn't ever lived in Paris.) | In a short answer to a yes/no question with the present perfect, the helping verb (**have** or **has**) is used. <br> In (c):  Speaker B is saying that he has been in London at some time in his lifetime. |
| (g)  I **haven't ever been** in Korea. <br> (h)  I**'ve never been** in Korea. <br> (i)  She **hasn't ever lived** in Paris. <br> (j)  She**'s never lived** in Paris. | (g) and (h) have the same meaning. <br> *haven't ever been = have never been* <br> (i) and (j) have the same meaning. <br> *hasn't ever lived = has never lived* |

■ **EXERCISE 33:**  Answer the questions.  Use short answers.

1. A: *(you, be, ever)* _____Have you ever been_____ in Russia?

   B: No, I ____haven't____. I *(be, never)* __'ve never been__ in Russia.

2. A: *(you, be, ever)* _____ in Turkey?

   B: Yes, I _____. I *(be)* _____ in Turkey several times.

3. A: *(you, visit, ever)* _____ the
   Metropolitan Museum of Art in New York City?

   B: No, I _____. I *(visit, never)* _____
   that museum.

4. A: *(Sam, be, ever)* _____ in Argentina?

   B: No, he _____. He *(be, never)* _____
   in Argentina.

5. A: *(Carmen, be, ever)* _____ in Canada?

   B: Yes, she _____. She *(be)* _____ there many times.

6. A: *(you, have, ever)* _____ a serious illness?

   B: No, I _____. I *(have, never)* _____
   a serious illness.  I've been very lucky.

7. A: *(your brother, live, ever)* _____
   in an apartment by himself?

   B: No, he _____.  He still lives with my parents.

8. A: *(you, talk, ever)* _____ to a famous
   person?

   B: No, I _____.  I don't know any famous people.

9. A: *(you, see, ever)* _____

   _____ a hummingbird?

   B: Yes, I _____.

■ **EXERCISE 34—ORAL (BOOKS CLOSED):**  Answer the questions.  Use short answers.
Several people should answer the same question.

*Example:*   Have you ever been in (Africa)?
STUDENT A:  No, I haven't.
STUDENT B:  No, I haven't.
STUDENT C:  Yes, I have.

 1. Have you ever been in (Egypt)?  (Italy)?
 2. Have you ever been to (Indonesia)?  (Venezuela)?★
 3. Have you ever been in (Washington, D.C.)?  (Tokyo)?
 4. Have you ever been to (Toronto)?  (Istanbul)?
 5. Have you ever had a pet?
 6. Have you ever had a bicycle?
 7. Have you ever had a *(kind of car)?*
 8. Have you ever had a purple umbrella?
 9. Have you ever lived in an apartment?  a dormitory?
10. Have you ever lived in a one-room apartment?
11. Have you ever lived in *(name of a city or country)?*
12. Have you ever touched an elephant?  a snake?  a cow?
13. Have you ever called ( . . . ) on the phone?
14. Have you ever stayed in a hotel in this city?
15. Have you ever watched *(name of a program)* on TV?
16. Have you ever been to *(name of a place in this city)?*
17. Have you ever seen a whale?

_____

★*Have you ever been* **in** *Indonesia* and *Have you ever been* **to** *Indonesia* have the same meaning.

## 10-17 THE PRESENT PERFECT: QUESTIONS WITH *HOW LONG*

| | |
|---|---|
| (a) A: *How long **have** you **been*** in this city?<br>B: For five months.<br><br>(b) A: *How long **has** Ali **had*** a mustache?<br>B: Since he was twenty-one years old.<br><br>(c) A: *How long **have** you **known*** Maria?<br>B: Since the beginning of the school term. | Question form of the present perfect:<br><br>***have** + subject + past participle* |

■ **EXERCISE 35:** Complete the sentences with the words in parentheses.

1. A: How long *(you, be)* _____*have you been*_____ at this school?
   B: Since the middle of January.

2. A: How long *(you, know)* _____ Shelley?
   B: For three years.

3. A: How long *(Mr. Lake, be)* _____ a teacher?
   B: Since he graduated from college in 1990.

4. A: How long *(you, have)* _____ your car?
   B: For a couple of years.

5. A: How long *(your roommate, be)* _____
   out of town?
   B: Since Friday.

■ **EXERCISE 36—ORAL:** Pair up with a classmate.

*PART I:*
STUDENT A: Ask questions with ***how long*** and the PRESENT PERFECT.
STUDENT B: Answer the questions.

*Example:* have a mustache
STUDENT A: How long have you had a mustache?
STUDENT B: I've had a mustache since I was seventeen years old.

1. be in *(this city/country)*
2. be in this class
3. know *(name of a classmate)*
4. be a student at *(this school)*
5. be in this room today
6. live at your present address
7. have *(something Student B owns)*
8. have *(something else Student B owns)*

*PART II: Switch roles.*

STUDENT A: Ask the questions. If the answer is yes, ask for more information, including **how long**. Use the PRESENT PERFECT in the question with **how long**. If the answer is no, think of other similar questions until Student B answers yes.

STUDENT B: Answer the questions.

*Example:* Do you have a pet?

STUDENT A: Do you have a pet?

STUDENT B: Yes, I do.

STUDENT A: What kind of pet do you have?

STUDENT B: A dog.

STUDENT A: How long have you had your dog?

STUDENT B: She's six years old. I've had her since she was a puppy. I've had her for six years.

*Example:* Do you have a pet?

STUDENT A: Do you have a pet?

STUDENT B: No.

STUDENT A: Do your parents have a pet?

STUDENT B: No.

STUDENT A: Does anyone you know have a pet?

STUDENT B: Yes. My brother does.

STUDENT A: What kind of pet does he have?

STUDENT B: A cat.

STUDENT A: How long has he had a cat?

STUDENT B: For five or six years.

9. Do you have a pet? (Do your parents? Does anyone you know have a pet?)

10. Are you a student at *(this school)?*

11. Do you live in an apartment? (a dormitory? a house?)

12. Do you have a roommate?

13. Do you have a briefcase or a bookbag? (a wallet? a purse?)

14. Do you know *(name of a classmate)?*

15. Do you have a car? (a bicycle? a personal computer? a calculator?)

16. Are you married? (Is the teacher married? Is anyone in this class married?)

| (a) I *have* never **touched** an elephant. | The past participles of regular verbs end in **-ed**. |
|---|---|
| (b) *Has* Jim ever **stayed** at a hotel in Bangkok? | Examples: *touched, stayed*. |
| (c) Tom *has* never **eaten** Thai food. | Irregular verbs have *irregular* past participles. |
| (d) *Have* you ever **gone** to a rock concert? | Examples: *eaten, gone*. |

THE PRINCIPAL PARTS OF SOME COMMON IRREGULAR VERBS

| Simple Form | Simple Past | Past Participle |
|---|---|---|
| be | was, were | been |
| eat | ate | eaten |
| go | went | gone |
| have | had | had |
| know | knew | known |
| lose | lost | lost |
| meet | met | met |
| read | read* | read* |
| see | saw | seen |
| speak | spoke | spoken |
| take | took | taken |
| teach | taught | taught |
| tell | told | told |
| wear | wore | worn |
| write | wrote | written |

* The simple past and the past participle of the verb **read** are both pronounced "red" — the same pronunciation as the color red.

### EXERCISE 37—ORAL (BOOKS CLOSED):   Add the PAST PARTICIPLE.

*Example:*   eat, ate, . . .
*Response:*   eaten

1. eat, ate, . . .
2. go, went, . . .
3. have, had, . . .
4. know, knew, . . .
5. lose, lost, . . .
6. meet, met, . . .
7. read, read, . . .
8. see, saw, . . .
9. speak, spoke, . . .
10. take, took, . . .
11. tell, told, . . .
12. wear, wore, . . .
13. write, wrote, . . .

■ **EXERCISE 38:** Complete the sentences with the correct form of the words in the list.

*PART I:*

| | |
|---|---|
| go | ✔ take |
| lose | tell |
| meet | write |

1. I've never _____*taken*_____ a physics class.

2. Have you ever _____ Maria's sister?

3. Have you ever _____ the keys to your apartment?

4. I've never _____ to a rock concert in my whole life.

5. Have you ever _____ a lie?

6. Have you ever _____ a poem?

*PART II:*

| | |
|---|---|
| eat | see |
| know | speak |
| read | wear |

7. How long have you _____ Abdul?  Have you been friends for a long time?

8. I've never _____ the movie *Gone with the Wind*.

9. Have you ever _____ the book *Gone with the Wind?*

10. Ann has never _____ raw meat.

11. Mr. Cook never dresses casually. He has never _____ blue jeans in his life.

12. Have you ever _____ to your teacher on the phone?

■ **EXERCISE 39—ORAL:** Pair up with a classmate.

STUDENT A: Your book is open. Ask a question beginning with *"Have you ever . . . ?"*
STUDENT B: Your book is closed. Give a short answer to the question.

*Example:*     be in *(name of a country)*
STUDENT A: Have you ever been in Malaysia?
STUDENT B: Yes, I have. OR: No, I haven't.

1. meet *(name of a person)*
2. go to *(a place in this city)*
3. lose the keys to your front door
4. be in *(name of a building in this city)*
5. read *(name of a book)*
6. wear cowboy boots
7. speak to *(name of a classmate)* about *(something)*
8. eat fish eggs
9. write a letter to *(name of a person)*
10. tell *(name of the teacher)* about *(something)*
11. see *(name of a movie)*
12. have *(name of a kind of food)*

*Switch roles.*
13. read *(name of a book)*
14. eat *(a kind of food)*
15. write a letter to *(name of a person)*
16. see *(name of a television program)*
17. go to *(a place in this city)*
18. have *(name of a kind of food)*
19. be in *(name of a place at this school)*
20. meet *(name of a person)*
21. wear *(a kind of clothing)*
22. speak to *(name of a teacher)* about *(something)*
23. lose *(name of something Student B has)*
24. tell *(name of a classmate)* about *(something)*

■ **EXERCISE 40—ERROR ANALYSIS:** Find and correct the mistakes.

1. Let's going to a restaurant for dinner tonight.

2. I've never see a whale.

3. The phone rang while I was eat dinner last night.

4. How long you have been a student at this school?

5. Ken doesn't has to go to work today.

6. I must to study tonight.  I can't going to the movie with you.

7. I have been in this city since two months.

8. Why you have to leave now?

9. You shouldn't to speak loudly in a library.

10. I've known Olga since I am a child.

11. You don't must be late for work.

12. Have you ever went to a baseball game?

13. I am in this class since the beginning of January.

■ **EXERCISE 41—WRITTEN:**  Write about your experiences as a member of this class. Suggestions of things to write about:
  - the first day of class
  - the teacher
  - your classmates
  - the classroom
  - your learning experiences
  - the textbook(s)
  - a memorable event in this class

# The English Alphabet

| | | | |
|---|---|---|---|
| A | a | N | n |
| B | b | O | o |
| C | c | P | p |
| D | d | Q | q |
| E | e | R | r |
| F | f | S | s |
| G | g | T | t |
| H | h | U | u |
| I | i | V | v |
| J | j | W | w |
| K | k | X | x |
| L | l | Y | y |
| M | m | Z | z★ |

Vowels = *a, e, i, o u.*
Consonants = *b, c, d, f, g, h, j, k, l, m, n, p, q, r, s, t, v, w, x, y, z.*

---

★The letter "z" is pronounced "zee" in American English and "zed" in British English.

| | | | | |
|---|---|---|---|---|
| 1 | one | 1st | first |
| 2 | two | 2nd | second |
| 3 | three | 3rd | third |
| 4 | four | 4th | fourth |
| 5 | five | 5th | fifth |
| 6 | six | 6th | sixth |
| 7 | seven | 7th | seventh |
| 8 | eight | 8th | eighth |
| 9 | nine | 9th | ninth |
| 10 | ten | 10th | tenth |
| 11 | eleven | 11th | eleventh |
| 12 | twelve | 12th | twelfth |
| 13 | thirteen | 13th | thirteenth |
| 14 | fourteen | 14th | fourteenth |
| 15 | fifteen | 15th | fifteenth |
| 16 | sixteen | 16th | sixteenth |
| 17 | seventeen | 17th | seventeenth |
| 18 | eighteen | 18th | eighteenth |
| 19 | nineteen | 19th | nineteenth |
| 20 | twenty | 20th | twentieth |
| 21 | twenty-one | 21th | twenty-first |
| 22 | twenty-two | 22nd | twenty-second |
| 23 | twenty-three | 23rd | twenty-third |
| 24 | twenty-four | 24th | twenty-fourth |
| 25 | twenty-five | 25th | twenty-fifth |
| 26 | twenty-six | 26th | twenty-sixth |
| 27 | twenty-seven | 27th | twenty-seventh |
| 28 | twenty-eight | 28th | twenty-eighth |
| 29 | twenty-nine | 29th | twenty-ninth |
| 30 | thirty | 30th | thirtieth |
| 40 | forty | 40th | fortieth |
| 50 | fifty | 50th | fiftieth |
| 60 | sixty | 60th | sixtieth |
| 70 | seventy | 70th | seventieth |
| 80 | eighty | 80th | eightieth |
| 90 | ninety | 90th | ninetieth |
| 100 | one hundred | 100th | one hundredth |
| 200 | two hundred | 200th | two hundredth |
| 1,000 | one thousand | | |
| 10,000 | ten thousand | | |
| 100,000 | one hundred thousand | | |
| 1,000,000 | one million | | |

APPENDIX *3*

# Days of the Week
# and Months of the Year

| DAYS | | MONTHS | |
|---|---|---|---|
| Monday | (Mon.) | January | (Jan.) |
| Tuesday | (Tues.) | February | (Feb.) |
| Wednesday | (Wed.) | March | (Mar.) |
| Thursday | (Thurs.) | April | (Apr.) |
| Friday | (Fri.) | May | (May) |
| Saturday | (Sat.) | June | (June) |
| Sunday | (Sun.) | July | (July) |
| | | August | (Aug.) |
| | | September | (Sept.) |
| | | October | (Oct.) |
| | | November | (Nov.) |
| | | December | (Dec.) |

Using numbers to write the date:

month/day/year
10/31/41 = October 31, 1941
4/15/92 = April 15, 1992

Saying dates:

| USUAL WRITTEN FORM | USUAL SPOKEN FORM |
|---|---|
| January 1 | January first/the first of January |
| March 2 | March second/the second of March |
| May 3 | May third/the third of May |
| June 4 | June fourth/the fourth of June |
| August 5 | August fifth/the fifth of August |
| October 10 | October tenth/the-tenth of October |
| November 27 | November twenty-seventh/the twenty-seventh of November |

# Ways of Saying the Time

| 9:00 | It's nine o'clock. |
| | It's nine. |

| 9:05 | It's nine-oh-five. |
| | It's five (minutes) after nine. |
| | It's five (minutes) past nine. |

| 9:10 | It's nine-ten. |
| | It's ten (minutes) after nine. |
| | It's ten (minutes) past nine. |

| 9:15 | It's nine-fifteen. |
| | It's a quarter after nine. |
| | It's a quarter past nine. |

| 9:30 | It's nine-thirty. |
| | It's half past nine. |

| 9:45 | It's nine-forty-five. |
| | It's a quarter to ten. |
| | It's a quarter of ten. |

| 9:50 | It's nine-fifty. |
| | It's ten (minutes) to ten. |
| | It's ten (minutes) of ten. |

| 12:00 | It's noon. |
| | It's midnight. |

A.M. = morning    It's nine A.M.
P.M. = afternoon/evening/night    It's nine P.M.

# APPENDIX 5

## Irregular Verbs

| SIMPLE FORM | SIMPLE PAST | PAST PARTICIPLE | SIMPLE FORM | SIMPLE PAST | PAST PARTICIPLE |
|---|---|---|---|---|---|
| be | was, were | been | keep | kept | kept |
| become | became | become | know | knew | known |
| begin | began | begun | lend | lent | lent |
| bend | bent | bent | leave | left | left |
| bite | bit | bitten | lose | lost | lost |
| blow | blew | blown | make | made | made |
| break | broke | broken | meet | met | met |
| bring | brought | brought | pay | paid | paid |
| build | built | built | put | put | put |
| buy | bought | bought | read | read | read |
| catch | caught | caught | ride | rode | ridden |
| choose | chose | chosen | ring | rang | rung |
| come | came | come | run | ran | run |
| cost | cost | cost | say | said | said |
| cut | cut | cut | see | saw | seen |
| do | did | done | sell | sold | sold |
| draw | drew | drawn | send | sent | sent |
| drink | drank | drunk | shake | shook | shaken |
| drive | drove | driven | shut | shut | shut |
| eat | ate | eaten | sing | sang | sung |
| fall | fell | fallen | sit | sat | sat |
| feed | fed | fed | sleep | slept | slept |
| feel | felt | felt | speak | spoke | spoken |
| fight | fought | fought | spend | spent | spent |
| find | found | found | stand | stood | stood |
| fly | flew | flown | steal | stole | stolen |
| forget | forgot | forgotten | swim | swam | swum |
| get | got | gotten/got | take | took | taken |
| give | gave | given | teach | taught | taught |
| go | went | gone | tear | tore | torn |
| grow | grew | grown | tell | told | told |
| hang | hung | hung | think | thought | thought |
| have | had | had | throw | threw | thrown |
| hear | heard | heard | understand | understood | understood |
| hide | hid | hidden | wake up | woke up | woken up |
| hit | hit | hit | wear | wore | worn |
| hold | held | held | win | won | won |
| hurt | hurt | hurt | write | wrote | written |

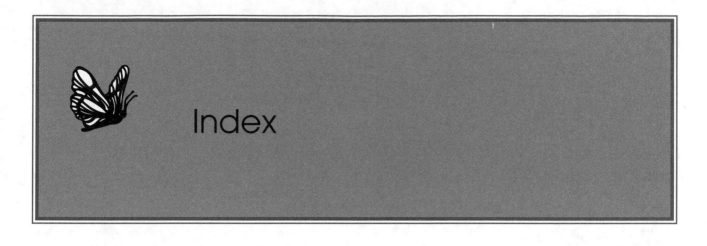

# Index